★★★★★★ ★★★★★★★★★★★★★★★★★★

NEAL R. PEIRCE **THE**

The Electoral College in American History

WITH A FOREWORD BY TOM WICKER

PEOPLE'S PRESIDENT

and the Direct-Vote Alternative

 SIMON AND SCHUSTER, NEW YORK

Contents

Foreword

Nobody knows to this day, or ever will, whom the American people really elected President in 1960. Under the prevailing system, John F. Kennedy was inaugurated, but it is not at all clear that this was really the will of the people or, if so, by what means and margin that will was expressed.

All history books record that Kennedy received 303 electoral votes to 219 for Richard M. Nixon. But electoral votes are determined by the popular votes of the states—basically, if not entirely, as we shall see—and in 1960, a shift of only 4,480 popular votes from Kennedy to Nixon in Illinois, where there were highly plausible charges of fraud, and 4,491 in Missouri, would have given neither man an electoral majority and thrown the decision into the House of Representatives. If an additional 1,148 votes had been counted for Nixon in New Mexico, 58 in Hawaii, and 1,247 in Nevada, he would have won an outright majority in the electoral college. Any experienced reporter or politician knows that that few votes can easily be "swung" in any state by fraud or honest error.

But, it will be said, Kennedy did win a plurality of the popular vote and even if the few votes that gave him his electoral majority were suspect, his election still had the legitimacy of popular approval. But that is not certain either, because of the result in Alabama. Nixon clearly got 237,981 popular votes in that unaccountable state. Depending on how one finally counts those Alabamians who voted for something called "unpledged electors," Kennedy got 324,050 or 318,303 or 147,295. Using the first two Kennedy totals would have given him a national popular vote plurality of either 118,000 votes or 113,000 (the figure usually cited); but using the lowest of the three totals—which

9

the Democratic National Committee actually did in 1964, in determining the size of the Alabama delegation to the national convention—would have given Richard Nixon a national popular vote plurality of 58,181 votes.

But the final decision in a Presidential election in which the electoral college fails to produce a majority is up to the House of Representatives, as presently required by the Constitution, and it is generally assumed that the Democratic Congress would have chosen Kennedy. The trouble with that assumption is that the House would have voted under an archaic provision giving each state delegation one vote, regardless of the size of the delegation, with a simple majority of 26 votes required for election. But at the time a Nixon-Kennedy choice would have been made, there were 23 delegations controlled by Democrats from Northern and border states, six by Democrats from the Deep South, 17 by Republicans, and four split evenly between the parties. Obviously the Democratic but anti-Kennedy Deep South states and the four split states would have held the balance of power, and it is impossible to say what would have happened after the bargaining, log-rolling and vote-buying had been completed. Kennedy might have become President only at the price of Senator James O. Eastland for Attorney General, or some other arrangement as grotesque.

Thus, it is not certain that Kennedy honestly won an electoral college majority, despite the history books and his inauguration; it is not clear that he won even a popular vote plurality; it is equally unclear that Nixon really was elected, either by the popular or electoral counts, and what would have happened had the whole mess been left to the House is too ghastly to think about.

The only thing that is clear, as Neal Peirce points out in this book, is that "the 1960 election summed up the evils of the electoral college in our times." Here is his indictment:

"First, [the 1960 election] showed once again the irrational, chance factors that decide a close election, when the shift of a few votes can throw huge blocs of electoral votes in one direction or the other. Secondly, it underscored the danger of fraud deciding a Presidential election, because Illinois, where the most ballot disputes arose, was the state that almost decided the entire election. Third, it showed the potentially decisive role that a narrowly based regional or splinter party [the unpledged electors] can play in the choice of a President and how the system actually encourages independent elector blocs.

Fourth, the election showed how a faceless elector, chosen to carry out a specific function, could suddenly break his trust and try to determine the choice of the chief executive for 180 million Americans. . . . And lastly, the election showed that as long as individual states have *carte blanche* in deciding how Presidential electors will be chosen, it may be difficult and sometimes impossible to compile accurate national popular vote totals (as in Alabama in 1960) and to learn whom the majority of Americans really wanted to be their President."

Obviously, this is a situation that ought to be rectified, and for the better part of two centuries American statesmen from Madison and Jefferson through Thomas Hart Benton to Lyndon B. Johnson have been trying to work out something better. None of the solutions commonly advanced, however, would have made much improvement for our time.

Had the nation, for example, been voting in 1960 under the often-proposed plan that would give each state two electoral votes and each Congressional district one, Nixon would have been elected by 278 to 245—a small but clear electoral majority that would have done nothing to clear up the clouded popular vote and might well have made him a minority President.

Under still a third system, just as often proposed, by which the electoral votes of a state would be apportioned according to the percentage of the popular vote won by each candidate, Nixon also would have squeaked in, 266.075 electoral votes to 265.623 for Kennedy, with the popular vote either in doubt or against him. If the constitutional amendment proposed in 1966 by President Johnson had been in effect in 1960, so that there could have been no defecting or unpledged human electors, the final electoral totals would have been changed to some undetermined figure, since it is not clear what would have happened in Alabama had there been a straight Nixon-Kennedy choice with no "unpledged electors" as an alternative. The controversy over who really won Illinois's 27 electoral votes would have been just as virulent, and the only thing that can firmly be said is that Nixon surely would have gained one additional electoral vote (because a Nixon elector in Oklahoma, which he easily carried, defected and voted for Harry F. Byrd, who was not even a candidate).

All of these proposed reforms have one fault in common. In some form each of them retains the electoral college, and that is the root of the trouble. Neal Peirce, whose researches and writings for *Congres-*

sional Quarterly have for years been the mainstay of Washington political writers and politicians, has got to that root in this book and has proved beyond reasonable doubt that the single reform that removes the inequities and perils of the present system without substituting others, that conforms to the long-range trend of American politics and society, is to eliminate the electoral college altogether and give the election of their President directly to the American people.

Under such a system of direct popular election, there could have been but a single controversy in 1960 and that on the irremovable question of fraud. There could have been no problem in Alabama, since unpledged electors could not have entered the picture and the choice would have been Nixon or Kennedy, one or the other. The Oklahoma defector could not have abandoned his trust (suppose, Peirce asks pertinently, his had been the *deciding vote* in the electoral college). There could have been no possibility of the House's selling the Presidency to the highest bidder. And even such vote frauds as might have been proven, unless on a scale more grandiose than any yet demonstrated to have occurred in American politics, could hardly have changed the outcome. Even if they had changed it, it could only have been to the numerical extent that fraudulent votes could have been proven to have been counted; there could have been nothing like the possibility of a few thousand shady votes in Illinois turning that state's entire 27 electoral votes (about five percent of the electoral college) from one candidate to another. To some extent, any or all of these potential defects can be found in any of the electoral college reform proposals except direct popular election.

In fact, as Peirce shows, the history of other systems proposed to reform the electoral college is an account of one or another of them coming to some popular favor and finally being defeated for lack of enough support; one by one, the district system, proportional electoral votes, automatic electors, have come out of the pack like challenging horses only to fall back in the homestretch. Now the American Bar Association has endorsed direct popular election; so has Senator Birch Bayh of Indiana, the chairman of the Senate Subcommittee on Constitutional Amendments; so has the influential Senator Everett McKinley Dirksen of Illinois, the Republican floor leader and formerly a believer in the district system. Thus, it seems clear that direct popular election, like the others before it, is beginning its run at the electoral college.

It seems to me that there are three fundamental reasons why this time the outcome may be different, and certainly should be. First, after so long a time and with 1960 fresh in mind, there has been ample demonstration of the pitfalls and perils of the electoral college as we know it, and there has been enough study of the older alternatives to discredit them as well.

Second, the best contemporary argument *for* the present system also has been discredited. It used to be contended that despite its inequities and dangers, the electoral college was justified because it was the only instrument in the American system weighted on behalf of the interests of the major states and the urban population, with their concentrations of minority groups. With each state having two Senators, with state legislatures dominated by rural interests, with these legislatures in turn malapportioning and gerrymandering Congressional districts, the electoral college had to be preserved to give New York and Detroit and Chicago a voice in national politics anywhere near proportionate to their popular voting power. This was a sound argument, but the one-man, one-vote decisions of the Supreme Court are putting it out of date. Legislatures and the House of Representatives are moving and will move further toward legitimate representation of urban interests; and while direct popular election of Presidents will reduce the power of the major states to *swing* elections through their huge electoral totals, it will not at all eliminate the necessity for candidates to campaign in such a manner as to win heavy support among the swollen populations of the major states.

Finally, it seems to me that the time of this particular idea has come. Can it any longer be pretended that this great people needs the electors to choose wisely for it? Of course not. Yet that was the original theory. The President is the only American official who represents the American people entire—the whole constituency, every one of us, from Maine to California, Dixiecrat and New Left, white and black, man and woman—and what real reason is there that we should not vote directly for him and have our votes counted directly for him? We may be 50 states in Congress but we are one people in the White House—or should be—and the President ought to be ours to choose.

There remain questions, of course. What effect will there be on minority parties? On the smaller, less populous states? Should there be a required minimum percentage of the vote for election, or should the high man be elected? If the former, what happens if no candidate reaches it? Is a runoff election feasible or is some other means of decision preferable?

Neal Peirce has explored all of these questions and many others—at length, in fascinating historical detail and with sound contemporary social and political research. His dispassionate and conclusive book might indeed be a milestone; for even when the time of an idea has come, its dimensions and importance still need to be made clear to all, doubters and proponents alike. After *The People's President*, there is little if anything left to be said about the way we choose our Presidents, and the way we ought to choose them.

Washington, D.C.   TOM WICKER

Preface

Since the Presidency is the grand prize of American politics, it is not surprising to find that narrow partisanship has often played a role in the debates about the way our chief executive should be elected. Yet since the first decades of the Republic, there have been some Americans who have labored tirelessly for true reform of our Presidential election system, without regard to their personal or partisan advantage. One thinks of men like Senators Thomas Hart Benton of Missouri and Oliver P. Morton of Indiana in the past century or Henry Cabot Lodge of Massachusetts and Estes Kefauver of Tennessee in our own. All failed in their effort to reform the system, yet all laid a groundwork for others to build on. As this book is written, a historic opportunity for leadership lies before those men of Congress who will lay partisan considerations aside in a new effort to reform our antiquated and dangerous electoral system and thus assure that the American President will truly be the man of the people.

This book was written both as a history of the electoral college in American history and as a statement of the major concerns—constitutional, political, social—that Americans and their leaders must consider as they debate the best way to elect a President in the last decades of the 20th century. If the book can help throw some light on those concerns and problems, then it will have served its purpose.

For their advice and counsel in the preparation of this book, I owe a special debt of thanks to three men who themselves have taken a special interest in electoral college reform: James C. Kirby, Jr., former counsel of the Senate Judiciary Constitutional Amendments Subcommittee and a member of the American Bar Association's Commission on Electoral College Reform; John D. Feerick, who was special adviser to the A.B.A. commission; and Robert G. Dixon, Jr., an authority in the reapportionment field. Others who read parts or all of the first-draft manuscript and offered valuable advice on many counts include Richard M. Scammon, former Director of the Census, and Joseph Foote, one of my colleagues on the staff of *Congressional Quarterly*.

My research associate, Roan Conrad, provided invaluable help in the search of historical sources, manuscript editing and the preparation of a number of charts. I am indebted also to Charles W. Bischoff for his statistical analysis of the chances for reversal of popular vote victories in the electoral college, which was prepared especially for this book and appears in Chapter 5. Professor Richard Claude of the University of Maryland was helpful in advising on suffrage problems, and Myer Zitter of the Census Bureau kindly prepared estimates of adult population in the early 19th century for the chart in Chapter 7. Robert L. Tienken and Elizabeth Yadlosky of the American Law Division, Library of Congress, assisted with a number of technical election law problems. My thanks go to a number of state election officials, especially Ohio Secretary of State Ted W. Brown and Ray Howard of his office for original Presidential election documents. The book's title, "The People's President," was suggested by an editorial in the Washington *Post*.

Others to whom a special word of acknowledgment is due include Charles Dennis McCamey, who assisted with final proofing; Sharon Marcus, who helped with a number of charts and research tasks; and my typists, Harriet M. Chadayammury and Marjorie Lash.

I deeply appreciate the advice and encouragement lent from time to time by a host of other friends and associates, including William Dickinson, David S. Broder, Martha Gottron, Charles Mack, Oliver Cromwell, Jean Allaway, Martha McGuinness, Shirley Seib—and, above all, my wife, Barbara.

My special thanks go to Tom Wicker, chief of the Washington bureau of *The New York Times*, for consenting to write the Foreword.

All evaluations, judgments and errors of fact are, of course, the responsibility of the writer.

Washington, D.C.   NEAL R. PEIRCE
October 1967

1 The People's President

AT 12:55 P.M. ON THE SIXTH OF JANUARY, 1961, THE DOORKEEPER OF THE House of Representatives announced the arrival in the House chamber of the Vice President and the members of the Senate for the purpose of counting the electoral votes cast for the next President and Vice President of the United States. Most Americans might have thought the previous November that they were voting directly for their Chief Executive, but this would be the legal, constitutionally dictated election.

Two handsome boxes of inlaid wood, holding the electoral votes submitted from all the states, had been brought by pages from the Senate chamber and were now taken down the center aisle of the House and placed on the desk of the Speaker's podium. For the Democrats it was a happy occasion, and their side of the chamber was almost filled, while only a few of the seats on the Republican side had been taken.

As the presiding officer of the Senate, Vice President Richard M. Nixon had the constitutional duty to preside at this joint session of Congress. It was the first time in a century that a Vice President had been called upon to preside over an electoral vote tally that certified the election as President of the man he had run against. The last occasion had been on February 13, 1861, when Vice President John C. Breckinridge, who had run unsuccessfully for President the previous autumn, certified the election of Abraham Lincoln.

Before ordering that the ballot count begin, Nixon threw his arm around the shoulder of the Speaker of the House, Sam Rayburn of Texas, and, as applause mounted, offered the congratulations of the Senate to the venerable Speaker on his 79th birthday. Then the official business of the joint session got under way. Four tellers had been appointed—a Republican and a Democrat from both the Senate and House. The senior man among them was Arizona's Senator Carl Hayden, whose Congressional service had begun 48 years before, when his state entered the Union. Representing the Senate Republicans was Carl Curtis of Nebraska, while Representatives Edna F. Kelly of New York and Frances P. Bolton of Ohio had been designated from the Democratic and Republican sides of the House respectively.

The returns from Alabama, the first state in alphabetical order, were withdrawn from the boxes and handed to Nixon, who opened the certification and then handed it to the tellers, who announced the result. The count for Alabama showed six electoral votes for Senator Harry Flood Byrd of Virginia and five for Senator John F. Kennedy of Massachusetts. Nixon nodded to Senator Byrd and said it seemed that "the gentleman from Virginia is now in the lead." (Having received the votes of the unpledged electors from Alabama and Mississippi, plus the vote of one renegade Republican elector in Oklahoma, Byrd would be accorded 15 of the total of 537 electoral votes.) The count proceeded uninterrupted until Nixon announced that three certificates had been received from Hawaii—one certifying the election of Republican electors, one certifying the election of Democratic electors, and a third, from the Governor of the state, certifying the proper election of the Democratic electors. The first official count in Hawaii had shown a Republican electoral victory by a margin of 141 votes, but on a recount the Democrats forged ahead by 115 votes. Nixon suggested that the Governor's certification of the Democratic electors be accepted, and there being no objection, it was so ordered.

The count then proceeded through the last state on the list—Wyoming. Nixon had sought, more or less successfully, to maintain a cheerful demeanor through the long ballot tally, but now he fidgeted as the tellers assembled the documents that showed the final results. The count, reported to him by the tellers, showed:

For President, John F. Kennedy, 303 electoral votes; Richard M. Nixon, 219 electoral votes; Harry F. Byrd, 15 electoral votes.

For Vice President: Lyndon B. Johnson, 303 electoral votes; Henry Cabot Lodge, 219 electoral votes; Strom Thurmond, 14 electoral votes, and Barry Goldwater, 1 electoral vote.[1]

Now the opportunity had come for Nixon to add a poignant footnote to the history of the American electoral college. Noting the rarity of the situation, Nixon asked "permission to impose upon the time of the Members of this Congress to make a statement which in itself is somewhat unprecedented." Proceeding without notes, Nixon said:

This is the first time in 100 years that a candidate for the Presidency announced the result of an election in which he was defeated and announced the victory of his opponent. I do not think we could have a more striking and eloquent example of the stability of our Constitutional system and of the proud tradition of the American people of developing, respecting and honoring institutions of self-government.

In our campaigns, no matter how hard fought they may be, no matter how close the election may turn out to be, those who lose accept the verdict and support those who win. And I would like to add that, having served in government for 14 years, a period which began in the House 14 years ago, almost to the day, which continued with two years in the Senate and eight years as Vice President, as I complete that 14-year period it is indeed a very great honor to me to extend to my colleagues on both sides of the aisle who have been elected, to extend to John F. Kennedy and Lyndon Johnson, who have been elected President and Vice President of the United States, my heartfelt best wishes, as all of you work in a cause that is bigger than any man's ambition, greater than any party. It is the cause of freedom, of justice, and peace for all mankind.

It is in that spirit that I now declare that John F. Kennedy has been elected President of the United States, and Lyndon Johnson Vice President of the United States.[2]

Moved by the magnanimity of Nixon's gesture, the members of both parties gave him a standing ovation as he declared the joint session adjourned at 1:48 P.M. After a warm pat on the back from Speaker Rayburn, Nixon descended from the rostrum, smiling and shaking hands with Congressmen on both sides of the aisle as they said their farewells. Fourteen days later, Kennedy and Johnson would be inaugurated and Nixon, for the time being at least, would retire to private life.

The substantial nature of John F. Kennedy's electoral college victory belied the suspense of election night, November 8, 1960, as the nation watched the popular vote reports in the most closely contested Presidential race of the century.

Early in the evening, as the polls began to close across the continent, it had looked like a national sweep for the Democrats. Led by bell-wether Connecticut, the industrial states of the Eastern seaboard had gone for Kennedy—Pennsylvania with its 32 electoral votes, New York

with its gigantic 45-electoral-vote bloc, and Kennedy's native Massachusetts with 16 electoral votes, the last by a staggering half-million
plurality in the popular vote.

But the East was not all of America, and the later the night grew,
the less certain the result appeared. Kennedy may have been strong in
his native East, but the Republican ticket of Nixon and Lodge showed
remarkable strength as the other regions began to report. To the
surprise of virtually every political analyst, Nixon won Ohio with her
25 electoral votes by a decisive margin of a quarter-million votes. The
"new South" states of Virginia, Kentucky, Tennessee and Florida were
his. The Midwestern Republican heartland delivered Indiana, Wisconsin and Iowa into Nixon's hands, and as the night progressed, it
became apparent that virtually every prairie state, from North Dakota
to Oklahoma, would be his and that he would capture every one of the
Western mountain states except Nevada. In addition, he defeated
Kennedy in the Pacific states of Washington, Oregon and Alaska.
Several days later it would become official that Nixon also had won his
native California, with her 32 electoral votes, by a fragile margin. In all,
he would win 26 of the 50 states of the Union.

John Kennedy's Eastern lead would never be overcome, however.
To that solid base, Kennedy added industrial Michigan with her 20
electoral votes; he captured Illinois, too—by a much-disputed margin
of 8,858 votes, which brought him 27 electoral votes. Border states like
Maryland, West Virginia and Missouri went for Kennedy, and his
victory was clinched by his ability to seize 81 electoral votes from
seven states of the Old Confederacy—aided in no small part by his
Vice Presidential running mate from Texas.

Kennedy's eventual total of electoral votes was 303, but later analysis would show that if 11,424 popular votes had shifted from him to
Nixon in certain key states, Nixon would have won a majority in the
electoral college—and become President. A mere shift of 8,971 votes
from Kennedy in two states would have deprived him—and Nixon—of
an electoral vote majority and given the Southern independent electors
the balance of power they had hoped for.[3] Strongly conservative and
segregationist in their views, those independent electors would probably have cast their votes for whichever of the leading candidates
agreed to compromise his personal views and his party's platform on
civil rights. If neither man had agreed, the independent elector votes
would probably have gone to Byrd anyway. The election would have
been thrown into the House of Representatives, where, under perhaps

the most undemocratic provision of the entire election machinery, each state would have had a single vote—Alaska and New York, Mississippi and California alike. No side would have controlled the 26 state delegations necessary for election, and prolonged deadlock might have resulted—to the peril of the Presidency and the people.[4]

What is this odd election machinery, this strange method of choosing a President we call the "electoral college"?[5] Through the annals of American history, one can find few men willing to defend it. An early analyst of the system called it "an abortive organism";[6] a modern-day political scientist depicts it as "a hoary and outworn relic of the stage-coach era."[7] One of the founding fathers believed it "the most pleasing feature of the Constitution,"[8] but only a few years later, one of the great reform advocates of the 19th century—Senator Thomas Hart Benton of Missouri—declared the system's operation "wholly incompatible with the safety of the people."[9] In our own times, the Supreme Court has declared that "the conception of political equality" behind the electoral college "belongs to a bygone day."[10]

The electoral college is a double-election system for the American Presidency. Instead of voting directly for their President, Americans vote for Presidential "electors" equal in number to the Representatives each state has in Congress plus each state's two Senators. The winning slate of electors in each state—Republican or Democratic—meets in the state capitol the first Monday after the second Wednesday of December in a Presidential election year to cast its votes. The results are forwarded to Washington, where they are opened in the joint session of Congress on January 6. If a candidate has a majority of the votes, he is declared elected. If there is no majority for a President, the choice is thrown into the House of Representatives, where each state has a single vote. If there is no majority for Vice President, the Senate makes the choice.

Once the people have selected the electors, they have nothing further to say about the election of the President. Three times in the last century—1824, 1876 and 1888—their will was frustrated and the man who had lost in the national popular vote was elevated to the Presidency. Three times in this century—1916, 1948 and 1960—we have come perilously close to another miscarriage of the popular will. Despite these experiences, we continue to rely, in the words of a foremost constitutional scholar, "on the intervention of that Providence which is said to have fools and the American people in its special care."[11]

But as illogical as the electoral college may appear for the United States in the latter 20th century, it *did* seem to make sense in 1787 when the founding fathers devised it at the Constitutional Convention in Philadelphia. Consider the differences between the country for which the Constitution was written and the America we know today.[12]

Then, the nation—if one could call it that at all—consisted of 13 contentious semisovereign states spread thinly along 1,300 miles of the Eastern seaboard, from Massachusetts and her province of Maine in the North to Georgia in the South. *Now*, the federal Union comprises 50 states, spanning the breadth of an entire continent and reaching into the Pacific to encompass Hawaii and Alaska.

Then, our frontier extended scarcely beyond the Appalachian Mountains; Pittsburgh was little more than a military post; Kentucky, just receiving her first great wave of migration; Cincinnati, a tiny village. Beyond these outposts there was little more than wilderness and solitude; no white man had yet beheld the source of the Mississippi River, and only a few men had seen the great Western plains. *Now*, our continental frontiers long since tamed, outer space is the only physical frontier that remains before us.

Then, communications and travel were torturously slow through the land; Philadelphia was two or three days by stagecoach from New York; from Boston to Philadelphia the traveler was obliged to disembark and ride crude "ferries" across no less than seven rivers and could well spend ten days on the road, dusty in summer, mired with ruts in spring, limited to 25 miles in a day by winter's snows. The postal service was slow and unsure; the nation's 80 newspapers, avidly read in every hamlet they reached, were the strongest link between the people and their nation. *Now*, jet air transportation has reduced travel time to a few hours between virtually any two points in the United States. We have an unparalleled system of rail, air and road transport; we complain when the mail takes more than a day, even between distant points; our newspapers, television and the telephone form a constant, almost instantaneous communications link between our people.

Then, we were an almost exclusively rural nation: 95 percent of the people lived independently on isolated farms or in villages of less than 2,500 persons, and eight in ten Americans took their living from the land. "At this time," wrote a not untypical farmer in 1787, "my farm gave me and my whole family a good living on the produce of it, and left me, one year with another, 150 silver dollars, for I never spent more than ten dollars a year, which was for salt, nails and the like. Nothing to wear, eat or drink was purchased, as my farm provided all."[13] *Now,* roughly three-quarters of our people live in great cities or towns of 2,500 or more. Six American cities have more than a million inhabitants; 21 metropolitan areas have passed the million mark. Our economy is totally interdependent.

Then, the land could boast but a handful of colleges, and public schooling was haphazard at the best. In New York and Pennsylvania a schoolhouse was never seen outside a village or town; in New England the little red schoolhouses were open but two months in the winter for the boys and two months in summer for the girls. Illiteracy was a critical problem, especially on the frontier. *Now,* free public education carries most American children through high school, we have a great network of universities, and illiteracy has been practically stamped out. The American electorate is immeasurably better informed than in the first years of the Republic.

Then, a clear class structure was apparent in America—less rigid than Europe's but still evident. It ranged from the distinct aristocracy of education and wealth from which the Constitution's framers sprang —landowners, merchants, lawyers—down through the great group known as the "middling sort"—farmers, shopkeepers, independent artisans—to a "meaner sort" of laborers, servants and hardscrabble farmers. And below all these, there were indentured servants and more than 600,000 Negro slaves. *Now,* we still find extremes of wealth and poverty, but the great mass of Americans form a dominant "middle class" in a land of pervasive affluence and extraordinary social mobility. Slavery is a century gone, though its scars remain.

Then, a myriad of property and tax qualifications imposed severe limitations on the right to vote. *Now,* we are approaching universal adult suffrage.

Then, the President of the United States was once removed from the people of the land—because men's primary loyalty was still expected to remain with their states; because the federal government was not expected to play a major role in taxation, education or economic affairs of most immediate import to the people; because of the nation's inadequate communications; because of the limited franchise; because we still lacked a party system to popularize American leaders. *Now,* the President is no longer removed but immediate—on our television screens, on the front page of every daily newspaper, in our consciousnesses because we relate to him directly, not as New Yorkers or

Nevadans, Vermonters or Oregonians, but as Americans. As we do a member of the family, we may like him or dislike him, we may praise him or curse him, we may support him or oppose him. But when all is said and done, he *is* our President until the next quadrennial election. The universal American reaction of sorrow and anger when John Kennedy was assassinated, from Kennedy's friends and foes alike, was ample demonstration of the strong attachment of the American people to their President.

If we would measure further the President's importance to us, we need only review the manifold functions he fulfills in modern American society. No one has summarized it better than the American historian Clinton Rossiter, who points to no less than ten major roles of the President:

He is *Chief of State,* a "one man distillation of the American people just as surely as the Queen is of the British people."

He is *Chief Executive,* the manager of the gigantic federal apparatus, the man with powers of appointment and removal, the person charged with the duty of seeing that the laws "be faithfully executed."

He is *Commander-in-Chief* of our military forces.

He is *Chief Diplomat,* the man with paramount responsibility for conducting the nation's foreign affairs.

He is *Chief Legislator,* proposing laws to Congress and devising the strategy to get them passed.

He is *Chief of Party,* the controlling figure behind national political party machinery, the inspirer of his partisans, his party's chief fund raiser.

He is *Protector of the Peace,* guarding the nation from internal revolt, moving swiftly to help when natural calamity strikes.

He is *Leader of a Coalition of Free Nations,* the newest responsibility added to those of our President, resulting from our emergence as the leading power of the Western world in the era since the Second World War.

He is *Manager of the Prosperity,* responsible under the Employment Act of 1946 and other statutes for maintaining a growing, stable economy.

He is the *Voice of the People,* "the leading formulator and expounder of public opinion in the United States."[14]

Indeed, the grand concept of the President as a man of all the people is not a 20th-century invention. More than a century ago, the Englishman John Bright wrote of our Presidency:

We know what an election is in the United States for President of the Republic. . . . Every four years there springs from the vote created by the whole people a President over that great nation. I think the whole world offers no finer spectacle than this; it offers no higher dignity; and there is no greater object of ambition on the political stage on which men are permitted to move. You may point, if you will, to hereditary rulers, to crowns coming down through successive generations of the same family, to thrones based on prescription and conquest, to sceptres wielded over veteran legions and subject realms,—but to my mind there is nothing more worthy of reverence and obedience, and nothing more sacred, than the authority of the freely chosen magistrate of a great and free people; and if there be on earth and amongst men any divine right to govern, surely it rests with a ruler so chosen and so appointed.[15]

Few Americans could have put it better than John Bright. But we must ask ourselves: to what world does our Presidential election system really correspond? Is it adapted to a modern technological society in a politically mature nation, where every American considers the ballot his birthright? Or is it more a vestige of the world of two centuries past, when voting was haphazard, the secret ballot scarcely known, the society disjointed and spread over a vast frontier? Have we adequately assured the sanctity of the franchise of all Americans? In short, have we placed within the body of our Constitution a foolproof system that will give the man whom most of us have chosen to be our President a universally understood, unequivocal mandate to govern and to lead?

As long as the antiquated electoral college system remains imbedded in our basic law, the answer must be "no." In any election the electoral college can misfire with tragic consequences. It can frustrate the will of the people, sending a man to the White House whom they have specifically rejected by a majority of their votes on election day. It can cause prolonged chaos and uncertitude by throwing an election into the House of Representatives. A malfunction of this awkward and outdated mechanism could undermine our prestige abroad. Just as serious, it could undermine the confidence of our own citizens in their Constitution, and it could raise serious questions about the sincerity of our democratic ideals. If the system went awry in times of peace and domestic tranquillity, it would be a monstrous embarrassment to us as a nation. If it misfired in a time of tension, in a time when we were close to open conflict with hostile powers, or when social divisions rent our nation, the consequences could be tragic and immeasurable. It would be foolhardy for us to expect that the goodwill and understanding of the American people would be so great that such a travesty would be tolerated. The electoral count "winner" could be placed under heavy pressures to step aside, from press and people alike. If he actually took office, his authority could be undercut at any moment by an opposition that honestly believed it had been "cheated" of the Presidency. The nation and the Presidency might well survive such an ordeal, but we would all be the losers for it.

Throughout history a variety of proposals for electoral college reform has been brought forward. Some would divide the national into small electoral "districts" that would vote separately for President. Others would divide each state's electoral vote proportionately, in the hope of at least approximating the popular will. But only one solution has ever been advanced that would assure that the man whom most Americans wanted would be President: a direct popular vote of the people, with no institutional obstacle between the people and their Chief Executive.

The time has come to amend our Constitution to implement the direct vote, so that in fact as well as in theory, in constitutional guarantee as well as by happenstance in the electoral college, the man we choose may truly be the People's President. This is not a new idea; it was advanced first in the Constitutional Convention, and in Congress as early as 1816. But when we have finally amended our Constitution to assure direct choice of the President by the people, future generations will surely look backward with amused tolerance and wonder whatever took us so long.

NOTES

1. The unpledged electors from Alabama and Mississippi had voted for Thurmond for Vice President, while the bolting Republican elector from Oklahoma, Henry D. Irwin, had cast his Vice Presidential vote for Goldwater.
2. *Congressional Record,* Jan. 6, 1961, p. 291. For a journalistic account of the joint session, see *N.Y. Times,* Jan. 7, 1961.
3. For further explanation of the vote shifts that would have changed the outcome of the 1960 election, see p. 108, below.
4. For a fuller discussion of what an election in the House might have meant following the 1960 election, see p. 106, below.

5. The terms "colleges of electors" or "electoral college" appeared first in Congressional debates around 1800. They were first incorporated in legislation in 1845. J. Hampden Dougherty, *The Electoral System of the United States* (New York, 1906), p. 74.

6. *Ibid.,* pp. 253–54.

7. Joseph E. Kallenbach, quoted in *Congressional Record,* 1949, p. 4449.

8. An opinion attributed to delegate Abraham Baldwin of Georgia, cited by Lucius Wilmerding, *The Electoral College* (New Brunswick, N.J., 1958), p. 4.

9. Senate Report No. 22, 19th Congress, 1st Session, Jan. 19, 1826, p. 4. Benton, author of the report, was referring specifically to the discretion given Presidential electors to vote for whomever they please.

10. *Gray v. Sanders,* 372 U.S. 368 (1963).

11. Edward S. Corwin, *The President, Office and Powers* (New York, 1957), p. 67.

12. For further background see: Clinton Rossiter, *1787—The Grand Convention* (New York, 1966), pp. 23–40; John Bach McMaster, *A History of the People of the United States from the Revolution to the Civil War,* 8 vols. (New York, 1893–1924), I, pp. 1–102; William Anderson, "Federalism—Now and Then," *State Government,* May 1943, pp. 107–12.

13. *American Museum,* Jan. 1787, quoted by McMaster, *op. cit.,* p. 26.

14. Rossiter, *The American Presidency* (New York, 1956), pp. 4–25.

15. *Ibid.,* p. 3.

2 The Birth of the Electoral College

THE AMERICAN PRESIDENCY AND THE ELECTORAL COLLEGE METHOD OF choosing our Chief Executive were first defined in the federal Constitution, written by the Constitutional Convention, which met in Philadelphia between May 25 and September 17, 1787. The 55 delegates from 12 states (Rhode Island refused to participate) had won their liberty—and their first sense of nationhood—in the crucible of revolution. Many had affixed their signatures to the Declaration of Independence with its ringing assertion that governments derive "their just power from the consent of the governed." But the founding fathers were also preoccupied with order and were determined to end the governmental chaos that had reigned under the Articles of Confederation.

This desire for order was nowhere more apparent than in Article II of the Constitution, starting with the words: "The executive power shall be vested in a President of the United States of America." The article spells out a wide range of Presidential powers: to be Commander-in-Chief of the Army and Navy, to appoint federal officers and require reports of the heads of executive departments, to make treaties, to appoint ambassadors, to report to Congress on the State of the Union and to "take care that the laws be faithfully executed." Proclaimed in an era when the legislative branches dominated the executive in almost every state, this grant of clear and independent executive authority was almost revolutionary in its impact. But the

Constitution's framers took care to guarantee liberty as well, by circumscribing the power of each branch of the new federal government—executive, legislative and judicial—to prevent a tyrannical exercise of power by any one of them. The delicate system of checks and balances written into the Constitution applied to the President as well as to Congress and the courts. The President could execute the laws but not make them. He could spend the federal government's money, but the specific appropriations would come from Congress. He could appoint federal officials and ambassadors, and he could make treaties, but only with the approval of the Senate.

In the course of our history as a nation, each of the branches of the federal government has come to exercise a degree of power scarcely dreamed of by the founders. There have been times when one of the branches seemed to dominate the others, when Presidential power seemed to eclipse that of Congress and the judiciary, or when Congress assumed such a dominant role that the Presidency faded in comparison, or when the judiciary made the vital national decisions. But the basic system of checks and balances has operated time and again to preserve this "balanced Constitution" and to make it safe and viable for a nation bearing little resemblance to the 18th-century union of new-born states.

More than a quarter of the Constitution's article on the Presidency is occupied with spelling out the complex mode by which he is to be chosen. From start to finish, the Convention had great difficulty in deciding the Presidential election problem. Delegate James Wilson of Pennsylvania commented on the Convention floor on September 4: "This subject has greatly divided the house and will also divide the people out of doors. It is in truth the most difficult on which we have to decide."[1]

Basic Issues

One reason that the Convention encountered such difficulty in devising a plan for electing the President was that no plan could be considered neatly on its own merits. A host of tangential issues, some of them crucial to the basic nature of the Constitution, presented themselves at every turn. The result, as one commentator put it, was to transform the debates into something resembling a game of "three-dimensional chess."[2]

THE SCOPE OF EXECUTIVE POWER. How much authority would it be desirable—or safe—to lodge in the executive branch of a strengthened federal Union? Should the national executive be one person or many? Should the executive be subservient to the legislative branch or equal in power to it? These questions were unsettled in the minds of most of the delegates when they arrived in Philadelphia.

Under British rule, the citizens of the Colonies utilized every means to wring concessions from the executive authority, then embodied in each colony's royal governor. The legislatures provided the best means the Colonials had to advance their own interests, and they used the opportunity to the fullest extent possible. When the Revolution came and the control of the British crown evaporated, most states shifted to the state legislatures the power that the royal governors had exercised. As the newly independent states drafted their charters of government, they placed stringent limitations on the power of their executives. Governors were generally chosen by the legislatures rather than the people, were elected for terms of just a single year (except for two years in South Carolina and three years in Delaware), and were hemmed in by executive councils that shared their power. Governor Edmund Randolph of Virginia said in 1786 that he was only "a member of the executive."[3] Most Americans seemed to share the sentiments of Tom Paine that the executive was "either a political superfluity or a chaos of unknown things" and should be "considered in [no] other light than as inferior to the legislative."[4]

Yet, by the time the Constitutional Convention was called, the shortcomings of exclusive legislative rule were becoming painfully apparent. Many legislative enactments were arbitrary or proscriptive in character, and the legislatures proved impotent or unwilling to deal with the financial crises that came in the wake of the Revolution, culminating in the debtors' revolt under Daniel Shays in Massachusetts in the autumn of 1786. Viewing the radical uprising in the Bay State, James Madison wrote of the rebels: "They profess to aim only at a reform of their Constitution, and of certain abuses in public administration; but an abolition of debts, public and private, and new division of property, are strongly suspected to be in contemplation."[5] The delegates gathering at Philadelphia were acutely aware of the need for some stronger executive authority to protect the interests of property and order. As Madison himself would comment on the Convention floor: "Experience has proved a tendency in our governments to throw all power into the legislative vortex. The executives of the states are in general little more than cyphers; the legislatures omnipotent. If no effective check can be devised for restraining the instability and encroachment of the [legislatures], a revolution of some kind or other would be inevitable."[6]

The nation's experience under the Articles of Confederation, which provided for no executive department whatever and rested on the principle of equal voting power for all states, large or small, had tended to confirm the delegates' misgivings about leaving all authority in the hands of a legislature. Under the Articles, Congress had shown serious inability to deal with crucial issues like taxation, Western lands, the regulation of commerce, paper money and Indian affairs. The problem was not only in getting effective legislation passed but in implementing it once it was approved. With no executive to entrust with implementation of laws, the Congress itself had to attempt the job. "Nothing is so embarrassing as the details of execution," Thomas Jefferson wrote. "The smallest trifle of that kind occupies as long as the most important action of legislation, and takes place of everything else. . . . The most important propositions hang over from week to week and month to month, till the occasion have past them and the thing never done." Jefferson said he hoped the Constitutional Convention would take care to separate the executive and legislative powers.[7]

Thus, many delegates to the Philadelphia Convention began their deliberations predisposed to the idea that the nation needed a strong, albeit safe, executive power. As a model, they could look to the constitution New York State had adopted in 1777, which provided for a popularly elected Governor in whom was vested "the supreme power and authority of the state." The New York Governor was freed from the burden of a privy council, enjoyed powers of convening and adjourning the legislature, and was given a qualified right of appointment and veto of legislative enactments.[8] Interestingly, New York's ability to act as a model for the entire Union was an early example— even before the Constitution's adoption—of the creative role that states were to play as testing grounds for new concepts under a federal system of government.

The Convention's first and most effective advocate of a strong executive was Pennsylvania's James Wilson. He took the floor early in June to urge that the chief magistracy be possessed by one man, "as giving the most energy, dispatch and responsibility" to the office. Wilson opposed hemming the President in with an executive council, "which oftener serves to cover than prevent malpractices." To place the executive on the same plane of power as the legislature, Wilson urged that both be chosen directly by the people, with similar short terms. The case was ably advanced by Gouverneur Morris, who declared that "we must either . . . renounce the blessings of the Union, or provide an executive with sufficient vigor to pervade every part of it."[9]

The Convention had a strong minority, however, with quite different ideas about the executive. Roger Sherman of Connecticut told his fellow delegates that he "considered the executive as nothing more than an institution for carrying the will of the legislature into effect," and that the legislature "should have the power to remove the executive at pleasure." Elbridge Gerry of Massachusetts thought that an executive council, like those then prevalent in the states, should be appended to the executive. Randolph of Virginia, who had presented the Virginia Plan for a relatively powerful national government early in the Convention's proceedings, believed that the executive should be composed of more than one person and appointed by the legislature. A single executive, he warned, would be "the foetus of monarchy."[10] The New Jersey Plan, constituting the small states' rejoinder to the Virginia Plan, provided specifically for a plural executive designated by Congress.

In the end, however, Wilson and the other advocates of a strong executive—including James Madison, who became a convert to their cause—would get most of what they wanted. On June 4 and again on July 17, the Convention voted for a single executive.[11] Later in July, as a member of the Convention's Committee of Detail, Wilson was able to write his concept of a strong and independent executive into the Constitution. In language that would be subjected to only stylistic improvement in the final days of the Convention, Wilson wrote: "The executive power of the United States shall be vested in a single person. His stile shall be 'The President of the United States of America.' . . ." Wilson's language excluded any executive council and spelled out Presidential powers in substantial detail.[12] The historian Charles Thach suggests that "when Wilson wrote into the report of the Committee of Detail the sentence, 'the executive power of the United States shall be vested in a single person,' it marked the final abandonment of the concept of the omnipotence of the legislature, and the substitution therefor of the characteristically American doctrine of coordinate departments."[13]

Wilson, Morris and Madison failed to get their way in the direct election of the President (see page 41, below), but they did succeed in scuttling the proposal for electing the President in the national legislature. In its place, a system of intermediate electors was substituted—a system they hoped would approximate a choice by the people.

REELIGIBILITY AND LENGTH OF TERM. The delegates had generally agreed that if the President were to be chosen by the legislature, he ought to be ineligible for a second term. Barring this limitation, George Mason of Virginia warned, there would be "a temptation on the side of the executive to intrigue with the legislature for a reappointment." The Virginia and New Jersey Plans, both stipulating election by the legislature, made the Chief Executive ineligible for reappointment.

Major objections arose, however, to a one-term limitation. Sherman warned that such a policy would result in "throwing out of office the man best qualified to execute its duties" and insisted that "he who has proved himself to be most fit for an office, ought not to be excluded by the Constitution from holding it."[14] Fears were also expressed that a man barred from running again might resort to unconstitutional maneuvers to prolong his hold on the Presidency.

To a degree, the possibility of a long term for the executive—the most common proposal was for seven years—seemed to reduce the disadvantages in limiting a Chief Executive to a single term. But even this alternative raised problems. Gunning Bedford of Delaware asked his fellow delegates "to consider what the situation in the country would be, in case the first magistrate should be saddled on it for such a period and it should be found on trial that he did not possess the qualifications ascribed to him. . . . An impeachment," Bedford said, "would be no cure for this evil, for an impeachment would reach misfeasance only, not incapacity." Gouverneur Morris said he favored making the executive reeligible lest one "destroy the great motive to good behaviour, the hope of being rewarded with a reappointment."[15]

In a speech to the Convention on June 18, Alexander Hamilton of New York suggested that the executive authority be vested in a Governor who would "serve during good behaviour." But when the Convention actually debated a similar resolution on July 17, Mason of Virginia said he considered "an executive during good behaviour as a softer name for an executive for life. And that would be an easy step to hereditary monarchy."[16] The motion for an executive term on good behaviour was rejected July 17 by a vote of 4 states in favor, 6 opposed.[17] When rumors began to circulate outside the Convention that a monarchy might be established under a royal European family—there had even been rumors that George Washington might be made a crowned head—a firm denial was issued. "Tho we cannot, affirmatively, tell you what we are doing; we can, negatively, tell you what we are not doing—we never once thought of a King," read the key part of a message "leaked" to the press by an unidentified delegate in mid-August.[18] This would be the only break in the policy of strict secrecy maintained during the four months that the Convention met.

The final Presidential election plan that the Convention would adopt was reported by a special committee on September 4. It was immediately apparent that the proposals for legislative election, long terms and ineligibility for reelection of the President had been defeated. The President would serve for a period of four years, and he would be indefinitely eligible for reelection. This remained the basic law of the land until ratification in 1951 of the 22nd Amendment, limiting the President to two four-year terms.

THE LARGE VERSUS THE SMALL STATES. There were enormous disparities in population and power between the states at the Constitutional Convention. Each state was jealous of its own prerogatives; each had existed for generations as a separate colony and, for better or worse, as a near-sovereign state under the Articles of Confederation. Small states, like the Carolinas, Delaware and Connecticut, were naturally the most apprehensive about a strong federal Union, fearing that their lordly neighbors—states such as New York, Pennsylvania and Virginia—might swallow them up.

The Convention's initial decisions in the area of large- versus small-state power did not relate to the Presidency but to representation in Congress. The Virginia Plan, presented early in the Convention by Randolph though its chief author was Madison, was based on the assumption that an entirely new Constitution was required—not just a rewriting of the Articles of Confederation—and that a strong national government ought to be established. Representation in both houses of Congress would be based chiefly on population. Little basic objection was raised to the principle of a powerful national government, but small state delegates did resent the apportionment scheme obviously written with the interests of the populous larger states in mind. "You see the consequences of pushing things too far," John Dickinson of Delaware told Madison on the Convention floor. "Some of the members of the small states wish for two branches of the general legislature and are friends to a good national government; but we would sooner submit to a foreign power than . . . be deprived of an equality of suffrage in both branches of the legislature, and thereby be thrown under the domination of the big states."[19]

The stage was then set for the presentation on June 15 by William Patterson of the so-called New Jersey Plan, based on the principle of equal representation for all the states in Congress with a significant strengthening of the Articles of Confederation. At this point the Convention appeared to be in real deadlock as the large states insisted on population-based apportionment and the small states held firm for equal representation. In a vote on June 19, seven states were in favor of continuing with the Virginia rather than the New Jersey Plan for the new government.[20] But the small states had established their case. As John Roche points out in an essay on the Convention, "from that day onward, it could never be forgotten that the state governments loomed ominously in the background and that no verbal incantations could exorcise their power."[21]

As early as June 20 the first glimmerings of compromise appeared when Sherman suggested that the national legislature "have two branches, and a proportional representation in one of them, provided each state had an equal voice in the other." But the "nationalists," led by Madison and Wilson, were reluctant to give ground. Madison tried to allay small-state fears by saying that the large states like Virginia, Pennsylvania and Massachusetts had no common economic and religious beliefs that would unite them against the smaller ones. Wilson asked the delegates, "Can we forget for whom we are forming a government? Is it for *men*, or for imaginary beings called *states?*"[22]

Political realities militated against a nationalist victory, however, since it was clear that ratification of a Constitution lacking strong guarantees for representation of the states *as states* would be difficult if not impossible. By July 2 the earlier majority for population-based apportionment had been reduced to a dead tie, and a special committee of one delegate from each state was appointed to work out a compromise. The result was the famed "Connecticut Compromise," reported to the Convention on July 5. The compromise provided population-based apportionment in the first branch of the legislature, which would have the authority to originate money bills. In the second branch of the legislature each state would have had an equal vote. After many more days of debate, the Connecticut Compromise was finally approved on July 16 by the narrow margin of 5 states to 4.[23] The Convention had faced and survived its most serious crisis.

The problem of large- versus small-state power appeared again in the Convention's debates on how the President should be elected. But the bulk of these debates took place *after* the Connecticut Compromise had been adopted, and they lacked the crisis atmosphere of the discussion and vote on Congressional representation. The alignments, though, were similar. The "nationalist" group favored a direct vote or some other system accurately reflecting population distribution. Small-state delegates feared that they would have no significant vote, under these circumstances, in the choice of a Chief Executive. "The most populous states by combining in favor of the same individual will be able to carry their points," Charles Pinckney of South Carolina warned. Ellsworth and Sherman of Connecticut voiced the same fears, and on August 24 Sherman opposed the plan for election by the national legislature (as reported by the Committee of Detail) because it would deprive "the states represented in the Senate of the negative intended them in that house." Madison defended the use of a joint ballot of members of both houses of Congress in choosing a President, saying that the rule of voting would "give to the largest state, compared with the smallest, an influence as four to one only, although the population is ten to one."[24]

The small states were not mollified by Madison's argument, however. Four of them opposed the proposal to have the Presidential election by joint ballot in Congress, and a motion by Jonathan Dayton of New Jersey to give each state one vote in the joint session to elect the President was barely defeated—5 states in favor, 6 opposed.[25] These votes made it clear that some further steps to appease small-state interests would have to be made in the Presidential election plan finally approved by the Convention.

These concessions were apparent when on September 4 the Committee of Eleven reported to the Convention the details of its intermediate elector plan, the plan that would become part of the Constitution. First, each state would have as many Presidential electoral votes as it had Representatives and Senators combined. This carried the Connecticut Compromise over into the Presidential election and gave the small states some relative advantage because of the two extra electoral votes corresponding to the number of Senators, regardless of how small a state's population might be. But it must be noted that this compromise was *not* considered crucial at the time. It had not been sufficient to mollify the small states when attached to a proposal for election of the President in Congress. At no time after the Committee of Eleven reported was any mention made on the Convention floor of the supposed advantage to small states of the Senatorial "counterpart" votes. Nor was this apparent concession mentioned in the subsequent ratifying conventions.

What *was* considered a major concession to the small states was the provision of the intermediate elector plan which stipulated that in the event there was no majority in the electoral college, the choice of the President would be transferred to the Senate, where each state would have equal voting power. (The Convention subsequently voted to shift the contingent election responsibility to the House of Representatives, but the provision for equality of state voting power was preserved.) The delegates apparently believed that many of the Presidential electors would vote for men from their own state and region, making a final choice in the electoral college unlikely and throwing most elections into Congress. The small states were expected to benefit further from the provision that the Senate (or later the House), when called upon to choose the President, would be required to choose from among the *five* persons who received the most electoral votes. There was a good chance that one or more of the five would be small-state candidates. Sherman of Connecticut, who had been a member of the Committee of Eleven, told the Convention that if the small states "had the advantage in the Senate's deciding among the five highest candidates, the large states would have in fact the nomination of these candidates."[26] Madison subsequently wrote that the Presidential election provisions were "the result of compromise between the larger and smaller states, giving to the latter the advantage of selecting a President from the candidates, in consideration of the former in selecting the candidates from the people."[27]

SUFFRAGE. A variety of complex voting qualifications existed in the states when the Constitutional Convention met. The Revolutionary period had resulted in some loosening of the restrictive suffrage requirements of the Colonial period, but most states still restricted the franchise to "freeholders"—men who possessed a specified amount of real property, with certain net value or annual yield. The stringency with which these requirements were enforced varied substantially from state to state. Some states were shifting to a simpler requirement that voters pay a certain amount of taxes. Vermont, entering the Union in 1791, would be the first state to permit all adult males to vote.

The major debate on suffrage at the Convention centered on qualifications to vote for the House of Representatives. (The Senate was not a problem, since it was agreed that its members should be selected directly by the state legislatures.) Gouverneur Morris proposed a national freeholder qualification, warning that if votes were given to the propertyless, they would sell them to the rich. John Dickinson of Delaware supported Morris, saying it was necessary to restrict the suffrage to freeholders "as a necessary defense against the dangerous influence of those multitudes without property and without principle." Madison predicted that "in future times a great majority of the people will not only be without land, but any other sort of property. . . . The freeholders of the country would be the safest depositories of republican liberty."[28]

The proposal to write property qualifications into the Constitution stirred spirited opposition, however. Ellsworth of Connecticut argued that "the right of suffrage was a tender point, and strongly guarded by most of the state constitutions. The people will not readily subscribe to the national Constitution if it should subject them to be disfranchised. The states are the best judges of the circumstances and temper of their own people." In one of his rare speeches at the Convention, Benjamin Franklin of Pennsylvania also opposed national freeholder qualifications: "It is of consequence that we should not depress the virtue and public spirit of our common people," said Franklin. "This class possess hardy virtues and great integrity."[29]

Morris' motion for a national freeholder qualification was defeated August 7 by a vote of 1 to 7, and the Convention decided to leave the matter in the hands of the states by approving the recommendation of its Committee of Detail that the voting qualifications in U.S. House elections should be the same as those for the most numerous branch of the state legislature in each state.[30] Even if they were personally disposed toward a freeholder qualification, the delegates feared that an effort to impose a national standard on the states could result in disapproval of the Constitution.

The suffrage problem in Presidential elections was circumvented by failure to guarantee any popular vote whatever for the Chief Executive. The final language of Article II simply provided that "Each state shall appoint, in such manner as the legislature thereof may direct, a number of electors. . . ." The failure to guarantee any popular vote for President was doubtless a conscious act of the Convention, since two plans for intermediate electors presented earlier in the summer had specifically stated that the Presidential electors should be chosen by the qualified voters in the various states.[31] The proposals for direct vote presented at the Convention had failed to specify just who were considered the "people" or "citizens" who would have the right to choose the President.

All the nation's Negro slaves were disfranchised, and the problem of their representation—both in the U.S. House and in Presidential elections—was a difficult one for the Convention. Madison acknowledged that it was the severest obstacle in the way of adopting a direct vote of the people for President.[32] The Convention finally compromised on counting three-fifths of the slave population in determining a state's Congressional representation, and the final elector plan carried the same principle into Presidential elections.

Thus the Convention washed its hands of the problem of voting qualifications for white men, refused to offer any guarantee whatever of a popular role in Presidential elections, and temporized on the question of representation to account for the slave population. The political exigencies of the time apparently made this the only feasible course. As a result, a whole revolution in human and political rights was left for future generations to cope with.

The Presidential Election Plans

Three major proposals for electing the President were debated during the Constitutional Convention: election by Congress (or the national legislature, as it was called through most of the debates), election by a direct vote of the people throughout the nation or election by intermediate electors. In addition, numerous alternative plans were brought forward, ranging from proposals that the state Governors choose the President to one that 15 members of Congress be chosen by lot to elect the next Chief Executive. None of these alternatives aroused much interest, and all were shunted aside with little debate.[33]

ELECTION BY CONGRESS. The idea of placing the choice of the President in the hands of the national legislature appeared in the original Virginia and New Jersey Plans, was specifically approved by votes of the Convention on four occasions, and was incorporated in the important Committee of Detail draft in the latter stages of the proceedings. Basically, it was favored by the delegates who backed a strong legislature and weaker executive, while proponents of a strong executive opposed it. In the end, it foundered on the shoals of executive independence and was rejected.

Sherman stated the definitive case for legislative election on June 1, the first day the Convention debated the mode of choosing the executive. He said the executive "ought to be appointed by and accountable to the legislature only, which was the depository of the supreme will of the society."[34] Looking to the state governments of the time, the delegates could see that no less than eight of the 13 states placed the choice of their executive directly in the hands of the legislature. Moreover, the members of the national legislature—who themselves had been selected by the people and state legislatures— would certainly be in the best position to judge the qualifications of the various candidates to be members of the national executive. The chief advocates of the legislative election, in addition to Sherman, were Randolph and Mason of Virginia, Charles Pinckney and John Rutledge of South Carolina, and William C. Houston of New Jersey.

The most vocal opponents of electing the President in Congress included Gouverneur Morris and Gerry, joined later by Madison. A Chief Executive chosen by the legislature, Morris warned, would be "the mere creature" of that body. Should the legislature elect, "it will be the work of intrigue, or cabal, and of faction: it will be like the election of a pope by a conclave of cardinals; real merit will rarely be the title of the appointment." There was an "indispensable necessity," Morris said, of "making the executive independent of the legislature." Gerry warned that election by the legislature would not only lessen executive independence but "would give birth to intrigue and corruption between the executive and legislature previous to election and to partiality in the executive afterwards to the friends who promoted him." Many delegates also feared the intervention of foreign powers if the legislature were to choose the President. Madison went to the heart of the opposition on July 17 when he said that "a dependence of the executive on the legislature would render it the executor as well as the maker of the laws; and then, according to the observation of Montesquieu, tyrannical laws may be made that they may be executed in a tyrannical manner."[35]

The first Convention vote on election of the President by Congress came June 1, when legislative election of an executive with a seven-year term was approved by a vote of 8 states to 2. The decision for legislative election was confirmed July 17 by a unanimous vote. On July 19 the Convention shifted to an intermediate elector scheme, but returned to election by the legislature on July 24 by a vote of 7 to 4. The motion for legislative election of the President with a single seven-year term was formalized July 26 by a vote of 7 to 3, and this provision was written into the report of the Committee of Detail, received by the Convention on August 6. But major dispute erupted on the Convention floor over the voting power in legislative election—whether it should be by joint ballot (a proposal accepted by a 7 to 4 vote) or by a system under which each state would have an equal vote (rejected by a 5 to 6 vote). The Committee of Eleven, appointed to break the deadlock, discarded the legislative election method in favor of inter-mediate electors. A motion by Rutledge to return to legislative election was rejected September 5 by a 2 to 8 vote, with one state divided, thus dooming the proposal that Congress choose the President.[36] But the final Constitution did preserve some element of the plan by providing that when the electoral college failed to produce a majority, the election would be thrown into the House of Representatives for decision.

DIRECT VOTE OF THE PEOPLE. Only a few delegates to the Constitutional Convention felt that American democracy had matured sufficiently for the choice of the President to be entrusted directly to the people. On the two occasions that the Convention voted on direct vote, the proposal was resoundingly defeated. But the advocates of direct vote were among the Convention's more illustrious members—James Wilson, Gouverneur Morris and James Madison. In retrospect, the arguments they offered seemed better suited to future generations than their own.

Wilson was the first to take the floor for direct election, arguing that "experience, particularly in New York and Massachusetts [two of the states then electing their Governors by direct vote], showed that an election of the first magistrate by the people was both a convenient and successful mode." Wilson said he wanted both houses of Congress and the President chosen by direct popular mandate, "to make them as independent as possible of each other, as well as of the states." Morris summed up the direct election argument by declaring that "the executive magistrate should be the guardian of the people, even of the lower classes, against legislative tyranny. . . . If he is to be the guardian of the people, let him be appointed by the people." Madison admitted that there were objections against virtually every possible mode of electing the President, but it was direct election, "with all its imperfections," that he "liked the best." After all, said Madison, "the

President is to act for the *people,* not the states." He recognized the problem raised by disfranchised slaves in the South, which would reduce his native Virginia's relative vote under direct election. But "local considerations," he said, "must give way to the general interest." As a Southerner, Madison said, he "was willing to make the sacrifice."[37]

Gerry, Sherman, Pinckney and Mason led the opposition to a direct vote of the people. "The people are uninformed and would be misled by a few designing men," Gerry warned. He found the proposal "radically vicious." Some cabal would control the Presidency, such as the Order of the Cincinnati, a unified and influential group with connections throughout the country. "They will in fact elect the chief magistrate in every instance, if the election be referred to the people," said Gerry. Mason declared that "it would be as unnatural to refer the choice of a proper magistrate to the people, as it would, to refer a trial of colors to a blind man. The extent of the country renders it impossible that the people can have the requisite capacity to judge . . . the candidates." Sherman found the proposal impractical because the people would "generally vote for some man in their own state, and the largest state will have the best chance for appointment." Voicing an argument to be heard time and again through U.S. history, Pinckney said he feared that "the most populous states, by combining in favor of the same individual, will be able to carry their points."[38] Moreover, the opponents warned, dangerous commotions might well accompany direct election.

Wilson and Morris took up the debate in rebuttal, arguing that there were no grounds to anticipate disorder in a national election, since it would occur in polling places across a wide land. If the people failed to produce a majority for a single candidate in the first election, Wilson argued, the legislature could then be authorized to choose among the men nominated by the people. Replying to the assertion that the people of the populous states might combine and elect their own man, Morris said: "Just the reverse. The people of such states cannot combine. If there be any combination it must be among their representatives in the legislature. It is said the people will be led by a few designing men. This might happen in a small district. It can never happen throughout the continent. . . . It is said the multitude will be uninformed. . . . But they will not be uninformed of the great and illustrious characters which have merited their esteem and confidence."[39]

Twice the alternative of a direct vote was put to the Convention, and each time the proposal was rejected—by a 1 to 9 vote on July 17 (only Pennsylvania in favor), and by a 2 to 9 vote on August 24 (only Pennsylvania and Delaware in favor).[40] But in the course of their arguments, the backers of popular election had destroyed the initial consensus for electing the President in Congress and laid the groundwork for a compromise proposal—the system of intermediate electors—that would eventually carry the nation most of the way down the road to a choice of the President by all the people.

THE INTERMEDIATE ELECTOR PLAN. The proposal for choosing the President by intermediate electors possessed the virtue of being the second choice of many delegates, though it was the first choice of few, if any, when the Convention began. The plan was first advanced on June 2 by Wilson when he decided that support was lacking for his proposal of a direct popular vote. Luther Martin of Maryland, a states'-rights man, next brought the idea forward on July 17. Gerry backed it as an alternative to direct election, suggesting that the state Governors choose the electors. On July 25 Ellsworth endorsed an elector system that would go into operation only when a President was standing for reelection. Otherwise, he favored election by Congress. Morris of Pennsylvania, a strong direct-election advocate, recommended the elector plan as second best on August 24. Some historians believe that the genesis of the intermediate elector plan was the scheme that Maryland wrote into its constitution in 1777 for the election of its Senate.[41]

When the Committee of Eleven reported the intermediate elector plan to the Convention on September 4, Morris, who served on the Committee, cited six grounds. They were all essentially negative, centering around the dangers of legislative election. The only real advantage Morris could cite for intermediate electors was that "the great evil of cabal" could be avoided since the electors "would vote at the same time throughout the U.S. and at so great a distance from each other."[42]

The elector plan had actually come up for Convention votes on frequent occasions before the Committee of Eleven devised its final form. As proposed by Wilson, with a provision for direct popular vote of the electors in districts, it was rejected June 2 by a 2 to 8 vote. When Martin suggested on July 17 that the President be chosen by electors designated by the state legislatures, the proposal was rejected by an identical 2 to 8 margin. But the mood of the Convention had changed perceptibly two days later when a proposal by Ellsworth for election of the President by electors was approved, 6 to 3 (with one state divided), and his motion that the state legislatures choose them passed, 8 to 2. The Convention then voted an apportionment scheme for electors, ranging between one and three a state, depending on population. On July 23, however, the Convention voted, 7 to 3, to reconsider its decision after William C. Houston of New Jersey pointed out "the extreme inconveniency and the considerable expense of drawing together men from all the states for the single purpose of electing the chief magistrate."[43]

The Committee of Eleven, picked by ballot of the entire Convention on August 31, included a remarkable aggregate of political talent— Rufus King of Massachusetts, Gouverneur Morris of Pennsylvania, James Madison of Virginia, Daniel Carroll of Maryland, John Dickinson of Delaware, Abraham Baldwin of Georgia, Pierce Butler of South Carolina, Nicholas Gilman of New Hampshire, David Brearley of New Jersey, Hugh Williamson of North Carolina and Roger Sherman of Connecticut. They set directly to work and four days later were able to present their ingenious compromise plan to the Convention. The framers' skill as practical politicians, well aware of what could be "sold" and what could not in their home states, was amply evidenced in the intermediate elector scheme they produced. As John Roche has pointed out, "everybody got a piece of the cake."[44] The big states got an element of population-based apportionment in choosing the President; the small states got equal voting rights in the contingent election plan when a majority of the electors failed to agree; the feelings of states'-rights advocates were acknowledged by giving the state legislatures the right to decide how the electors should be chosen; and those who wanted to entrust the choice of the President to the people could see at least the potentiality for popular vote in the scheme presented.

In a relatively brief debate ending September 7, the Convention approved the Committee of Eleven plan and incorporated it into the final Constitution. A few changes were made, the most significant in the method of contingent election. The analysis below shows in italics the wording of the final Constitution in regard to electing the President, together with a comparison to the original Committee of Eleven plan where different, and key votes.

Article II, Section 1. . . . [The President] shall hold his office during the term of four years, and, together with the Vice President, chosen for the same term, be appointed in the following manner: . . .

The four-year term (with indefinite reeligibility) and the idea of having a Vice President were inventions of the Committee of Eleven. A motion to return to the idea of a seven-year Presidential term that the Convention had favored during most of its proceedings was offered by Williamson and Richard Spaight of North Carolina but rejected by a vote of 3 states to 8. The North Carolinians then moved for a six-year term but lost on a 2 to 8 vote. The four-year term was then formally approved with all states but North Carolina in favor.[45]

The Convention spent little time debating the desirability of having a Vice President. Williamson commented that "such an officer as the Vice President was not wanted. He was introduced only for the sake of a valuable mode of election which required two to be chosen at the same time."[46]

Each state shall appoint, in such manner as the legislature thereof may direct, a number of [Presidential] electors, equal to the whole number of Senators and Representatives to which the state may be entitled in Congress. . . .

In opting for this intermediate elector scheme, the Committee of Eleven rejected the much-discussed legislative mode of election and returned to a proposal that had encountered stiff resistance earlier in the proceedings. Predictably, several delegates announced their opposition to the new scheme in its entirety. Rutledge of South Carolina moved on September 5 to return to the proposal for Congressional election of a President limited to a single seven-year term. But the weary delegates were in no mood to return to that deadend. They rejected his motion by a vote of 2 states to 8. The only states supporting Rutledge were North Carolina and his own South Carolina, with New Hampshire divided.[47]

Interestingly, there was no debate in the Convention on the elector apportionment formula recommended by the Committee of Eleven. Nor was there any debate on how the state legislatures should or would select electors—whether they would appoint the electors themselves, require that they be chosen by popular vote in districts, or provide for popular vote statewide. This knotty problem, which would cause endless debates and maneuvers in the state legislatures in the ensuing years, was completely ignored. The legislatures were simply granted complete discretion in the matter.

Nor was there any debate on the real role of electors. Should they be wise men endowed with a wide knowledge of the country and thus best entrusted with choosing a President? Or should they simply be representatives of the legislatures or the people who would designate them? The delegates may have debated the question after hours at the Indian Queen, the local tavern where many spirited discussions took place after the formal sessions. But they barely touched on the question on the Convention floor, if Madison's meticulous notes are to be trusted. The nearest they came to the issue was when Pinckney of South Carolina charged that the electors would "be strangers to the several candidates" for President and thus be "unable to decide on their comparative merits." Wilson replied that "continental characters will multiply as we more and more coalesce, so as to enable the electors in every part of the Union to know and judge of them."[48]

. . . but no Senator or Representative, or person holding an office of trust or profit under the United States, shall be appointed an elector.

This wording was not included in the text of the Committee of Eleven but proposed on the Convention floor by King and Gerry of Massachusetts as a way to prevent Congressmen or federal officials from having a hand in the election of the President with the bribery and intrigue they feared might result. It was approved unanimously.[49]

The electors shall meet in their respective states, and vote by ballot for two persons, of whom one at least shall not be an inhabitant of the same state as themselves. And they shall make a list of all the persons voted for, and of the number of votes for each; which list they shall sign and certify, and transmit sealed to the seat of the Government of the United States, directed to the President of the Senate. . . .

This wording, as recommended by the Committee of Eleven, was left almost untouched by the Convention. The requirement that electors meet in their respective states resolved an objection to earlier forms of intermediate elector plans, which had aroused opposition because of the inconvenience of traveling to the national capital simply to cast ballots. Also, the framers had feared "cabal and corruption" if all the electors actually met at one place, a problem this new wording neatly solved—or so it seemed in the world of 1787, before the growth of national political parties.[50]

Electors were required to cast their ballots for two persons for President—the votes to be of equal weight—in the hopes that at least one of them would be a man of "continental reputation" rather than a fellow citizen of the elector's home state. This requirement would raise enormous difficulties in the first elections, necessitating the 12th

Amendment in 1804 with its provision for separate voting for President and Vice President.

> . . . *The President of the Senate shall, in the presence of the Senate and House of Representatives, open all the certificates, and the votes shall then be counted. The person having the greatest number of votes shall be the President, if such number be a majority of the whole number of electors appointed; . . .*[51]

This section would cause prolonged disputes during the 19th century, because it did not say *who* should actually count the electoral votes—the President of the Senate or the members of the two houses of Congress—and did not stipulate who would have the authority to decide in the event that some electoral votes were challenged. It was little debated by the Convention.

The majority requirement was expected to throw many elections into Congress for decision (see below). A move by Mason of Virginia to strike out the requirement of a majority for election by the electors was rejected on September 5 by a vote of 2 states to 9, and the Convention by the same margin turned down a motion by Madison and Williamson to substitute "one third" for a majority. Gerry argued that a one-third requirement would "put it in the power of three or four states to put in whom they pleased."[52]

> . . . *If there be more than one [candidate for President] who have such a majority, and have an equal number of votes, then the House of Representatives shall immediately choose by ballot one of them for President; and if no person have a majority, then from the five highest on the list the said House shall in like manner choose the President. But in choosing the President, the votes shall be taken by states, the representation from each state having one vote. A quorum for this purpose shall consist of a member or members from two-thirds of the states, and a majority of the states shall be necessary to a choice. . . .*

The Committee of Eleven draft had differed in that it vested the contingent election authority in the Senate—a provision that aroused much opposition and the most debate on the Committee's report. The provision was considered crucial, since many delegates apparently agreed with Mason "that 19 times in 20, the President would be chosen by the Senate."[53] Pinckney warned that with no limit on Presidential terms, the President "will become fixed for life under the auspices of the Senate." Williamson feared that the foundation was being laid "for corruption and aristocracy." The Senate, after all, would itself be chosen by the state legislatures, not by the people directly. But when

Wilson moved on September 5 to shift the contingent election to the House instead, he was defeated on a vote of 3 states to 7 (with one divided). The bulk of the opposition came from the smaller states.[54]

Undaunted, Wilson returned to the attack the next day, warning of the excessive power being placed in the hands of the Senate if control of the Presidency were added to its powers over treaties, impeachments and approval of appointments. Wilson saw a danger of blending the legislative, executive and judicial functions into one branch of government. "According to the plan as it now stands, the President will not be the man of the people as he ought to be, but the minion of the Senate," Wilson warned. But again he was defeated, the Convention voting 6 to 4 to retain the contingent election power in the Senate.[55]

The final compromise was then brought forward by Williamson and Sherman, who proposed that the contingent election be decided in the House but that each state have but a single vote. The Convention quickly seized on this alternative by an affirmative vote of 10 states, with only Delaware opposed.[56]

The great debate on the election of the President was now over, but Madison the next day (September 7) warned of the problem of election in the House with each state enjoying a single vote. In some instances, he said, a single man might cast his state's vote. This led to a "further weighty objection, that the representatives of a *minority* of the people might reverse the choice of a *majority* of the states and of the people." Gerry moved to require that a majority of the state delegations be obtained to elect a President in the House, thus meeting one part of Madison's objection, and the Convention agreed.[57] But it would still be possible for a minority of the people to elect a President in this manner. Madison had detected the profoundly undemocratic potentialities of a contingent election in which each state would have a single vote—a problem the nation would still have to face 180 years later.

Another problem of this section was the provision that the contingent election should be from among the *five* candidates receiving the most electoral votes—a clear concession to the smaller states, since a restriction of the number of candidates to the two or three receiving the most electoral votes would more likely have confined the choice to candidates from the larger states. Mason and Gerry moved to reduce the number of candidates in the contingent election from five to three, but lost on a 2 to 8 vote. A small-state countermove to make the choice from 13 candidates—apparently on the assumption that each state could then "nominate" a man—was rejected, with only the Carolinas in favor.[58]

Another floor amendment, that the contingent election take place "immediately" in instances where it was required, was approved without objection, probably in the belief that the outcome of the electoral vote would not be known until the count in Congress was announced and that quick runoff would prevent corruption and cabal among the members of Congress called on to make the choice.[59]

. . . In every case, after the choice of a President, the person having the greatest number of votes of the electors shall be the Vice President. But if there should remain two or more who have equal votes, the Senate shall choose from them by ballot the Vice President.

This proposal, from the Committee of Eleven, was not altered by the Convention. It is interesting to note that a majority electoral vote for Vice President was not required. A separate vote for Vice President, together with a majority requirement, would be established by the 12th Amendment.

The Congress may determine the time of choosing the electors, and the day on which they shall give their votes, which day shall be the same throughout the United States.

The last phrase, requiring that the electors meet on the same day, was inserted from the Convention floor September 6 on an 8 to 3 vote.[60] It was apparently another device to prevent what the framers saw as "the great evil of cabal" between the electors.

No person except a natural born citizen, or a citizen of the United States at the time of the adoption of this Constitution, shall be eligible to the office of President; neither shall any person be eligible to that office who shall not have attained the age of thirty-five years, and been fourteen years a resident within the United States.

This language, from the Committee of Eleven, was accepted without debate.

In case of the removal of the President from office, or of his death, resignation or inability to discharge the powers and duties of the said office, the same shall devolve upon the Vice President, and the Congress may by law prescribe for the case of removal, death, resignation or inability, both of the President and Vice President, declaring what officer shall then act as President, and such officer shall act accordingly, until the disability be removed, or a President shall be elected.

This provision was suggested on the Convention floor September 7 by Randolph of Virginia and approved by a vote of 6 states to 4, with one (New Hampshire) divided.[61] The questions of what constitutes Presidential "inability," who shall decide when it has begun and ended, and whether a Vice President succeeding to the office would enjoy its full powers were to provide major problems for Presidential administrations and the Congress for the next 180 years. The Constitution would not be definitively clarified on this point until the ratification in 1967 of the 25th Amendment to the Constitution, providing that the Vice President "shall become President" on the death or resignation of the President, authorizing the President to nominate a new Vice President (subject to approval of the Congress) when the latter office should become vacant, and spelling out steps to be followed in the event of a temporary or permanent Presidential inability.[62]

The Ratification Debates

With the hindsight that history affords, it is remarkable to note how little the opponents of the new Constitution attacked the Presidential election system in the sometimes tumultuous ratifying conventions that followed submission of the document to the states in September 1787.[63] In the Pennsylvania convention James Wilson went unchallenged when he declared that "the manner of appointing the President of the United States, I find, is not objected to."[64] In *The Federalist* paper No. 68, published the following March, Alexander Hamilton would confidently state: "The mode of appointment of the chief magistrate of the United States is almost the only part of the system, of any consequence, which has escaped without severe censure, or which has received the slightest mark of approbation from its opponents." The more reasonable opponents, Hamilton said, had even admitted "that the election of the President is pretty well guarded."[65]

The silence of the Constitution's enemies, who were utterly forthright in their critique of so many other portions of the document, is all the more remarkable in light of the inherent contradiction in the way that Madison, Hamilton and the Constitution's other advocates explained the system. On the one hand, they suggested that the President would be the man of the people and spring almost directly from them. On the other hand, they would either suggest that wise electors would make the choice or that the real power would lie in the hands of the state legislatures.

Madison was foremost in suggesting an essentially democratic election procedure. The President, he told the Virginia ratifying convention, "will be the choice of the people at large." It was only because of the difficulties of direct vote in as large a land as America, he indicated, that the indirect system was proposed, but the people would choose the electors.[66] In *The Federalist* paper No. 39, Madison announced: "The President is indirectly derived from the choice of the people."[67] Wilson told his fellow Pennsylvanians: "The choice of this officer is brought as nearly home to the people as practicable. With the approbation of the state legislatures, the people may elect with only one remove."[68] And Hamilton wrote in *The Federalist* No. 68: "It was desirable, that the sense of the people should operate" in choosing a President, and that the President should be dependent for his continuation in office on none "but the people themselves."[69]

Reading only these portions of the debate, one would assume that the people's voice was to be almost direct in choosing the Chief Executive. But the same proponents had another message to deliver. Wrote Madison in *The Federalist* paper No. 45: "Without the intervention of the state legislatures, the President of the United States cannot be elected at all. They must in all cases have a great share in his appointment, and will perhaps in most cases of themselves determine it." And Hamilton would depict the Presidential electors as men of special "information and discernment" who would not be as corruptible as the people themselves might be and would be able to choose a Chief Executive "free from any sinister byass."[70]

Thus there was never a clear definition of how much electors should rely on their own inclinations rather than the popular will. Perhaps the issue lacked importance in the minds of many, since it was universal knowledge that George Washington would be picked as the first President with the virtually unanimous support of his countrymen.

Nor was there any substantial challenge to the "double balloting" system that would lead to the 12th Amendment 17 years later, or to the Constitution's total silence on how state legislatures should arrange for selection of the Presidential electors. In the Virginia convention Randolph did proclaim that "the electors must be elected by the people at large," but he could point to no provision of the Constitution to support his assertion. James Monroe, a future President, told the same Virginia convention: "I believe that he [the President] will owe his election, in fact, to the state governments, and not to the people at large."[71]

The most frequent argument which the Constitution's supporters presented in favor of the electoral system was that it would prevent what Hamilton called the "heats and ferments . . . tumult and disorder . . . cabal, intrigue and corruption" which might well accompany the election of a President. No corruption would be possible, he claimed, because of the "transient existence" and "detached situation" of the electors.[72]

Even though the country still lacked any semblance of an organized party system, it is hard to believe that hardheaded politicians like Alexander Hamilton could have believed that election of a President would operate in a political vacuum. The historian Carl Becker has commented: "If the motives of the founding fathers in devising the electoral system were of the highest, it must be said that their grasp of political realities, ordinarily so sure, failed them in this instance. Of all the provisions of the federal Constitution, the electoral system was the most unrealistic—the one provision not based solidly on practical experience and precedent. It was in the nature of an academic invention which ignored experience in the vain expectation that, in this one instance for this high purpose, politicians would cease to be politicians, would divest themselves of party prejudice and class and sectional bias, and be all for the time being noble Brutuses inspired solely by pure love of liberty and the public good."[73]

The most basic reason that the electoral college was invented was that the Convention was deadlocked on simpler schemes like direct election and choice by Congress and thus invented a system that could be "sold" in the immediate context of 1787. The electoral college, John Roche has commented, "was merely a jerry-rigged improvisation which has subsequently been endowed with a high theoretical content. . . . The future was left to cope with the problem of what to do with this Rube Goldberg mechanism."[74]

James Madison, the "father of the Constitution," perhaps was as frank about the problem as any of the framers could ever be when he wrote some 36 years later: "The difficulty of finding an unexceptionable process for appointing the Executive Organ of a Government such as that of the U.S., was deeply felt by the Convention; and as the final arrangement took place in the latter stages of the session, it was not exempt from a degree of the hurrying influence produced by fatigue and impatience in all such bodies; tho' the degree was much less than usually prevails in them."[75]

N O T E S

1. Max Farrand (ed.), *The Records of the Federal Constitutional Convention of 1787,* 4 vols. (New Haven, 1911, 1937) (referred to hereafter as "Farrand"), II, p. 501.
2. John P. Roche, "The Founding Fathers: A Reform Caucus in Action," *American Political Science Review,* Dec. 1961, p. 810.
3. Letter to George Washington, Nov. 24, 1786, cited by Charles C. Thach, *The Creation of the Presidency, 1775–1789* (Baltimore, 1922), p. 29.
4. *Rights of Man* (Everyman ed.), p. 207, cited by Thach, *op. cit.,* p. 30.
5. Letter to his father, Nov. 1786, *Madison's Works* (Cong. ed.), I, p. 253, cited by Thach, *op. cit.,* p. 19.
6. Farrand, *op. cit.,* II, p. 35.
7. Letter to Carrington, Aug. 4, 1787, *Jefferson's Writings* (Ford ed.), IV, p. 424, cited by Thach, *op. cit.,* p. 71. Jefferson was the United States minister to France at the time of the Constitutional Convention, and thus did not serve as a delegate.
8. Thach, *op. cit.,* pp. 36–37. The chief authors of the New York Constitution were John Jay, Robert Livingston and Gouverneur Morris. Morris left New York following his 1779 defeat for reelection to the Continental Congress and settled in Philadelphia. He was designated as one of the Pennsylvania delegates to the Constitutional Convention. Subsequently, he served as a U.S. minister in Europe and resettled in New York, serving as a U.S. Senator from that state from 1800 to 1803.
9. Farrand, *op. cit.,* I, pp. 52, 65, 97.
10. *Ibid.,* I, pp. 65–66, 85.
11. *Ibid.,* I, p. 97; II, p. 29. The June 4 vote was 7–3, the July 17 vote, 10–0.
12. *Ibid.,* II, p. 171. The title "President" appears to have been proposed to the convention by Charles Pinckney of South Carolina, to whom it may have been suggested by the title at that date of the chief magistrate of Delaware. See Thach, *op. cit.,* p. 109.
13. Thach, *op. cit.,* pp. 166–67.
14. Farrand, *op. cit.,* I, p. 68; II, p. 55.
15. *Ibid.,* I, p. 69; II, p. 33.
16. *Ibid.,* I, p. 292; II, p. 35.
17. A summary of other Convention voting on the length of term and reeligibility:
    Under proposals for election of the President by the national legislature: Proposals for a seven-year term with reeligibility unspecified were approved by the Convention June 1 on a 5–4 vote, with one state divided, and June 2 by an 8–2 vote (Farrand, *op. cit.,* I, pp. 69, 77). The Convention June 2 voted 7–2, with one state divided, to limit the executive to a single seven-year term (*ibid.,* I, p. 88). On July 16, the Convention voted 6–4 to permit

the Chief Executive to seek reelection (*ibid.*, II, p. 35). Proposals to make him ineligible for reelection but extend his term up to 8, 11, 15 or even 20 years were considered July 24 (*ibid.*, II, p. 102). The Convention July 26 voted to return to the seven-year term with a one-term limit, by a vote of 7–3 (*ibid.*, II, p. 120). The report of the Committee of Detail, submitted August 6, contained an identical provision.

Under proposals for election by intermediate electors: Under an early version of this plan, the Convention voted 8–2 on July 19 to make the Chief Executive eligible for reelection, and voted to reduce the term from seven to six years (*ibid.*, II, pp. 58–59). The final plan, submitted by the Committee of Eleven on September 4, provided for a four-year term and indefinite reeligibility. The Convention September 6 voted 3–8 to reject a motion to extend the term to seven years, and 2–9 against a motion to extend it to six years. The four-year provision was approved by a 10–1 vote (*ibid.*, II, p. 525). The provision for indefinite reeligibility was not challenged during this final stage of the debate.

18. Clinton Rossiter, *1787—The Grand Convention* (New York, 1966), pp. 222–23.
19. Farrand, *op. cit.*, I, p. 242.
20. Three states were opposed and one divided. The vote could not be characterized completely as a large- versus small-state decision, since New York joined Delaware and New Jersey in voting to use the New Jersey Plan as the basis for further debate.
21. Roche, *loc. cit.*, p. 808.
22. Farrand, *op. cit.*, I, pp. 343, 447–48, 483.
23. *Ibid.*, II, p. 15. Voting in favor were Connecticut, New Jersey, Delaware, Virginia and North Carolina. Opposed were Pennsylvania, South Carolina, Maryland and Georgia. Massachusetts was divided. New York did not vote, since two of its three delegates (Robert Yates and John Lansing, Jr.), both of whom were strongly antinationalist and out of sympathy with the effort to write a strong constitution, had departed Philadelphia early in July. Alexander Hamilton, the third member of the New York delegation, attended sporadically but could not cast a vote for the state.
24. *Ibid.*, II, pp. 30, 111, 401, 403.
25. *Ibid.*, II, p. 404. Both votes occurred Aug. 24.
26. *Ibid.*, II, p. 513.
27. Jonathan Elliott, *The Debates in the Several State Conventions on the Adoption of the Federal Constitution*, 2nd ed. (Washington, 1836), II, pp. 495, 464.
28. Farrand, *op. cit.*, II, pp. 201–4.
29. *Ibid.*, II, pp. 201, 204, 208.
30. *Ibid.*, II, pp. 206, 216. Scraps of memoranda of the members of the Committee of Detail indicated they had considered such voter qualifications as "possession of real property," "inrolment in the militia" and "freeholders." *Ibid.*, II, pp. 140, 151.
31. *Ibid.*, I, p. 81; II, p. 404.
32. *Ibid.*, II, pp. 57, 111.

33. The proposal for election by state Governors was advanced by Elbridge Gerry of Massachusetts and rejected by the Convention, 9 states opposed and 1 divided (Farrand, *op. cit.,* I, pp. 175–76). Gerry subsequently proposed that state Governors appoint the President with the advice of the Governors' councils, but if the state had no council (all but New York did at the time), then by the state legislature. The motion never came to a vote (*ibid.,* II, p. 109). A proposal for electing the President by 15 members of Congress chosen by lot was advanced, perhaps ironically, by Wilson of Pennsylvania, otherwise a strong backer of direct election by the people. Wilson commented candidly that his proposal for choice by 15 Congressmen was "not a digested idea and might be open to strong objections." It was not brought to a vote (*ibid.,* II, p. 103). Other hybrid plans included a proposal by Oliver Ellsworth of Connecticut that the President be chosen by Congress unless the incumbent had been in office for a whole term and would be eligible for reelection, in which case electors selected by the state legislatures would choose. The proposal was rejected, 4 states to 7 (*ibid.,* II, pp. 108, 112). John Dickinson of Delaware suggested that each state be allowed to choose its best citizen, and of the 13 men so designated, the President would be chosen by Congress or electors appointed by Congress. The proposal never came to a vote (*ibid.,* II, pp. 114–15).
34. *Ibid.,* I, p. 65.
35. *Ibid.,* II, pp. 29, 34, 175, 500.
36. *Ibid.,* I, p. 81; II, pp. 33, 101, 120, 185, 404, 511.
37. *Ibid.,* I, pp. 68–69; II, pp. 29, 52–53, 111, 403.
38. *Ibid.,* II, pp. 29–31, 57, 114.
39. *Ibid.,* II, pp. 30–31.
40. *Ibid.,* II, pp. 32, 402.
41. Under the Maryland plan, the state Senate was chosen by an electoral college of 40 members—two from each county, plus one additional from Baltimore City and one additional from Annapolis. The electors were charged with selecting persons "of the most approved wisdom, experience and virtue." The electors were required to choose nine of the 15-member Senate from the Western Shore of Maryland and six from the Eastern Shore. They could choose persons from their own number as Senators, or any number from any given county, as long as the 9–6 ratio was preserved. Within a generation, one Maryland historian records, the state Senate was not only "free from the gusts of popular passions" (a phrase Alexander Hamilton used in defending the institution), but also "not open to decent ventilation" (a phrase used by the Jeffersonian Democrats in attacking it). Matthew Page Andrews, *History of Maryland* (Garden City, N.Y., 1929), pp. 330–31.
42. Farrand, *op. cit.,* II, p. 500.
43. *Ibid.,* I, p. 81; II, pp. 33, 58, 64, 95.
44. Roche, *loc. cit.,* p. 810.
45. Farrand, *op. cit.,* II, p. 525.
46. *Ibid.,* II, p. 537.
47. *Ibid.,* II, p. 511.

48. *Ibid.*, II, p. 501.
49. *Ibid.*, II, p. 521.
50. In debate on this section, a motion was made that the electors meet at the seat of the national government, but only one state (North Carolina) voted for it. *Ibid.*, II, p. 525.
51. The word "appointed" did not appear in the Committee of Eleven draft. It was inserted on the motion of Dickinson of Delaware "to remove ambiguity" —and, as experience would demonstrate in the early years, to make it easier to achieve a majority if some states failed to appoint electors. Dickinson's motion was approved by an 8–2 vote. *Ibid.*, II, p. 515.
52. *Ibid.*, II, pp. 513–14.
53. A more perspicacious observer was Baldwin of Georgia, who thought the Senate would "be less and less likely to have the eventual appointment" because of "the increasing intercourse among the people of the states," making candidates well known to all. *Ibid.*, II, p. 501.
54. *Ibid.*, II, pp. 512–13.
55. *Ibid.*, II, pp. 522–23, 527.
56. *Ibid.*, II, p. 527. Williamson's first proposal was actually for choice of "the legislature," apparently meaning both houses. Sherman suggested the modification to choice by the House, which was approved.
57. *Ibid.*, II, p. 536.
58. *Ibid.*, II, pp. 514–15.
59. *Ibid.*, II, p. 526.
60. *Ibid.*, II, p. 526.
61. *Ibid.*, II, p. 535.
62. *Congressional Quarterly 1965 Almanac* (Washington, 1966), pp. 573–81; John D. Feerick, *From Failing Hands: The Story of Presidential Succession* (New York, 1965).
63. The major opposition arguments—such as they were—did not appear until the convention in Virginia, the tenth of the 13 original states to ratify. It was claimed that foreign states might interfere in Presidential elections or that the President would conspire with Congress to stay in office for life or that he would become a despot. One of the more cogent arguments was that if an election were thrown into the House, the majority could consist of 15 Representatives constituting a majority of the delegations of seven states—outvoting 50 other Representatives from the other six states. George Mason contended that the elector system "was a mere deception—a mere *ignis fatuus* on the American people,—and thrown out to make them believe they were to choose" the President. "The people will, in reality, have no hand in the election," Mason said. Elliott, *op. cit.*, III, pp. 492–93.
64. *Ibid.*, II, p. 511.
65. *The Federalist*, Jacob E. Cooke (ed.), (Middletown, Conn., 1961), pp. 457–58.
66. Elliott, *op. cit.*, III, pp. 487, 494.
67. Cooke, *op. cit.*, p. 252.
68. Elliott, *op. cit.*, II, p. 512.

69. Cooke, *op. cit.*, pp. 458, 460.

70. *Ibid.*, pp. 311, 458–59.

71. Elliott, *op. cit.*, III, pp. 486, 488. Monroe opposed ratification.

72. Cooke, *op. cit.*, pp. 458–59.

73. Carl Becker, "The Will of the People," *Yale Review*, March 1945, p. 389.

74. Roche, *loc. cit.*, p. 811.

75. Letter to George Hay, Aug. 23, 1823, cited in Farrand, *op. cit.*, III, p. 458.

3 The First Elections

THE TENDER GREENS OF A VIRGINIAN SPRING HAD BEGUN TO COVER THE land as General George Washington departed Mount Vernon on April 16, 1789, for his trip to New York to be sworn in as the first President of the United States. Normally, the stagecoach trip might have taken five days. But Washington would not reach Manhattan until the 23rd of the month. Everywhere, the people turned out to welcome their new Chief Executive. Washington was feasted at Alexandria, warmly entertained at Georgetown, and when he arrived in Philadelphia was welcomed by the Governor and his troops as the city's church bells rang and a *feu de joie* was ignited. At Trenton, the women of that city erected a triumphal arch at the Assumpink bridge over which Washington had led his little army 12 years earlier, on the night before the Battle of Princeton.

Local militia companies—veterans of the Revolutionary War and some of the French and Indian wars—escorted Washington through New Jersey: the Hunterdon Horse from Trenton to Rocky Hill, the Somerset Horse to Brunswick, the Middlesex Horse from Brunswick to Woodbridge, and finally the Essex Horse to Elizabethtown Point. Thirteen pilots rowed the General's barge across the harbor to Murray's wharf, where Governor Clinton and the new United States Senators and Representatives were present to escort him through throngs of cheering New Yorkers to the house made ready for his use.

Seven days later, when the final touches had been completed on the refurnished Federal Hall, which would house the first Congress, Washington appeared on the building's balcony to take the now-familiar oath of office, as prescribed in the Constitution: "I do solemnly swear that I will faithfully execute the office of President of the United States, and will to the best of my ability preserve, protect and defend the Constitution of the United States." Chancellor Robert Livingston of New York administered the oath, and when the ceremony was finished, turned to the multitude filling Broad and Wall streets and cried, "Long live George Washington, President of the United States!" As the crowd took up the cry and the cannon roared on the Battery, Washington withdrew to the Senate chamber to deliver his inaugural address. The Presidency was born.[1]

It was 19 months since the Constitutional Convention had completed its work. The framers stipulated that nine states would be required for ratification, and by the end of 1787, the first three had ratified—Delaware, Pennsylvania and New Jersey. Often in heated debate, the other states followed suit until New Hampshire became the ninth on June 21, 1788. But without Virginia and New York, no viable Union would have been possible. To the joy and relief of the Constitution's backers, these states followed suit on June 26 and July 26, 1788.[2] Now the initial steps could be taken to elect the first Congress and President of the United States.

The old Congress of Confederation bogged down in a dreary debate on where the new seat of government should be located, but on September 18 finally decided on New York and passed a resolution proclaiming the new Constitution to be in effect. The first Wednesday of January 1789 was set as the date for the Presidential electors to be appointed, and they were directed to meet in their own states and ballot for President on the first Wednesday in February. The meeting day for the new Congress was set for March 4, 1789.

In reality it would be April 6 before both houses of the new Congress could muster a quorum and proceed to their first business: counting the electoral votes for President. In joint session the electoral returns from the states were opened and the temporary President of the Senate, John Langdon of New Hampshire, announced that 69 votes—a unanimous tally—had been cast for George Washington. John Adams of Massachusetts received 34 electoral votes and was elected the nation's first Vice President.

Thus, on its first try, the electoral college seemed to be a successful institution. But the appearance was deceptive. Two major sources of difficulty were already apparent.

The first difficulty lay in the method by which the Presidential electors were chosen. The Constitution provided simply that each state would appoint electors "in such manner as the legislature thereof may direct." Did this mean that the legislatures should appoint the electors directly? Or would the people choose the electors? And if the people made the choice, would they choose by districts? Or would the election be on a statewide basis—a method that would come to be known as the general ticket system? In this first Presidential election, five legislatures—those of Connecticut, New Jersey, Delaware, South Carolina and Georgia—simply appointed the electors without reference to the people. The New York Legislature undertook to do the same, but its two houses argued so long about the choice that the deadlock could not be broken before the day on which the electors were to vote. Thus New York lost its vote completely.

In Massachusetts the General Court (legislature) let the people choose electors in districts but appointed two at-large electors itself. Only four states decided to entrust the selection of the electors exclusively to the people—Maryland and Virginia on a district basis, and Pennsylvania and New Hampshire on the general ticket system. But under New Hampshire's complicated election requirements, none of the candidates for elector received a popular vote majority and the legislature ended up appointing the electors itself.[3] Thus, while the President was to be the chief magistrate of all the people, there would be no uniformity in the way that the electors who chose him were elected. Acting under the specific mandate of the Constitution, the state legislatures had an open invitation to manipulate the electoral system in any way they thought might satisfy their immediate partisan purposes.

The second problem related to the system of "double balloting" prescribed by the Constitution. Each elector was required to cast two votes for President. He could not differentiate and indicate he wanted one of those votes to be for President and the other for Vice President. Yet the fact was that every elector, from the first election on, had a distinct preference for President and another distinct preference for Vice President. In this year of 1789, there was no opposition to the selection of the revered George Washington as the first President. Yet there would have to be a Vice President as well. A man from the North was sought to balance Washington's Virginia, and Adams of Massachusetts became the prevailing choice. Yet no one thought of Washington as a possible Vice President, and no one at this point (except perhaps Adams himself) thought of Adams as a candidate for President.[4] The problem was that if all the electors had voted for *both* Washington and Adams, the two men would have been tied in the electoral vote and the choice would have been thrown into the House of Representatives. To avert such an outcome, Alexander Hamilton sent word to several states urging that a few of the electors withhold their votes from Adams. His counsel appears to have been followed directly by some Connecticut and New Jersey electors. In retrospect, Hamilton's action was probably not necessary, since Adams received no votes at all from Delaware, Maryland, South Carolina and Georgia. Indeed, Adams was accorded less than half the electors' "second votes." The tally was 34 for Adams, with most of the remaining 35 votes split among various states' "favorite sons." (For voting in all Presidential elections, see Appendix A.) But the Constitution had no majority requirement for Vice President, so Adams was elected.

If all 13 states had voted, there would have been 91 votes—corresponding to the 65 Representatives and 26 Senators. But Rhode Island and North Carolina, with three and seven votes respectively, had not yet ratified the Constitution. New York's delay in appointing electors cost that state its eight votes, and two electors in both Maryland and Virginia failed to appear on the day of voting. Thus the total number of electoral votes was reduced to 69. According to one historian's account, the absenteeism in Maryland was explained by the ice on the rivers and the Chesapeake Bay, which prevented one elector from reaching Annapolis, while an attack of gout kept the other at home.[5] Had the election been close, such irrational factors could have swayed the future of the republic.

The Elections of 1792 and 1796

Despite the vagueness of the Constitution on the electoral base of the President, the idea of the President as the one, great national representative of the American people began to assert itself from the very year of the nation's birth. The welcome accorded George Washington wherever he went surely demonstrated the people's direct support for him—not simply as citizens of a particular state but as citizens of the United States. In the first Congress, Representative

Thomas Hartley of Pennsylvania declared: "The President is the representative of the people in a near and equal manner; he is the guardian of his country. The Senate are the representatives of the state legislatures." Representative Thomas Scott of Pennsylvania found the President "justly and truly denominated the man of the people. Is there any other person who represents so many of them as the President? He is elected by the voice of the people of the whole Union. . . . No man in the United States has their concurrent voice but him."[6]

But if the concept of the people's President was gaining ground in many quarters, the state legislatures still had a different idea. In the election of 1792 the legislatures of nine of the 15 states then in the Union took onto themselves the function of appointing the Presidential electors directly. (See chart, Appendix B.) In New Hampshire and Massachusetts some of the electors were chosen by the people, others by the legislatures. Only four states—Pennsylvania, Maryland, Virginia and Kentucky—left the choice of electors entirely in the hands of the people. (Pennsylvania and Maryland used the general ticket system, Virginia and Kentucky the district system.)

By the time of this election the first party lines were becoming apparent. The ruling Federalist party was encountering more and more opposition from the group centered around Thomas Jefferson— the anti-Federalists, or as they soon named themselves, the Republicans (and still later, the Democrats). This group did not criticize Washington directly or try to prevent his reelection. Instead, the chief criticism was aimed at Adams. The Republicans' 1792 candidate to oppose Adams for the Vice Presidency was George Clinton of New York. In most states, the choice of electors turned into a strict party contest. The Federalists had solid control of New England, while New York was moving toward the Republican column. The middle states were more Federalist, while North Carolina and Georgia supported Clinton. The final 1792 count showed that each of the 132 electors had cast a vote for Washington. Adams received 77 electoral votes, followed by Clinton with 50, Jefferson with 4, and Aaron Burr of New York with one.

Again in 1796 a majority of the state legislatures appointed the Presidential electors directly. There were now 16 states. Only six gave the people the exclusive right to pick electors—Pennsylvania and Georgia under the general ticket system, Maryland, Virginia, North Carolina and Kentucky under the district method. A popular general ticket election was held in New Hampshire, but when no elector candidates amassed a majority, the legislature picked the electors. Massachusetts again had a mixed system of popular district elections and electors chosen at large by the legislature.

Early in 1796 Washington told his intimates that he would not run for a third term—establishing a tradition that would remain unbroken until the election of Franklin D. Roosevelt for a third term 144 years later. Washington's decision did not become public until September, but the Federalist members of Congress had already caucused during the summer and decided to nominate Adams as their candidate for the Presidency and Thomas Pinckney of South Carolina for Vice President. A Republican Congressional caucus selected the party's natural leader, Thomas Jefferson, for the Presidency and decided to back Burr for Vice President. These Congressional caucuses were of special interest because they established the method of nominating candidates for the Presidency that would survive until the overthrow of "King Caucus" in the 1820s. The rise of the caucus system destroyed forever any lingering pretense that the Presidential electors, chosen later in the election year in each state, would be dispassionate searchers for the men of "continental character" who were fit to be Chief Magistrate of the republic. The founding fathers' conception of the disinterested elector vanished quietly into history, leaving its traces only in the Constitution they created. Henceforth the electors would be little more than political puppets, mere tools of the political parties that had already decided on the nominees.

Now that there would be two bona fide candidates for President, the "double-balloting" system in the electoral college would cause even more difficulties. Not only was there the possibility—recognized since Washington's first election—that the man generally supported for Vice President would get as many votes as the man intended for the Presidency, thus throwing the election into the House with unpredictable results. But now, with two clearly defined parties, each putting forward its candidates for President and Vice President, the winning party might discover that if it instructed a number of electors to withhold their votes from the Vice Presidential choice to prevent an electoral college tie, then the opposing party's Presidential candidate might win the Vice Presidency instead. The result would then be a President of one party and a Vice President of the other.

In fact, this is just what happened in 1796. The dominant Federalists, anxious that their Vice Presidential choice, Pinckney, would not receive as many votes as their Presidential candidate, Adams, withheld

18 electoral votes from Pinckney in New England and 3 in Maryland. Pinckney received 8 votes with Jefferson in South Carolina and one more than Adams in Pennsylvania. The net result was that while Adams won 71 electoral votes, Pinckney lagged 12 votes behind with 59. But Jefferson's over-all total was 68. Thus Jefferson, the Republican, became Vice President in the administration of Adams, the Federalist. (Burr, the Republicans' Vice Presidential choice, received only 30 votes, and another 48 were scattered.) The election results also revealed a clear regional split. The Federalists carried all the states north of Pennsylvania, while the Republicans won all those from Virginia southward. The Federalists won 6 of the 10 Maryland districts, one of them by a margin of only 4 votes. A change of less than 100 popular votes in Pennsylvania, which unexpectedly elected 13 Republican electors out of 15, would have resulted in the election of Pinckney instead of Jefferson as Vice President.[7]

The year 1796 also produced the first faithless elector. He was picked as one of the two Federalist electors in Pennsylvania, so that everyone expected he would vote for Adams, the Federalist candidate. But instead he decided to cast his vote for Jefferson. An exasperated Federalist complained in the *United States Gazette:* "What, do I chuse Samuel Miles to determine for me whether John Adams or Thomas Jefferson shall be President? No! I chuse him to *act,* not to *think.*"[8]

The next winter, when Congress met in joint session for the official count of the electoral votes, Adams—the outgoing Vice President and thus President of the Senate—presided and had the pleasure of declaring his own election as Chief Executive. Adams may have felt a few pangs of nervousness that day, however. An essential part of his majority was comprised of Vermont's four electoral votes, but there was an apparent deficiency in the Vermont electoral law. (The Vermont Legislature proceeded to appoint electors without first passing legislation specifying that designation would be by the Legislature itself rather than by another method.) Happily for Adams, no objection was raised. If the Vermont votes had been invalid, Adams would have had only 67 votes. The total number of valid electoral votes would then have been reduced to 134, and Jefferson—with 68—would have possessed a bare majority and thus won the election.[9]

Commenting in February 1797 on the election results, the *New York Diary* wrote: "Mr. Adams' election is not owing to a fair, decided expression of the public voice, but to the different modes prescribed in the several states for the appointment of electors. A uniform rule on this subject is a desideratum of our Constitution. Accident alone gave Adams the Presidency."[10]

Thus the electoral college's propensity for razor-thin decisions and its susceptibility to political manipulation was abundantly clear as the nation headed for the climactic election of 1800.

The Election of 1800

The four years of John Adams' Administration had witnessed a rapid disintegration of the Federalist party. The disruption of relations with France, leading to talk of war in 1797–98, darkened the foreign scene, while at home the Federalists stirred up bitter opposition by enacting the repressive Alien and Sedition Laws. The brilliant Alexander Hamilton sought to maintain his influence over the Adams Administration, of which he was not a member, a practice that led in 1800 to the dismissal of two of Adams' Cabinet officers who followed Hamilton's lead on policy.[11] This was followed closely by a Republican victory in the New York elections in the spring of 1800 and the appearance of a letter by Hamilton attacking the President.

As the long-dominant party, however, the Federalists were not to be taken lightly, and the country girded itself for a heated contest. In 1799 some Federalist circles sought to induce General Washington to emerge from retirement and run again, but he refused. On December 14, 1799, Washington was dead. The Federalists really had no alternative to Adams, and a party caucus of the Federalists in Congress decided early in 1800 that their party's ticket would consist of Adams and General Charles Cotesworth Pinckney, a brother of Thomas Pinckney, the 1796 candidate. The selections were not authoritatively announced until June, however. Vice President Jefferson was the Republicans' obvious candidate, but a small Congressional caucus was held to confirm his selection as the party's Presidential candidate and to settle on Aaron Burr for Vice President. Jefferson later wrote that Burr had been put on the ticket "out of respect for the favor he had obtained with the Republican party by his extraordinary successes in the New York election in [April] 1800."[12]

The closeness and bitterness of the impending campaign prompted the leading politicians of both parties to rig the methods of choosing Presidential electors in their respective states to maximize their own electoral vote and minimize that of the opposition. Ironically, several members of the Constitutional Convention, men who had declared so confidently in 1787 that they had protected the election of the President against all intrigue and cabal, were at the forefront of the effort.

In Virginia, where the ruling Republicans had witnessed a number of Federalist inroads since 1796, James Madison introduced a bill in the House of Delegates to shift from the district system Virginia had employed in the first three elections to a general ticket system. The change was to be made "until some uniform mode of choosing a President and Vice President of the United States shall be prescribed by an amendment to the Constitution," and the preamble to the bill actually condemned the general ticket system. But Madison told the House of Delegates that necessity had impelled the change. Jefferson had summed up the reasons for the move in a letter to Monroe: "All agree that an election by districts would be best if it could be general, but while ten states choose either by their legislatures or by a general ticket, it is folly or worse for the other six not to follow."[13] The effect of the change in Virginia in 1800, of course, was to assure all the state's 21 electoral votes for Jefferson in that fall's election.

In New York state, where the Legislature had chosen the Presidential electors in the previous elections, the Federalists viewed with alarm the results of the April 1800 elections that had put Republicans in control. Alexander Hamilton wrote to Governor John Jay on May 7 urging that the lame-duck Federalist Legislature be called quickly into session to adopt a popular vote district system that would prevent a solid New York electoral vote for Jefferson. Hamilton told Jay he was aware there were "weighty objections to the measure," but that "in times like these in which we live, it will not do to be overscrupulous." So long as nothing was proposed that integrity would forbid, he said, the scruples of propriety "ought not to hinder the taking of a legal and constitutional step to prevent an atheist in religion, and a fanatic in politics, from getting possession of the helm of state." Jefferson's party, Hamilton warned, was "a composition, indeed of very incongruous materials, but all tending to mischief—some of them to the *overthrow* of the government, by stripping it of its energies; others of them, to a *revolution* after the manner of Bonaparte." The text of Hamilton's letter found its way into the public prints, occasioning strong criticism. The original letter was found years later among Jay's papers, on the back of which the Governor had written: "Proposing a measure for party purposes, which I think would not become me to adopt."[14] In the fall the new Republican Legislature would vote to cast all of New

York's 12 electoral votes for Jefferson and Burr—a crucial factor in the Republican ticket's 8-vote lead in the electoral college.

In Pennsylvania, another key state, the old law providing for popular election of electors on a general ticket had expired and the Senate—under Federalist control by a 2-vote margin—refused to agree to renewal of the statute, fearing that the Republicans would capture the state's electoral votes. The Republicans already controlled the Assembly by a large margin and had won decisive control of both houses of the Legislature and of the Governorship in the 1800 elections. The refusal of the lame-duck Federalists in the Pennsylvania Senate—a group of 13, known as the "Spartan band"—to agree on an election system prompted the Republican newspaper *Aurora* of Philadelphia to comment that because the Constitution lacked "explicitness on the momentous object of choosing electors of a chief magistrate, it is almost in the power of two or three abandoned individuals, by disenfranchising our state, perhaps, to impose a President on the Union contrary to the strongest wishes of the people."[15] Finally, a compromise was arranged that allowed the Senate to choose seven electors and the Assembly to pick eight. Predictably, the Senate picked Federalists, the Assembly Republicans, so that the votes nearly canceled themselves out. "Thus," commented one observer of the past century, "was the vote of a state bargained away."[16]

In Massachusetts, to save the whole ticket for Adams and Pinckney, the General Court was summoned into special session and took on itself the appointment of electors. New Hampshire also withdrew the privilege of voting for electors from the people and appointed six Federalist electors by action of the legislature.[17]

In the end, legislatures picked the Presidential electors in 10 of the 16 states. The only states with popular election were Virginia and Rhode Island (employing the general ticket system) and Maryland, North Carolina and Kentucky (under the district system).

The Federalists had remained confident that they could eke out another victory, and on December 13, 1800—after the electors had already met to cast their votes—the *Columbian Centinel* of Boston confidently asserted that "there cannot be a doubt" of the election of Adams and Pinckney. (This journalistic blunder would go unmatched until the night of November 2, 1948, when the banner headline of an early edition of the Chicago *Tribune* proclaimed: "Dewey Elected President.") One week later the *Centinel* was obliged to "concede" the "bad news" that Jefferson and Burr were chosen. The results were finally determined by the votes of South Carolina, which went for Jefferson and Burr despite the Federalists' expectations of victory.[18] The final electoral count would show 73 votes each for Jefferson and Burr. In amassing its victory, the Republican ticket had won New York, half of Pennsylvania, and every state from Maryland southward.[19] The Federalists were confined to their solid base of support in New England, plus scattered support in the middle states. Adams received 65 electoral votes, Pinckney 64 and John Jay one.

The Republicans, however, could not rejoice. For they had failed to take the precaution of having just one of their electors withhold a vote from Burr. The result was that Jefferson and Burr were in a dead tie, and there was no decision on a President in the electoral college. Ironically, the duty fell to Jefferson, as the Vice President and President of the Senate, to preside over the joint session of Congress on February 11, 1801, where the electoral votes were opened and this unhappy result confirmed.

Now, for the first time in United States history, the House of Representatives was required to choose the President, acting under the contingent election procedure spelled out in the Constitution. Each state would have but a single vote, and if its Representatives were equally divided, the state would lose its vote.

Since late December, when the outcome of the electoral vote had become common knowledge throughout the country, the Federalists had been laying plans to thwart Jefferson's election. The lame-duck Congress, with a strong Federalist majority, would still be in office, and the possibilities for intrigue were all too apparent. An initial Federalist plan was to block any candidate from receiving a majority of the states' votes in the House until March 4, when the offices of President and Vice President would become vacant and a new election could be required under a 1792 law and the original Constitutional language regarding Presidential elections, which was still in effect.[20] This course of action was soon abandoned, however, perhaps because such a naked power play would backfire and result in an easy election for Jefferson in any runoff.

The next plan developed was to throw the support of the Federalist House delegations to Burr, thus electing a cynical and pliant politician over a man the Federalists considered a "dangerous radical."[21] This became the general Federalist strategy, even though Alexander Hamilton remonstrated against it. "I trust the Federalists will not finally be so mad as to vote for Burr," Hamilton wrote to Gouverneur Morris. "I speak with intimate and accurate knowledge of his character. His elevation can only promote the purposes of the desperate and the profligate. If there be a man in the world I ought to hate, it is Jefferson. With Burr I have always been personally well. But the public good must be paramount to every private consideration." In a letter to Albert Gallatin, Hamilton said he "could scarcely name a discreet man of either party" who did not think "Mr. Burr the most unfit man in the United States for the office of President."[22]

When the House of Representatives retired to its own chamber to choose a President on February 11, it became apparent that Hamilton's powerful efforts to dissuade the Federalists from supporting Burr had been only partly successful. A majority of the Federalists in the House insisted on backing Burr over Jefferson, the man they despised the most. Indeed, if Burr had given clear assurances that he would run the government as a Federalist, he might well have been elected. But Burr was unwilling to make those assurances; as one chronicler has put it, "no one knows whether it was honor or a wretched indecision which gagged Burr's lips."[23]

In all, there were 106 members of the House at this time, consisting of 58 Federalists and 48 Republicans. If the ballots had been cast per capita, Burr would have received 53 to Jefferson's 51. But the Constitutional rule was for a single vote for each state, with a requirement that a majority of the states vote for a man before his election could be declared. On the first ballot, Jefferson received the votes of eight states—one short of a majority of the 16 states then in the Union. Six states backed Burr, while Vermont and Maryland were evenly divided, so that their votes could not be counted. The rules of the House required that it remain in continuous session until a President was elected, but by midnight on the first day of balloting, 19 ballots had been taken and the deadlock remained.[24] In all, 36 ballots would be required before the House came to a decision on February 17.

In the meantime, frantic efforts were under way to resolve the deadlock. Two men backing Burr held it in their power to switch their states to Jefferson—James A. Bayard of Delaware and Lewis R. Morris of Vermont. One more state for Jefferson would have given him nine and thus the election. On the other hand, Burr could have gained three states and thus been elected President if two Federalists from New York and one each from New Jersey and Maryland had decided to withdraw their support from Jefferson. Predictably, there were men who sought to exploit the situation for personal gain. Jefferson wrote to

Monroe on February 15: "Many attempts have been made to obtain terms and promises from me. I have declared to them unequivocally that I would not receive the government on capitulation; that I would not go in with my hands tied."[25]

Hamilton directed his efforts of persuasion, which were considerable, on Bayard of Delaware, who initially voted for Burr in the hope Burr would govern as a Federalist. Bayard finally became convinced that Burr's Republicanism was unshakable, however, and announced to one of the Federalist caucuses that he intended to vote for Jefferson. "You cannot well imagine the clamor and vehement invective to which I was subjected for some days," Bayard wrote later.[26] Bayard was persuaded to hold off for a day, but on the 36th ballot on February 17, the impasse was broken. Morris of Vermont turned in a blank ballot, permitting his sole Vermont colleague, Matthew Lyon, to vote the state for Jefferson. The Burr backers in Maryland, sensing that the deadlock had been broken, also cast blank ballots, permitting the four Jefferson backers from that state to switch its support to Jefferson. Delaware and South Carolina also withdrew their support from Burr by casting blank ballots. Thus, at the completion of the 36th ballot, Jefferson had ten states and Burr four. Jefferson was elected the third President of the United States.[27]

But the nation had not survived its constitutional crisis without danger. The Republican Governors of Pennsylvania and Virginia had reportedly been ready to call out their militia to block a Federalist usurpation of the Presidency. Two years later Senator James Jackson of Georgia declared that if the scheme to elect Burr had "been pursued to consummation," Georgia "would have flown to arms, and South Carolina would have joined her to do justice in the interest of the nation."[28]

Once the Presidency was decided in Jefferson's favor, Burr's name stood highest on the list of persons receiving electoral votes and he became Vice President. But Jefferson refused to consult Burr in patronage matters and the Republicans dropped him from their ticket in 1804. Burr returned to New York, bargained for Federalist support in an unsuccessful race for Governor of that state, and darkened his name forever by killing Hamilton in a duel on July 11, 1804.

As for the Federalist party, its day of power was finished. The Congress to take office on March 4, 1801, which had been elected the previous autumn, would have strong Republican majorities in both houses. In the next Presidential election only two states would cast their electoral votes for the Federalist candidate. The Federalists would never again elect a President.

The 12th Amendment

The election of 1800 had demonstrated both the impracticality and the dangers in the Constitution's requirement that each Presidential elector cast two equal, undifferentiated votes for President. The system had been designed in the hope that the Vice President chosen would be a man of high character and ability who could easily assume the Presidency if needed. But the early rise of the party system had altered the situation entirely. Each party decided on the man it wanted for President and selected another—often of inferior quality—for the Vice Presidency. The dangers in the system were threefold. First, there might be a tie vote, as occurred in 1800—bringing an inferior man like Burr perilously close to the Presidency through the kind of intrigue and cabal the founding fathers had hoped most to prevent. Second, if some electoral votes were withheld from the man intended for Vice President, there was a chance that the opposing party's candidate for President might win the Vice Presidency. This occurred with Jefferson's election as Vice President in 1796 over Pinckney, the man the winning Federalists favored that year. And third, the minority party could, if it so chose, switch some of its votes to the Vice Presidential candidate of the opposing party and thus make him President. If Jefferson had received a few less votes than Pinckney in 1796, a solid bloc of Southern Republicans might well have cast votes for Pinckney, making him President instead of Adams. This was seriously considered by many Southern Anti-Federalists.[29] Thus, after only three Presidential elections, an inherent weakness of the electoral system had been demonstrated. By a number of numerical vagaries, the will of the country could be frustrated in any relatively close election.

The first constitutional amendment proposing that electors vote separately for President and Vice President was introduced in Congress in January 1797 by Representative William Smith of South Carolina. In 1798 John Marshall of Kentucky proposed a similar amendment in the Senate, and the following year Representative Abiel Foster of New Hampshire sought unsuccessfully to get the House to debate the proposition. The Vermont Legislature in November 1799 and the Massachusetts General Court in early 1800 proposed similar amendments, but the Congress failed to take action on any of these proposals.[30]

After the 1800 election, pressure for an amendment to the Constitution to avoid the pitfalls of "double-balloting" was renewed. In 1801 and 1802 the New York Legislature, partly on the urging of Alexander Hamilton, passed resolutions asking for a constitutional amendment obliging the electors to vote separately for President and Vice President. (The New York proposals also urged that the system of choosing electors by popular vote in districts be made mandatory, but Congress failed to act affirmatively on this aspect of the recommendation.) An amendment incorporating the separate vote for President and Vice President cleared the House on May 1, 1802, by a 47 to 14 vote, but the Senate failed to get the required two-thirds majority for approval in voting two days later.[31] The Senate vote would have been a bare two-thirds in favor if Gouverneur Morris of New York had not opposed the amendment. Morris explained his vote in a letter to the president of the New York Senate, referring to his role as a delegate to the Philadelphia Convention: "The Convention not only foresaw that a scene might take place similar to that of the last Presidential election [1800], but even supposed it not impossible that at some time or other a person admirably fitted for the office of President might have an equal vote with one totally unqualified, and that, by the predominance of faction in the House of Representatives, the latter might be preferred," Morris said. "This, which is the greatest supposable evil of the present mode, was carefully examined, and it appeared that, however prejudicial it might be at the present moment, a useful lesson would result from it for the future, to teach contending parties the importance of giving both votes to men fit for the first office."[32] Morris' argument is an interesting one, but the records of the Convention indicate that if any such discussion did take place, it was not on the Convention floor. Hamilton easily demolished Morris' argument with the comment: "One such fact as the late election is worth a thousand theories." If Morris saw a danger, however, in degrading the Vice Presidency, he was correct. Opposing the amendment in the House the same year, Roger Griswold of Connecticut warned prophetically: "What will be the effect of this principle? The office of Vice President will be carried to market to purchase the votes of particular states."[33]

The proposed amendment was brought up again and considered at length by the first session of the Eighth Congress, which met in October 1803. By this time, five legislatures were on record as favoring it—New York, Vermont, Massachusetts, North Carolina and Ohio.[34] The opposition seemed to spring from two sources—from the fear of some small states that their voice in the Presidential election would be undercut, and the fear of some Federalists that they would have less chance of electing a Vice President.

Senator William Plumer of New Hampshire, expressing the small-state fears, said that under the proposed amendment "the large states can with more ease elect their candidates." The reason was that there would be less chance of tie votes and thus less chance that the election might be thrown into the House, where the small states enjoyed equal voting power. Yet the Constitution, Plumer said, "is the great plan of compromise between the jarring and contending interests of the great and small states." Seeking to rebut the small-state attack, Senator Samuel Smith of Maryland said that no law could be found in the country's statute books that was produced by such a combination of large-against-small or small-against-large states. But Senator Jonathan Dayton replied angrily that under the proposed amendment, the smaller states would be "degraded to the dependent position of satellites." The people of his New Jersey, Dayton said, "will never willingly submit to such degradation."[35]

The Federalist opposition to a change was based on that party's hope that it could compel the Republicans to scatter enough of their second votes in the Presidential election of 1804 so that the Federalist candidate for President could at least be elected Vice President. Thus the Federalists hoped to exploit the anomalies of the electoral system to elect a Vice President just as the Republicans had done in 1796. The Federalist John Quincy Adams said he considered the proposed amendment "as intending to prevent a federal Vice President being chosen." In the Senate, a dissident Republican, Pierce Butler of South Carolina, sought to pinpoint the motives for the Federalist opposition by saying: "If you do not alter the Constitution, the people called Federalists will send a Vice President into that chair; and this, in truth, is the pivot upon which the whole turns."[36]

The party lines were apparent when the Senate approved the 12th Amendment by a 22 to 10 vote on December 2, 1803, with almost all the Republicans in favor and the Federalists almost solid in opposition. The House then approved after considerable debate on a vote of 84 to 42, with the Speaker (Nathaniel Macon of North Carolina) casting the deciding vote to achieve the required two-thirds. After some differences in wording were ironed out, the Amendment was submitted to the states on December 8, 1803. The states ratified with unexpected rapidity, and the Amendment was declared in effect September 25, 1804, in time for that year's election.[37]

The text of the 12th Amendment—which, with slight changes, remains the law of the land today—appears in Appendix G. It effected the following changes from the original Constitution:

1. The Presidential electors must vote separately for President and Vice President, instead of casting two undifferentiated votes.

2. If an election is thrown into the House of Representatives because no candidate has a majority, the House shall pick from the *three* top electoral vote recipients, rather than the five stipulated in the original Constitution.

3. If the House is called on to pick the President and does not make a selection by March 4 (this date was changed to January 20 by the 20th Amendment, ratified in 1933), then the new Vice President will become President. The original Constitution had no comparable provision.

4. A majority of electoral votes is also required for election as Vice President. The original Constitution had simply provided that the person receiving the second highest number of electoral votes, regardless of whether they constituted a majority, would be elected Vice President. The 12th Amendment left the contingent election for Vice President in the Senate. (The original Constitution had contemplated throwing the Vice Presidential choice into the Senate only if there was a tie for that office.)

5. The age, citizenship and residence requirements of a Vice President are to be the same as those for a President. The original Constitution was silent on this point.

Choosing Electors: From Variety to Uniformity

The practice of shifting the method of choosing Presidential electors from year to year for the benefit of ruling circles in each state, so apparent in the election of 1800, would continue for another quarter-century. The Constitution had given the state legislatures an absolute *carte blanche* in this regard, and the state legislatures seemed to place partisan interests first whenever they had a choice. Massachusetts, for example, shifted its system of choosing electors no less than seven times during the first ten elections. In 1826 a Senate report authored by Thomas Hart Benton noted that the various states' methods of choosing electors "change with a suddenness which defies classification," a practice producing "pernicious effects."[38] The case was put even stronger by Senator Mahlon Dickerson of New Jersey in 1818. "The discordant systems adopted by the different states," he said, "are the subject of constant fluctuation and change—of frequent, hasty and rash experiment—established, altered, abolished, re-established, according to the dictates of the interest, ambition, the whim or caprice, of party and faction."[39] (See chart showing various states' usage, 1789–1836, Appendix B.)

Direct choice by the legislature was the most widely used method in the first four elections and was employed by a significant number of states until the 1820s. For the dominant political circles in a state, it was the simplest method, since it involved no reference to the people— that unpredictable and sometimes fickle electorate. In fact, when state legislatures saw a chance that the candidate of their party would be defeated in a popular choice of electors, they sometimes revoked previous laws permitting popular election and took the appointment of electors back into their own hands. This is exactly what the lame-duck Federalists in the Pennsylvania Senate succeeded in doing in 1800, though they were unable to elect Federalists to more than half the elector slots because the Republicans controlled the other part of the legislature at the time (see page 67). The New Jersey Legislature, under Federalist control, effected an even bolder coup in 1812, repealing the state law for popular choice of electors and designating the electors itself on the very eve of the statewide election. Dickerson of New Jersey related six years later in the Senate: "Expresses were sent into the different parts of the state, to give notice of this repeal, but not in time, for the citizens in many towns met and gave their votes for electors and Representatives without knowing of the repeal of the law. The Legislature appointed eight electors, not one of whom would have been appointed by the people under the late election law—and this the Legislature well knew; otherwise they would not have taken from the people the right of choosing the electors under the law."[40]

When the legislatures did appoint electors directly, there were many ways in which to do so. Sometimes the appointments were made by the joint vote of the two houses; sometimes the choice was by concurrent vote, requiring a majority of each house for each elector chosen. Under a New York law in effect from the first elections to 1825, each house nominated a slate of electors by majority vote. The two houses then met in joint convention to reconcile their differences, again by majority vote.[41] This procedure was spelled out in statute to prevent a recurrence of the circumstances in the first election, when neither house of the New York Legislature would concur in the other's choice for electors and the state lost its vote for President altogether.

The rise of democratic sentiment in the early 19th century was to doom the direct legislative choice of electors, however. In several instances, parties that used the legislative election to control a state's electoral votes subsequently found themselves thrown out of office by an enraged populace. Between 1812 and 1820, nine state legislatures still chose the electors for their states. In 1824, though, the figure dropped to six states, in 1828 to only two, and from 1832 to 1860, only one state—South Carolina—resisted the trend to democratic selection of the electors. After the Civil War, finally, democracy came to that state as well.

Popular choice of electors by district was the system personally favored by many of the nation's most distinguished early statesmen, including Jefferson, Hamilton, Madison, Andrew Jackson, John Quincy Adams and Daniel Webster.[42] Madison wrote in 1823 that "the district system was mostly, if not exclusively, in view when the Constitution was framed and adopted."[43] Yet in practice the district system was never employed by a majority of the states in any election. Only two states adopted it in the first two elections. It reached its height in 1820 when six states utilized it. By 1836 it had disappeared completely from the scene.

When the district system was employed, it appeared in many forms. Sometimes there was a district for each elector; sometimes a state had only two or four superdistricts, each electing several electors. Sometimes a majority of the district vote was required for election; sometimes a plurality was sufficient. Sometimes two electors were chosen statewide, either by direct vote or by the legislature, while the remainder were chosen by popular vote in districts. Variations of this plan were tried several times in Massachusetts. Popular election was the basis of choosing electors in the great majority of district plans, but Tennessee offered a major exception in 1796 and 1800. So that the "electors may be elected with as little trouble to the citizens of the state as possible," the Tennessee Legislature decreed that the state should be divided into three districts and that the appointment of the

Presidential elector from each district be given in turn to a group of "electors"—three citizens from each county, men whom the Legislature itself had selected.[44]

Popular vote under a general ticket system, the plan under which all Presidential electors run for election on a statewide basis, was the simplest system used in the early years. It was employed by two to three states in the first four Presidential elections and by five to seven states in the years between 1804 and 1816. Then it rapidly gained the center of the stage, as its usage rose from nine states in 1820 to 18 states in 1828 and 25 states (all but South Carolina) in 1836.

Why did the general ticket win this wide acceptance? There appear to be two major reasons. First, its provision for the popular choice of electors—whose party loyalties were generally well known—corresponded in substantial measure to the developing ideas of the people's President. By the 1820s, democratic ideals had advanced so far in the United States that the people of most states were simply unwilling to leave the crucial choice of Presidential electors in the hands of state legislatures.

Secondly, the general ticket system suited the purposes of the ruling political faction in any state. No longer would it be necessary (as under the district system) to share the state's electoral votes with the opposing party. By the general ticket system, the ruling party could deliver an absolutely solid electoral vote bloc to its national candidates—and then be in a position to demand the dividends in patronage and power that the contribution warranted. Once the opposition party could be subdued within the individual state, it would have absolutely no voice in the Presidential election. Thus the dominant politicians almost invariably lined up in favor of the general ticket system. The politicians out of power usually preferred the district system so that they could retain some voice. But lacking power, they naturally had little to say about the system the state would adopt—and the general ticket system gradually prevailed.

The adoption of the general ticket in some states, moreover, virtually compelled the others to follow suit so that their strength in the electoral college would not be diluted. In the words of the Benton Committee in the Senate in 1826: "If uniformity by districts is not established by free consent of the states, uniformity by general ticket or legislative ballot must be imposed by necessity. For, when the large states consolidate their votes to overwhelm the small ones, those, in turn, must concentrate their own strength to resist them. A few states may persevere for some time, in which they believe to be the fairest system; but, when they see the unity of action which others derive from the general ticket and the legislative modes of election, they will not, they *cannot*, resist the temptation to follow the same plan."[45] (See Jefferson's comments along the same line, page 66.)

The first decades of the 19th century witnessed the first major effort in U.S. history to write into the Constitution some specific plan, such as the choice of electors by district, that would prevent the abuses so apparent in the early years of the republic. But the attempt would fail, because it was in the interest of the ruling political circles in some states to adopt the general ticket system, and once some states had taken the step, the others were eventually obliged to follow. The general ticket was not adopted out of high constitutional principle. Indeed, as Lucius Wilmerding points out in his study of the period, "the question of reform tended to be debated on grounds of state power rather than national principle."[46] Ironically, most Americans today—if they are aware of the electoral college at all—usually think that the general ticket system is part of the Constitution. The truth is that any state could abandon it in any election. But none is likely to do so, until the day the electoral college is finally abolished. The arguments against change by any single state—arguments that spring from simple motives of political self-preservation—are the same today as they were a century and a half ago.

N O T E S

1. John Bach McMaster, *A History of the People of the United States from the Revolution to the Civil War,* 8 vols. (New York, 1893–1924), I, pp. 538–40.
2. Edward Stanwood, *A History of the Presidency from 1788 to 1897* (Boston, 1898), p. 20. North Carolina and Rhode Island refused to ratify until Congress proposed a series of 12 amendments, 10 of which were adopted—the "Bill of Rights." Neither participated in the first election.
3. *Ibid.,* pp. 22–23.
4. *Ibid.,* p. 26.
5. *Ibid.,* p. 27.

6. In debate on the President's power to remove federal officers. *Annals of Congress*, I, p. 550, 554. Elbridge Gerry of Massachusetts took a different view. *Ibid.*, I, p. 557.

7. Stanwood, *op. cit.*, p. 48.

8. *Ibid.*, p. 51.

9. *Ibid.*, p. 52.

10. *New York Diary*, Feb. 15, 1798, cited by Charles A. O'Neil, *The American Electoral System* (New York, 1887), p. 66.

11. Stanwood, *op. cit.*, pp. 54–57; O'Neil, *op. cit.*, p. 83.

12. Jefferson, *Works*, I, p. 381, cited by Lucius Wilmerding, *The Electoral College* (New Brunswick, N.J., 1958), p. 32. Burr had contributed to the Republican cause by helping to persuade George Clinton to come out of retirement and head up a "blue ribbon" ticket of Republican candidates for the state Assembly (which chose the Presidential electors). Under Clinton the Republicans scored an upset victory.

13. Letter of Jan. 12, 1800, cited by J. Hampden Dougherty, *The Electoral System of the United States* (New York, 1906), p. 286.

14. Cited by O'Neil, *op. cit.*, pp. 71, 261–62.

15. Issue of Nov. 4, 1800.

16. O'Neil, *op. cit.*, p. 73.

17. *Ibid.*, pp. 74–75.

18. Stanwood, *op. cit.*, p. 59.

19. *Ibid.*, p. 63. A slight exception to the Southern sweep was the victory of four Federalist electors in North Carolina (out of the state's total of 12).

20. *Ibid.*, p. 70. The 1792 law provided that whenever the offices of President and Vice President both became vacant, a special election should be held. Paragraph 6 of Article II, Section 1 of the Constitution provided that Congress might appoint an officer to act as President "until . . . a President shall be elected." The original proposal for this section of the Constitution, as considered by the Convention on September 7, 1787, had read, "until the time of electing a President shall arrive." Madison had objected that this "would prevent a supply of the vacancy by an intermediate election of the President," and moved to substitute the wording, "until . . . a President shall be elected." (Max Farrand, ed., *The Records of the Federal Constitutional Convention of 1787*, 4 vols. [New Haven, 1911, 1937], II, p. 535.) Until 1947, Presidential succession laws permitted a special election in the event of a dual vacancy. See John D. Feerick, *From Failing Hands: The Story of Presidential Succession* (New York, 1965), pp. 146, 209.

21. Samuel Eliot Morison and Henry Steele Commager, *The Growth of the American Republic* (New York, 1950), I, p. 381.

22. Cited by Stanwood, *op. cit.*, p. 70, and Wilmerding, *op. cit.*, p. 32.

23. Sidney Hyman, *The American President* (New York, 1954), p. 128.

24. O'Neil, *op. cit.*, pp. 87–88.

25. Cited by O'Neil, *op. cit.*, pp. 88–89.

26. Cited by Stanwood, *op. cit.*, p. 72.

27. For state-by-state balloting chart, see Stanwood, *op. cit.*, p. 72.

28. Eugene H. Roseboom, *A History of Presidential Elections* (New York, 1959), p. 46; *Annals*, XIII, p. 158.

29. See Wilmerding, *op. cit.*, p. 36.

30. Herman V. Ames, "The Proposed Amendments to the Constitution of the United States During the First Century of Its History," *Annual Report of the American Historical Association for 1896* (Washington, 1897), pp. 77–78.

31. The Senate vote was 15–8 in favor. Ames, *op. cit.*, p. 78.

32. Farrand, *op. cit.*, III, pp. 393–95.

33. Cited by Stanwood, *op. cit.*, pp. 79–80.

34. Ames, *op. cit.*, p. 78.

35. *Annals*, XIII, pp. 155, 194–195.

36. *Annals*, XIII, pp. 87, 128.

37. Ames, *op. cit.*, p. 79.

38. Senate Report 22, 19th Congress, 1st Session, Jan. 19, 1826, p. 2.

39. *Annals*, XXXI, p. 180.

40. *Annals*, XXXI, pp. 182–83; see also Stanwood, *op. cit.*, p. 103.

41. Wilmerding, *op. cit.*, p. 46.

42. *Ibid.*, p. 58.

43. Letter to George Hay, Aug. 23, 1823, printed in Farrand, *op. cit.*, III, p. 459.

44. Wilmerding, *op. cit.*, pp. 45–46.

45. 1826 Senate Report, p. 17. See also comment by Jefferson, p. 46, above.

46. Wilmerding, *op. cit.*, p. 59.

4 Years of Controversy

ANY ELECTORAL SYSTEM IN A DEMOCRATIC COUNTRY, WHERE ELECTIONS ARE marked by competing political parties and free expression of the popular will, is likely to produce "close calls" and cliff-hanger elections in which a slight shift in votes can alter the final result. Yet the American electoral system, with its two stages in choosing a President—first through the votes of the people and then by the votes of the Presidential electors whom they have chosen—can magnify the uncertainties in any close election, and through our history it has fostered uncertainties and the kind of unsavory intrigue that can only weaken the American Presidency and the unity of the American people behind their Chief Executive.

We have already seen how, in 1796, the defeated Federalist candidate for Vice President might have been propelled into the Presidency by scheming electors of the other party if 100 votes had shifted in a single state, Pennsylvania (page 64, above). The 1800 tie vote in the electoral college and the pressures for unprincipled agreements by the Presidential contenders during the subsequent 36 ballots in the House have also been reviewed (pages 68–70). The 12th Amendment was intended to correct the chief deficiencies, yet all it really did was to reduce sharply the possibilities of a tie in the electoral balloting. The mathematical vagaries and uncertainties of the electoral college have reasserted themselves through our history.

In the era since ratification of the 12th Amendment, six Presidential elections have illustrated most clearly the anomalies, ambiguities and undemocratic consequences of the system. The first three—those of 1824, 1876 and 1888—showed how the electoral college could elect the man whom the people rejected. The 1824 election also showed the special danger of elections in the House, while that of 1876 illustrated the ugly consequences of widespread disputed returns. Three later elections—1916, 1948 and 1960—demonstrated how close we have come to a miscarriage of the popular will in our own century, and the dangers still inherent in vote frauds, splinter parties and electors who may suddenly break the traces and exercise their own will against that of the people. Each of these elections deserves closer scrutiny.

The Election of 1824

Thomas Jefferson's election began a quarter-century of Virginian Presidents, all members of his Republican party—or, as it was known by the 1820s, the Democratic party. James Madison won relatively easily in 1808 and 1812, and by the time James Monroe ran in 1816 and 1820, the once-powerful Federalist party was so weak that it could offer no organized opposition. The rise of new national issues—slavery in the new Western states, tariffs, public works—brought an end to the "Era of Good Feeling" at the end of Monroe's second administration. But the Democratic party was the only recognizable national party, and thus the search for a new President was an entirely intraparty affair.

Though as many as 17 men were prominently mentioned for the Presidency, the field by the time of the election was narrowed down to four men: John Quincy Adams of Massachusetts, the Secretary of State and son of the former President; Henry Clay of Kentucky, who had won national prominence as Speaker of the House; William H. Crawford of Georgia, the Secretary of the Treasury; and Andrew Jackson of Tennessee, known to his countrymen as the hero of the Battle of New Orleans in 1815. Though each candidate sought a national following, their appeals were primarily sectional in character. Adams' major source of support lay with the Eastern industrialists, Western businessmen tended to favor Clay, Crawford was the favorite of the Southern planters, and Jackson had the Western farmers on his side.

Through 1823 and into 1824 there was widespread controversy over the desirability of holding a Congressional caucus to nominate candidates for President and Vice President. Defenders of the caucus system, which had received increasing criticism over the years, argued that it was a tried method that offered the best expression of nationwide rather than strictly sectional interest in the Presidential nomination. Opponents claimed that the caucus was simply a device to permit rule by powerful Congressional cliques and that it would not represent the will of the people. In 1824, however, special opposition to the caucus developed because it was common knowledge that one of the candidates—Crawford—would probably receive its support. In a strategic blunder, Crawford's supporters did call a Congressional caucus in February 1824. Supporters of the other contenders boycotted the caucus, making it a rump affair. Of the 216 party members in Congress, only 66 attended. Crawford was nominated with 64 votes. Not only the dispute over the caucus, but Crawford's physical condition— he had suffered a paralyzing stroke in September 1823—would work to his disadvantage in the ensuing campaign.[1]

In the meantime, in November 1822, the Kentucky Legislature had nominated Clay. Jackson was nominated by the lower house of the Tennessee Legislature in 1822 and then by mass conventions of people in various parts of Tennessee and in other parts of the country. Adams' name was placed in nomination by most of the New England legislatures early in 1824. The names of two other men were also put forward: John C. Calhoun of South Carolina and De Witt Clinton of New York. But both withdrew before the election, Calhoun to run for (and win) the Vice Presidency.

In 18 of the 24 states, there was a popular vote for President. For the first time in U.S. history, something approximating a national popular vote could be compiled. The vote showed 152,933 for Jackson, 115,696 for Adams, 46,979 for Crawford and 47,136 for Clay. The accuracy of this count as a valid reflection of the popular will is open to serious challenge, however, because the states still choosing their Presidential electors by legislature included mighty New York. Even in Virginia, where there was a popular election, only 14,955 votes were cast from a white population of 625,000, and the vote was similarly low in many other states.[2] The popular vote count was important, however, for it would give Jackson's supporters an opportunity to claim that their man was the real choice of the people.

RESULTS OF THE 1824 ELECTION

	Popular Votes*	Electoral Votes
Andrew Jackson	152,933	99
John Quincy Adams	115,696	84
William H. Crawford	46,979	41
Henry Clay	47,136	37

* Returns from 18 of the 24 states then in the Union. In the other 6 states, the legislatures chose the Presidential electors.

Since no candidate received an electoral vote majority, the election was thrown into the House, where Adams won on the first ballot. The count: 13 states for Adams, 7 for Jackson, 4 for Crawford.

The electoral count was widely split. Jackson won Pennsylvania, New Jersey and a majority of the Southern states; Adams all of New England; Crawford drew his main support from Virginia and Georgia; Clay had little support outside of Kentucky and Ohio. On February 9, 1825, when the electoral votes were officially counted, it was apparent that no candidate had received a majority, and it fell to the House of Representatives—for the first time since 1801—to select the President. The House would have to choose from the three top candidates—Jackson, Adams and Crawford. The real choice lay between Jackson and Adams, the top contenders, and the key man whose support had to be obtained was Henry Clay. From the start, Clay apparently intended to support Adams as the lesser of two evils; he is known to have regarded Jackson as a hotheaded military man with little qualification for the Presidency.[3]

But before the House vote, a great scandal erupted. The *Columbian Observer* of Philadelphia published an anonymous letter alleging that Clay had agreed to support Adams in return for being made Secretary of State. The letter said that Clay would have been willing to make the same deal with Jackson. Clay immediately denied the charge and pronounced the writer of the letter to be "a base and infamous character, a dastard and a liar." Clay urged the anonymous letter writer to make himself known and challenged him to a duel. Representative George Kremer of Pennsylvania announced that he had written the letter but failed to take up the duel challenge. A slow-witted man, Kremer probably was a "front" for the Jackson faction. Jackson himself believed the charge and his suspicions were clearly vindicated when Adams, after the election, actually did appoint Clay as Secretary of State. "So you see the Judas of the West has closed the contract and will receive the thirty pieces of silver," Jackson wrote to a friend. "His end will be the same. Was there ever witnessed such a bare faced corruption in any country before?"[4] Representative John Randolph of Virginia termed the Adams-Clay alliance "the coalition of Blifil and Black George—the combination, unheard of till then, of the puritan with the black-leg." Clay challenged Randolph to a duel, which actually took place, though neither was hurt.[5]

As the day of decision in the House approached, Adams seemed assured of the six New England states and, in large part through Clay's backing, of Maryland, Ohio, Kentucky, Illinois, Missouri and Louisiana. Thus he had 12 of the 24 states and needed only one more to win the election. The likeliest state to add to the Adams column appeared to be New York, since 17 members of its 34-man delegation were already reported ready to vote for him. Clay decided that the one uncommitted member of the delegation was Stephen Van Rensselaer, an elderly, deeply religious member of one of New York's aristocratic families. Van Rensselaer was invited into the Speaker's office the morning of the crucial vote and personally urged by Clay and Daniel Webster to vote for Adams. The entreaties from these two powerful men were reportedly unsuccessful, but the story is told that as Van Rensselaer sat at his desk in the House before the vote, he bowed his head in prayer to seek divine guidance. As he did this, his eyes fell on a slip of paper inadvertently left on the floor. The name "Adams" was written on the slip. Interpreting this as a sign from above, Van Rensselaer voted for Adams. Thus was New York's vote cast for the man from Massachusetts. Added to the 12 states he already had, Adams thus enjoyed the support of 13 of the 24 states—and was elected President by the House on the first ballot.[6]

In his reply to the committee that notified him of his election, Adams alluded to the circumstances under which he had been chosen and expressed his wish to decline the office and submit the question once again to the people. But he noted that this avenue was not open, for "the Constitution has not so disposed of the contingency which would arise in the event of my refusal."[7] Like his father, Adams would have but a single term in the Presidency. The controversy and allegations that accompanied Adams' election would hang over him like a cloud for the next four years. This handicap, together with his natural limitations as a popular leader, would make Adams' term a trying one.

Losing no time, the Tennessee Legislature in 1825 nominated Jackson for the Presidency in 1828. As the campaign approached, the Jacksonians harped increasingly on the basic issue given them by the 1824 election: that Jackson had won the most popular votes and had been the choice of the people, but the House of Representatives had frustrated the will of the people. This simple, emotional appeal was more than Adams could withstand, and the 1828 election results would show an overwhelming triumph for Jackson, both in popular and electoral votes.

The Election of 1876

The American nation was little more than a decade past the throes of its great Civil War as it prepared to elect its 19th President in 1876, and the bitterness lingered on, both in North and South. While the states of the old Confederacy labored to cast off the last remnants of Reconstruction, Republican orators in the North waved the "bloody shirt" and warned of dire consequences if the Democratic party, the party of the former rebels, were to return to power. The country had come on hard times and many had suffered in the great financial panic of 1873. The midterm elections of 1874 had carried the Democrats into control of the House of Representatives, much to the dismay of Republican President Ulysses S. Grant and his Administration, especially as committees of the House began to disclose corruption in high places. Against this background, the country entered the Presidential campaign of 1876—a contest that would not be decided until two days before the inauguration in 1877, following a historic dispute over the counting of the popular and electoral ballots. Two decades later, Edward Stanwood, the distinguished historian of the Presidency, would write: "It is to be hoped that the patriotism of the American people and their love of peace may never again be put to so severe a test as that to which they were subjected in 1876 and 1877."[8]

Meeting in Cincinnati the week of June 14, 1876, the Republican National Convention balloted seven times before it could agree on Ohio's Governor, Rutherford B. Hayes, as its Presidential nominee. A dark horse when the Convention convened, Hayes received only 61 of the 754 votes on the first ballot but gradually drew ahead of James G. Blaine of Maine and other early favorites. Into the campaign Hayes would carry a reputation as an efficient three-term Governor and Ohio's top vote-getter and a record free from any taint of scandal.

The Democrats met in St. Louis two weeks later and nominated Governor Samuel J. Tilden of New York on the second ballot. A corporate lawyer who had won a high reputation by his warfare against the "Tweed ring" in New York City, Tilden was known as a competent reform Governor of his state. But he was an austere bachelor of 62 who lacked much of the fire and verve needed for an effective onslaught on the entrenched Republicans.

RESULTS OF THE 1876 ELECTION

| | Popular Votes | | Electoral Votes, Count After Decisions of Electoral Commission |
	Republican Count	Democratic Count	
Samuel J. Tilden (Dem.)	4,285,992	4,300,590	184
Rutherford B. Hayes (Rep.)	4,033,768	4,036,298	185
Minor Parties		94,935	

Tilden Plurality: 252,224 (Republican count); 264,292 (Democratic count)

The above figures are based on contemporary accounts.[9] For slightly differing figures, based on modern-day analysis, see Appendix A.

Following a relatively spiritless campaign, the people went to the polls on Tuesday, November 7. The real excitement began as the returns started to pour in. The Republicans' one-time strongholds in Connecticut, New York, New Jersey and Indiana went for Tilden, and with the expected outpouring of Southern votes for the Democrats, Tilden looked like a winner on election night. Republican National Chairman Zachariah Chandler, discouraged with the reports, went to bed, and Hayes admitted his defeat in his diary.[10] The general expectation was that Tilden would have 203 electoral votes to Hayes's 166.

Early the next morning, however, Republican hopes began to revive. If South Carolina, Florida and Louisiana could be held for Hayes, he would defeat Tilden by a single electoral vote—185 to 184. Chandler proclaimed Hayes's victory. Telegrams were rushed to Republican leaders in the doubtful states warning them not to accept the early returns, which were favorable to the Democrats, and Republican agents supplied with money were soon on their way South to help local Republican political leaders in the impending disputes over contested returns. In each of the disputed Southern states, Reconstruction was still in force and the Republicans controlled the state governments and election machinery. Republicans counted on masses of Negro votes to win, while the Democrats employed threats and intimidation and even violence on occasion to prevent the Negroes from casting ballots. The ensuing struggle would find agents of both parties using illegal and corrupt tactics to achieve their ends; there were even reports of a Democratic offer of a million dollars to a member of the Louisiana election board to achieve the certification of at least one Democratic elector from that state.[11] Both sides were keenly aware that the choice of *a single* Tilden elector in the disputed states would upset Hayes's alleged one-vote lead and result in a Democratic victory.

Eventually, double sets of elector returns were sent to Congress from four disputed states. In South Carolina, it was alleged that Army detachments stationed near the polls had prevented a fair election. The official returns showed a slight lead for the Hayes elector slate, and the state board of canvassers so certified. But the state's Democratic elector candidates met the same day, voted for Tilden and forwarded their ballots to Washington. In Florida, both sides charged fraud, and though the canvassing board and Governor certified the election of Hayes electors, the Democrats won a court challenge and submitted electoral votes for Tilden. Anarchy reigned in Louisiana, where there were two Governors, two canvassing boards, two sets of returns showing different results and two electoral colleges. In Oregon, where the Republicans received a clear majority, Democratic Governor L. F. Glover discovered that one of the Republican electors chosen was a postmaster and thus ineligible under the U.S. Constitution. Glover thereupon certified the election of the top-polling Democratic elector candidate. But the Republican electors met, received the resignation of the ineligible Republican elector, and then elected the same man to the vacancy, since in the meantime he had resigned as postmaster. Two sets of returns were sent from the state to Washington.[12]

On two previous occasions, Congress had faced the problem of disputed electoral votes, but this was the first time in U.S. history that a decision would have to be made on competing sets of elector returns which would determine the actual outcome of the election. Nor would the conflict be easy to resolve, for while the House of Representatives was under Democratic control, Republicans still held a majority in the Senate. The fear of the time, expressed by Senator George F. Edmunds of Vermont in the *American Law Review* of October 1877, was that "the Senate would declare Hayes President, the House Tilden." In that case, he continued, "each of these gentlemen would have taken the oath of office, and attempted to exercise its duties; each would have called upon the Army and the people to sustain him against the usurpations of the other. . . . The solemn ceremonies and the grand pageant of inauguration would be only the first act in the awful tragedy and anarchy of civil war."[13] Indeed, there were threats that thousands would march on the Capitol to demand an honest count, and calls of "Tilden or Blood" came from some Democrats.

These dangers were keenly felt when Congress met in December 1876. The leaders of both political parties quickly resolved that some compromise would have to be reached for the good of the whole country. No clear precedent existed for resolving electoral disputes. In fact, a rule that would have disqualified the returns of any state where one house of Congress objected had been allowed to lapse at the start of 1876. If the former rule had been in effect, the House could easily have objected to any of Hayes's disputed votes and thus brought about Tilden's election.

With a need for immediate action because of the impending electoral vote disputes, a joint committee was established to write a rule on resolving electoral disputes "by a tribunal whose authority none can question and whose decision all will accept as final." The Electoral Commission Law, to apply to the count of the 1876 electoral votes only, passed both houses late in January and was signed by President Grant on January 29—three days before the appointed day for opening and counting the electoral votes, February 1.[14]

Under the new law, both houses would have to agree to reject the electoral votes from any state for those votes to be disqualified. A special blue-ribbon commission of 15 members—five from the Senate, five from the House and five from the membership of the Supreme Court—was established to judge those cases in which more than one return from a state had been received. The decisions of this Electoral Commission would be final, unless overruled by both houses of Congress.

All commission members were required to take a solemn oath that they would unquestionably "dismiss every consideration that would cloud their intellects or warp their judgments." This heroic attempt to achieve nonpartisanship was underpinned, however, by a clear understanding of all parties concerned that the members appointed by the Senate would include three Republicans and two Democrats, while those from the House would include three Democrats and two Republicans. The names of four Supreme Court Justices were designated in the bill—two Democrats and two Republicans. Thus it was known that the commission would have seven Republicans and seven Democrats. The crucial selection—on which the entire election was to turn—was the fifth Justice. The bill specified that he would be selected by the four Supreme Court Justices already designated, and it was generally understood that this final member would be Justice David Davis, a Lincoln appointee who was regarded as a political independent.[15]

If Davis actually had served, it is quite likely that he would have agreed with the Democrats in at least one of the disputed elector cases and thus brought about Tilden's election. But on January 26, the very day the commission bill passed Congress, startling news arrived from Springfield, Illinois. The afternoon before, the Illinois Legislature had named Davis to a seat in the U.S. Senate. The historian Eugene Roseboom comments that "fortune seemed to reserve her smiles for the Republicans during these years, but in this case asinine blundering by the Illinois Democrats would seem to be a more logical explanation."[16] The four Justices designated in the bill eventually chose another colleague, Justice Joseph P. Bradley, as the commission's 15th member. Democratic leaders approved of the choice, feeling Bradley was as independent as any of the remaining members of the Court. But the fact of the matter was that Bradley was a Republican, and on every disputed vote before the commission, he would take the Republican side—giving the Republican cause an 8 to 7 edge and bringing about Hayes's election. Even though eight million people voted for President, as one newspaper charged, "the vote of one man—Justice Bradley— nullifies the voice of the majority and places the usurper in the chair."

As the electoral count began in Congress on February 1, each party was confident—the Democrats believing that at least *one* Hayes vote would be found invalid, the Republicans hopeful that the commission would confine itself to deciding which state elector certificates were official, without investigating the circumstances surrounding the actual balloting. As each disputed state was reached in the official count in the joint session of Congress, objections were raised to both the Hayes and Tilden certificates that had been submitted. The disputes were then automatically referred to the electoral commission, which met and made a decision on each of the disputes. In every instance, the commission split 8 to 7 in favor of accepting the Hayes votes and rejecting the Tilden votes. The decision was then referred back to each house of Congress, and in every instance the Democratic House voted against the electoral commission decision while the Republican Senate voted to uphold it. Under the new law, the result was that the Commission's decision was sustained in every case.[17]

This long process of count and challenge stretched over a month and a day, and the final result was not announced until four o'clock in the morning on March 2. That same day, Hayes arrived in the capital, and took the oath the next evening at the White House, because March 4 fell on a Sunday. A formal inauguration followed on Monday.[18]

As the disputed South Carolina votes were being counted, some Democrats in the House suggested launching a filibuster that would block resumption of the joint sessions and the regular count beyond inauguration day—with unpredictable consequences. The crisis was never to develop that far, however, because negotiations had already been under way between associates of Hayes and a number of Southern conservatives. Under the terms of the agreement, the Democrats would permit the electoral count to proceed without obstruction. In return, Hayes would agree to a number of concessions, the most important of which were the withdrawal of federal troops from the South and the end of Reconstruction. In return, the Southerners pledged that Negro rights would be respected. Within a few months, Hayes had lived up to his part of the bargain by withdrawing the remaining federal troops in the Confederacy.[19] But the conservative Southerners were unable to protect Negro rights. More violent forces in the South were soon to seize power and to deprive Southern Negroes of their most basic right—the right to vote. It would be almost a century until the nation began to rectify the injustices to the Southern Negro which stemmed from the price that was paid for peace in the land in 1877.

No public disturbances followed the announcement of Hayes's election. Even Tilden refused to offer public protest. "I can return to private life," he said, "with the consciousness that I shall receive from posterity the credit of having been elected to the highest position in the gift of the people, without any of the cares and responsibilities of the office."[20]

Democrats continued for years thereafter, however, to denounce the outcome as a fraud. A Democratic-controlled committee of the U.S. House reached this very conclusion in 1879. Many newspapers refused to speak of Hayes as the rightful President. That the public will had been frustrated, there could be little doubt. For whether one accepted the Republican or Democratic version of the correct vote count, it was clear that Samuel Tilden had received some quarter-million more votes for President than Rutherford Hayes, the man whom the electoral college and political happenstance made President.

Moreover, the 1876 election had demonstrated a grave defect in the Constitution: its failure to spell out exact responsibility for counting the electoral votes and resolving disputes, so that the resolution of the entire Presidential election can swing on the intrigues and maneuvers in a partisanly motivated Congress, to the detriment of the people and the Presidency alike. Even today, that basic constitutional defect remains uncorrected.

The Election of 1888

From 1876 through 1900 the country experienced an unbroken line of exceptionally close Presidential elections. In 1876 the shift of one state—indeed, the shift of one electoral vote—would have altered the outcome. Single state outcomes also dictated the results in 1880, 1884 and 1888. Strategically placed shifts of less than 75,000 popular votes would also have altered the outcome in 1892, 1896 and 1900. But the election of 1888 has the distinction of being the last election, up to the present time, in which the electoral college clearly elected a man to the Presidency over the candidate whom most of the people favored.

In itself, the campaign of 1888 offered little excitement. Grover Cleveland was completing his first term in the White House, and the Democratic Convention in St. Louis nominated him by acclamation for a second term—the first time since Martin Van Buren's renomination in 1840 that a roll call had not been necessary. James G. Blaine could probably have had the Republican nomination for the asking; he had barely lost to Cleveland in 1884 and was still the party's most popular leader and powerful orator. But Blaine announced that he would not be a candidate, and when the Republicans met in Chicago in June, eight ballots were required until General Benjamin Harrison of Indiana, a grandson of President William Henry Harrison, emerged as the nominee. The tariff was the great issue of the campaign, with the Democrats pressing for freer trade and the Republicans pledging that they would sweep away the entire internal revenue system before they would lower the protective duty on imports. With the end of Reconstruction the Democrats had seized complete control of the South and the question was whether the Republicans could prevent enough Northern defections to overcome the solid South. The election turned on the doubtful states of Indiana and New York. Cleveland lost Indiana, and crucial New York also went to Harrison—by a margin of 13,373 votes out of the 1,321,897 cast in that state. Had Cleveland carried New York, he would have won the election.* Across the nation, Cleveland led Harrison by 95,096 popular votes. But the electoral college rendered a different decision: Harrison would be the next President, winning 233 electoral votes to Cleveland's 168.[21]

RESULTS OF THE 1888 ELECTION

	Popular Votes	Electoral Votes
Benjamin Harrison (Rep.)	5,445,269	233
Grover Cleveland (Dem.)	5,540,365	168
Minor Parties	404,205	——
Cleveland Plurality: 95,096		

The Election of 1916

No American President of the 20th century has been chosen by the electoral college after a definitive defeat in the popular vote. But on three occasions in this century, the nation has come perilously close to such an unjust outcome of the national election. The first occurred in 1916.

* Four years before, in the election of 1884, the national result had also swung on the outcome in New York. Two trivial occurrences appear to have delivered the state to Cleveland over Blaine. The first occurred October 29, when Blaine, in an informal meeting with a group of ministers in New York City, failed to take exception to the allegation of one of the clerics that the Democrats were the party of "rum, Romanism and rebellion." Cleveland forces moved quickly to exploit Blaine's failure to object, and the incident may well have cost Blaine enough Irish votes to lose the state. Possibly even more important, election day brought a driving rain upstate and cut down the rural Republican vote. Cleveland's margin in the state was only 1,149 votes out of 1,167,169 cast. With New York, he won the nation and became the first Democratic President since the Civil War.[22]

The election of 1912 had witnessed a historic schism in the Republican party between the Old Guard, under President William Howard Taft, and the Progressives, led by former President Theodore Roosevelt. The split opened the way for Woodrow Wilson to become the first Democratic President in two decades. As the 1916 contest approached, the Republicans sought a candidate who would be acceptable to both factions of the party. In Supreme Court Justice Charles Evans Hughes, they felt they had the ideal candidate. Hughes had proven his administrative abilities as a reform Governor of New York state, yet had been isolated from the internecine Republican warfare as a member of the bench since 1910. Against a split field, Hughes was nominated on the third ballot at the Republican National Convention in Chicago the second week of June. Roosevelt was nominated by the Progressives for a second time, but he declined the honor and campaigned for Hughes. No organized opposition materialized against Wilson in his own party, and he was renominated at the Democratic National Convention in St. Louis a week after Hughes.

Labor unrest and tariffs figured as campaign issues, but the overriding appeal on which the Democrats won, spelled out in their platform and repeated countless times up to election day, was that Wilson had "kept us out of war." Most Americans genuinely abhorred the idea of becoming involved in the great European war, even though the sinking of the *Lusitania* and other submarine horrors had aroused serious resentments against Germany. The Republicans found themselves occupying a middle ground between the country's pro- and anti-German factions, while the Democrats campaigned as the party that could preserve peace. The issue had great appeal, especially in the farm areas, known for their isolationism, and among women voters. Wilson carried nearly all the states in which the franchise had already been extended to women.

The best hope for Hughes was that the country's basic Republicanism, disrupted in 1912, could reassert itself in the Presidential balloting. Roosevelt's decision to support Hughes increased his chances substantially. Indeed, as the first returns began to pour into New York on election night, a Hughes victory seemed imminent. The East, including New York with her 45 and Pennsylvania with her 38 electoral votes, went Republican, and when the Midwestern returns showed only Ohio in the Democratic column, President Wilson told his close associates that he was relieved to see the burdens of office lifted from him.[23]

RESULTS OF THE 1916 ELECTION

	Popular Votes	Electoral Votes
Woodrow Wilson (Dem.)	9,131,511	277
Charles Evans Hughes (Rep.)	8,548,935	254
Minor Parties	855,786	—
Wilson Plurality: 582,576		

As more states reported, however, the race for electoral ballots grew closer and closer. The solid South held steadfastly Democratic, and Wilson won Kansas, most of the border states and all of the mountain states. Finally, the outcome hinged on California and her 13 electoral votes. Excluding California, the electoral count stood at 264 for Wilson, 254 for Hughes. Whichever man won California would be President. An agonizing delay in the vote count now occurred, and it was not until several days later that the California vote was finally tallied and Wilson found to be the victor. But Wilson had carried California by only 3,806 votes out of almost a million cast in the state. A shift of less than one-fifth of one percent of the California vote would have elected Hughes, despite Wilson's national popular vote plurality of well over half a million votes.

The nation was apparently spared this electoral travesty by a chance occurrence early in the campaign. Hughes, on a tour of California, had let the more reactionary Republican leaders plan his itinerary and failed to meet with Republican Governor Hiram Johnson, who had been the Progressive nominee for Vice President in 1912 and was running for the Senate in 1916. Johnson gave at least nominal support to Hughes in the campaign that followed, but his more enthusiastic backing could well have delivered California to Hughes. Johnson won his own campaign for the Senate by almost 300,000 votes.

The Election of 1948

Except for President Harry S Truman, virtually everyone in the country expected the Republicans to take over the White House in 1948, thus ending the period of Democratic dominance that had begun with Franklin D. Roosevelt's first election in 1932. Truman, a Missouri Senator until Roosevelt chose him for the Vice Presidential nomination in 1944, had suddenly been catapulted into the Presidency by Roosevelt's death in office in April 1945. But under Truman's leadership the Democrats were thrown for staggering losses in the 1946 mid-term elections, relinquishing control of Congress for the first time since the early 1930s.

Truman and the newly elected Republican 80th Congress were able to work together fairly well on foreign problems and indeed launched such historic programs as the Marshall Plan to aid war-torn Europe. But bitter feuding erupted between President and Congress on domestic issues. In 1947, over the President's veto and the angry protests of organized labor, the 80th Congress passed the landmark Taft-Hartley Labor-Management Relations Act. Congressional investigation of Communist infiltration of the government in the 1930s further exacerbated White House–Capitol Hill relations. In his 1948 State of the Union Address, Truman shocked a budget-conscious Congress by simultaneously urging new social welfare legislation that would cost $10 billion and a $40 tax cut for every man, woman and child in the nation. Republicans promptly accused him of gross political opportunism, and that dispute had scarcely cooled before the President in February advocated a sweeping civil rights program that drew embittered protests from the Southern Democrats. Truman had already won the enmity of the Democratic left wing by adopting a stiff policy against Soviet advances in Europe.

By the summer of 1948 the President's popularity had plummeted to such depths that many Democrats—conservatives and liberals alike—had cast around for another nominee to head the party's ticket. In the end, however, Truman was able to exert the massive political powers of an incumbent President and force his own renomination by the Democratic National Convention in Philadelphia on July 15. In his acceptance speech, Truman lashed out at the Republicans as "the party of special interests" that "favors the privileged few and not the common everyday man." Truman used the occasion to announce that he would call Congress back into special session on July 26 ("Turnip Day in Missouri") to enact an almost incredible array of social welfare bills. "What that worst 80th Congress does in its special session will be the test," the President said. Naturally, the Republican Congress did little that Truman asked, and throughout the campaign Truman could concentrate his fire on the "do-nothing Republican Congress." The Republicans, Truman declared, were "predatory animals who don't care if you people are thrown into a depression." They had "murdered" housing legislation, he said, and the farmers should oppose the Republicans because "this Republican Congress has already stuck a pitchfork into the farmer's back." Truman made a special appeal to minority religious and racial groups, calling for strong civil rights legislation and condemning Republicans for passing the Displaced Persons Act, which he said discriminated against Catholics and Jews.[24]

One reason for the near-universal predictions of Truman's defeat was the split-off from the Democratic party of the Southern segregationists on one side and the left-wingers on the other. The Southern defection, brewing several months, came to a head at the Democratic National Convention when a tough civil-rights plank was adopted at the instigation of Minneapolis Mayor Hubert H. Humphrey and other party liberals. The Alabama and Mississippi delegations walked out on the spot, and rebellious Southerners from 13 states subsequently held a rump convention at Birmingham, Alabama, to nominate Governor Strom Thurmond of South Carolina as the States' Rights (Dixiecrat) party candidate. On the other extreme of the party, former Vice President Henry A. Wallace organized a new Progressive party opposed to the United States' Cold War foreign policies. Though no one doubted Wallace's own loyalty, his new party was heavily influenced by Communists and others of the extreme left. Both the Dixiecrat and Progressive candidacies posed serious dangers for Truman. The former could deprive him of regular Southern electoral votes counted on by Democratic Presidential candidates ever since 1880, while the latter could cost him enough votes to lose a number of strategic urbanized states of the North.

Regardless of how they felt personally about Truman, most Americans had to admire his courage in launching an exhaustive, 31,000-mile "barnstorming" whistle-stop train tour, crisscrossing the country in the face of almost unanimous predictions from pollsters, reporters and sundry political "experts" that Thomas E. Dewey would win an overwhelming victory. A Republican of moderate persuasion in his second term as Governor of New York, Dewey had emerged as his party's nominee on the third roll call at the Republican National Convention in Philadelphia on June 24. In New York, Dewey had first won fame as a tough and effective district attorney and was respected as an able state administrator. In 1944 he had run a creditable race against Roosevelt for the Presidency. These factors helped him outrun Senator Robert A. Taft of Ohio, leader of the Republican conservative wing, and Harold E. Stassen, a younger liberal leader, in the competition for the nomination. But in the fall campaign, Dewey made the fateful mistake of believing his election was already assured and thus refused to join Truman in a sharp partisan debate on substantive issues. Instead, Dewey concentrated on diffuse calls for "national unity," failed to excite the Republican partisans, and left most of the country indifferent to his fate.

RESULTS OF THE 1948 ELECTION

	Popular Votes	Electoral Votes
Harry S Truman (Dem.)	24,179,345	303
Thomas E. Dewey (Rep.)	21,991,291	189
Strom Thurmond (States' Rights)	1,176,125	39
Henry A. Wallace (Prog.)	1,157,326	—
Minor Parties	289,739	—
Truman Plurality: 2,188,054		

As the first returns came in from the Northeastern states the night of November 2, Truman seized the lead in the popular vote. As the night hours wore on, state after state that observers had marked as "safe Republican" moved into the Truman column. Massachusetts went Democratic, as did the border states. Truman lost only four Southern states—Alabama, Louisiana, Mississippi and South Carolina—to the Dixiecrat ticket. About half the farm belt was Truman's, and he ran ahead in California despite the presence of that state's popular Governor, Earl Warren, as the Vice Presidential nominee on the Republican ticket. Among the larger states, Dewey won only New York, Michigan and Pennsylvania. When Ohio went conclusively for Truman at 11 o'clock on Wednesday morning, Dewey conceded.

The national popular vote total showed Truman had won by more than two million popular votes while he ran 114 votes ahead of Dewey in the electoral college. Truman's electoral vote margin was deceptive, however. A shift from Truman to Dewey of only 24,294 votes in three states (16,807 in Illinois, 8,933 in California and 3,554 in Ohio) would have made Dewey President instead. The election would have gone into the House of Representatives for final resolution with a shift of only 12,487 votes in California and Ohio.

Even with the hindsight that history affords, it is impossible to determine just what might have happened if the House had been called upon to pick a President in the wake of the 1948 election. Control of 25 delegations (a majority) would have been required to elect. Loyalist Democrats would have controlled 21 delegations, Republicans 20, the Dixiecrats four. Three delegations would have been divided equally between the major parties. In fact, an election by the House was precisely what Thurmond and his Dixiecrats had hoped for. They would undoubtedly have brought pressure on Truman to hold back on civil rights legislation or other steps designed to further racial integration, in return for which the Dixiecrat states would have thrown their support to Truman and made him President. Thus a splinter party that won only 2.4 percent of the national popular vote might have forced its terms on a President. The Dixiecrats probably would have been amenable to a similar deal with the Republicans, but even if their votes had been added to his, Dewey would have been one state short of a majority. These calculations assume, of course, that House members would invariably vote for their own party's Presidential candidate or, in the case of the Southerners from the four Dixiecrat states, the way the people of their states had voted in the fall elections. There might have been "breaks" in this lineup or peculiar types of deals under the pressures of the moment.

One scarcely believable but distinct possibility, if the 1948 election had gone into the House, is that no decision at all would have been made there. Had the House deadlock held from the day of the electoral count, January 6, until inauguration day, January 20, then the new Vice President would have assumed the Presidency under the terms of the 20th Amendment to the Constitution. (That amendment, ratified in 1933, provided in part that "if the President elect shall have failed to qualify, then the Vice President elect shall act as President until a President shall have qualified.") But who would have been the new Vice President? If Truman had failed to win an electoral majority, his Vice Presidential running mate, Senator Alben W. Barkley, would also have failed to win a majority. Under the Constitution the Senate would have had the task of electing the new Vice President. The party lineup in the Senate was 54 Democrats, 42 Republicans. The Senators would have had only two choices: Barkley or Warren. Barkley was a highly respected fellow-Senator and member of its inner "club." Thus he could have expected solid backing from all the Northern Democrats and probably from all but one or two of his colleagues and long-time associates from the Dixiecrat states. The chances are very high that Barkley would have been chosen as the next Vice President. And if the House had failed to break its deadlock by January 20, Barkley would have assumed the powers of the Presidency—even though not a single

American had voted to elect him to that position.[25] But Barkley would have been only Acting President and would have been obliged to relinquish the office at any time in the following four years that the House resolved its deadlock and chose a new President.

But the 1948 election did more than demonstrate anew the dangers of throwing an election into the House. It also provided a striking example of how the electoral college permits splinter parties, which receive only tiny percentages of the national popular vote, to play a decisive role in the ultimate allocation of large blocs of electoral votes. Truman apparently lost a massive bloc of 74 electoral votes—those of New York, Michigan and Maryland—because Henry Wallace was on the ballot in those states. The Wallace vote, liberal and basically Democratic-inclined, accounted for more than the difference between Dewey and Truman in each of those states. Thus the electoral college permits splinter parties in big states to occupy the balance of power in the election of an American President.

The Election of 1960

Republican President Dwight D. Eisenhower, the first man of his party to win the Presidency since the 1920s, was ineligible to seek a third term in 1960 because of the two-term limitation written into the Constitution through the 22nd Amendment. The Democrats also felt obliged to come up with a new nominee because Adlai E. Stevenson, their standard-bearer in 1952 and 1956, had a record of two successive defeats behind him. For the Republicans, the choice of a Presidential candidate was comparatively easy. Vice President Richard M. Nixon had been in the public eye for eight years, had been an exceptionally active Vice President and enjoyed strong support in the Republican organizations throughout the country. New York Governor Nelson A. Rockefeller, the only potential opponent to Nixon who might have amassed significant delegate strength, decided the odds against success were too high and declined to make the effort. Nixon was nominated by an almost-unanimous vote of the Republican National Convention on July 27 in Chicago.

Four formidable candidates entered the race for the Democratic nomination—Senator Hubert H. Humphrey of Minnesota, a leading spokesman for the party's liberal wing; Senator John F. Kennedy of Massachusetts, a liberal, strong vote-getter and the first Roman Catholic to be seriously considered for the Presidency since Alfred E. Smith in 1928; Senator Stuart Symington of Missouri, a former Secretary of the Air Force; and Senate Majority Leader Lyndon B. Johnson of Texas, a skilled and powerful Democratic legislative leader since 1953. By winning the most important Presidential primaries of the year and obtaining the support of the party's big-city leaders, Kennedy was able to win nomination on the first ballot at the Democratic National Convention in Los Angeles on July 13. In a surprise move, Kennedy picked Johnson as his Vice Presidential running mate. Many liberal leaders in the party expressed consternation at the selection of Johnson, but later it became evident that Johnson's presence on the ticket was probably an essential element in holding most of the South behind Kennedy and effecting Democratic victory in one of the closest elections of U.S. history.

Kennedy promised the voters a "New Frontier" to cope with "uncharted areas of space and science, unsolved problems of peace and war, unconquered pockets of ignorance and prejudice, unanswered questions of poverty and surplus." The central issue, he asserted repeatedly, was the need for strong Presidential leadership to reverse the nation's declining prestige abroad and lagging economy at home. Nixon, on the other hand, pledged to "build on" the achievements of the Eisenhower Administration and pictured himself as a man trained for the Presidency and its trying problems, especially in the field of international diplomacy. He described Kennedy as "immature" and "impulsive" and said the Democratic platform pledges would add $18 billion to the government's annual budget. As the campaign entered its final weeks, Kennedy was thought to have gained significantly from an unprecedented series of four face-to-face encounters between the Presidential candidates on national television.[26]

The suspenseful election night of 1960 has already been described in Chapter 1. In some respects, the outcome was similar to that of 1948. The Democratic candidate won a substantial margin of electoral votes—303 compared to 219 for his Republican opponent. There was no left-wing splinter party of any consequence in the 1960 balloting, but the Southern unpledged elector movement, a successor to the Dixiecrat movement of 1948, won 14 electoral votes in two Southern states. The unpledged electors eventually cast their votes for Senator Harry Flood Byrd in the electoral college. In one major respect, however, the results were markedly different from those of 1948. While Truman had amassed a popular vote plurality of over 2 million votes, Kennedy's popular vote margin was one of the smallest in the history of Presidential elections—apparently just over 100,000 out of a total of 68,738,000 ballots cast in the country.

In fact, it was impossible to determine exactly what Kennedy's popular vote plurality—if it existed at all—really was. With the exception of Alabama, where unprecedented difficulties arose in determining the popular vote, the national count was 33,902,681 for Kennedy and 33,870,176 for Nixon—a Kennedy lead of 32,505. In Alabama, the state law provided that the names of the individual candidates for Presidential elector would appear separately on the ballot, with the voter allowed to vote for as many or as few members of any electoral slate as he liked. (For ballot diagram, see Appendix K.) Each elector slate consisted of 11 men—the number of electoral votes to which the state was entitled. All the Republican electors were pledged to vote for Nixon, and the highest Republican elector received 237,981 votes in the general election—establishing a clear Nixon popular vote total in the state.[27] There had been stiff competition in Alabama to determine who would be placed on the ballot as Democratic electors— men pledged to support the party's national nominee or unpledged electors opposed to the national policies of the party. A Democratic primary and runoff held in the spring had resulted in the selection of six unpledged and five loyalist elector candidates to compose the 11-man Democratic elector slate in the general election. Thus the question arose: For whom should the votes cast for the Democratic elector slate be counted in the national popular-vote tally—for Kennedy or for the unpledged elector movement? On election day the highest unpledged elector on the Democratic slate received 324,050 votes while the highest loyalist or Kennedy elector received 318,303 votes. It appeared that, with few exceptions, the same people had voted for both the unpledged and the loyalist electors. The national wire services chose to credit Kennedy with the highest vote cast for any Democratic elector in the state—the 324,050 that one of the unpledged members of the Democratic slate received. The wire service accounts made it appear that no unpledged elector votes at all were cast in Alabama. The result, of course, was a gross misstatement of the actual vote in the state, an error that followed over into the wire associations' reports that Kennedy won the national popular vote by some 118,000 votes. The figure was open to criticism on two counts: first, because it included some 6,000 votes which were specifically cast *against* Kennedy by Alabama Democrats who would not support loyalist electors, and secondly because it totally disregarded the unpledged elector vote, even though it was higher than Kennedy's.

A preferable method of reporting the Alabama vote, adopted by *Congressional Quarterly* and noted as "First Method" (see below), was to report the vote for the highest Kennedy elector (318,303) as part of his national count and the vote for the highest unpledged elector (324,050) as part of the national unpledged elector vote (eventually credited to Byrd). The result was a Kennedy plurality nationwide of 112,827 votes. In reporting this result, *Congressional Quarterly* took care to note, however, that it was actually reporting the votes of the citizens who supported Democratic electors in Alabama two times— once for Kennedy, once for unpledged electors. The result involved a serious distortion, since it resulted in a double count of the votes of the Democratic voters in Alabama while the Republican voters in the state—and the votes of citizens in every other state of the Union— were reported but once.

RESULTS OF THE 1960 ELECTION

	Popular Votes	Electoral Votes
First Method		
John F. Kennedy (Dem.)	34,220,984	303
Richard M. Nixon (Rep.)	34,108,157	219
Harry F. Byrd*	638,822	15
Minor Parties	188,559	——
Kennedy Plurality: 112,827		
Second Method		
Kennedy	34,049,976	303
Nixon	34,108,157	219
Byrd*	491,527	15
Minor Parties	188,559	——
Nixon Plurality: 58,181		

First Method involves counting split Alabama elector slate both for Kennedy and unpledged electors; *Second Method* involves dividing vote for Alabama Democratic elector slate proportionately according to its composition. See below.

  * Byrd was accorded the votes of 14 unpledged electors from Alabama and Mississippi, plus one vote by a Republican elector in Oklahoma.

An alternative method, developed by *Congressional Quarterly* and noted as "Second Method" (see above), was to take the highest vote for any Democratic elector in Alabama—324,050—and divide it proportionately between Kennedy and unpledged electors. Since loyalists held five of the 11 spots on the slate, they were credited with 5/11ths of the party total—147,295 votes. The unpledged electors, holding six elector slots, were credited with 6/11ths of the Democratic vote—176,755. This procedure, while somewhat arbitrary, had the virtue of avoiding any double count of the Democratic votes in Alabama. The state totals would now read: Nixon 237,981; Kennedy 147,295; unpledged electors (Byrd) 176,755. But when these totals were added to the popular-vote results from the other 49 states, a significant change took place. Kennedy no longer led in the national popular vote at all. Instead, Nixon was the popular vote winner by a margin of 58,181 votes.[28]

Interestingly, Nixon never sought to use these figures to argue that he had been the people's choice for President in 1960. Since Kennedy was clearly the electoral college winner, Nixon may have felt that claiming a popular-vote victory would simply have made him out as a poor loser. Moreover, the complex issues raised by the Alabama count were not the kind that many people would fully understand. Thus, little public debate took place on the question of how Alabama's votes should be counted, and it seemed likely that the issue would not be raised again.

But in 1964 the problem of determining the 1960 Alabama vote appeared once more. The Democratic National Committee, in allocating the number of delegate seats each state would have to the 1964 Democratic National Convention, employed a formula that rested in part on the number of popular votes the party's nominee—Kennedy—had received in the last Presidential election. The Northern Democrats in control of the Committee were anxious to minimize the weight of the Southern states, especially those that had been disloyal to the national ticket in the 1960 election. So when it came to determining the number of Kennedy votes with which Alabama should be credited in determining the delegate apportionment, the National Committee used exactly the same formula that *Congressional Quarterly* had used following the 1960 election. It took the highest vote for a Democratic elector in Alabama, divided it in 11 parts, and credited five parts to Kennedy and six to the unpledged electors. As a result, the size of the Alabama delegation to the 1964 Convention was reduced. But by employing this stratagem, the Democratic National Committee was accepting the rationale of a counting system under which Nixon was the clear popular vote winner in 1960.

In the days and weeks following the 1960 election, however, the nation's attention was focused not on the Alabama vote count but rather on the question of fraud. Two days after the election, Republican National Chairman Thruston B. Morton sent telegrams to party leaders in 11 states asking them to look into allegations of voting irregularities. A Republican spokesman said many complaints alleging fraud, payment of money and other irregularities had been received, most of them from Illinois, Texas, North and South Carolina, Michigan and New Jersey. Republicans were especially bitter over the outcome in Illinois, where Kennedy had won by 8,858 votes out of 4,757,409 cast and there were allegations of irregularities in the count in heavily Democratic Cook County (Chicago). The Cook County Republican chairman alleged that 100,000 fraudulent votes had swung Illinois to Kennedy through "systematic" looting of votes in 12 city wards and parts of two others.[29] Republicans laid stress on one precinct, virtually deserted because of highway demolitions, where the vote reported was 79 for Kennedy and 3 for Nixon though there were less than 50 registered voters on election day.[30] Widespread "tombstone" voting and tampering with voting machines were alleged. The Democrats replied angrily that the Republicans had no proof of substantial irregularities and that they were darkening the name of the city before the nation. The recounts in the city soon bogged down in legal maneuvering, and the Republicans were never able to produce hard evidence to show that fraud had been a big enough factor to give the state to Kennedy. (In 1962, however, three Democratic precinct workers in Chicago did plead guilty to "altering, changing, defacing, injuring or destroying ballots" in the 1960 election.[31]) Republicans were even less hopeful of a reversal in Texas, where the Kennedy-Johnson ticket led by 46,233 votes, though Republicans charged that the Democratic-controlled election boards had consistently invalidated Republican ballots with slight defects while counting Democratic ballots with identical deficiencies.

Despite the closeness of the election, the Republicans never publicly claimed that the alleged vote irregularities were sufficient to reverse the outcome. But for a while between November 8 (election day) and December 19 (when the electors met to vote), there was speculation that if Illinois' 27 electoral votes were lost to Kennedy through proof of vote fraud, thus reducing Kennedy's electoral votes to 273—only four more than the 269 needed for victory—Southern electors might bolt and withhold votes from the Kennedy-Johnson ticket, thus throwing the election into the House of Representatives. This immediate fear was dispelled, however, when the Illinois electoral board, consisting of four Republicans and one Democrat, certified the election of the Kennedy electors from the state on December 14.

The close elections in the Northern states had been watched with special interest by conservative Southerners who hoped to thwart Kennedy's election. On December 10, Alabama's six unpledged electors met in Birmingham and announced their desire to cast their Presidential vote "for an outstanding Southern Democrat who sympathizes with our peculiar problems in the South." They stated that "our position remains fluid so that we can cooperate with other unpledged electors for the preservation of racial and national integrity." The Alabamans specifically deplored the role of Southerners who "ally themselves with a candidate [Kennedy] who avowedly would integrate our schools, do away with literacy tests for voting," and "otherwise undermine everything we hold dear in the South."[32]

Two days later, a joint meeting was held in Jackson, Mississippi, between the six unpledged electors from Alabama and the eight who had been chosen in Mississippi. The decision was made to throw the unpledged elector support to Senator Byrd of Virginia, and a joint statement was drafted calling on Presidential electors from the other Southern states to join the vote for Byrd in the hope that enough electoral votes might be withheld from Kennedy to throw the election into the House of Representatives. A defection of 35 additional Southern electors from Kennedy would have been necessary to send the election to the House. Mississippi's Governor Ross Barnett, one of the South's strongest segregationists, sent letters to six other states asking for support in the move to block Kennedy. In Louisiana, leaders of the White Citizens Council were at the forefront of a move to have the state's Democratic electors withhold their support from Kennedy.[33] The stated hope of the unpledged electors was that if the election reached the House, all Southerners would vote for Byrd and that the Republicans, "being fundamentally opposed to the liberalism of Senator Kennedy," would follow suit.[34] The new party lineup in the House would consist of 23 states controlled by Northern and border state Democrats, six controlled by Deep South Democrats, and 17 controlled by Republicans. Another four delegations were evenly split between the parties. Thus it is highly problematic what would have happened, even if the election had reached the House.

As it turned out when the electors actually cast their votes on

December 19, the only vote Byrd got outside of the anticipated ones from Alabama and Mississippi came not from another Southern Democrat but from a Republican. He was Henry D. Irwin, who had been elected as a member of the winning Republican elector slate pledged to Nixon in Oklahoma. Irwin subsequently stated on a nationwide television program that he had performed "his constitutional duty" as a "free elector." The next July, subpoened to appear before a U.S. Senate Judiciary Subcommittee, Irwin said he had never planned to vote for Nixon, whom he "could not stomach." Irwin revealed that he had worked in concert with R. Lea Harris, a Montgomery, Alabama, attorney, in a national movement to get the members of the electoral college to desert Nixon and Kennedy in favor of a strongly conservative candidate. An alternative considered by Harris was to support a plan reportedly considered by some conservatives in the Louisiana Legislature to call a meeting of conservative Southern Governors in Baton Rouge, to which Kennedy would have been invited and presented with the following conditions which he would have to meet to receive the Southern electoral votes he needed for election: "(1) Eliminate the present sizable foreign aid we presently give to the Communist economy; (2) adhere to the spirit of the 10th Amendment [reserving powers not specified in the Constitution to the states], and (3) appoint one of these Southern Governors Attorney General."[35]

On November 20, Irwin had telegraphed all Republican electors in the country saying, "I am Oklahoma Republican elector. The Republican electors cannot deny the election to Kennedy. Sufficient conservative Democratic electors available to deny labor Socialist nominee. Would you consider Byrd President, [Barry] Goldwater Vice President, or wire any acceptable substitute. All replies strict confidence." Irwin received approximately 40 replies, some of them favorable, but most of the electors indicated they had a moral obligation to vote for Nixon. Irwin subsequently asked the Republican national committeemen and state chairmen to free Republican electors from any obligation to vote for Nixon, but received only three sympathetic replies. Republican National Committeeman Albert K. Mitchell of New Mexico wired Irwin that he had taken up the idea "with some of the leaders of the Republican National Committee level and found that while everyone was in favor of the move, they felt that it should not be sponsored by the Republican organization." Mitchell encouraged Irwin, however, to take further steps to "eliminate Kennedy from the Presidency." Later, Republican National Chairman Morton said that if

Irwin "had the support of the Republican National Committee, I knew nothing about it." Not a single additional Republican elector in the country followed Irwin's lead.[36]

Thus every move to upset the results of the 1960 election—from a Republican challenge of vote returns to the efforts of the Southern unpledged electors and the machinations of Henry Irwin of Oklahoma—was to prove fruitless. But it was only by chance that the country was spared weeks or months of indecision following the 1960 contest. A shift of but 8,971 popular votes—4,480 in Illinois and 4,491 in Missouri—would have thrown the election into the House of Representatives. If an additional 1,148 votes had shifted from Kennedy to Nixon in New Mexico, along with 58 in Hawaii and 1,247 in Nevada, Nixon would have become President. Whether that would have violated the popular will, one cannot say, because there is no obviously clear and fair way to count the popular vote for the 1960 election. Had it not been for the electoral college, each man might have conducted his campaign in a somewhat different manner, and one candidate or the other might have won a clear-cut popular vote victory.*

In many ways, the 1960 election summed up the evils of the electoral college in our times. First, it showed once again the irrational, chance factors that decide a close election, when the shift of a few votes can throw huge blocs of electoral votes in one direction or the other. Secondly, it underscored the danger of fraud deciding a Presiden-

---

* Kennedy's strategy was to carry the Midwest and Eastern industrial states, plus California, while counting on the normal Democratic vote from the majority of Southern states. The Nixon strategy was to carry the normally Republican farm areas, run strongly in the Far West, and make sufficient inroads in the major industrial states and normally Democratic South to win a majority of the electoral votes. Perhaps one reason Kennedy won was that he and his advisers ever since 1956 had shown an extraordinarily keen perception of the workings of the electoral college and understood how an appeal centered on the major industrial states might win for a Democratic candidate. Nixon, on the other hand, pledged to visit every one of the 50 states in his campaign, a pledge that would bedevil him on the final weekend before the election as he spent valuable hours in a visit to Alaska (a state with 3 electoral votes) instead of concentrating on big doubtful states like Michigan and Illinois (with 20 and 27 electoral votes respectively). In retrospect, neither candidate could say his strategy had been completely effective. Kennedy, to be sure, did carry most of the big states. But he lost Ohio and California and, by his failure to win the prairie or mountain states, came perilously close to defeat. Nixon did win a majority of the states, a fitting conclusion for a campaign in which he visited every state. But Nixon had diffused his effort and fell short of victory. Without the electoral college, the campaigns might have been somewhat less oriented to specific states or blocs of states.

tial election, because Illinois, where the most ballot disputes arose, was the state that almost decided the entire election. Third, it showed the potentially decisive role that a narrowly based regional or splinter party can play in the choice of a President and how the system actually encourages independent elector blocs. Fourth, the election showed how a faceless elector, chosen to carry out a specific function, could suddenly break his trust and try to determine the choice of the chief executive for 180 million Americans. (What if Henry Irwin's vote had been *the deciding vote* in the electoral college in 1960?) And lastly, the election showed that as long as individual states have *carte blanche* in deciding how Presidential electors will be chosen, it may be difficult and sometimes impossible to compile accurate national popular vote totals (as in Alabama in 1960) and to learn whom the majority of Americans really wanted to be their President.

N O T E S

1. Eugene H. Roseboom, *A History of Presidential Elections* (New York, 1959), p. 82; Edward Stanwood, *A History of the Presidency from 1788 to 1897* (Boston, 1898), pp. 127–31.
2. Stanwood, *op. cit.*, pp. 135–36.
3. *Ibid.*, p. 139; Roseboom, *op. cit.*, p. 84.
4. Cited by Roseboom, *op. cit.*, p. 88. See also Stanwood, *op. cit.*, pp. 138–39.
5. Cited by Samuel Eliot Morison and Henry Steele Commager, *The Growth of the American Republic* (New York, 1950), I, p. 464.
6. Richard C. Baker, "On Becoming President by One Vote," *American Bar Association Journal*, May 1962, p. 455; Roseboom, *op. cit.*, p. 86. For text of rules under which the House operated in choosing a President, see Appendix J.
7. Cited by Charles A. O'Neil, *The American Electoral System* (New York, 1887), p. 124.
8. Stanwood, *op. cit.*, p. 393.
9. See Stanwood, *op. cit.*, p. 383.
10. Roseboom, *op. cit.*, pp. 242–43.
11. *Ibid.*, pp. 243–45.
12. Stanwood, *op. cit.*, p. 381; Roseboom, *op. cit.*, p. 245.
13. Cited by J. Hampden Dougherty, *The Electoral System of the United States* (New York, 1906), p. 108.
14. *Ibid.*, pp. 109–10, 126–35.

15. *Ibid.*, pp. 110–16.
16. Roseboom, *op. cit.*, p. 247.
17. Stanwood, *op. cit.*, pp. 390–91.
18. Roseboom, *op. cit.*, p. 249.
19. *Ibid.*, pp. 248–49.
20. Cited by Sidney Hyman, *The American President* (New York, 1954), pp. 29–30.
21. Stanwood, *op. cit.*, pp. 457–83.
22. *Ibid.*, pp. 447–49.
23. Roseboom, *op. cit.*, p. 387.
24. For more detailed background on the 1948 campaign, see *Congress and the Nation* (Congressional Quarterly Service, Washington, 1965), pp. 5–8; also Jules Abels, *Out of the Jaws of Victory* (New York, 1959).
25. Richard M. Scammon, "How Barkley Became President," *Northern Virginia Sun*, March 7, 1960.
26. For further background on the 1960 campaign, see Theodore H. White, *The Making of the President, 1960* (New York, 1961); also *Congress and the Nation*, as cited, pp. 32–39.
27. The commonly accepted practice in determining popular votes for President is to credit the Presidential candidate with the number of votes received by the highest-polling elector pledged to him in the state. See pp. 136–37, below.
28. *Congressional Quarterly Weekly Report*, Feb. 17, 1961, pp. 285–88. See also U.S. Senate, Committee on the Judiciary, Subcommittee on Constitutional Amendments, *Hearings, Nomination and Election of President and Vice President and Qualifications for Voting*, 87th Congress, 1st Session, 1961, pp. 391–99. Cited hereafter as 1961 Senate *Hearings*.
29. Chicago *Tribune*, Nov. 14, 1960.
30. N.Y. *Herald Tribune*, July 14, 1961.
31. N.Y. *Times*, March 4, 1962.
32. *Ibid.*, Dec. 11, 1960.
33. Wash. *Evening Star*, Dec. 12, 1960.
34. Associated Press dispatch, Dec. 12, 1960.
35. 1961 Senate *Hearings*, p. 622.
36. For Irwin's testimony, which includes copy of his correspondence with other Republican electors and Southern unpledged elector leaders, see 1961 Senate *Hearings*, pp. 562–655.

5 Electing a President Today

THE PROCESS BY WHICH THE AMERICAN PEOPLE SELECT THEIR CHIEF EXECU-tive has two distinct aspects: the highly visible, popular campaign, which is seen, experienced and participated in by millions of citizens, and, at the same time, the almost invisible workings of the constitutional mechanisms for elections, which go unnoticed by the vast majority of Americans. In most elections the electoral college manages to mirror the popular will, so that the two systems coincide in their results. But there are always the dangers that the electoral system may go awry and that the popular choice for President will be rejected by the electoral college. The interplay between these two systems—popular and constitutional—defines the subject of Presidential election in America today. It is a necessary prelude to any discussion of the possibilities for reform and change.

The Popular Campaign

Early in the year preceding a Presidential election, the would-be candidates of each party begin their preliminary soundings across the nation, wooing influential party leaders and trying to establish a public image that will help them win the greatest prize the American electoral system has to offer. The first objective is to win the Presidential nomination of one of the dominant national political parties, for no other road leads to the Presidency under the country's prevailing two-party system.

THE NATIONAL NOMINATING CONVENTIONS. The historian Carl Becker has commented that "the national nominating convention is something unknown to the Constitution and undreamed of by the founding fathers. It is an American invention, as native to the U.S.A. as corn pone or apple pie. A Democratic or a Republican nominating convention, once it gets going, emits sounds and lights that never were on land or sea. Superficially observed, it has all the variety of a Slithy Tove. At different hours of the day or night, it has something of the painted and tinseled and tired gaiety of a four-ring circus, something of the juvenile inebriety and synthetic fraternal sentiment of a class reunion, something of the tub-thumping frenzy of a backwoods meeting." This is only the semblance, the picture to the outer world, however. "What goes on beneath the surface and behind locked doors," Becker adds, "is something both realistic and important. For it is here, unexposed to the public eye, that deals and bargains, the necessary compromises are arranged—compromises designed to satisfy as well as possible all the divergent elements within the party. . . . What really goes on in a national nominating convention is the attempt, by the party leaders, to forecast the intangible and uncertain will of the people, as it will be registered in the state pluralities, and to shape the party policies in conformity with it."[1] Thus in many important respects, the national conventions perform the task for the people that the Constitution's framers thought would be performed by the electors. But instead of settling on one candidate, the nominating conventions—and only those of the two dominant parties are usually of any lasting importance—propose the two Presidential candidates from which the people and their agents, the electors, will choose the following autumn.

The Constitution's framers never contemplated national conventions for two reasons: because nationally organized political parties were unknown at the time, and because they dreaded the idea of partisan coalition and sought in the charter of government they wrote to isolate the Presidential election from any pressures of faction or party.

By the early 1900s, however, national political parties were a fact of life in the United States. Institutions had to be developed by which each party could decide on its candidates for President and Vice

President, rather than fragmenting its support in the election. The Congressional caucus, operating from 1796 until 1824, was the first answer to this problem (see pages 63 and 83, above). Functioning in the era before the railroad, when travel from one part of the country to another was arduous and time consuming, the Congressional caucus provided the only logical national forum for a political party. Ironically, the caucus placed the nomination of the President precisely where the Constitutional Convention had been determined not to place it: in Congress. Significantly, it was the supporters of frontier democracy and egalitarianism, grouped around Andrew Jackson, who effectively killed the caucus system in 1824. The caucus (or King Caucus, as its opponents derisively called it) could not survive an era of expanding democracy, because its power base was too narrow: Congressmen were chosen by the people to make laws, not Presidents.

In 1828, Jackson and Adams were nominated by a combination of state legislatures, public meetings and irregular conventions scattered throughout the Union. The time was ripe for national nominating conventions to appear, and the first was held by the Anti-Mason party in Baltimore in September 1831. The short-lived coalition called the National Republican party met in Baltimore in December 1831 to nominate Henry Clay for the Presidency, and the Democrats held their first national convention in the same city in May 1832, nominating Andrew Jackson for a second term. The first Whig Convention was in 1839, the last in 1852. The first Republican National Convention was held in Philadelphia in 1856, nominating John C. Frémont for the Presidency.

The delegates to each national convention come from every state and thus represent a broad geographic cross section of their parties. Some are Governors, Congressmen and other prominent leaders from nonpolitical professions; many are simply party hacks who come to vote as party leaders tell them to. Most are chosen by state party conventions, but a significant minority are elected in popular Presidential primaries currently held in about 16 states. Collectively, the delegates to a national convention represent the continuing entity of the national political party, a continental alliance that will continue to function and flourish only as long as it represents a significant cross section of the American people.[2]

THE PRESIDENTIAL CAMPAIGN. In the early days of the Republic, the candidates for President remained quietly in their home cities and awaited the decision of the people. Today, every American is aware of the whirlwind of activity surrounding a Presidential campaign. The candidates for President and Vice President cover the face of the continent again and again, by air, rail and motorcade, visiting every major population center at least once and even the smallest states of the Union. With the advent of radio, and especially of television in the years since World War II, the Presidential campaign has been carried into the homes of all but a handful of the people. Whether the issues brought forth by the candidates be great or petty, the battle is distinctively national in character and is recognized by all as the decisive plebiscite on the course of the nation for four years to come.

ELECTION DAY. The grand climax of the race for the Presidency comes as the people register their votes, starting with the stroke of midnight in a few early-voting hamlets in New England and ending some 26 hours later with the close of the last polling place in Alaska, four thousand miles to the west. In early American elections, it was days or weeks until the result was known; now, with quick reporting through the News Election Service, a cooperative ballot-counting operation of the three major television networks and the two major wire services, and rapid computer calculations by the national television networks, the result is generally known by mid-evening. A few hours later, except in the closest of contests, the losing candidate will concede, wishing his opponent all success in office and urging the nation to unify behind the winner. The drama seems to be closed for another four years.

The Constitutional System

As far as the Constitution is concerned, the popular election every fourth November is only the first step in a complex procedure that should culminate in the declaration of a winner a full two months later. In fact, under the Constitution, the November election is not for the Presidential candidates themselves but for the electors who subsequently choose a President. And all the Constitution says of this stage of the election process is that "each state shall appoint, in such manner as the legislature thereof may direct, a number of electors, equal to the whole number of Senators and Representatives to which the state may be entitled in Congress." Thus the major controversies over the way the President is elected have centered on the Presidential elector.

HOW MANY ELECTORS ARE THERE? Since each state's representation in the electoral college is equal to its representation in Congress, a state is guaranteed three electoral votes: two corresponding to the number of its United States Senators, and one corresponding to the minimum of one seat in the U.S. House which the Constitution assures each state. Additional House seats are apportioned on the basis of population following each decennial Census. Congress has the power to decide the over-all size of the House. The total number of Representatives was set provisionally at 65 in the Constitution, rose to 106 after the 1790 Census, and then increased gradually until the current level of 435 seats was established following the 1910 Census. At the present time, with 50 states in the Union, the electoral college consists of 538 persons—435 corresponding to the number of Representatives, 100 to the number of Senators, and an additional three for the District of Columbia under the 23rd Amendment to the Constitution.[3]

The relative power of various states in the electoral college has risen and fallen dramatically in the course of U.S. history (see Appendix C). Virginia, the early "mother of Presidents," swung the heaviest weight in the first years of the nation—21 out of a total of 138 electors in the last decade of the 18th century. Today, Virginia contributes only 12 electors in a vastly enlarged college. New York had 12 of the 138 electors in the 1791–1800 period, but rose to a high for any state—47 electors—between 1931 and 1950. California, starting with only 4 electors when she entered the Union in 1850, has 40 electoral votes in the 1960s, and in the 1970s is expected to control 46 of the 538 electoral positions.

A state's Congressional apportionment—and thus its electoral vote— tends to lag behind actual population shifts. Since each Census takes place in the first year of a decade (1790, 1960, etc.), the new apportionment cannot take effect until two years later. Thus the population figures from the 1790 Census were not reflected in a new Congressional apportionment until 1792, and the House elected under that apportionment did not take office until 1793. The same two-to-three-year gap has occurred after each subsequent Census, except in the 1920s, when Congress failed to provide for any new apportionment whatever. If a Presidential election falls in the same year as a Census, it is still governed by the apportionment based on the Census of a full

decade before. The first Presidential election under a new apportionment will take place either two years after the apportionment (as in
1952 and 1972) or a full four years later (as in 1944 and 1964),
depending on the quadrennial cycle.

WHO PICKS THE ELECTORS? In practice, the people of the states have
been given the power to choose the electors in statewide elections since
the 1830s (see pages 74–78, above). The last instances in which a
legislature chose the electors directly were in South Carolina through
1860, the newly reconstructed state of Florida in 1868, and the newly
admitted state of Colorado in 1876. With these minor exceptions, the
people have chosen the electors.

If any state legislature chose to, however, it would have the right
under the Constitution to take the choice of the electors away from the
people and do the job itself or deputize some other body to make the
selection. In the words of a Senate committee in 1874, "The appointment of these electors is thus placed absolutely and wholly within the
legislatures of the several states. They may be chosen by the legislature, or the legislature may provide that they shall be elected by the
people of the state at large, or in district; . . . and it is, no doubt,
competent for the legislature to authorize the Governor, or the supreme court of the state, or any other agent of its will, to appoint these
electors." This language was quoted approvingly by the U.S. Supreme
Court in a landmark 1892 case, *McPherson v. Blacker,* in which a
group of Michigan citizens challenged the right of that state's Legislature to shift to a district system for the 1892 elections.[4] The Court rejected the appeal, saying that the word "appoint" in the Constitution
conveys the "broadest power of determination" to the legislatures.
"There is no color for the contention," said the Court, that "every male
inhabitant of a state being a citizen of the United States has from the
time of his majority a right to vote for Presidential electors." The Court
said the state legislatures have "plenary power" over appointing electors and could indeed refuse to provide for appointment of any electors at all if they so chose. During a debate in the U.S. House in 1826,
Representative Henry R. Storrs of New York commented that nothing
in the Constitution prevented a state legislature from vesting the power
to choose Presidential electors "in a board of bank directors—a turnpike
commission—or a synagogue."[5]

Despite such sweeping language, there are some limitations on the
discretion of state legislatures in setting the mechanism for Presiden-

tial election in their respective states. Even *McPherson v. Blacker* recognized that *if* a state permits the people to choose the electors, then the 14th Amendment protects citizens from having their vote denied or abridged. Congressional enactments designed to prevent fraud or regulate campaign expenditures in connection with Presidential elections have been upheld by the U.S. Supreme Court.[6] The Governor of a state, moreover, might well veto a legislative act abolishing popular election for Presidential electors. In referendum states, a law abolishing popular election could be referred to the people, where it would almost certainly be defeated. Initiative measures could be used in a similar way.[7]

For the most part, however, it is not state or federal constitutional guarantee that assures the people the right to choose Presidential electors. First of all, it would probably never occur to modern-day state legislatures to take the power of appointment of the electors directly unto themselves. And even if the temptation presented itself, fear of retribution at the polls would restrain the state legislators. After the 1960 election, segregationist forces in the Louisiana Legislature suggested revoking the choice of the regular Democratic electors already elected by the people and substituting a new elector slate that would oppose Kennedy's election. But despite the strong conservative sentiment in the Legislature, the motion was withdrawn before it could come to a vote. Even if the motion had passed, it could probably have been subjected to successful challenge in the courts because it would have violated the Congressional requirement that the electors be chosen on a uniform date—which had already passed. But a move by a legislature to take the appointment of the electors into its own hands before the nationally established date for choosing the electors would not be open to similar challenge.

WHO ARE THE ELECTORS? The Constitution merely says that "no Senator or Representative, or person holding an office of trust or profit under the United States, shall be appointed an elector." The probable intent of the founding fathers was that the electors would be distinguished citizens, and such they were in some early elections. But in 1826 a Senate select committee said that electors were "usually selected for their devotion to party, their popular manners, and a supposed talent for electioneering."[8] As late as 1855, it was noted that the electors in Alabama and Mississippi were among the state's ablest men and went among the people to instruct, excite and arouse them on the issues of the campaign.[9] Today, it is probable that not one voter in thousands knows who the electors are. Persons are usually nominated for elector on the basis of their service to their party. Since the only payment is normally a small per diem allowance on the day they cast their votes, some small measure of prestige is about all that electors can hope for from their selection. Democratic National Chairman John M. Bailey acknowledged in 1961 that the elector's role was "almost purely ceremonial" but said that the office should be continued because it "provides an honorary role for the people who devote themselves to making our political system work, and our society has too few such rewards."[10] Based on an entirely unscientific perusal of the pictures of electoral colleges convened in several states, it appears that such "rewards" are often reserved for women and party workers in the twilight of their lives. Many octogenarians are apparent. Thomas O'Connor was 93 years of age when he was elected president of the Massachusetts electoral college in 1960.

A modern-day exception to the practice of anonymous electors occurred in New York State in 1936, when the Democratic party put several trade-unionists, including Ladies' Garment Workers' chief David Dubinsky on its electoral slate as a means of attracting the labor vote to Franklin D. Roosevelt. At the time, some fears were expressed that a "Tammanyizing" of electoral slates might occur, with the introduction of class, racial and religious appeals through giving each of these groups some of the electoral nominations.[11] But the fears have not proved real; indeed, fewer and fewer states actually list the names of the electors on their ballots.

NOMINATION AND ELECTION OF THE ELECTORS. Presidential electors for each party are today nominated by a variety of methods. The most widely used procedure—now in effect in 35 states—is for state conventions of the parties to nominate the electors. In five states and the District of Columbia, nominations are made by the state political committees. Two states, Arizona and Alabama, authorize nomination of the electors in primary elections. The remaining eight states use a variety of combination methods. The most unusual nomination law is Pennsylvania's, which authorizes the Presidential nominee of each political party to nominate electors on his behalf in the state (see Appendix J for state-by-state listing).

Before 1845, Congress refrained from setting any specific day for actual election of the electors. The Act of 1792, spelling out procedures for Presidential election, stipulated only that the electors must be chosen within 34 days preceding the first Wednesday in December every fourth year.[12] A uniform national election date was established in 1845, however: the first Tuesday after the first Monday in November.[13] The date was especially appropriate for an agrarian society, for it fell after most of the autumn harvest had been gathered yet before the rigors of winter set in. The date has been observed in every subsequent Presidential election.

Since the advent of Jacksonian democracy, the general ticket for choosing electors has been used almost exclusively by the states. Under this system, electors are chosen "at large" (on a statewide basis) and the party with the most votes receives all the state's electoral votes.* Since 1832, only one state has reverted to the district system of choosing electors that several states used in the first years. This occurred in 1892 in Michigan, where Democrats were temporarily in control of the Legislature and hoped to divide the state's electoral votes so that they would not go *en bloc* to the Republicans, who normally had a majority in the state. Each of the state's 12 Congressional districts became a separate elector district, and two "at large" districts, one Eastern and one Western, were established for the votes corresponding to Michigan's two Senators. The plan was successful in dividing the Michigan electoral vote: nine electoral votes went for the Republican Presidential ticket and five for the Democratic ticket in that year's election. But the national outcome was not close enough to be influenced by the Michigan returns. It was this Michigan plan that the Supreme Court refused to invalidate in *McPherson v. Blacker* (see page 116, above). No state has since used the district plan.

The virtual anonymity of the Presidential elector has been reinforced in recent years by the marked trend, apparently spurred by the desire to simplify the vote count and the spread of voting machines, toward the use of the Presidential "short ballot" in the November election. Instead of facing a ballot or voting machine with long lists of elector candidates, the voter sees the names of the parties' Presidential candidates written in large type, usually preceded (in small type) by the words, "Presidential electors for . . ." Many states even omit the wording about Presidential electors altogether, so that the voter, unless

---

* A plurality is sufficient for election of electors in all states except Georgia, which requires an absolute majority. Georgia officials have ruled that if no elector slate won a majority, the two leading slates would participate in a runoff two weeks after the general election.

he is well versed politically, has no way of knowing that he is actually voting for electors rather than directly for President and Vice President (see sample state ballots, Appendix K). The Presidential short ballot was employed by 15 states in 1940, by 26 in 1948, and was prescribed by the laws of 35 states in 1966. The names of both the Presidential candidates and the electors appear on the ballots in 14 states. Most of these states require that the voter choose one slate or another as a unit, though some permit the voter to pick and choose among electors on various slates and permit write-ins. Only one state—Alabama—prints the names of the electors but makes no mention of the Presidential candidates (for state-by-state listing, see Appendix J).

One beneficial result of the short ballot is to cut down the chances for voter confusion in marking ballots. History abounds with examples of spoiled ballots resulting from voter confusion over how to vote for electors. In the 1904 Presidential election in Florida, the 20 candidates for elector, five from each of the four parties that qualified, were printed in a close column, one name below the other, with no line or space to separate the parties. Nor did the ballot carry any emblem or name to indicate which party each candidate for elector represented. The Democratic voter had to mark the first five electoral candidates, the Republican numbers six through ten, the Populist numbers 11 through 15, and so on. Naturally, a large number of voters were muddled, and 4,300 out of the 39,300 voters in the state failed to mark all the electors of their parties.[14] In Maryland in 1904 some 2,000 Republican voters marked only the square for the first Republican elector, thinking that that square represented a vote for all eight Republican elector nominees. The result was that the Republicans received only one instead of all eight Maryland electoral votes.[15] One of the most serious voter mix-ups of modern times occurred in Ohio in 1948. The state normally employs the short ballot, so that the names of the Republican and Democratic electors do not appear on the ballot. Henry Wallace's Progressive party was unable to qualify as a regular party for the general election ballot, however, so that the Wallace electors appeared on the ballot as individual names. Thousands of voters were confused by the double system and voted for some Wallace electors as well as marking ballots for Dewey or Truman. It has been estimated that more than 100,000 Ohio Presidential ballots were invalidated for this reason. The confusion could well have determined the outcome in the state, which Truman won by a margin of only 7,107 votes.[16]

Under the general ticket ballot as employed by most states, the voter chooses one entire elector slate as a unit and there is no chance for a split result—some electors elected from one slate and some from another. But where an elector can split his elector ticket, there is a chance for a divided result. As noted above, that result occurred in Maryland in 1904. It also resulted in California in 1912, when two Democratic electors and 11 Progressive electors were victorious because of slight differences in the vote cast for the various elector candidates on those two slates.[17] The spreading use of the short ballot has minimized the chances for such occurrences.

ELECTORS: BOUND OR NOT? Since the first election, there has been controversy about the proper role of Presidential electors. Are they to think and act independently, or are they merely agents of the people who choose them? History records that in 1792 the electors chosen in North Carolina met and debated the respective merits of John Adams and George Clinton and finally decided to support Clinton.[18] Debates among the Virginia electors in the same year were reported to have shifted six votes from Adams to Clinton.[19] But even in the first elections, few electors really acted as independent agents. The journal *Aurora* said in 1796: "The President must not be merely the creature of a spirit of accommodation or intrigue among the electors. The electors should be faithful agents of the people in this very important business; act in their behalf as the people would act were the President and Vice President elected immediately by them. . . . Let the people then choose their electors with a view to the ultimate choice."[20]

With the passage of the 12th Amendment in 1804, any semblance of the electors as independent agents faded. In his 1826 Senate committee report, Thomas Hart Benton of Missouri said that the founding fathers had intended electors to be men of "superior discernment, virtue and information," who would select the President "according to their own will" and without reference to the immediate wishes of the people. "That this invention has failed of its objective in every election," Benton said, "is a fact of such universal notoriety, that no one can dispute it. That it ought to have failed," he concluded, "is equally uncontestable; for such independence in the electors was wholly incompatible with the safety of the people. [It] was, in fact, a chimerical and impractical idea in any community."[21]

Thus by the early 19th century, the function of the electors was little more than ministerial. Benton said the electors had "degenerated into mere agents"; and Justice Bradley, the famed "15th man" on the

Electoral Commission of 1877, characterized electors as mere instruments of party—"party puppets" who are to carry out a function which an automaton without volition or intelligence might as well perform.[22] Senator John J. Ingalls of Kansas commented in the same era that electors are like "the marionettes in a Punch and Judy show."[23] Reviewing the historical failure of the electors to be free agents as contemplated by the founding fathers, Supreme Court Justice Robert H. Jackson wrote in 1952: "Electors, although often personally eminent, independent and respectable, officially become voluntary party lackeys and intellectual nonentities to whose memory we might justly paraphrase a tuneful satire:

> "They always voted at their Party's call
> And never thought of thinking for themselves at all."[24]

Jackson concluded that "as an institution, the electoral college suffered atrophy almost indistinguishable from *rigor mortis*."[25] Senator Henry Cabot Lodge of Massachusetts said in 1949 that electors "are mere rubber stamps—and inaccurate rubber stamps at that. The people know the candidates for President and Vice President; rarely do they know the identity of the electors for whom they actually vote. Such 'go-betweens' are like the appendix in the human body. While it does no good and ordinarily causes no trouble, it continually exposes the body to the danger of political peritonitis."[26]

Nevertheless, under the Constitution the elector remains a free agent and, if he chooses, can vote in any way he likes. At least as far as the law is concerned, Senator Benton warned, the elector "may give or sell his vote to the adverse candidate, in violation of all the pledges that have been taken of him. The crime is easily committed, for he votes by ballot; detection difficult, because he does not sign it; prevention is impossible, for he cannot be coerced; the injury irreparable, for the vote cannot be vacated; legal punishment is unknown and would be inadequate. . . . That these mischiefs have not yet happened, is no answer to an objection that they may happen."[27] Since Benton's day, some efforts have been made to restrict the elector's independence, but his basic point still holds. In 1898 former President Benjamin Harrison suggested that "an elector who failed to vote for the nominee of his party would be the object of execration, and in times of high excitement might be the subject of a lynching."[28]

In fact, there have been isolated instances where Presidential electors have broken their pledges. The first known case was recorded in Pennsylvania in 1796, when Samuel Miles, chosen as a Federalist, voted for Jefferson, prompting the much-quoted voter's remark that Miles had been chosen "to act, not to think" (see page 64, above). In 1820 former Senator William Plumer of New Hampshire cast his electoral vote for John Quincy Adams rather than James Monroe, to whom he was pledged. Accounts vary about Plumer's motivation; he is reported to have said he felt only George Washington "deserved a unanimous election"; but biographers also report he wanted to draw attention to his friend Adams as a potential President and to "protest against the wasteful extravagance of the Monroe administration."[29] In 1824, North Carolina's 15 electors voted *en bloc* for Jackson, despite a reported agreement to divide their votes according to the result of a Presidential preference vote, which the voters were allowed to make by writing on the ballot the name of the man they preferred. Adams' name was written in by about a third of the state's voters, so that he should have received about five electoral votes, according to the historian J. B. McMaster. Other authorities maintain, however, that it was understood that all of the state's votes would go to the more popular candidate.[30] In the same election the New York Legislature picked a mixed slate of electors, including seven electors expected to back Clay (from the state total of 36 in that election). One of the Clay electors was elected to Congress, however, and the man who replaced him voted for Adams. By the time the New York electors actually cast their ballots, they already knew that Clay would not even qualify for the runoff in the House. Two of the remaining six Clay electors from the state then deserted him—one to vote for Crawford, one to support Jackson.[31]

In recent times, three electors have broken their pledges. The first was Preston Parks, who was nominated on two elector slates in Tennessee in 1948—the regular Democratic (pledged to Truman) and the States' Rights (pledged to Thurmond). The regular Democratic slate, including Parks, was elected, but he voted for Thurmond anyway. In 1956, W. F. Turner of Alabama, a Democratic elector, voted for a local circuit judge, Walter E. Jones, for President, instead of supporting the regular Democratic nominee, Adlai E. Stevenson, to whom he was pledged. Turner subsequently commented: "I have fulfilled my obligations to the people of Alabama. I'm talking about the white people."[32] The most recent instance of a renegade elector was Henry D. Irwin—the 1960 Republican elector in Oklahoma who voted for Harry Byrd for

President despite his pledge to vote for Nixon (see pages 107–108, above). Irwin, who listed his occupation as "slave labor for the federal government," explained his action on a national television program: "I was prompted to act as I did for fear of the future of our republic form of government. I feared the immediate future of our government under the control of the socialist-labor leadership. . . . I executed my constitutional right . . . as a free elector." Irwin went on to say that the founding fathers were landowners and propertied people who never intended "that the indigent, the nonproperty owners should have a vote in such a momentous decision" as election of the President.[33]

Fortunately for the nation, neither Henry Irwin nor any of the self-willed men who broke electoral pledges before him have been able to change the outcome of a Presidential election. Statistically, the chances are not very high. Between 1820 and 1964, 15,245 electoral votes were cast. Only four votes in all those years were indisputably cast "against instructions." If one also includes the disputed 1824 votes in New York and North Carolina, the total of bolting electors rises to 12.

Most electors consider themselves irrevocably bound to support the Presidential candidate on whose party ticket they were elected. In the disputed Hayes-Tilden election of 1876, James Russell Lowell, who had been chosen as a Republican elector in Massachusetts, was urged to switch his vote from Hayes to Tilden—a move that would have given Tilden the election, since only one vote divided the men in the national count. Lowell refused to take the step, however. "In my own judgment I have no choice, and am bound in honor to vote for Hayes, as the people who chose me expected me to do," Lowell wrote to a friend. "They did not choose me because they have confidence in my judgment but because they thought they knew what the judgment would be. If I had told them that I should vote for Tilden, they would never have nominated me. It is a plain question of trust."[34] At the meeting of the California electoral college in Sacramento in 1960, former Governor Goodwin Knight told his fellow Republican electors: "Before coming here today, many of us received messages by mail and wire urging that we cast our ballots for prominent Americans other than Richard Nixon and Henry Cabot Lodge. Among those mentioned were former Governor Allan Shivers of Texas, Senator Barry Goldwater of Arizona, and Senator Harry Byrd of Virginia. Conceding that these gentlemen have merit as statesmen," Knight said, "the fact remains it is our solemn duty, in my humble judgment, to vote for those men the people selected on November the eighth."[35]

In an effort to prevent runaway electors, the party organizations in a few states require specific pledges by electors that they will support the national nominees of the party in electoral college balloting. Electors must now make such pledges in Alaska, Oregon, Oklahoma and Florida—the latter two by formal oath.[36] In a number of other Southern states, the party committees are given sufficient discretion by state law to demand party loyalty pledges whenever they wish. Alabama has demanded such pledges in several elections, but not in the last few years because the party machinery generally supports the unpledged elector movement. In 1944 some Texas Democratic electors indicated that they might bolt the national ticket. A special party committee was convened. One of its members, Representative Wright Patman, later said the committee had "tried the proposed electors for disloyalty" and "put most of them off the ticket and put loyal ones on."[37]

In addition, a sharply increased number of states now have specific statutory provisions directing electors to vote for the Presidential candidates of the party that nominated them. Only five states had such laws in the 1940s, but today the list has expanded to 15, including the nation's two largest states, California and New York. In the wake of the bolt by Republican elector Irwin in 1960, the Oklahoma Legislature added a new section to its election code stipulating that each elector candidate must take an oath to support his party's Presidential and Vice Presidential candidates, and that if he votes for another person he will be guilty of a misdemeanor and fined up to $1,000.[38]

Serious constitutional questions are raised as soon as any effort is made to bind or control electors. Custom may have made electors into little more than instruments of party, but the Constitution provides that they shall vote by ballot, a procedure which would seem to imply that they are free agents. In 1952 the Supreme Court was called upon to judge the constitutionality of a requirement laid down by the Democratic Executive Committee of Alabama that candidates for elector pledge to support the Presidential and Vice Presidential candidates of the party's national convention as a condition to being certified as a candidate in the Democratic primary. The Court, in a 5 to 2 opinion, held that the pledge requirement represented a legitimate exercise of the state's right to appoint electors under Article II. The majority opinion noted the popular expectation that electors would vote for the party nominees and implied that the states' power to control electors was supported by the traditional practice of elector pledges. Even if a loyalty pledge were unenforceable, the Court said, it would not follow that a party pledge as a requisite for running in a primary was unconstitutional, since any person not wishing to take the oath could run independently of party.[39] But the Court did not rule on the constitutionality of state laws that require electors to vote for their party's candidates, or indicate whether elector pledges, even if given, could be enforced. The preponderance of legal opinion seems to be that statutes binding electors, or pledges that they may give, are unenforceable. "If an elector chooses to incur party and community wrath by violating his trust and voting for some one other than his party's candidate, it is doubtful if there is any practical remedy," in the view of James C. Kirby, Jr., an expert on electoral college law. Once the elector is appointed, Kirby points out, "he is to vote. Legal proceedings which extended beyond the date when the electors must meet and vote would be of no avail. If mandamus were issued and he disobeyed the order, no one could change his vote or cast it differently. If he were enjoined from voting for anyone else, he could still abstain and deprive the candidate of his electoral vote."[40]

CONDITIONALLY PLEDGED OR UNPLEDGED ELECTORS. Quite separate from the problem of elector fidelity is that of electors who either announce before the election that in certain circumstances they may support an alternative candidate, or who simply refuse to be pledged in any way. An example of electors' announcing alternatives came in 1912, when South Dakota electors, nominally pledged to Theodore Roosevelt, let it be known before the election that if the returns from the rest of the country made it clear that Roosevelt could not be elected and the contest was between Woodrow Wilson and William Howard Taft, they would vote for Taft. The voters apparently found this assurance satisfactory, for the Roosevelt slate was victorious on election day in South Dakota. But Taft had run so far behind across the country that the state's electors stuck with Roosevelt anyway.

The concept of totally unpledged electors disappeared from the political scene around the time of the 12th Amendment, only to reappear in the mid-20th century as a device by conservative, segregationist-minded Southerners to force the major parties to pay more heed to Southern views. The genesis of the movement can be traced to the abortive States' Rights (Dixiecrat) third-party movement in the 1948 election (see pages 97 and 99, above). The Dixiecrat goal of 1948 was revived by the unpledged elector movement of 1960: to prevent either of the major party nominees from receiving a majority of the electoral votes. With the power to dictate the result of the election in their hands, the Southerners then could extract pledges from one of the major party candidates with respect to Southern positions on segregation and other issues, in return for the swing elector support from the South. If that strategy failed, the election would be thrown into the House of Representatives, where the Southern states might also find themselves in a crucial bargaining position.

In 1948 the Dixiecrat nominees, Strom Thurmond (South Carolina) and Fielding Wright (Mississippi), won the elector votes of the four states where they actually appeared on the ballot as the Democratic nominees—Alabama, Louisiana, Mississippi and South Carolina. Presumably, Thurmond and Wright would have released their electors to vote for one of the national party nominees if they had achieved enough votes to occupy a balance of power, and could have struck off a bargain with Truman or Dewey. Thus the Dixiecrat electors were technically pledged but would quickly have become unpledged if such an action had suited their purposes. In 1960 the unpledged electors chosen in Alabama and Mississippi decided to cast their votes for Harry Byrd when it appeared they had been unable to achieve a balance-of-power position. Major preparations were made to launch another unpledged elector movement in 1964, but they were discarded when the Republicans nominated Barry Goldwater for President.[41] Goldwater's general conservatism and stand against civil-rights legislation satisfied most of the segregationist Southerners, and of the six states he carried, four were the same ones that had gone Dixiecrat in 1948. If the Southern conservatives in the future decide to repeat their previous strategy, they may put unpledged elector slates on the ballot—as the law now specifically permits in Alabama and Mississippi—or may run a Southern leader like Alabama's George C. Wallace, who would then use his electors as a bargaining tool if both major parties failed to get an electoral college majority.

THE ELECTORS CAST THEIR VOTES. The Constitution, in Article II and the 12th Amendment, provides that the electors shall meet in their respective states to vote by ballot for President and Vice President. Congress is given the power to determine the day of voting, "which day shall be the same throughout the United States." This system of simultaneous elections in each state was adopted, according to one of the delegates to the Constitutional Convention, in the hope that "by apportioning, limiting and confining the electors within their respective states, . . . that intrigue, combination and corruption would be effectively shut out, and a free and pure election of the President of the United States made perpetual."[42] The founding fathers had apparently hoped that the electors would be unaware of, and thus not influenced by, the action of their counterparts in all the other states.

Even in the first election, of course, the curiously naïve hope for absolutely independent action by the electors in the various states was not fulfilled. But the form of election which the Constitution's framers prescribed has remained unchanged for almost two centuries, and on a specified day every fourth year a separate group or "college" of electors meets in each state capital to vote for President. In 1792 Congress decreed that the day should be the first Wednesday in December. This provision remained in effect until 1877, when Congress shifted the date to the second Monday in January, reportedly to allow a state more time to settle any election disputes.[43] The final adjustment, to the first Monday after the second Wednesday in December—still the law today—was set by Congress in 1934 following ratification of the 20th Amendment, which shifted inauguration day from March 4 to January 20.[44]

On the appointed day in December, the electors then convene, in most states at 12 noon. The meeting takes place in the state legislative chambers, the executive chambers or the office of the secretary of state. Under federal law, the Governor of the state must by this time have sent to the Administrator of General Services in Washington a certificate showing the names of the electors appointed and the number of popular votes cast for them (for sample certification, see Appendix K). Copies of these certificates are presented to the electors when they convene, and the Governor or secretary of state generally makes a short speech welcoming the electors to their august duty.[45]

Frequently, however, some of the electors fail to appear for their great day. Congress, in a law first passed in 1845, has authorized the states to provide for filling of vacancies. In almost all the states today, the electors themselves are authorized to choose replacements.[46] Sometimes the replacements are found by scouring the hallways of the state capitol for likely candidates. This process was followed by the Michigan electoral college in 1948, when only 13 of the 19 chosen electors—all pledged to Dewey and Warren—appeared. But one of the substitutes recruited on the spot, a Mr. J. J. Levy of Royal Oak, had to be restrained by his colleagues from voting for Truman and

Barkley. "I thought we had to vote for the winning candidate," Levy was quoted as saying.[47] Substitute electors must frequently be designated because federal office holders have been chosen as electors, in violation of the Constitution.

While they have but one function—to vote for President—the electors in many states go through an elaborate procedure of prayers, election of temporary and permanent chairmen, speeches by state officials, appointment of committees and the like. Robert G. Dixon, in an interesting review of electoral college procedures, points out that the secretary of state is the "shepherd and guiding spirit of the electoral college in all states . . . the high priest who knows the ritual prescribed by laws and usages, federal and state, and under his prompting the electors go through their paces like obedient children."[48] In a speech accepting chairmanship of the Ohio electoral college (for the fifth time) in 1948, Alfred M. Cohen said: "Our task is purely perfunctory if we are faithful to the trust confided in us." Cohen had apparently developed little love of the institution he headed, however, because he told his colleagues that he favored abolishing the system altogether in favor of direct popular voting for President.[49]

The Constitution provides specifically that the electors shall vote "by ballot" for President and Vice President, which would seem to require a secret vote. In reality, the voting is not at all secret in many states. Dixon's survey showed that in 17 of the 40 states from which he received a response in 1949, the electors voted either by signed ballot, by oral announcement only (with no ballot whatever!) or by unsigned ballot accompanied by a public announcement of how each of them was voting. Fourteen states used paper ballots, 12 employed type-written ballots, eight printed ballots, two engraved ballots and five the obviously unconstitutional practice of oral voting. Many of the printed ballots, in fact, actually list the names of the Presidential and Vice Presidential candidates of the party that carried the state, thus destroying even the semblance of a free vote[50] (see sample electors' ballots, Appendix K). In 1800 one New York elector, Anthony Lispenard, insisted on his right to cast a secret ballot. It was reported, however, that Lispenard intended to forsake Jefferson and cast his double vote for Burr and someone else—a maneuver that would have given Burr the Presidency. The prestigious De Witt Clinton was then brought into the meeting and his presence had such an impact that the participants showed each other their ballots before placing them in the ballot box. Lispenard hesitated but finally exhibited his ballot, marked properly for Jefferson and Burr.[51] Thus by common practice since the earliest days, the ballot is not secret and sometimes is not even a ballot at all. Actual use of the secret written ballot, as one observer has noted, "is an anti-democratic provision which may cause a blunder, and could be easily used to cover a crime. An agent of the people should never be permitted to act secretly in transacting their business, except in cases where the public safety may require."[52]

After balloting separately for President and Vice President, as required by the Constitution, the electors are required to send lists of their votes by registered mail to the President of the Senate in Washington. This constitutional requirement has been amplified by statute to safeguard against loss of the first copy. Two copies are kept by the secretary of state of the state, two go to the General Services Administrator and one to the judge of the local district court.[53]

THE COUNT IN CONGRESS; DISPUTED VOTES. Once the electors have balloted and the certificates of their votes have been forwarded to Washington, the scene shifts to Congress, where the votes are to be counted. The Constitution and 12th Amendment provide simply that "The President of the Senate shall, in the presence of the Senate and House of Representatives, open all the certificates and the votes shall then be counted." In 1792, Congress provided that the joint session for counting the votes should take place on the second Wednesday in February; since passage of the 20th Amendment, the date has been January 6 following each Presidential election. The count takes place in the hall of the House of Representatives, with the President of the Senate (who is the Vice President of the United States) presiding.

Throughout the 19th century the major controversy regarding the entire electoral college procedure centered on the technicalities of the vote count in Congress. By one theory, the President of the Senate had authority to count the votes; by another, the two houses present in joint session had the responsibility for counting; by still another theory, there was a *casus omissus* in the Constitution on who actually should do the counting.[54] The question was of great importance because of the number of disputed electoral votes. Obviously, the officer (or officers) responsible for the actual count enjoyed tremendous power, because, in effect, he was able to disqualify disputed electoral votes or to decide in the event of double returns from a state. During the first two decades of the 19th century it was the unquestioned custom for the President of the Senate "to declare the votes."

But from 1821 onward, his authority was undercut, and in the Reconstruction period, Congress itself exercised the power to judge disputed returns.

The major 19th-century ballot controversies centered on whether a state was fully admitted to the Union at the time its electoral ballots were cast (Indiana in 1817, Missouri in 1821, Michigan in 1837); whether certain Southern states were properly readmitted to the Union when they sought to cast electoral votes immediately following the Civil War, and which ballots should be counted when two sets of returns were submitted by a state. Some of the objections raised during the century seem to have bordered on the trivial. In 1856, Wisconsin's electors met and voted one day later than the date set by Congress because of a blizzard that prevented their assembling on the proper date. The certificate of their vote was transmitted to the President of the Senate with an explanation of the circumstances that precluded their meeting on the appointed day. But though Wisconsin's vote would not have changed the national result, spirited argument began when the presiding officer in the joint session of Congress announced the count of the tellers "including the vote of Wisconsin." The arguments were ruled out of order, but the two houses withdrew to their own chambers for two days of bitter and inconclusive argument over whether the Constitution was inexorable in its requirement of the casting of the electoral vote on a single day.[55] Among the more arbitrary actions of Congress was its vote in 1873 to exclude the electoral vote of Arkansas because the certificate of returns bore the seal of the secretary of state instead of the great seal—an article that the state did not possess at the time.[56]

In 1877, Congress finally enacted a law covering procedure in all disputed vote cases—a law still largely in force today. It seeks to shift the onus of decision in disputed vote cases back onto the states by providing that if a state has established a mechanism to resolve disputes, the decisions of the state officials will be binding on Congress. Congress may refuse to count votes from a state only if the two houses decide concurrently that the certification is invalid or that the electoral votes were not "regularly given" by the certified electors (for the text of existing statutes on the electoral count, see Appendix H). No vote counts in Congress have been disputed since the celebrated battle over the returns of the 1876 election.

Over the years the role of the President of the Senate has been reduced to little more than presiding at the joint session and breaking the seals on the ballots. The ballots are then given to tellers—two from each house—who actually announce each state's votes and make the national tally. The President of the Senate then has the honor of announcing the names of the new President and Vice President of the United States—assuming that there has been a majority vote.

CONTINGENT ELECTION. If no Presidential candidate receives a majority of the electoral votes, the task of choosing a new Chief Executive is transferred to the House. This phenomenon has occurred twice in our history, following the elections of 1800 and 1824 (see pages 68–70, 84–85, above). A minor shift of popular votes in the nation would have sent a number of other elections—including those of 1860, 1892, 1948 and 1960—into the House for decision. Under the 12th Amendment, the House must choose among the three leading electoral vote recipients, rather than the top five originally stipulated in the Constitution. But the original system giving each state one vote in the House, regardless of size, remains in effect, and any state whose delegation is evenly divided loses its vote altogether (for rules of the House in a contingent election, see Appendix I).

Except for the founding fathers, few Americans have ever found much commendable in the system of contingent election in the House. Thomas Jefferson wrote in 1823: "I have ever considered the constitutional mode of election ultimately by the legislature voting by states as the most dangerous blot on our Constitution, and one which some unlucky chance will some day hit."[57] Martin Van Buren in 1826 declared that "there is no point on which the people of the United States were more perfectly united than upon the propriety, not to say the absolute necessity, of taking the election away from the House of Representatives."[58] Senator Oliver P. Morton of Indiana said in an 1873 Senate speech: "The objections to this constitutional provision for the election of a President need only to be stated, not argued. First, its manifest injustice. In such an election each state is to have but one vote. Nevada, with its 42,000 population, has an equal vote with New York, having 104 times as great a population. It is a mockery to call such an election just, fair or republican." Morton showed that under the apportionment then in effect, 45 members of the House, drawn from 19 states, could control an election in a House then consisting of 292 members representing 37 states. The 19 states with an aggregate 1870 population of a fraction over 8 million people would be able to outvote 18 states with an aggregate population of 30 million. Morton declared that "the rotten-borough system was a mild and very small bagatelle" in comparison.[59] The comparable figures based on the 1960 Census showed that 76 members of the House, drawn from 26 states, could elect a President in a House of 435 members representing 50 states. The 26 states with an aggregate population of 30.7 million people would be able to outvote 24 states with a total population of 148.6 million.

A number of other objections to election by the House are also apparent. First, Representatives are elected not with an eye to their preference for President but for very different reasons. Many districts and states elect Congressmen of one party and vote for the Presidential candidate of another. Secondly, the choice of the President by Congress could place the Chief Executive under heavy obligations to the legislative branch. Third, the whole election could swing on one or two men from one or two key states, as it did in 1825. Fourth, the Constitution does not explain the procedure if a tie for third place occurs in the electoral balloting. Would the House consider just the top two, or in reality the top four candidates? After extensive research on these questions, a reputable political scientist noted, somewhat wryly, "A certain amount of perseverance is needed in order to discover something good to say about the possibility of an election of the President in the House of Representatives."[60]

The rules of the House provide for continuous House balloting on President until a winner is declared. The balloting would start January 6, leaving 14 days until the scheduled inauguration. In most cases, a speedy resolution could be hoped for. But a prolonged deadlock could occur, so that no President would be chosen by January 20. In that event the new Vice President would become Acting President under the specific mandate of the 20th Amendment. If, as would be likely, there had also been no majority in the electoral college vote for Vice President, he would have been chosen by the Senate. Since only the top *two* Vice Presidential elector candidates could be considered by the Senate, with each member having a single vote, a choice would almost certainly have occurred.

Only once in history has the Senate been called on to choose a Vice President. In 1837, Van Buren won 170 of the 294 electoral votes in a split field. But his Vice Presidential running mate, Colonel Richard M. Johnson of Kentucky, had only 147 electoral votes—one less than a majority. Johnson, who had been hailed as the man who personally killed the Indian leader Tecumseh in the Battle of the Thames during the War of 1812, was boycotted by the Virginia electors, who voted for Van Buren for President but reportedly wanted to register disapproval of Johnson's social behavior.[61] The Senate proceeded to elect Johnson by a vote of 33 to 16 over Francis Granger of New York, the runner-up in the electoral vote for President.[62]

If a Presidential election should ever be thrown into Congress again, at least the decision would not be made by lame-duck legislators as it was in 1801 and 1825. Under the 20th Amendment, ratified in 1933, a new Congress—elected the same day as the Presidential electors—takes office on January 3, three days before the official count of the electoral votes.

DEATH OF A PRESIDENTIAL CANDIDATE OR PRESIDENT-ELECT. Under the United States' multistage process of electing a President—stretching from the day that the national party conventions nominate candidates to the day in January that a new Chief Executive is inaugurated—a number of contingencies can arise through the death or withdrawal of a prospective President or Vice President.

The first contingency may arise through the death of one of the nominees between the adjournment of the convention and the day in November when the electors are officially chosen. No law covers this contingency, though both the Democratic and Republican parties have adopted procedures to cover the eventuality. The rules of the Democratic party, approved by its national conventions, provide that the 108-member Democratic National Committee shall have the power to fill the vacancy, with each state or territory's delegates empowered to cast the same number of votes that the state or territory had at the original nominating convention. A resolution adopted by each Republican National Convention authorizes the Republican National Committee to fill any vacancy, with the same assignment of voting power to the committee members to correspond to voting strength at the convention. Alternatively, the Republican National Committee is authorized to call a new convention, a step it might well take if the election was not imminent.[63] Should they be called on to fill a vacancy caused by the death of a Presidential candidate, the national committees might in most instances select the Vice Presidential nominee as the candidate for President, and substitute a new candidate for Vice President. If the death of a candidate took place just before election day—especially if he were one of the major Presidential candidates—Congress might decide to postpone the day of the election, allowing the national party

time to name a substitute and the new candidate at least a few days to
carry his campaign to the people.

At no time in our history has a Presidential candidate died before
election day. In 1912, however, Vice President James S. Sherman, who
had been nominated for reelection on the Republican ticket with
President Taft, died on October 30. No replacement was made before
election day, but thereafter the Republican National Committee met
and instructed the Republican electors (only eight had been elected)
to cast their Vice Presidential votes for Nicholas Murray Butler.[64] In
1860 the man nominated for Vice President by the Democratic National Convention, Benjamin Fitzpatrick of Alabama, declined the
nomination after the convention had adjourned. By a unanimous vote,
the Democratic National Committee named Herschel V. Johnson of
Georgia to fill the vacancy.[65]

The second major contingency may arise if a Presidential or Vice
Presidential candidate dies between election day and the day that the
electors actually meet—under current law, a period of approximately
five weeks. Theoretically, the electors would be free to vote for anyone
they pleased. But the national party rules for the filling of vacancies by
the national committees would still be in effect, and the electors would
probably respect the decision of their national committee on a new
nominee. Again, the elevation of the Vice Presidential candidate to the
Presidential slot would be likely but not certain.

The only time that a candidate died in this period was in 1872, when
the defeated Democratic Presidential nominee, Horace Greeley, died
on November 29—three weeks after the election and a week before the
electors were to meet. Sixty-six electors pledged to Greeley had been
elected, and they met to vote on the very day that Greeley was laid in
his grave. Sixty-three of them scattered their votes among a variety of
other eminent Democrats, but three Greeley electors in Georgia insisted on marking their ballots for him despite his demise. Congress
refused to count the votes in the official national tally.[66]

The third contingency may occur through the death of a President-
or Vice President-elect between the day the electors vote in mid-
December and January 6, the day that the votes are counted in
Congress. There would likely be debate about whether the votes cast
for a dead man could be counted, but most constitutional experts
believe that the language of the 12th Amendment gives Congress no
choice but to count all the electoral votes cast, providing the "person"
voted for was alive when the ballots were cast.[67] The U.S. House

committee report endorsing the 20th Amendment sustains this view. Congress, the report said, would have "no discretion" in the matter and "would declare that the deceased candidate had received a majority of the votes." The operative law would then be Section 3 of the 20th Amendment, which states: "If, at the time fixed for the beginning of the term of the President, the President-elect shall have died, the Vice President-elect shall become President."[68] And when the Vice President-elect took office as President, he would be authorized under the 25th Amendment to nominate a new Vice President.

Similarly, if the Vice President-elect should die before the count in Congress, he would still be declared the winner, and the new President would be able to nominate a replacement.

A fourth contingency may be caused by the death of either the President- or Vice President-elect between the day the votes are counted in Congress and inauguration day. If the President-elect died, the foregoing provisions of the 20th Amendment would elevate the Vice President-elect to the Presidency. In the event of the death of the Vice President-elect, the 25th Amendment would similarly authorize the new President to nominate a Vice President, subject to the approval of Congress.

No President-elect has ever died in this period. But on February 15, 1933, a week after his election had been declared in joint session of Congress, and three weeks before his inauguration, President-elect Franklin D. Roosevelt barely escaped a would-be assassin's bullets in Miami, Florida.

In the event that neither a President nor a Vice President qualified on inauguration day, January 20, then the Automatic Succession Act of 1947 would go into effect, placing the Speaker of the House, the President pro-tempore of the Senate and then the various Cabinet officials in line for the Presidency.

Popular Votes versus Electoral Votes

Though the term "popular vote" would seem to be simple and self-explanatory, its calculation can be quite complicated. As reported and generally understood in the United States, it is determined by taking the number of votes cast by the people on election day for each slate of electors in each state—Republican, Democratic or minor party—and then adding up the totals on a national basis. If a state requires that an elector slate be chosen as a unit, then the popular vote represents the number of ballots cast for that slate.[69] Thus in the 1964 election, 7,057,586 Californians voted for President. Of that total, 4,171,877 marked their ballots for the Democratic elector slate, and Lyndon Johnson was thus credited with that number of popular votes. The Republican slate pledged to Barry Goldwater received 2,879,108 votes, and he was credited with that total in the state. Minor party elector slates received 6,601 votes and were credited appropriately in the count. If a state permits its voters to ballot separately for Presidential electors, then each elector is likely to have a slightly different total vote. In this case, the modern practice is to credit the Presidential candidate with the number of votes received by the highest-polling elector pledged to him in the state.[70] The national popular vote total for any particular candidate consists of the aggregate of the votes cast for the electoral slates pledged to him in the various states.

With rare exceptions, this gives an accurate picture of the national will. There have been instances, however, in which a candidate's national vote was unnaturally reduced when state party rules or state laws prevented a slate of electors pledged to him from qualifying. In 1860 no electoral slate was pledged to Lincoln in ten of the 33 states then in the Union. In 1912 the only way for California voters to cast ballots for President Taft was to write in the names of 13 elector candidates, since the Republican slot had been seized by Theodore Roosevelt's Progressives. In 1948 and again in 1964 the Dixiecrat and unpledged elector movements controlled the Alabama Democratic party machinery and appropriated the Democratic electoral slate for their own purposes. The Alabama voter had no way to register a vote for the national Democratic nominees in those years.

The percentage of electoral votes received by a candidate on a nationwide basis rarely coincides with his percentage of the popular vote for three reasons: (1) The general ticket (or unit vote) system, in which all the electoral votes of a state are credited to whichever elector slate receives a plurality of the state vote. Minority votes in a state are washed out completely in the national electoral vote count. (2) The distortions caused by the existence of the two "Senatorial" electoral votes in each state. (3) The fact that each state casts the number of electoral votes accorded it in the national apportionment, regardless of how few or how many citizens actually go to the polls.

DISPARITIES FROM THE GENERAL TICKET (UNIT VOTE) SYSTEM. The operation of the general ticket system is said to result in massive disfranchisement of minority voters. In 1960, 3,446,419, or 47.3 percent, of New York's voters cast their ballots for Nixon, but Kennedy's elector slate received a majority and Nixon failed to receive a single one of the state's 45 electoral votes. In California, Kennedy won 3,224,099 votes, or 49.6 percent of the state total, but Nixon received all the state's 32 electoral votes. One calculation shows that in the 11 Presidential elections from 1908 through 1948, a total of 372 million votes were cast for President, but 163 million (44 percent) of these votes were cast by minority voters in various states who failed to see a single electoral vote cast representing their votes.[71]

A study of the impact of the general ticket system on a small number of states demonstrates its inherent inequality. For example, in the neighboring states of Illinois and Indiana in 1960, Nixon won a total of 3,554,108 votes to Kennedy's 3,330,204. But Kennedy had narrowly won Illinois, thus receiving her 27 electoral votes, while Nixon won a strong victory in Indiana, bringing him 13 electoral votes. Thus the two-state electoral vote was 27 for Kennedy, 13 for Nixon—or 67.5 percent for Kennedy, based on only 48.4 percent of the two-state popular vote total. In the adjoining states of Maryland and Virginia, the discrimination worked the other way. Kennedy won 50.9 percent of the two-state popular vote, but he received only 43 percent of the two states' electoral votes because he won by a large majority in Maryland (with 9 electoral votes) but lost by a smaller margin in Virginia (with 12 electoral votes).[72] Reviewing the operation of the general ticket system half a century ago, one observer said: "A plurality or majority in one section may, it is true, at times be counteracted by one in another section, and thus the net result be a rude approximation to fairness, taking the country as a whole; but this theory of averages may not work constantly, and the steady suppression of minority conviction in a state is an undisputed evil."[73]

EFFECT OF TWO ADDITIONAL ELECTORAL VOTES CORRESPONDING TO THE NUMBER OF SENATORS. The weight of the population factor is further diminished in the electoral vote count by the two Senatorial "counterpart" electoral votes that each state enjoys, no matter how few inhabitants it has. Based on the 1960 Census, an electoral vote in Alaska corresponds to 75,389 persons, while one in California corresponds to 392,930 persons. On this basis, 35 states and the District of Columbia are technically "overrepresented" in the electoral college and 14 states are "underrepresented." The table below shows the disparities.[74]

RATIO OF ELECTORAL VOTES TO POPULATION IN EACH STATE AND THE
DISTRICT OF COLUMBIA FOR 1964 AND 1968 PRESIDENTIAL ELECTIONS
(BASED ON 1960 CENSUS)

Rank and State	Ratio	Rank and State	Ratio
1. Alaska	75,389	28. Kansas	311,230
2. Nevada	95,093	29. Connecticut	316,904
3. Wyoming	110,022	30. Washington	317,024
4. Vermont	129,960	31. Tennessee	324,281
5. Delaware	148,764	32. Louisiana	325,702
6. New Hampshire	151,730	33. Alabama	326,674
7. North Dakota	158,112	34. Georgia	328,593
8. Hawaii	158,193	35. Wisconsin	329,315
9. Idaho	166,798	36. Virginia	330,579
10. Montana	168,692		
11. South Dakota	170,129	National average	333,314
12. Rhode Island	214,872		
13. Utah	222,657	37. Kentucky	337,573
14. New Mexico	237,756	38. Minnesota	341,386
15. Maine	242,316	39. North Carolina	350,473
16. District of Columbia	254,652	40. Florida	353,682
17. Arizona	260,452	41. New Jersey	356,870
18. West Virginia	265,774	42. Indiana	358,654
19. Nebraska	282,266	43. Missouri	359,984
20. Oklahoma	291,036	44. Massachusetts	367,756
21. Colorado	292,325	45. Michigan	372,533
22. Oregon	294,781	46. Ohio	373,325
23. Arkansas	297,712	47. Texas	383,187
24. South Carolina	297,824	48. Illinois	387,736
25. Iowa	306,369	49. New York	390,286
26. Maryland	310,069	50. Pennsylvania	390,323
27. Mississippi	311,163	51. California	392,930

VOTER TURNOUT DISPARITIES. Since each state has a set number of
electoral votes, the actual vote total in a state has no relevance to its
electoral votes. The electoral votes of a state will all be counted,
whether one person or all the eligible persons go to the polls. In
Mississippi, for example, only 25.5 percent of the adult citizens voted
for President in 1960, so that 37,271 voters controlled one electoral
vote. In Kansas, which had an identical number of electoral votes, 70.3
percent of the adult population voted, so that there was a ratio of
116,103 popular votes to every electoral vote.[75]

The net result of these distorting factors is that there is a gross
disparity in most elections between the popular vote a candidate

receives and his percentage of the electoral vote. The following tables illustrate the three elections in which the disparities were the greatest:[76]

THE ELECTION OF 1860

	Lincoln	Douglas	Breckinridge	Bell
Popular Vote	1,867,000	1,379,000	854,000	591,000
Electoral Vote	180	12	72	39
Percentage of Popular Vote	39.8	29.4	18.2	12.6
Percentage of Electoral Vote	59.1	3.9	24.0	13.0

Although Douglas was second in popular votes, he was last in the electoral college. And despite the fact that he won 74 percent as many popular votes as were cast for Lincoln, his electoral vote was only $6\frac{2}{3}$ percent of Lincoln's. Douglas' popular vote was 162 percent of Breckinridge's, but he received only $16\frac{2}{3}$ percent of the number of electoral votes for Breckinridge. Douglas' popular vote exceeded Bell's by more than twice, but Bell had three times as many votes in the electoral college.

THE ELECTION OF 1912

	Wilson	Roosevelt	Taft	Debs (Socialist)
Popular Vote	6,301,000	4,128,000	3,486,000	901,000
Electoral Vote	435	88	8	0
Percentage of Popular Vote	41.9	27.4	23.2	6.0
Percentage of Electoral Vote	82.0	16.5	1.5	0

Taft had 85 percent as many popular votes as Roosevelt, but he carried only two small states, Vermont and Utah, with a total of eight electoral votes, or exactly one-eleventh of the Roosevelt electoral vote.

In 1936 Landon received 36.5 percent of the total popular vote but only $1\frac{1}{2}$ percent of the electoral vote (see chart, next page).

Indeed, in few elections have the percentages of electoral votes received by candidates shown any reasonable semblance to the popular-vote breakdown. Since 1916 there has been only one election—that of 1948—in which the winning Presidential candidate failed to run at least 10 percentage points better in the electoral college than he did in the popular vote (see chart, Appendix D).

THE ELECTION OF 1936

	Roosevelt	Landon	Others
Popular Vote	27,757,000	16,680,000	1,213,000
Electoral Vote	523	8	0
Percentage of Popular Vote	60.8	36.5	2.7
Percentage of Electoral Vote	98.5	1.5	0

Chances of a Misfire

Despite the apparent tendency of the electoral count to inflate a winner's margin of victory, the fact is that in any close election, the disparity between popular and electoral votes can easily cause the man who lost the popular vote to win in the electoral college. In fact, in the seven Presidential elections in which the leading candidate had a popular-vote lead of less than 3 percentage points over his closest competitor, the electoral college has elected the "wrong man"—the popular-vote loser—in two instances, or almost 30 percent of the time.*

Careful analysis shows that the danger of an electoral college misfire is not just historical but immediate in any close contest. In fact, only sheer luck has saved the nation from the choice of the popular-vote loser in the electoral college in several recent elections. These dangers lurking in the dual count system emerged clearly from a statistical analysis of Presidential voting patterns commissioned for this book and prepared by Charles W. Bischoff of the Department of Economics,

* The elections included in this count are 1844, 1876, 1880, 1884, 1888, 1916 and 1960. The two which clearly "misfired" were those of 1876 and 1888. The count excludes the election of 1824, when Jackson ran 10.3 points ahead of Adams in the rather incomplete national popular-vote count, yet lost in the electoral college.

Massachusetts Institute of Technology. The experience of the past 50 years, Bischoff concluded, shows that in an election as close as that between Kennedy and Nixon, there is no better than a 50–50 chance that the electoral vote will agree with the popular vote as to the winner. When the leading candidate has a plurality of about 500,000 (or 0.57 percent, based on a 70-million-vote turnout), the verdict would still be reversed about one time in three. Even a plurality of 1 to 1½ million votes (a percentage point lead of 1.1 to 1.7) would provide not quite three chances out of four of winning the election, and a 2-million-vote plurality might not suffice one time out of eight. Projected 40 years hence (to the election of 2008), when the voter turnout will probably be at least 140 million, even a 1-million-vote plurality will fail to elect the popular vote winner in one election out of three. A plurality of 2 to 3 million votes will not quite provide three chances out of four of winning the election. A 4-million-vote plurality may still fail to elect the winner in one election out of eight.

Bischoff counsels that it is not possible to make precise probability statements because the chance of a reversal depends in substantial measure on the particular candidate and the particular political climate in which an election takes place. For instance, as long as the South remained solidly Democratic, the Democratic party almost invariably needed more than 50 percent of the national major-party popular vote to win an election—a result of large Democratic pluralities in Southern voting, which in effect were "wasted" because they could not increase the region's electoral votes.

But Bischoff was able to arrive at some fascinating conclusions about the elections of recent decades by assuming various shifts in the popular votes between the two leading candidates in each contest. These conclusions, in turn, cast light on the possible problems of the next decades, regardless of what the exact political conditions of the time may be.

Bischoff's method postulated a range of uniform shifts in the percentages of popular votes received by major party candidates in each election. The impact of these assumed shifts on the electoral vote results was then calculated for each election. In 1948, for example, Truman received 52.38 percent of the major-party vote. If his vote had been reduced by 1 percent, he would have received 51.86 percent of the major-party vote (52.38 percent less 1 percent of 52.38 percent, or .5238 = 51.86 percent). The method further assumes that the percentage reduction occurred uniformly in each state, with a corresponding increase in the popular vote for the opposing major-party candidate—in this example, Dewey—in each state.* Minor-party votes in each election were assumed to remain unchanged. In the 1948 example, the question may then be asked, would Truman still have won in the electoral college? The answer is "no," for with a reduction of 1 percent of his vote total in all states, Truman would have lost Ohio, California and Illinois—three of the states he carried by the narrowest margins. This would have left him with only 225 electoral votes and would have given Dewey 267 electoral votes and the election. By repeating this experiment with different percentages, Bischoff discovered the minimum percentage of the major-party vote needed by each party to win an electoral college majority in the elections between 1920 and 1964:

MINIMUM PERCENTAGE OF MAJOR-PARTY POPULAR VOTE
NEEDED TO CARRY THE ELECTORAL COLLEGE

Year	Needed by Democrats	Needed by Republicans
1920	51.34	48.66
1924	50.36	49.64
1928	48.75	51.25
1932	50.14	49.86
1936	52.25	47.75
1940	51.71	48.29
1944	51.36	48.64
1948	52.24	47.99
1952	50.32	49.68
1956	49.71	50.29
1960	49.82	50.31
1964	48.67	51.33

It is interesting to note that with growing two-party competition in the South, the Republicans have lost the comparative advantage they enjoyed up to the early 1950s. If the year 1960 could be taken as a norm for elections in the immediate future, the parties would seem to be on a fairly even footing in terms of the percentage of the vote they need to win election.

But it would be incorrect to assume that the haphazardness of the system depends only on phenomena like solid-party voting in the South. Bischoff concludes that the more important, and perhaps more permanent, feature of the system depends on the existence of strong two-party systems in the large states of the Union like New York,

* Bischoff notes that some assumption about the distribution of the reduced vote is needed and that this symmetrical assumption seems to be the *most reasonable* one to make.

California and Illinois. As long as these states are likely to swing either way, thus throwing large blocs of electoral votes into one column or the other, the electoral college will often fail to reflect the popular vote in a close election. By rearranging and summarizing the data in the table above, Bischoff developed this chart showing the number of electoral vote victories each party would have enjoyed at set percentages of the national vote in the 12 elections since 1920:

ELECTIONS WON BY EACH MAJOR PARTY SINCE 1920 ASSUMING
THE SPECIFIED DIVISION OF MAJOR-PARTY POPULAR VOTES*

Division of Major-Party Vote	Democratic Victories	Republican Victories
Democratic 52.5% (5% Point Lead)	12	0
Democratic 52.0% (4% Point Lead)	10	2
Democratic 51.5% (3% Point Lead)	9	3
Democratic 51.0% (2% Point Lead)	7	5
Democratic 50.5% (1% Point Lead)	7	5
Democratic 50.4% (0.8% Point Lead)	7	5
Democratic 50.2% (0.4% Point Lead)	5	7
Tie Vote	4	8
Republican 50.2% (0.4% Point Lead)	3†	8†
Republican 50.4% (0.8% Point Lead)	2	10
Republican 50.5% (1% Point Lead)	2	10
Republican 51.0% (2% Point Lead)	2	10
Republican 51.5% (3% Point Lead) (or greater)	0	12

* The preceding chart, which was developed by applying uniform percentage shifts to the votes of each party, showed the percentage of the popular vote that would have given it a bare majority in the electoral college in each election. The chart on this page simply "adds up" the number of elections either party would have won at any set percentage of the national popular vote. For instance, there were seven elections when the Democrats needed 51.0 percent *or less* of the popular vote to win the election—1924 (when they needed only 50.36 percent), 1928 (48.75 percent), 1932 (50.14 percent), 1952 (50.32 percent), 1956 (49.71 percent), 1960 (49.82 percent) and 1964 (48.67 percent). But in five other elections, the Democrats needed *more* than 51.0 percent of the popular vote to win, and thus would have lost, even if they had polled that much—1920 (when they needed 51.34 percent), 1936 (52.25 percent), 1940 (51.71 percent), 1944 (51.36 percent) and 1948 (52.24 percent). Therefore the fourth line on this chart, which assumes that the Democrats had received 51.0 percent in *all* elections between 1920 and 1964, shows that in that event, the Democrats would have won seven elections and the Republicans five. The notation of a percentage-point lead on the chart is simply a translation of the absolute percentage-point figure. If a party has 51.0 percent of the major-party vote, the other party has 49.0 percent—2.0 points less.

† One election would have gone to the House of Representatives for decision.

The dangers of electoral defeat the Democrats faced in every close election, even when they won the most votes, are clear from the figures. But even with the advantage the Republicans generally enjoyed because of the Democrats' "wasted" popular votes in the one-party South, the Republicans would have lost from a third to a fifth of the elections in which they received from 50.2 to 51.0 percent of the total popular vote.

The American public may have failed to notice the haphazard nature of the electoral college because of the "runaway" nature of many recent elections. But almost any halfway reasonable electoral system, Bischoff notes, can elect the right man in a landslide election. The times in which a good electoral system is needed are precisely those times in which it *does* make a difference—that is, in close elections. With spirited two-party competition in every region of the country, there is every possibility that the nation may experience a string of close elections like those of the 1870s and 1880s. And if history and mathematics can be our guide, the country will run a high chance of electoral disaster in every such election.

N O T E S

1. Carl Becker, "The Will of People," *Yale Review,* March 1945, pp. 389, 399.
2. For a comprehensive background on political conventions, see Paul T. David, Ralph M. Goldman and Richard C. Bain, *The Politics of National Party Conventions* (Washington, 1960). For a shorter review, with details on current delegate apportionment, see *CQ Convention Guide,* Supplement to June 12, 1964, *Congressional Quarterly Weekly Report.* For details on Presidential primary laws, see *Presidential '68,* Supplement to *C.Q. Weekly Report,* Sept. 29, 1967, pp. 1893–1901.
3. For data on Congressional apportionment procedures and patterns, see *Representation and Apportionment* (Congressional Quarterly Service, 1966), pp. 51–61; also Floyd M. Riddick, *The United States Congress, Organization and Procedure* (Manassas, Va., 1948), pp. 6–10.
4. 481 U.S. 1 (1892).
5. U.S. Congress, Register of Debates, II, p. 1405, cited by Lucius Wilmerding, *The Electoral College* (New Brunswick, N.J., 1958), p. 43.
6. *Ex parte Yarbrough,* 110 U.S. 651 (1884); *Burroughs and Cannon v. United States,* 290 U.S. 534 (1934).

7. See James C. Kirby, Jr., "Limitations on the Power of State Legislatures over Presidential Elections," *Law and Contemporary Problems,* Spring 1962, pp. 497–504.

8. Senate Report No. 22, 19th Congress, 1st Session, Jan. 19, 1826, p. 4.

9. Wilmerding, *op. cit.,* p. 175.

10. U.S. Senate, Committee on the Judiciary, Subcommittee on Constitutional Amendments, *Hearings, Nomination and Election of President and Vice President and Qualifications for Voting,* 87th Congress, 1st Session, 1961, p. 546. Cited hereafter as 1961 Senate *Hearings.*

11. Robert G. Dixon, Jr., "Electoral College Procedure," *The Western Political Quarterly,* June 1950, p. 216.

12. The Congress apparently refrained from setting a specific date for two reasons: because it would be inconvenient for state legislatures that might choose the electors themselves, and would need more than a single day to complete their debates and action, and because states'-rights advocates said Congress should not place unnecessary restrictions on the states. See Charles A. O'Neil, *The American Electoral System* (New York, 1887), pp. 41–43.

13. *Ibid.,* pp. 43–44.

14. J. Hampden Dougherty, *The Electoral System of the United States* (New York, 1906), pp. 392–93.

15. Dixon, *loc. cit.,* p. 217.

16. "The Electoral College: Operation and Effect of Proposed Amendments," memorandum prepared by the staff of the Senate Judiciary Committee, Subcommittee on Constitutional Amendments, Oct. 10, 1961, p. 16. (Referred to hereafter as 1961 Senate Committee Memorandum.)

17. Dixon, *loc. cit.,* p. 217. Other instances where close votes resulted in election of split elector slates: North Dakota in 1892 (1 Republican, 2 Democratic electors); Maryland in 1908 (2 Republican, 6 Democratic); Ohio in 1892 (22 Republican, 1 Democratic); West Virginia in 1916 (7 Republican, 1 Democratic); California in 1880 (5 Republican, 1 Democratic); California in 1892 (8 Democratic, 1 Republican). See Wilmerding, *op. cit.,* p. 74.

18. O'Neil, *op. cit.,* p. 48.

19. Wilmerding, *op. cit.,* p. 174.

20. Cited by O'Neil, *op. cit.,* p. 56.

21. 1826 Senate Report, p. 4.

22. Cited by Dougherty, *op. cit.,* p. 250.

23. *Ibid.,* p. 251.

24. Justice Jackson's inspiration obviously came from a song by Sir Joseph Porter and the chorus in Act I of Gilbert and Sullivan's *Pinafore:*

> I grew so rich that I was sent
> By a pocket borough into Parliament.
> I always voted at my party's call,
> And I never thought of thinking for myself at all. . . .

W. S. Gilbert and Arthur Sullivan, *H.M.S. Pinafore, or, The Lass That Loved a Sailor* (Boston, 1880), p. 36.

25. *Ray v. Blair,* 343 U.S. 214.

26. *Rotarian* magazine, July 1949.

27. 1826 Senate Report, p. 5.

28. Cited by Edward S. Corwin, *The President, Office and Powers* (New York, 1957), p. 41.

29. Everett S. Brown, *William Plumer's Memorandum of Proceedings in the United States Senate* (New York, 1932), p. vii, cited by Wilmerding, *op. cit.*, p. 176.

30. John Bach McMaster, *A History of the People of the United States from the Revolution to the Civil War,* 8 vols. (New York, 1893–1924), V, pp. 74–75; A. R. Newsome, *The Presidential Election of 1824 in South Carolina* (Chapel Hill, N.C., 1939), Ch. 8, cited by Wilmerding, *op. cit.*, pp. 177–78.

31. Wilmerding, *op. cit.*, pp. 178–79.

32. *N.Y. Times,* Dec. 18, 1956.

33. 1961 Senate *Hearings,* pp. 445–46, 634. The television program, reprinted in the *Hearings,* was a "CBS Reports" program of Jan. 5, 1961.

34. Letter from Lowell to Leslie Stephen, quoted in Horace Elisha Scudder, *James Russell Lowell* (Boston, 1901), II, p. 217.

35. 1961 Senate *Hearings,* p. 446 (in transcript of "CBS Reports" program).

36. Robert L. Tienken, *Proposals to Reform Our Electoral System,* Legislative Reference Service, Library of Congress (Washington, 1966), pp. 9–11. Cited hereafter as 1966 LRS Report.

37. U.S. House, Committee on the Judiciary, Subcommittee No. 5, *Hearings, Amending the Constitution with Respect to Election of President and Vice President,* 81st Congress, 1st Session, 1949, p. 148. Cited hereafter as 1949 House *Hearings.*

38. The 15 states that require electors by law to vote for their party's Presidential candidate: Alaska, California, Connecticut, Colorado, Florida, Hawaii, Idaho, Maryland, Nevada, New Mexico, New York, Oklahoma, Oregon, Tennessee, Virginia and the District of Columbia. See 1966 LRS Report, pp. 13–17.

39. *Ray v. Blair;* see also, "Presidential Electors," *Columbia Law Review,* April 1965, p. 696.

40. Kirby, *op. cit.*, p. 509.

41. Before the 1964 election, substantial efforts were made to open the way for the entry of unpledged elector slates in Florida, South Carolina, Virginia and Georgia, in addition to Alabama and Mississippi. In each case, an effort was made to get the legislature, or party committees if they had sufficient authority under state law, to authorize unpledged states. Democrats loyal to the national party were able to thwart most of these moves, however. In the case of Florida, President Kennedy reportedly made a personal telephone call to the House Speaker to prevent passage of enabling legislation for independent electors. See *Congressional Quarterly Weekly Report,* June 14, 1963, p. 969, and Sept. 13, 1963, p. 1572. Alabama Gov. George C. Wallace announced on July 4, 1964, that he had "definite, concrete plans" to run for President in 16 states: Alabama, Arkansas, Florida, Georgia, Illinois, Indiana, Kentucky, Louisiana, Mississippi, Missouri, New York, North Carolina, South Carolina, Tennessee, Virginia and Wisconsin. But he withdrew

July 19, four days after Goldwater's nomination. See *C.Q. Weekly Report*, July 17, 1964, p. 1499, and July 24, 1964, p. 1547. For further background on the 1960 effort, see *C.Q. Weekly Report*, April 1, 1960, p. 569; 1961 Senate *Hearings*, pp. 562 ff., especially pp. 622–25, showing plans to mobilize independent electors for subsequent elections.

42. Rufus King in 1824. See *Annals of Congress*, 18th Congress, 1st Session, I, p. 355.

43. Dougherty, *op. cit.*, p. 226.

44. See U.S. Code, Title 3, Ch. 1, for statutory provisions regarding the meeting of electors, reprinted in Appendix H, below.

45. Dixon, *loc. cit.*, p. 218.

46. *Ibid.*, p. 219.

47. Ann Arbor *News*, Dec. 14, 1948, cited in *Congressional Record*, April 13, 1949, p. 4449.

48. Dixon, *loc. cit.*, p. 220.

49. Cited by Dixon, *loc. cit.*, p. 221. Using the 1948 Ohio electoral college as an example, Dixon listed the array of political paraphernalia sometimes involved in electoral college proceedings: (1) opening of session with secretary of state presiding; (2) calling of roll to ascertain if quorum is present; (3) prayer; (4) election of temporary chairman; (5) calling of the official roll and swearing in of members (the point at which vacancies are filled, if necessary); (6) oral statement by Governor of electors' duties; (7) appointment of four committees—rules and order of business, permanent organization, mileage and per diem, resolutions; (8) recess for lunch; (9) reconvening, report of committee on permanent organization, election of permanent chairman and of the secretary of state as *ex officio* secretary of the college; (10) address by the permanent chairman; (11) reports of committees on rules and order of business, on mileage and per diem, and on resolutions; (12) casting and counting of ballots for President and Vice President of the United States; (13) signing of the requisite certificates of votes and provision for their disposition; (14) authorization for printing the proceedings of the college; (15) reading of a letter regarding a dinner planned in Washington for members of all the electoral colleges in the various states, to take place on the eve of the inauguration; (16) adjournment. (Pp. 219–20.)

50. *Ibid.*, pp. 220–21.

51. James Cheetham to Thomas Jefferson, Dec. 10, 1801, in *Proceedings of the Massachusetts Historical Society*, 3rd series, I, p. 47; cited by Wilmerding, *op. cit.*, p. 183.

52. William Purcell, cited by Dougherty, *op. cit.*, p. 253.

53. See U.S. Code, Title 3, Ch. 1, in Appendix H, below; also Dixon, *loc. cit.*, p. 222.

54. David A. McKnight, *The Electoral System of the United States* (Philadelphia, 1878), p. 15.

55. Dougherty, *op. cit.*, pp. 51–57.

56. *Ibid.*, pp. 86–87; 1949 House *Hearings*, p. 15.

57. Letter to George Hay, Aug. 17, 1823, in Paul L. Ford (ed.), *The Works of Thomas Jefferson* (New York, 1905), XII, p. 303.

58. Cited by John B. Andrews, "Should the President Be Elected by Direct Popular Vote? Yes!," *Forum,* Oct. 1949, p. 231.

59. Cited by Dougherty, *op. cit.,* pp. 23–24.

60. Paul J. Piccard, "The Resolution of Electoral Deadlocks by the House of Representatives," in *Selecting the President: The 27th Discussion and Debate Manual* (1953–54), Vol. I, reprinted in 1961 Senate *Hearings,* pp. 826–43.

61. Sidney Hyman, *The American President* (New York, 1954), p. 145; Wilmerding, *op. cit.,* p. 209.

62. Edward Stanwood, *A History of the Presidency from 1788 to 1897* (Boston, 1898), pp. 187–88.

63. John D. Feerick, *From Failing Hands: The Story of Presidential Succession* (New York, 1965), pp. 271–72; 324–25.

64. *Ibid.,* pp. 161, 271.

65. *Ibid.,* pp. 271–72.

66. Corwin, *op. cit.,* pp. 339–40; Stanwood, *op. cit.,* pp. 353–54.

67. Feerick, *op. cit.,* p. 274. The 1873 precedent, in which Congress refused to count the Greeley votes, would not be binding, because Greeley was already dead when the electors cast their votes.

68. For further background, see *C.Q. Weekly Report,* Nov. 18, 1960, p. 1901.

69. In an attempt to show that voters in population-heavy states have inordinate power in the Presidential election, the Committee on Electoral College Reform of the American Good Government Society and Senator Karl Mundt have advanced a most curious method of computing "votes" as opposed to "voters." In the 1960 election, for instance, it is claimed that 7,290,823 voters in New York state actually cast an astronomical 328,000,000 "votes" for President since each voter chose 45 Presidential electors. But the voters of Alaska, 60,762 in number, are claimed to have cast only 182,286 votes, since each voter chose only three Presidential electors. This remarkable way of counting may be an interesting mathematical game, but it is no substitute for serious analysis. The method overlooks the fundamental—and important—fact that the number of voters per electoral vote is actually much less in Alaska (where there were 20,254 voters for each electoral vote) than in New York (where there were 162,018 voters per electoral vote), a situation which arises, of course, from the "extra" votes corresponding to the Senators, which effectively gives individual voters in smaller states greater proportionate power than their counterparts in more populous states. Therefore, the fact that New Yorkers in 1960 voted for 45 electors, while Alaskans voted for only three, is more than overbalanced by the relevant fact of the population disparity between the two states.

70. In the 19th century a few states followed the practice of averaging the number of votes received by the various members of an electoral slate, rather than taking the highest electoral vote. The practice has since been discontinued. The only difficulty in the prevailing method arises in rare instances, like that of Alabama in 1960, when the members of the same electoral slate in a particular state favor different candidates. See pp. 102–104, above.

71. Figures presented by former Rep. Clarence F. Lea of California in 1949 House *Hearings,* p. 28.

72. See plaintiff's complaint in *Delaware v. New York*, a legal challenge to the general ticket system filed in the U.S. Supreme Court in 1966; quoted in *C.Q. Weekly Report*, Aug. 19, 1966, p. 1812.
73. Dougherty, *op. cit.*, p. 73.
74. Reprinted from 1961 Senate *Hearings*, p. 670.
75. See 1961 Senate Committee Memorandum; also fact sheet on Voting Participation, *C.Q. Weekly Report*, Sept. 18, 1964, p. 2181.
76. Adapted from material presented by C. S. Potts, Dean Emeritus, Southern Methodist University, 1949 House *Hearings*, p. 181.

6 Reform Efforts of Two Centuries

"THE ROAD TO REFORM IN THE METHOD OF CHOOSING THE PRESI-
dents and Vice Presidents of the United States is littered with the
wrecks of previous attempts," Arthur Krock commented in *The New
York Times* some years ago. "Though the inequalities and other defects
of the present system are generally conceded," he said, "it has been
protected from change for more than 100 years by a mixture of natural
American conservatism where the letter of the Constitution is concerned and a bipartisan political combination effected by what some
major party politicians believe to be self-interest."[1] The actual count
shows that in the first century of the Republic, 224 resolutions were
introduced in Congress to amend the Constitutional provisions for
electing a President.[2] In the succeeding seventy-seven-year period,
through 1966, another 289 amendments were offered, making a grand
total of 513 to that point in American history.[3] Yet of all these proposals, only one has been successful—the 12th Amendment, ratified
in 1804, which was significant mainly in its requirement that Presidential electors vote separately for President and Vice President (see
page 71, above).

In addition to the glaring objections to the existing system—the
possibility of minority Presidents, the problem of faithless electors, the
possibility that state legislatures might take the popular vote from the
people, the serious consequences of fraud in a state that might swing

an entire election, and the undemocratic aspects of contingent elections in the House, with the invitation such elections offer for political manipulation and corruption—most of the reformers over the years have centered their fire on the general ticket or "winner-take-all" system of casting state electoral votes, with its resultant disfranchisement of the minority in each state in each election. This is particularly unfair, critics have said, in large states where some sections are urban and industrial, others rural and agricultural, some markedly Republican and some as heavily Democratic. In the words of Senator Thomas Hart Benton of Missouri in 1824, "To lose their votes is the fate of all minorities, and it is their duty to submit; but this is not a case of votes lost, but of votes taken away, added to those of the majority, and given to a person to whom the minority is opposed."[4]

In the 20th century, many reformers have criticized the general ticket system for allegedly inflating the bargaining power of splinter parties and pressure groups, especially in large states fairly evenly divided between the parties. This criticism has grown in significance with the urbanization of the country and the tension between various minority ethnic and economic groups, centered in the cities, and the remainder of the U.S. population. The current system, Senator Henry Cabot Lodge said in 1950, "not only permits but actually invites the domination of Presidential campaigns by small, organized, well-disciplined pressure groups within the large so-called pivotal states."[5]

Other criticisms of the existing general ticket system are that it effectively limits the choice of Presidential candidates to men from the larger states and that it leaves no incentive for citizens to vote in states that are supposedly "safe" for one party or the other.

The District System

The proposal to divide each state into separate districts for the casting of electoral votes was first made by Representative John Nicholas of Virginia on March 14, 1800, and was the subject of extensive debate in Congress and the state legislatures during the first decades of the 19th century. A significant minority (though never a majority) of the states employed the system during the first few elections (see page 76, above) and it was favored in some form by many leaders in the first half-century of the Republic. The major backing for the district system has always come from those who saw the general ticket or unit vote system of casting electoral votes as a chief evil of the American electoral system. Writing to George Hay in 1823, Madison said that "the district mode [of choosing electors] was mostly, if not exclusively, in view when the Constitution was framed and adopted; it was exchanged for the general ticket and the legislative election, as the only expedient for baffling the policy of the particular states which had set the example."[6]

The exact form of district system plans has varied widely over the years. The first proposal, which was the subject of some 30 resolutions in Congress between 1800 and 1826, would have created as many electoral districts in each state as the state had Representatives and Senators combined. Thus even if a state had only three electoral votes altogether, corresponding to two Senators and one Representative, it would have been divided into three distinct districts for the choosing of electors. A second form, first advanced by Senator Mahlon Dickerson of New Jersey in 1817, called for the choice of one elector in each Congressional district and the election of two more, corresponding to the state's two Senators, by some other method—usually statewide popular vote.[7] As a variant of both these plans, some proposed amendments retained the office of elector, while others abolished the office of elector, provided for direct vote of the people, but retained the basic form of the electoral system by providing that each candidate would be credited with as many electoral votes as the number of districts he carried. The first form, retaining the elector, was prevalent during the first decades of the 19th century, but the second, based on a direct vote by districts, gained popularity after Benton first introduced it in 1823.

The first district system plan, which contemplated retaining the electors and subdividing the states into the whole number of electors to which they were entitled, was proposed in resolutions by the legislatures of Vermont, New York and North Carolina in 1802. But it was brushed aside in order to get a consensus for the 12th Amendment, which provided simply for separate electoral votes for President and Vice President. After the 1812 election, in which several state legislatures—notably those of Massachusetts, New Jersey and North Carolina—arbitrarily shifted electoral systems for partisan advantage, another major effort was made to get this amendment through Congress. A newly elected legislature in North Carolina instructed Senator James Turner of that state to introduce the amendment in the Senate, where it passed by a 22 to 9 vote in 1813. But the House failed to take any action. The Legislature of Massachusetts endorsed the district system in 1816, but despite the urgings of many Senators and Representatives, sponsors saw they could not achieve the required two-thirds vote. Commenting on the failure of Congress to act on these proposals to establish a uniform national elector system, the *Niles Register* noted in an editorial: "And we jog on in the old way, swindling and to swindle."[8]

The next major push for reform effort began in 1817 with Senator Dickerson's proposal—brought forward at the instruction of the New Jersey Legislature—for a district system with two electors chosen at large. North Carolina instructed its Senators to switch their support to the New Jersey Plan, and when it was brought to a vote in the Senate in March 1818, it achieved majority support but fell short of the required two-thirds. By the next session the legislatures of New York, New Hampshire and Connecticut had added their weight to the movement. The Dickerson amendment finally passed the Senate in February 1819, on a 28 to 10 vote, but the House—as in 1813—again failed to act. Dickerson introduced his proposal again, however, and it passed the Senate early in 1820. The House refused to consider it at first but later in the year voted on a similar amendment by Representative James S. Smith of North Carolina. But the amendment fell just short of two-thirds—92 to 54—in House voting. If the House had approved the amendment, the Senate would surely have agreed to the House language and the amendment would have gone to the states for ratification. The district system would never again come so close to success.[9]

Dickerson continued to introduce his amendment through 1826, but Thomas Hart Benton had entered the Senate with the admission of Missouri to the Union in 1821 and became the great reform leader of the succeeding 30 years. Benton's first proposed Constitutional amendment on Presidential election, introduced in 1823, broke fresh ground by proposing a district system based on a direct vote of the people rather than intermediate electors. A uniform election system throughout the United States, Benton told the Senate, would "give to each mass of persons entitled to one elector the power of giving an electoral vote to any candidate they preferred." Both the general ticket system and the choice of electors by state legislatures, he said, violated the rights of minorities, because "a majority of one in either case carries the whole state." But when a select committee of five Senators reported Benton's amendment early in 1824, it was opposed by Martin

Van Buren, then a Senator from New York, who said that division into districts would tend "to reduce greatly the present weight of the large states in the general scale" by "preventing them from bringing their consolidated strength to bear upon the Presidential question."[10] This fear in the large states, that their comparative power in the electoral college might be reduced, helped to defeat the district plan whenever it was brought forward.

Benton not only failed to muster enough Senate support to risk bringing his amendment to a vote in 1824, but also failed to do so after an enlarged special committee he headed reported a widened plan for consideration in 1826, just a year after the Jackson-Adams election had been thrown into the House of Representatives for decision. In an effort to replace the fallen caucus system with an election process that gave the people the right of nomination, as well as election, Benton's committee recommended not only a first election by direct vote of the people in districts but a runoff by the identical system if no candidate received a majority in the first contest. "No intervening bodies should stand between" the people and their President, Benton said in his report. "The President should be nothing but an emanation of their will." A uniform district system, Benton claimed, would "give to every state and to the several sections of the state, and, as far as possible, to every individual citizen of the whole Union, their legitimate share and due weight in the election of the chief officers of their country."[11] Similar arguments were raised by Representative George McDuffie of South Carolina in a six-week-long House debate during the 1826 session.

The entrenched forces that saw an advantage in the prevailing systems of choosing electors by general ticket or legislature action were too strong to be overcome, however. In 1826 the House rejected the district system proposal on a 90 to 102 roll call, and Benton withdrew his resolution when he saw that he could not muster the required two-thirds vote for Senate approval. But Benton refused to accept final defeat, saying he "would pledge himself to the Senate and to the American people to continue the subject with all the energy he was master of till he brought it to a conclusion."[12] Benton remained true to his word, presenting his district system amendment at different times down to 1844. Among his allies over the years was President Jackson, a close friend and supporter of the Missouri Senator. In his first annual message to Congress, Jackson urged that the people be allowed to vote directly for President, for, he said, "in proportion as agents to execute the will of the people are multiplied there is danger of their wishes being frustrated; some may be unfaithful, all liable to err."[13] Jackson repeated his plea in each of his succeeding messages to Congress. Special Senate committees again reported the Benton amendment in 1834 and 1836, but it was never brought to a vote.

Benton's plan for a direct vote of the people by districts was advanced again by Andrew Johnson, then a Member of the House, in the early 1850s, and was debated extensively by the House in 1854— again without a conclusive vote. As President, Johnson urged a similar amendment in a special message to Congress in 1868, and repeated the recommendation in his annual message the following winter.[14]

The case for electoral reform was taken up and ably advanced during the 1870s by Senator Oliver P. Morton of Indiana. Like Benton, Morton was for abolishing the office of elector and letting the people vote directly for President by districts. But he modified the Benton formula by requiring that the statewide popular vote winner receive two electoral votes, and that the number of districts correspond exactly to the number of Representatives the state had in Congress. The provision for two statewide Presidential votes corresponding to the Senators was similar to Dickerson's plan earlier in the century, except that Dickerson had contemplated retaining the office of elector. In a major Senate floor debate on his amendment in 1875, Morton said that the theory of the electoral college had failed completely: "It has turned out in practice that the electors are pledged in advance to vote for a particular candidate. . . . The reasons for the electoral college have gone. Why not let the people vote themselves for the Presidential candidates, instead of voting for electors who are pledged to do the same thing?" asked Morton. He acknowledged that "by the election of districts you do not bring the vote absolutely home to the people, as you would by a vote as one community, but you come as near to it as possible." Morton explained that his amendment preserved two votes at large for each state so that "the autonomy and power of the small states" might be preserved. He sought to avoid the problem of contingent election altogether by eliminating the majority vote require-ment, simply providing that the candidate with the most district and state votes would be elected.

Morton's amendment had reached the Senate floor in 1875 with the endorsement of the Senate Committee on Privileges and Elections, which he headed. A district system amendment similar to Morton's was also brought to the House floor for debate in the same Congress, and aroused considerable interest. But neither the Senate nor the House actually reached a vote on the merits of the proposals, for the general opinion was that the greatest immediate danger relating to the electoral college lay in the count of disputed electoral votes in Congress. In fact, Morton's opening remarks in the 1875 debate presaged the disputed election of 1876: "No more important question can be considered by the Senate at this session of Congress," said Morton, "for in my opinion, great dangers impend, owing to the imperfection of the present system of electing the President and Vice President. . . . Though the election may be distinguished by fraud, notorious fraud, by violence, by tumult, yet there is no method for contesting it."[15] Morton would see the problem at first hand as a member of the 15-man Electoral Commission established to decide the Hayes-Tilden election.

As soon as the disputed election of 1876 had been resolved, Morton renewed his campaign for electoral reform. In the *North American Review* of May 1877, he declared: "Experience, as well as reason, now suggests that the rubbish of the electoral college be brushed away entirely."[16] But eight months later, at 54 years of age, Morton succumbed to a chronic disease. With his death, the cause of electoral reform lost its most eloquent spokesman of the latter 19th century. Indeed, it would be almost three-quarters of a century before an electoral reform leader of comparable stature emerged.

After Morton's death, the district system was incorporated from time to time in amendments proposed in Congress, but it aroused little interest. When it finally was revived, in the era following World War II, the district system emerged in a form closer to that of the very early 19th century than the more democratic forms advocated by Benton and Morton. The first postwar sponsor was Representative Frederic R. Coudert, Jr., a conservative Republican representing Manhattan's "silk-stocking" East Side Congressional district. Coudert submitted his amendment on several occasions, starting in 1949, and was joined in 1953 by an equally conservative Republican, South Dakota's Senator Karl E. Mundt. The Mundt-Coudert plan, as it came to be known, retained two features of the original Constitution that Benton and Morton had sought to abolish: the office of elector and contingent election in Congress. Mundt and Coudert did advocate, however, that the responsibility for a contingent election be expanded from the House to both the House and Senate, in joint session, with each member entitled to a single vote. Under their plan, each Congressional district would choose one elector, and two electors would be chosen at large in each state, corresponding to its number of Senators.[17] A majority of electoral votes would be necessary for election.

The roster of supporters for the Mundt-Coudert plan was heavily weighted with conservative Republicans and former Dixiecrats. Senator Strom Thurmond of South Carolina, the 1948 Dixiecrat Presidential candidate, became a sponsor, as did Senator Barry Goldwater of Arizona and a number of Representatives from the Deep South states.[18] In 1956 the plan was reported to the Senate as part of a hybrid package giving each state a choice between a proportional plan of dividing its electoral votes and the district system. (For details on proportional plan, see below.) Arguing for the compromise package on the Senate floor, Mundt said that it "would restore and preserve the balance of voting power between the rural and urban areas, between great states and small states, which was intended by our Constitutional forefathers."[19]

At the crux of Mundt's argument was the assertion that both the President and the Congress should have the same "constituency." The Congress, he said, was elected on an individual district system basis, while its counterparts in the electoral college were chosen in multi-member districts consisting of entire states. As a result, the political complexion of the electoral college, chosen at large in each state, could differ radically from the political complexion of the House of Representatives chosen in the same election. The district system, Mundt claimed, would end the political disparity between the "Presidential United States" and the "Congressional United States" and lead to more harmony in relation between the executive and legislative branches of government.

It was precisely this "counterpart" theory that Mundt's opponents, led by Democratic Senators Paul H. Douglas of Illinois and John F. Kennedy of Massachusetts, objected to. The nation's big cities and the many minority groups within them, Douglas and Kennedy argued, were seriously underrepresented in the state legislatures and in both houses of Congress. "In the 48 state legislatures," Kennedy said, "the urban areas representing about 60 percent of the nation's population are allotted 25 percent of the seats in the popularly contested houses." Douglas produced figures showing a ratio of 540 to one in population between the most heavily populated and the least heavily populated districts in Connecticut. The ratios were 94 to one in Florida, 25 to one in Wisconsin, and 296 to one in California, he said.

These rurally dominated state legislatures, it was alleged, in turn create Congressional districts that are malapportioned and gerrymandered to favor rural areas and conservative interests. The populations of the Congressional districts in Texas, for instance, varied in the 1950s from 226,739 to 806,701, while Georgia had a disparity of 246,227 to 618,431 between the smallest and largest districts. In addition, the Constitutionally mandated requirement for two Senators for each state, regardless of population, overbalanced that body to the small, predominantly rural states. The cities of the United States, Douglas said, simply "do not have their fair and just representation." The effect of the proposed amendment, he argued, would be "to deliver the cities, bound hand and foot, into the power of the rural sections of the country" by removing the sole advantage of the urban areas in the existing electoral system—their power to swing the vote in the largest states and thus influence the Presidential election in a significant way. Kennedy summarized the opposition argument in these much-quoted words: "It is not only the unit vote for the Presidency we are talking about, but a whole solar system of governmental power. If it is proposed to change the balance of power of one of the elements of the solar system, it is necessary to consider the others."[20]

Thus the 1956 debate resolved itself into a fundamental power struggle along liberal-conservative, urban-rural and party lines. The district system's opponents were able to show that it would increase the power of the conservative elements in both the Democratic and Republican parties. Since the heavily populated, two-party states of the North would split their electoral votes fairly evenly, the balance of power in the Democratic party would shift to the conservative Southern states that would still cast almost all their electoral votes for Democratic Presidential candidates. And in the Republican party, conservative rural interests would increase their influence because of the decreased importance of the large states and large cities where liberal Republicanism had previously flourished. "If political realignment is the real purpose of electoral change," Douglas said, "let us debate the merits of a political realignment rather than sneak realignment under the cloak of 'electoral reform.' "[21]

As it had been reported from the Senate Judiciary Committee, the 1956 amendment incorporated the proportional plan only. Its sponsors had subsequently agreed to attach the district system as an alternative, and the debate was technically on the motion to substitute the hybrid proportional-district plan. On March 27 that motion passed by a 48 to

37 vote, enough to carry as a substitute but substantially short of the two-thirds vote that would be needed for final passage. Facing defeat, the sponsors then moved to recommit the whole package to the Judiciary Committee. No Constitutional amendment for changing the electoral college system has since reached the floor of either house of Congress.

Coudert dropped out of Congress at the end of 1958, but Mundt remained in the Senate and continued to introduce his district system amendment in every Congress. In 1961 it was considered with other proposed reforms in extensive hearings before the Constitutional Amendments Subcommittee of Senate Judiciary, chaired by Tennessee's Estes Kefauver. Appearing before the Kefauver Subcommittee, Mundt said his resolution had been altered to meet previous criticism by inclusion of a provision requiring that Presidential elector districts be composed of compact and contiguous territory, containing as nearly as practicable equal population. These districts, he said, might coincide with Congressional districts, but then the Congressional districts would naturally have to meet the same standards. Mundt contended that the antigerrymandering requirement in Presidential elector districts could be enforced by a suit of a state's citizens in state courts, by a similar suit in federal courts because of the possible violation of a federal Constitutional provision, and by the authority that Congress would have to reject any electoral votes improperly cast because of the failure to establish equally populated and compact districts. Kefauver replied, however, that "the same political pressures and opportunity for political advantage would operate on the legislatures in this Presidential electoral districting as now influence Congressional redistricting." Professor Robert G. Dixon, Jr., of the George Washington University Law School warned that there was "a strong line of federal precedent against judicial action in legislative or electoral district cases," and that if Congress tried to enforce standards, "interminable wrangles and interstate reprisals" would result, making the sanction "both inadvisable and politically unfeasible." Thus the districts might well lack real standards of population equality and compactness, Dixon warned, and "we shall have gerrymandered the Presidency."[22]

In a letter to the Kefauver Subcommittee, former President Harry S Truman endorsed the district system. "The problem we face today is that of the emergence of the big cities into political overbalance, with the threat of imposing their choices on the rest of the country,"

Truman said. (Ironically, the big city vote had been a key factor in his own victory in 1948.) Other backers of the district system included the National Association of Manufacturers and William E. Miller, chairman of the Republican National Committee and the 1964 Vice Presidential candidate. The NAM contended that "the district system would make the President the man of all the people; would reduce the effect of accident and improper election practices; would reduce the exaggerated influence of groups and individuals in control of bloc votes; and eliminate the unfair system of having the votes of large minorities cast opposite to their wishes."[23]

In the wake of the Judiciary Subcommittee's 1961 hearings, its chief counsel, James C. Kirby, Jr., prepared a detailed memorandum showing the impact which any of the proposed reforms might have on the operation of Presidential elections.[24] Under the district system, he pointed out, the five states with one Representative in the U.S. House (Alaska, Delaware, Nevada, Vermont and Wyoming), plus the District of Columbia, would constitute three-elector districts in which the entire vote would go to the plurality winner. In the other 45 states, 90 electoral votes, representing the two Senators from each, would continue to be awarded to the statewide plurality winner in the same manner as the existing unit vote or general ticket practice. Each of the remaining 430 elector votes would go to the winners in individual districts of states. If party strengths were uniform throughout a state, all the votes would still go to the winner of the statewide plurality.

Historically, Kirby noted, the district system had had mixed results in breaking up state unit votes. Between 1789 and 1892 there were 52 instances in which states used some form of the district system. In 36 of these cases, all of the state's votes had been cast as a unit. In the 1960 elections, if existing Congressional districts had been employed as Presidential elector districts, 21 states with a total of 119 electoral votes would still have cast their electoral votes as a bloc under the district system. In another seven states with 51 electoral votes, only one vote would have gone contrary to the state unit. In six states, with a total of 75 electoral votes, the minority party would have captured less than 25 percent of the state electoral vote. But in many states, especially the most populous ones, the district system would have effectively split the state's votes. New York would have split, 25 to 20; California, 19 to 13; Illinois, 15 to 12; Pennsylvania, 17 to 15; and Michigan, 10 to 10. Kirby's analysis would seem to bear out the charge of critics that the district system would magnify the comparative strength of smaller one-party states and dilute that of large states that are balanced relatively evenly between the parties. For instance, New York's effective vote—the lead it gave one candidate over another—would have been five votes, Pennsylvania's two and Michigan's zero. But in states where one candidate won all the districts, a solid block of electoral votes would still have been cast. Massachusetts would have had a relative weight of 16 votes in the 1960 election, Georgia 12, North Dakota 4, Oregon 6 and Wyoming 3.

By the same token, the disfranchisement of minority voters within any state could still continue under the district system. In a state with just three electoral votes, minority voters would never have a chance to capture electoral votes for their Presidential candidate. In large states that split their electoral votes, the minority in each district would be just as effectively disfranchised as minorities are on a statewide basis today. As Thomas Jefferson said in 1800 (basing his comment on the then-existing size of the Union and number of districts), "It is merely a question of whether we will divide the United States into 16 or 137 districts."[25]

Under other circumstances the vote of a *majority* of a state's voters could also be negated under the district system. This would occur if one Presidential candidate won a minority of the districts by overwhelming margins while losing a majority of the districts by small margins. Though such a candidate might emerge with a substantial victory in the state's popular vote, the distribution of district strengths might be such as to give his opponent a majority of the state's electoral votes.

The district system would also not prevent the election of a minority President. Two of the three distortions of the existing system—the wide disparity in the number of votes representing one elector between large and small states, and the inequalities stemming from variations in the voter turnout—would continue in full force (see pages 138–39, above). The general ticket system, as noted, would in effect remain in operation in the substantial number of states that could be expected to cast all their district votes for one Presidential candidate. This, in turn, could have a profound political impact. Most of the states that could be expected to continue casting their electoral votes *en bloc* would be the smaller states, which are predominantly conservative in political complexion. The states whose electoral votes would be split up would be the larger states, which on the whole tend to contain larger metropolitan areas and be more liberal politically.

Thus the district system would likely benefit small-state, rural conservatism and harm big-state, urban liberalism. It is hardly surprising to note that in 1960, while Kennedy won a substantial electoral majority under the existing system, Nixon would have been the clear winner under a district system—278 electoral votes to 245. Since Nixon won 26 states, including most of the more lightly populated ones in the Union, he would have had a solid small-state base (with its inflated electoral vote) to which he could add the substantial number of individual Republican-oriented districts in the large, industrial states (New York, Illinois, Michigan, etc.) that Kennedy carried under the existing general ticket system.

The basic conservative bias of the district system could be expected to reassert itself in election after election because the balance of the existing general ticket system—the inflated electoral vote power of conservatives in small states versus the swing power of liberal groups in the large states—would be erased. Conservatives, moreover, would frequently win more of the districts in large states than their percentage of the statewide vote would justify, because the popular vote majorities in conservative suburban and rural districts generally tend to be less than the liberal majorities in center-city districts. These factors would continue to operate even with an end to the malapportionment of Congressional districts on which opponents of the district system centered their arguments in earlier years. There would be a continuing danger of minority Presidents in close Presidential elections.

Statistics based on the past four Presidential elections show clearly that under a district system there would still be major disparities between a candidate's percentage of the national popular vote and his electoral vote. Reliable Congressional district breakdowns for President are not available for the elections before 1952, but the figures since then show a wide disparity between the percentage of popular vote and vote under the district system.[26]

Winning Candidate	Electoral Vote Under District System	Percentage of District System Vote	Percentage of Popular Vote	Disparity
1952 (Eisenhower)	375	70.6	55.1	15.5
1956 (Eisenhower)	411	77.4	57.4	20.0
1960 (Kennedy)	245	45.6	49.7	4.1
1964 (Johnson)	466	87.1	61.1	26.0

The pivotal state, Kirby noted in his survey, would be of less importance under the district system. In fact, states as units would cease to be the targets of special campaign efforts. The national campaigns would instead be concentrated on the seriously contested districts—depending on the political circumstances of any year, probably 100 to 200 of the 435 House districts. The votes of minority blocs in the large two-party states would be of substantially less importance, because they would lose any balance-of-power position they may enjoy under the existing system. The potentialities for fraud or accidents of weather to influence a large state's vote would likewise be minimized, with such factors confined to a more limited number of districts.

Mundt's district system amendment was reported to the full Senate Judiciary Committee by the Kefauver subcommittee on a 4 to 2 vote in 1962, but no further action was taken on it.

In 1966, Mundt appeared before the Constitutional Amendments Subcommittee to press his amendment again, once more decrying the power of big-state minorities under the existing system. Mundt pointed out that the Supreme Court decisions of the early 1960s requiring equally populated Congressional districts had removed any possibility of gerrymandering under a district system. "The judicial branch," Mundt said, "has very clearly and vigorously indicated they not only can but will enforce districting standards." Mundt said the district system should be approved because it was the only electoral reform proposal that would "bring about a needed reform without a basic change in our constitutional system."[27]

The Proportional Plan

The proportional plan for choosing a President would retain the Constitutionally mandated apportionment of electors to the states, based on their representation in Congress, but would divide each state's electoral vote to reflect the share of the popular vote for President cast by the voters of the state. The plan was first introduced in Congress by Representative William T. Lawrence of New York on December 11, 1848. Lawrence envisaged abolishing the office of elector and assigning each Presidential candidate the proportion of each state's electoral votes that would reflect the popular vote. No action was taken on Lawrence's proposal, but 21 years later Representative James M. Ashley of Ohio suggested an almost identical plan, except that the office of elector would be retained and the state legislatures would be called on to appoint electors who would divide their votes proportionately to reflect the popular vote in each state.[28]

Between 1875 and 1889, 20 proportional system amendments were suggested in Congress. The first of them, by Representative H. Boardman Smith of New York, was designed as a substitute for the district system amendment reported by the House Committee on Elections in 1875. His amendment, Smith said, was framed "for the purpose of obviating the danger and difficulty of a large accumulation of contested election cases in the electoral districts proposed by the plan of the Committee on Elections, and to prevent the gerrymandering of states by partisan majorities in the construction of election districts, and to dispense with the cumbersome machinery of electoral districts, while preserving the autonomy of the states in the election of President and Vice President."[29]

Major interest in the proportional plan was aroused in the wake of the disputed election of 1876, as Congress sought a way to avoid the difficulties of disputed elector votes. Among the chief sponsors were Representatives Levi Maish of Pennsylvania, William Springer of Illinois and Jordan E. Cravens of Arkansas. Most of the 19th-century proportional plans would have retained whole electoral votes, dividing each state in proportion to the largest fraction. Thus if a candidate received 54 percent of the popular vote in a state with 10 electoral votes, he would get 5 electoral votes; if he polled 56 percent, he would receive 6 electoral votes. The plan introduced by Cravens in 1877, however, contained the first formula for carrying the computation out to the nearest one-thousandth. This formula has been utilized in most proportional plans advanced since.[30]

Writing in the *North American Review* in 1877, Senator Charles R. Buckalew of Pennsylvania claimed numerous beneficial results in a proportional system amendment: "It will greatly reduce, in fact, almost extinguish, the chance of a disputed election, by causing the electoral vote of the state to be very nearly a reflex of the popular vote, by confining the effect of fraud and other sinister influences within narrow limits, and by withdrawing the compact, undivided power of any one state from the contest. . . . Popular disfranchisement within a state will be swept away, while the supporters of no candidate will control more than their due share of electoral power." He said the amendment would "exclude the temptation to falsify or manipulate election returns, by which the whole vote of the state may be wielded in the interest of a party. Under it there would be no rival electoral colleges, or double returns of electoral votes, and pivotal states, inviting to profuse money expenditure, to fraud and to false returns, would no longer be known as a conspicuous feature of Presidential contests. It will render almost impossible the election of a minority candidate."[31]

In 1878 and again in 1880 a select committee of the House reported favorably on the proportional election plan. The 1878 report asserted that "it was not intended by the framers of the Constitution . . . that the state, as an entity, should cast the electoral vote *in solido* for a particular candidate." The select committee's minority, however, discerned a major threat to states' rights and declared that "the right to speak by a majority, when its fundamental laws permit, is a right inherent in every republic. This plan takes away from these republics, the states, this right *to speak by their majorities,* and confers upon the United States the right to say by a majority of the whole who shall be President and Vice President."[32] As reported to the House, the proportional plan required a simple plurality of electoral votes to win election. But it failed to come to a vote in the House in either year that it was reported.

It was almost 50 years before Congress again gave serious consideration to the proportional plan. In 1928, and in succeeding Congresses in a 30-year Congressional career that ended in 1948, Representative Clarence F. Lea of California introduced proportional plans and pushed for adoption of the reform. In 1933, at the end of the 72nd and again early in the 73rd Congress, committees of the House reported favorably on the Lea amendment, but it never came to a vote on the floor. Senator George W. Norris of Nebraska also introduced a proportional plan, and his proposal was debated fully by the Senate Judiciary Committee in 1934. But the committee decided instead to report out a resolution simply abolishing the office of elector while retaining the state unit vote system.[33]

Interest in electoral reform increased significantly following World War II, and the leadership for the proportional plan was undertaken by Senator Henry Cabot Lodge of Massachusetts and Representative Ed Gossett of Texas. The Lodge-Gossett plan, as it came to be known, was reported favorably by the Judiciary Committees of both the Senate and House in 1948, but no further action was taken in that Congress. Lodge and Gossett renewed their efforts the following year, however, and the Judiciary Committees of the two houses reported favorably on the proposal in the summer of 1949.

On January 25, 1950, the plan was brought before the Senate and

Lodge delivered a major speech reviewing the deficiencies of the existing electoral college system and the benefits to be derived from a proportional plan. Under the proposed amendment, Lodge said, the anachronistic and potentially dangerous institution of the Presidential elector would be abolished. The electoral vote per state, equal to its number of Senators and Representatives, would be retained, "but purely as an automatic counting device." The possibility that an election would be thrown into the House of Representatives would be eliminated, together with all "the turmoil, unrest, intrigue and possible frustration of the popular will by an election of the President in Congress."[34]

Because each state's electoral vote would be automatically divided to reflect the popular will, Lodge said, "all the evils inherent in the unit-rule method of counting electoral votes" would be eliminated. "No longer would millions of voters be disfranchised and their votes appropriated to the candidate against whom they voted. No votes would be lost. Every vote for President would count." The big pivotal states, Lodge said, would no longer receive a disproportionate share of Presidential campaign efforts and spending. The proportional plan would "spread the campaign . . . into all the 48 states." As a result, it would "break up so-called solid or one-party areas," since votes anywhere would have an impact on the national tally.

The major opposition raised against the Lodge-Gossett plan on the Senate floor came from Senators Homer Ferguson of Michigan and Robert A. Taft of Ohio. Ferguson charged that proportional voting would weaken federalism because the states, by being forced to break up their electoral vote to reflect popular sentiment, would be "required to surrender their sovereignty over the disposition of their own electoral votes." The idea of proportionalizing the vote of various states, Ferguson said, was "revolutionary" and should not be undertaken because one could not foretell the political consequences.[35]

Taft said he would vote against the proportional plan "principally on the one ground, that it would give a tremendously disproportionate weight to one-party states." Taft was especially worried about the one-party Democratic South and the relative weight the Southern states, voting overwhelmingly Democratic, would have as compared to the Northern states, where the vote is more evenly divided. Under the proportional system in 1900, Taft said, Mississippi would have had a relative weight of 7 electoral votes while Ohio, more closely divided, would have had a weight of only 1.6 electoral votes.[36]

Lodge dismissed the idea that the proportional plan might help one party over the other, pointing out that minority parties in one-party states would be encouraged if their votes counted nationally and that "the question of partisan advantage depends on the energy, imagination and ability of American party leadership. These are qualities which cannot be created by constitutional amendment." At any rate, Lodge contended, if one agreed that "the present system is wrong, dangerous and unfair, then it should be reformed regardless of party advantage."[37]

A major argument of the opponents was that the nation's two-party system would be endangered by proportional voting. Minority political groups, Ferguson charged, usually lacked enough power to carry states and thus win electoral votes under the existing system. But with proportional voting, he said, "their share of electoral votes in each state and accumulated total across the nation would provide a score card for their progress. The shining goal would be to divide and conquer the major parties by splintering."[38] Ferguson's argument paralleled, though it lacked a bit of the flamboyance evident in, a similar charge by Representative Wright Patman of Texas a year earlier that under Lodge-Gossett there would be "the rise of many new parties—the Communist, the Dixiecrat, the Ku Klux Klan; parties representing the North, East and West; parties representing the farmers, the manufacturers, the laborers; parties representing racial and religious minorities,"[39] all because they would now be able to obtain electoral votes. Replying to the splinter party argument, Lodge said the minor parties' hopes would actually be minimized, because they would no longer enjoy a balance-of-power position enabling them to throw large blocs of electoral votes one way or the other through their swing power in the big states—the practice that Henry Wallace's Progressives followed in 1948. On a related point, Lodge was obliged to deal with the argument that proportional voting for President might lead to a multiplicity of ideologically oriented splinter parties. Proportional voting for a single official, Lodge said, bears no resemblance to proportional representation in a legislative body. "Even the cleverest surgeon cannot divide one man up—proportionately or otherwise—and expect him to live," Lodge said.[40]

Lodge acknowledged that a man receiving a minority of the national popular vote could also be elected under a proportional system. That possibility, he said, could never be entirely eliminated without doing away with the two-electoral-vote bonus awarded each state regardless of population and resorting to direct popular election of the President.

But Lodge said he thought the possibility would be much less likely under the proportional system.[41]

After rejecting alternative proposals for a direct vote or a general ticket system without electors, on February 1, 1950, the Senate approved the Lodge-Gossett amendment by a vote of 64 to 27, three votes over the required two-thirds majority. It was the first time in 130 years that the Senate had approved a constitutional amendment to alter the electoral college.[42] But, as time would show, it was the high-water mark for the proportional system.

In the 1950 Senate vote, the Lodge-Gossett plan had been supported almost solidly by Democratic Senators and by moderate and liberal Republicans. The opposition came almost completely from conservative Republicans. But in the House, more Republicans moved to the opposition side, apparently sharing Taft's fear of increased electoral power in the Democratic South. And an even more significant block of opposition arose: from Northern Democrats who likewise feared the political repercussions of the amendment. In the wake of the affirmative Senate vote, the Americans for Democratic Action in April 1950 went on record against Lodge-Gossett unless it was modified to make a state's vote dependent on the actual voter turnout rather than population. In large part because of the growing Northern Democratic opposition, Lodge-Gossett became bottled up in the House Rules Committee, which exercised wide discretion in deciding which bills could be sent to the House floor for a vote. Of the 11 members of the Rules Committee, seven opposed reporting out the amendment—four Northern Democrats and three Northern Republicans. A minority of four favored reporting the bill for House debate—three Southern Democrats and one Republican, Representative Christian A. Herter of Massachusetts.

In a last-ditch effort to circumvent the Rules Committee, Gossett moved on July 17, 1950, to suspend the rules and bring the amendment to the floor. Motions to suspend the rules on controversial bills are rarely successful, and this was no exception. But Gossett in his introductory speech to the House adopted an additional strategy that only helped to solidify opposition: he actually named—"at the danger of stepping on some toes," as he put it—those minority groups in the large pivotal states who were said to have inordinate power under the existing unit vote system. "Is it fair, is it honest, is it democratic, is it to the best interest of anyone in fact," Gossett asked, "to place such a premium on a few thousand labor votes, or Italian votes, or Irish votes, or Negro votes, or Jewish votes, or Polish votes, or Communist votes, or big-city machine votes, simply because they happen to be located in two or three large, industrial pivotal states? Can anything but evil come from placing such temptation and such power in the hands of political parties and political bosses? . . . Both said groups and said politicians are corrupted and the nation suffers." The exaggerated electoral power of Negroes, Gossett said, had led to inclusion of fair employment practices platforms in the 1944 and 1948 national platforms. Likewise, "the radical wing of organized labor" in the Congress of Industrial Organizations had been appeased. And Jews had improperly influenced the parties by inclusion of planks backing the Zionist position on Palestine because "there are 2.5 million Jews in the city of New York alone."[43] Not surprisingly, only a handful of Northern Democrats voted for Gossett's proposal.

The opposition to Lodge-Gossett on the House floor was led by Representative Clifford P. Case of New Jersey, a liberal Republican. Case warned that the proposal would "reduce the Republican party to impotence" because it would need 52 to 54 percent of the popular vote to overcome the weight of Southern electoral votes that would still be cast against its candidates. In the 1948 election, Case said, the electoral margin given by the state of Georgia alone would have been larger than the combined electoral margin given either party by the 11 most populous states of the country outside the solid South.[44] Republican Minority Leader Joseph W. Martin, Jr., of Massachusetts, who had been Speaker in the preceding Congress, warned that the amendment would "make it impossible for the election of a Republican President for a good many years." Martin said he held no "fetish and belief that the existing electoral college cannot be improved," but that a legitimate two-party system would first have to develop in the South.[45]

The final House vote, after the short 40 minutes of debate permitted under the rules, was 134 in favor of Lodge-Gossett, 210 opposed.[46] No electoral reform amendment has since come to the floor of the House of Representatives.

In another round of hearings on electoral reform before the House Judiciary Committee in 1951, Gossett and Representative Lea (now retired but still active at the age of 76) presented the familiar arguments for the proportional system. The hearings were more significant, however, for statements submitted by liberals explaining their opposition to the Lodge-Gossett plan. James Loeb, Jr., national executive secretary of the ADA, charged that the Lodge-Gossett proposal would "make more secure the continued control of the government by the Democratic party, because of the disproportionate weight given the Southern states. But it would make even more certain the control of the Democratic party by the Southerners, including the Dixiecrats whose moribund movement would receive new life and influence. It would do all this without liberalizing the Republican party." Republicans, Loeb said, would be motivated to nominate more conservative men for the Presidency to bid for their share of the Southern vote— men like Robert Taft or John Bricker instead of Thomas Dewey or Wendell Willkie. Enacting a proportional plan would be unthinkable, Loeb said, as long as "the Fielding Wright machine in Mississippi and the Talmadge machine in Georgia remain free to maintain poll taxes, literacy tests, economic coercion or just plain terrorism in the electoral process." It would be like a united Germany with democratic elections in Western Germany and one-party rule in the East, he contended.[47]

The National Association for the Advancement of Colored People, in a statement submitted by its Washington director, Clarence Mitchell, said the Lodge-Gossett amendment would "effectively draw the political eye teeth of all independent voters, including the Negro voter, as far as Presidential elections are concerned," since independent voters can swing doubtful states into one party column or the other. "Since 1909, in ever increasing numbers, the Negro has been migrating out of the South to the large industrial states of the North," most of which have large blocs of electoral votes and are doubtful politically, the NAACP noted. "If the Gossett proposal goes through, the Negro vote and the vote of other minority, national and religious groups will no longer be important in the great pivotal states of New York, New Jersey, Pennsylvania, Ohio, Indiana, Michigan, Illinois, California, West Virginia, Kentucky and Tennessee." But, said the NAACP, the solid South would continue to deliver a solid Democratic vote. "The only offset the Negro has to disfranchisement in the South . . . has been his political influence in the Northern pivotal states. The Gossett proposal would rob him of his influence without enfranchising him in the South." Thus, the NAACP concluded, "the Gossett proposal is antiurban, antinorthern and antiliberal."[48]

In 1951 the Lodge-Gossett plan was again endorsed by both the House and Senate Judiciary Committees, but the proposal was not brought out for floor debate in either house. The Senate Judiciary Committee held hearings again in 1953–1954, but no further action was taken.

The next significant effort came in 1955, when the Senate Judiciary Committee, after a full round of hearings, reported out a Lodge-Gossett type of amendment. Lodge, however, had been defeated for re-election to the Senate in 1952 by John F. Kennedy, and the chief sponsorship of the proportional plan had been undertaken by Senators Estes Kefauver of Tennessee and Price Daniel of Texas. (Gossett had retired from Congress in 1950, but no prominent House advocate of the proportional plan arose to take his place.) A total of 30 Senators sponsored the Kefauver and Daniel proportional amendments. By the time the measure was brought up for Senate floor action in March 1956, however, the supporters of the proportional and district methods had joined forces in an effort to gain enough votes for passage. The so-called "Daniel substitute," giving each state a choice between the proportional and district methods, had an astounding total of 54 Senate sponsors. Kefauver took the lead in floor debate, echoing many of the arguments for the proportional plan that Lodge had presented six years before.[49]

Senators Douglas and Kennedy, spearheading the opposition, employed basically the same arguments against the proportional plan aspect of the Daniel substitute that they employed against the district system alternative. Southern states could still be expected to cast the great bulk of their electoral votes for the Democratic candidates, while the closely divided Northern states would split their votes more evenly. Thus a conservative bias would be introduced into Presidential elections, compounding the alleged conservatism flowing from mal-apportionment of state legislatures and Congressional districts. The proportional plan, Kennedy charged, "has been discredited in the past and . . . promises only doubt and danger for the future."

Seeking to demonstrate the danger of the proportional plan to the Republican party, Douglas produced statistics to show that in 17 of the 19 Presidential elections between 1880 and 1952, the Democratic candidate would have received a larger electoral vote under the plan than he was entitled to by his percentage of the popular vote. Conversely, the Republican candidate's portion of the electoral vote would have been smaller than his popular vote percentage in all 19 elections.[50] "The Lodge-Gossett formula would handicap the Republicans because the Democrats could secure large blocs of electoral votes in the South, where relatively few popular votes will capture an electoral vote," Douglas said. "In contrast, the Republicans would have to win the bulk of their electoral votes in the North, where more popular votes are required to gain an electoral vote."[51] Douglas also argued that many elections would have been thrown into the House under the proportional plan, because no party would have achieved 50 percent of the electoral vote in eight and possibly nine elections between 1880 and 1948. As reported to the Senate floor, the Daniel substitute required a majority of electoral votes for choosing a President, although other versions of the same plan in 1956 had alternatively set 40 and 45 percent of the electoral vote as the requirement for election.[52]

Kennedy and Douglas also took issue with the conservatives' allegation that minority voting blocs actually controlled elections under the existing electoral college system. "In politics," Kennedy said, "minority pressure groups almost always refer to those on the other side of an issue. Some of the proponents [of the proposed amendment] have been frank enough to admit they are talking about Negroes, Jews, Catholics and labor unions. . . . But to others, the term 'pressure groups' refers to farmers, doctors, veterans, the aged or someone else." Douglas quoted a 1948 editorial in the Vernon (Texas) *Times* to show the political motivation of some proportional system backers: "If the Republican party succeeds in having the Gossett-Lodge resolution adopted," the editorial said, "that will put an end to the bipartisan contest for Negro votes in pivotal states and eliminate the so-called civil rights issue from national politics." As for himself, Douglas had a quite different image of the minority groups in urban centers: "In our big cities, Americans of various races, religions and ethnic origins all live side by side as close neighbors," Douglas said. "The broadmindedness and tolerance which emanates from our cities is a leaven of our political parties. . . . Under the proposal before us, the major parties would give less attention to the legitimate interests of these minority groups; and this in turn would weaken our two-party system."[53] Ironically, the breakup of the minority vote alliance between Negroes and foreign ethnic groups like Poles, Italians and Irish would contribute to Douglas' own defeat for reelection to the Senate ten years later, in 1966.

Aside from their political attack on the proposed amendment, Kennedy and Douglas had two factors in their favor: the complex nature of the proposed compromise amendment, which Kennedy could label a "hybrid monstrosity," and natural disinclination to amend the Constitution without wide-ranging agreement on the change to be made and its necessity. Of the Daniel substitute, Kennedy said: "The two schemes joined together by this shotgun wedding . . . are wholly incompatible, the sponsors of each having thoroughly and accurately assailed the merits of the other over the years. The Mundt proposal multiplies the general ticket system; the Daniel proposal abolishes it. The Mundt proposal continues the importance of states as units for electoral purposes; the Daniel proposal reduces it. And yet it is now proposed that the Senate, being unable to give its approval to either system, should lump them together and give each state its choice. No surer method of introducing confusion and loss of public confidence in our electoral system could be devised."[54]

Douglas recognized evils in the electoral college system and personally favored a direct vote. But Kennedy saw no real need for reform at all. "No urgent necessity for immediate change has been proven," he said. "No minority Presidents have been elected in the 20th Century; no elections have been thrown into the House of Representatives; no breakdown in the electoral system, or even widespread lack of confidence in it, can be shown. . . . There is obviously little to gain—but much to lose—by tampering with the Constitution at this time." Kennedy then added: "It seems to me that Falkland's definition of conservatism is quite appropriate—'When it is not necessary to change, it is necessary not to change.' "[55]

On March 27, after a full week's debate, the Senate moved to final voting on the amendment. Proposed substitutes that would have instituted a direct vote were rejected, as was a proposal by Senator Clifford P. Case of New Jersey that the electoral vote of each state depend on the percentage of its eligible voters who actually vote. Case's amendment, which would have applied both to states using the proportional and to those opting for the district plan, was rejected by a 20 to 66 vote. The Senate then voted, 48 to 37, to accept the Daniel substitute, giving each state its choice of using the district or proportional plan. Significantly, six fewer Senators voted for the Daniel substitute than the 54 who had placed their names on it as cosponsors before it came to the Senate floor. The margin of approval was substantially below the two-thirds needed for final passage, and the Senate by voice vote approved a motion by Daniel and Kennedy to recommit the amendment to the Judiciary Committee. In 1960, Kennedy would seek and win the Presidency on a strategy geared to winning the large pivotal states of the North—a strategy that would have been denied him under either the proportional or district plans that he was instrumental in defeating in the 1956 debate.

Interest in electoral reform in Congress lagged seriously after the 1956 reverse and was not revived until the close 1960 election outcome raised questions about the safety of the existing system. In 1961 hearings before the Senate Judiciary Constitutional Amendments Subcommittee, Kefauver restated the classic arguments for the proportional system: It would, he said, "come nearer reflecting the popular will and would make each state just as important as any other. It would bring about a substantial two-party system in the United States. It would eliminate the evil that has grown up in the past of each party selecting the pivotal states and concentrating the election there."[56] Senator Thomas H. Kuchel of California supported the Kefauver position, saying that "a proportional system undeniably provides the best reflection of popular desire in the framework of a federal system that retains the states as voting units."[57]

The familiar argument about the threat to the two-party system in proportional voting was raised by Assistant Attorney General Nicholas deB. Katzenbach. "The chief and overriding objection against proportional division of electoral votes is that it would encourage the development of splinter parties," Katzenbach said. Senator Sam J. Ervin, Jr., of North Carolina took a different view, saying he saw no danger in splintering or other radical changes in the parties because, "after all, most Americans like to be on the winning side."[58] Kefauver later took the argument further, saying that the American voter, "whether his vote is counted out at the state or district level by a unit rule, or at the national level where it is insufficient by virtue of its total, . . . is not likely to waste his vote on a third party candidate who has no chance of winning."[59]

In a perceptive critique of the various proposals presented to the Kefauver Subcommittee, Professor Paul J. Piccard of Florida State University said proportional voting would actually discourage splinter parties because they would lose their potential to "determine the outcome in a whole state and thereby control the balance of power in the entire nation," a practice Piccard said sometimes bordered on "political blackmail."[60] Nor did Piccard think that electoral vote counts reflecting minor party votes would encourage proportional representation. "As far as public opinion is concerned, all the candidates get credit under the present system anyway, for as soon as the election is over people discuss the size of the vote received by such gentlemen as Eugene V. Debs," said Piccard. (Debs was the Socialist candidate for President in five elections between 1900 and 1920 and actually polled 901,255 votes in 1912.) Debs wanted to poll a million votes, Piccard said, "and he was not discouraged by the electoral college system which deprived him of official votes. Giving him a few electoral votes, calculated to three decimal places, would hardly have offered him new inducements." But Piccard did not endorse the proportional system. He suggested that fractionalized electoral votes would only create confusion, and that he would "not like the job of explaining to the losers the significance of the third- or fourth-place decimal. . . . The question arises, is the labor of constitutional amendment justified for such an imperfect compromise?"[61]

The possibility that minority Presidents might be elected under the proportional plan was also brought out in the 1961 hearings. In 1880, Winfield S. Hancock trailed James A. Garfield by more than 9,000 votes, but Hancock would have won by a margin of 6 to 8 electoral votes if the proportional system had been in effect. In 1896, William McKinley won nearly 51 percent of the popular vote to less than 47 percent for William Jennings Bryan. But proportionate voting would have elected Bryan by an electoral vote margin of 6. In 1900 the proportional division between Bryan and McKinley was so close— 217.3 for McKinley, 217.2 for Bryan—that minuscule vote shifts could have determined the outcome, even though McKinley ran more than 6 percentage points ahead of Bryan in the popular vote. In 1960 the proportional result would apparently have been 266.075 for Nixon, 265.623 for Kennedy, at least if one can assume that the voting patterns would not have changed with another electoral count system in effect[62] (see Appendix M).

Since 1961 the proportional system has made little headway in Congress and won few new adherents. During a brief round of hearings before the Senate Judiciary Constitutional Amendments Subcommittee in 1966, Senator Spessard L. Holland of Florida did point to "new evidence and new developments" that he thought had removed some of the political objections to proportional voting for President—the decisions of the Supreme Court requiring equal apportionment on the basis of population at every governmental level, and the eclipse of the one-party system in the Southern states that culminated in Republican victories or near-wins in all the states of the old Confederacy in 1964. Holland predicted that the Republican party would "continue to grow and thrive in the South" and that in a few more elections there would be no substantial difference between the percentage of the total vote cast in the South and in the other states of the Union. The effort to overhaul the ancient electoral college machinery should be a bipartisan one, Holland suggested, adding: "No plan has yet been advanced, which preserves and safeguards our federal system, that better achieves the result of fair and democratic reform of the electoral system, than does the proportional plan."[63]

Opposition to the reform remained, however. Katzenbach, then the Attorney General, opposed the proportional system because the existing balance—overrepresentation of the small states through the Constitutional apportionment formula on the one hand, and the unit rule advantage enjoyed by the large states on the other—would be destroyed. There would be a shift of power, Katzenbach charged, "to the rural states and perhaps those few states with historically a one-party political structure."[64]

The Automatic System

In September 1801, just six months after he had taken office as President, Thomas Jefferson wrote of an "amendment which I know will be proposed, to wit, to have no electors, but let the people vote directly, and the ticket which has a plurality of the votes in any state to be considered as receiving the whole vote of the state."[65] It was a quarter of a century, however, until Representative Charles E. Haynes of Georgia in 1826 introduced this most modest of all electoral college reforms. Known by many names over the years, the proposal has best been described as "the automatic system," since it would simply write the general ticket or "winner take all" system of casting state electoral votes directly into the Constitution and abolish the actual office of elector.

Haynes's proposal was a progressive one at the time it was offered, since it guaranteed to the people the right, by their vote, to decide for which Presidential candidate the state's electoral votes should be cast. The state legislatures would have lost the right—which many of them still exercised—to appoint electors themselves, or to provide for district system elections as an alternative to the general ticket. Amendments similar to Haynes's were proposed 11 times over the succeeding two decades, and three state legislatures—those of Georgia, Missouri and Alabama—endorsed the idea. The Georgia General Assembly, however, took care to note that it favored a uniform method of electing the President and Vice President through the suffrage of the people, "provided such alterations can be so made that the sovereignty of the states be not invaded and the weight of the states and the present basis of representation be retained according to the existing conditions of the Constitution." The Alabama and Missouri resolutions were similar in tone.[66]

An even more minimal proposal was put forth by Representative Thomas Whipple of New Hampshire in 1828. He suggested that the general ticket system be made mandatory for all states, but he would have retained the office of elector. Congress showed little interest in any of these proposals, however, and between 1844 and 1889 only two resolutions of a similar character were even proposed.[67]

When Michigan broke the national pattern of voting by general ticket by decreeing a district system for the 1892 election, there was concern that other states might follow suit. President Harrison, in his annual message to Congress on December 9, 1891, recommended that the permanency of the prevailing general ticket system should be secured by a constitutional amendment. If states went to the district system, Harrison warned, the evil influence of the gerrymander would be felt in Presidential elections as well as those for Congress, and eventually the Supreme Court, indirectly through the power of appointment, would be infected as well. Again, Congress showed little interest in the proposal.[68]

Senator George W. Norris of Nebraska was a foremost advocate of the automatic system during the 1920s and 1930s.[69] In 1922 he wrote a provision abolishing the office of elector and formalizing the general ticket system into a constitutional amendment that he was pushing to eliminate lame-duck sessions of Congress. But when opposition to the electoral college feature developed, Norris struck it from his amendment. After the 1932 election Norris advocated a proportional system, but the Senate Judiciary Committee modified it to an automatic system before reporting it for Senate consideration early in 1934, and Norris said he approved of the change (see p. 166, above). Even this minimal reform could not pass, however. The Senate vote on May 21, 1934, was 42 in favor, 24 opposed—7 votes short of the required two-thirds. Most of the opposition came from conservative Senators who opposed any substantive change in the Constitution. Senator Arthur H. Vandenberg of Michigan charged that the automatic system would make it easier for independent candidates to get on the ballot, thus endangering the two-party system through a plethora of splinter parties, the "curse" and "plague" of European politics.[70]

During debate on the Lodge-Gossett plan in 1950, Senator Homer Ferguson of Michigan offered an automatic system as a substitute for the more comprehensive proportional plan then being debated by the Senate. The reformers, led by Lodge, rightly understood Ferguson's amendment as a move to block more thoroughgoing reform and combined to defeat it on a 20 to 71 roll-call vote.[71]

The possibility of an automatic system amendment was next raised seriously by Senator Kennedy during the 1956 Senate debate on electoral reform.[72] Kennedy said such an amendment would abolish the unnecessary office of elector and provide a more democratic manner of contingent election by having the entire Congress vote for the President if no candidate won a majority in the electoral college. But it would retain the state unit vote system, which Kennedy thought essential to the country's electoral balance. Kennedy did not bring this amendment to a vote during the 1956 debate, however, and did not actually introduce it in Congress until more than a year later.[73]

In the 1960 election the "winner-take-all" system of casting state electoral votes worked distinctly to Kennedy's advantage, and he showed little interest in the more comprehensive reform proposals urged in the wake of that year's elections. Assistant Attorney General Katzenbach supported Kennedy's earlier automatic system amendment in the Senate hearings of 1961. Senator Gale McGee of Wyoming, sponsor of a similar amendment, said the office of elector should be abolished because electors, "with sufficient collusion, . . . could even overthrow the intent of the popular will on a nationwide scale." But the automatic system amendment, McGee said, "preserves that which has contributed so much to our political stability; namely, the great compromise among the diverse states and regions of the country." Little support was engendered for the Kennedy type of amendment, however. Professor Robert G. Dixon commented at the hearings that the breaking of pledges by electors "has been so infrequent and also so ineffective, that it may be questioned whether it warrants going through the whole process of constitutional amendment."[74]

The automatic system proposal was next revived by President Lyndon B. Johnson in a message to Congress on January 28, 1965. "Today there lurks in the electoral college system the ever-present possibility that electors may substitute their will for that of the people. I believe that possibility should be foreclosed," Johnson said. But he emphasized his support for the general ticket system: "Our present system of computing and awarding electoral votes by states is an essential counterpart of our federal system and the provisions of our Constitution which recognize and maintain our nation as a union of states." Johnson also maintained that the unit vote system supported the two-party system. The Presidential proposals were incorporated into resolutions by Senator Birch Bayh of Indiana, chairman of the Senate Judiciary Constitutional Amendments Subcommittee, and Representative Emanuel Celler of New York, chairman of the House Judiciary Committee. The resolution provided that each state would have an electoral vote equal to its number of Senators and Representatives, and that all of a state's electoral votes would go to the plurality winner in the state. Voters would cast their vote for President and Vice President by one ballot. If no candidate won a majority of the national electoral vote, the choice would be made from among the top three electoral-vote winners by the Senate and House meeting jointly. The amendment also provided that if at the time of the Congressional counting of electoral votes the winning Presidential candidate had died, the Vice Presidential candidate who ran with him would become President. Congress was authorized to provide by law for the case of the death of both the President- and Vice President-elect.[75]

Early in 1966, President Johnson reiterated his proposal in another special message to Congress, and it was considered in hearings before Bayh's subcommittee in the Senate. Opening the hearings, Bayh endorsed the automatic system and said that alternative proposals for reforming the electoral college "pose far greater dangers to the nation than the state-by-state, winner-take-all system." Katzenbach cautioned against discarding a tried and tested system of electing the President for proposals that would "change the basic system itself" with "grave risks" to the country's political structure. Senator Robert F. Kennedy of New York endorsed the Administration proposal, saying he believed "our electoral system on the whole has worked quite well." But Kennedy noted that a switch of a few thousand votes in key states in 1960, when his brother John F. Kennedy defeated Richard M. Nixon, "might have given a few electors the power to control the outcome. . . . It would be tragic for us as a nation if such a situation ever did come to pass."[76]

Even with full Presidential backing, however, the automatic system gained little support. The advocates of virtually all the other proposed reforms opposed the automatic system because it would have given Constitutional cognizance—for the first time in U.S. history—to the very "winner-take-all" system of casting state electoral votes which reformers have considered the chief evil of the existing system. The Chamber of Commerce of the United States, which had come out for comprehensive reform of the electoral college, said that the automatic system "would be worse than having no reform at all. Not only would it write into the Constitution the evils of the unit vote system, but its adoption would undoubtedly preclude meaningful reform indefinitely."[77] Opponents also said the automatic system incorporated such minor changes that it might never have a bearing on any election. "Indeed," said Senator Ervin on the Senate floor, "it is hardly worth cranking up the complex and protracted amendment process to accomplish so little—it would be almost like chasing a fly with an elephant gun."[78]

The death knell for the automatic system was apparently sounded on May 18, 1966, when Senator Bayh, the Constitutional Amendments Subcommittee chairman and chief Senate sponsor of the Administration's plan, announced he was abandoning it in favor of direct popular vote of the people. "It may well be that mere procedural changes in the present system would be like shifting around the parts of a creaky and dangerous automobile engine, making it no less creaky and no less dangerous," Bayh said. "What we may need is a new engine, because we are in a new age."

Direct Popular Vote

Of the more than 500 constitutional amendments proposed in Congress through the course of U.S. history, well over 100 have envisaged the simplest solution of all to election of the President: a direct vote of all people, with no intermediate electors or electoral count standing between them and the choice of their Chief Executive. The arguments for and against this solution have changed greatly in weight and significance over the years, but most of them were already clear on March 20, 1816, the day that direct national election was first proposed in Congress.

On that occasion, the Senate was debating the merits of a proposed district system amendment to the Constitution. Fittingly, it was Senator Abner Lacock of Pennsylvania, the state whose delegates had offered the strongest support for direct election in the Constitutional Convention, who offered the direct vote amendment.[79] Lacock said he could see no reason why agents such as the electors "should be employed between the people and their votes."

Supporting Lacock's position, Senator Rufus King of New York, who had been a delegate to the Constitutional Convention, said: "In time of difficulty and peril to the nation, when it is in utmost need of superior talent for its high stations, no tribunal is more competent to discern and select it than the people." In his judgment, King said, "the people are . . . the best keepers of their own rights; and any device to remove that power from them weakens the security of it."

Opposition was voiced immediately, however. Senator Jeremiah Mason of New Hampshire said the great disparities between voting qualifications in the various states would make direct election impracticable. Senator William W. Bibb of Georgia wanted to know what "would be the condition of the slave-holding states? They would lose the privilege the Constitution now allows them, of votes upon three-fifths of their population other than freemen. It would be deeply injurious to them." Senator James Barbour of Virginia warned of a "destruction of the balance of power in the Confederacy" because "it has pleased God to give the Southern country a population anomalous, having the double character of person and property; other states had none such."

Yet another objection was raised by Senator Eligius Fromentin of Louisiana. "Look at the vast expanse of our country, from Maine to Louisiana—no such election could here be made in case of emergency; before it could be consummated we should be devoured by the monster which threatened us."

It was left to Senator Robert G. Harper of Maryland to present the states'-rights argument, one that would return to plague direct election proposals for another century and a half. Election per capita, Harper charged, "threw out of view altogether the federal principle by which the states are represented, as well as the people, in the present mode of election. . . . It would destroy that influence of the smaller states in the Presidential election, which arises from their representation of the sovereign characters of the states—and thus destroy a very important principle of the Constitution."

Attempting to rebut the opposition arguments, Lacock admitted that there might be difficulties in instituting a direct national election, but asked: "What could make us so much one people, as to give to all the people this equal privilege? It will produce in the national habits, manners and love of country, more harmony than any other political measure which could be possibly adapted."

Whatever the merits of direct election might have been, the Republic was clearly not prepared for it. Lacock's motion went down to defeat, only 12 Senators in favor to 21 in opposition.[80]

The election of 1824, which resulted in the election of Adams despite Jackson's lead in the recorded national popular vote, rekindled interest in a direct national election. On January 3, 1826, Representative William McManus of New York presented a direct vote resolution that declared: "Inasmuch as the people of the United States are subject to two distinct governments and their laws (the one state and the other national), and are citizens of, and owe allegiance to each government, they have the same equal and just right to elect, by their individual votes, the President and Vice President of the Union, that they have to elect the Governor and Lieutenant Governor of their respective states." McManus proposed that the plurality choice of the people of all the states be sufficient to elect the President and Vice President.[81] Within the following four years the proposal was introduced eight more times in the House, twice on the instigation of individual state legislatures—those of Ohio and Missouri. Senator George M. Bibb of Kentucky made a similar proposal in 1833, but the committee to which it was referred recommended a district system instead.[82]

Though he was willing to let the states retain their weight in electoral voting, President Andrew Jackson can be counted as the spiritual godfather of the direct vote movement. "To the people belongs the right of electing their chief magistrate," Jackson said in his first annual message to Congress. "It was never designed that their choice should, in any case, be defeated either by the intervention of the electoral colleges, or by . . . the House of Representatives." Indeed, said Jackson, "the first principle of our system" is "that the majority is to govern. . . . It must be very certain that a President elected by a minority cannot enjoy the confidence necessary to the discharge of his duties."[83] Obviously, Jackson had the disputed election of 1824, and the election of Adams with fewer popular votes than he (Jackson) had received, in mind.

In the three decades from the mid-1830s to 1865, little interest in direct vote was apparent in Congress.[84] But in the period immediately following the Civil War, it was frequently proposed. The chief exponents of the direct vote in this era were Senator Charles Sumner, Massachusetts' great reform leader and civil rights advocate, together with Representative James M. Ashley of Ohio and Senator Luke P. Poland of Vermont. Sumner advocated a direct vote because he found the existing system "artificial, cumbrous, radically defective and unrepublican." A direct election amendment, Sumner said, "would give every individual voter, wherever he might be, a positive weight in the election. It would give minorities in distant states an opportunity to be heard in determining who shall be chief magistrate."[85] Sumner's amendment, along the lines of Senator Benton's recommendations in earlier years, provided for a first election in the spring and then a national runoff in the autumn if no candidate won a majority on the first round. The intention—though it is questionable if it would have been realized—was to supersede the convention method of nominations.

Of the 25 direct vote resolutions in the immediate postwar era, 12 proposed a runoff popular election if no candidate received a majority in the first election, while four others provided for contingent election in Congress and several others required a mere plurality of the national vote for election. The greatest number of resolutions were proposed between 1872 and 1878, the majority of them by Congressmen from the Western states.

In the three-quarters of a century following the Reconstruction period, occasional proposals were advanced in Congress to abolish the electoral college and go to direct vote, but none of them made significant headway. A major reason seems to have been the almost universally held belief that a popular vote amendment would never be ratified by the required three-quarters of the states, because a majority of them would lose some percentage of their relative weight under the existing electoral college apportionment (see pages 138–39, above).

This gloomy belief failed to deter a number of prominent American statesmen from endorsing the idea of a direct vote. "I have favored the popular voting system for President and Vice President for 40 years," Senator (and former Vice President) Alben W. Barkley said in the 1950s. "One of the first measures I introduced in Congress in 1913," he added, "was a resolution to adopt a constitutional amendment which would have allowed the people to vote directly for President and Vice President. . . . It took a long time before the Constitution was amended to provide for the popular voting for United States Senators." Barkley said he realized the difficulties of achieving ratification, but "they do not dampen my belief or feeling that some of these days we shall have to give the American people the right to vote directly for President and Vice President."[86]

Indeed, by the 1950s Barkley was not alone among leading politicians who said they would accept popular vote for President. Senator Henry Cabot Lodge of Massachusetts introduced such an amendment in 1941, and in 1950 Senate debate (while pushing for the Lodge-Gossett proportional plan) said he had "never ceased to believe that this would be a desirable change." He had shifted to support of the proportional system, Lodge said, because he believed direct vote "utterly impossible of accomplishment, because it diminishes the relative importance of smaller states in a Presidential election. But I would not want it to appear that I oppose direct election." Lodge actually voted for direct vote amendments offered by other Senators to the Lodge-Gossett bill.[87] In the same 1950 debate, Senator Robert A. Taft of Ohio said, "Personally I will be willing under some circumstances to vote for a resolution based simply on the popular vote. Certainly it would be logical and reasonably defensible."[88] Senator (and later Vice President) Hubert H. Humphrey was one of the most prominent supporters of the direct national vote in the postwar era, offering an amendment to that effect during 1950 Senate debate on electoral reform. Under direct vote, Humphrey said, "every voter casts one vote, a whole vote, which is just as good and just as important as the vote cast by any other voter in the country. . . . This is the final step in the constitutional evolution which began with the Declaration that all men are created equal, and continued with the assertion that no man or woman may be denied the right to vote for arbitrary reasons. Now we must make the suffrage an equal suffrage, and repudiate arbitrary and discriminatory geographical bases for denying or reducing the importance of the votes of some of our citizens."[89] Senator Paul Douglas of Illinois, a leader in the 1956 Senate debate that ended in defeat of the Daniel proportional district system substitute, was a strong supporter of the direct vote alternative. And Senator Estes Kefauver of Tennessee, associated for years with the proportional system, said in 1950 Senate debate: "I, too, would be very happy if the President and Vice President could be elected by popular vote. . . . I would support . . . popular vote if it were possible to have the Constitution so amended."[90]

The prevailing mood of Congress in the postwar years was hostile to the direct vote alternative, however. In 1947 a combination direct vote–national nominating primary amendment was offered as a substitute for the proposal for a two-term limit on the President, then being debated in the Senate. It was rejected by a 14 to 66 vote.[91] In this instance, the vote for direct vote was doubtless reduced because it was not germane to the topic at hand, and because it was sponsored by two political mavericks—Senators William Langer of North Dakota and Glen Taylor of Idaho (the latter subsequently ran for Vice President on Henry Wallace's Progressive ticket in 1948).

During 1950 debate on the Lodge-Gossett proportional plan, two direct vote amendments were offered. The first, by Langer, would have substituted direct vote along with national nominating primaries. It was rejected by a vote of 31 to 60. The second, offered by Humphrey, provided only for election by direct national vote. It went down to defeat as well, by a vote of 28 to 63.[92]

Again in 1956, when the Senate was debating the Daniel substitute, amendments were offered to substitute a direct vote plan. On this occasion, they were defeated by even larger margins than in 1950. Langer's combined national primary–direct vote amendment was rejected by a margin of 13 to 69, and a simple direct vote amendment authored by Senator Herbert H. Lehman of New York lost by a vote of 17 to 66. John Kennedy was a leading opponent of direct vote in 1956. The Langer amendment, he said, "while purporting to be more democratic, would increase the power of and encourage splinter parties, and I believe it would break down the federal system under which most states entered the Union, which provides a system of checks and balances to insure that no area or group shall obtain too much power." Kennedy took a strong states'-rights view on the electoral college, saying, "I should hate to see the abolishment of state lines. . . . The Presidential election is determined on the basis of 48 separate units. I think the election should be decided in each one of them."[93]

One of the most fascinating parts of the 1956 debate, little noted at the time, was this colloquy between Kennedy and Senator John Pastore of Rhode Island, who favored direct vote:[94]

PASTORE: Why should one state be a pivotal state? Why should a group of states be pivotal states?

KENNEDY: Under the Senator's plan the pivotal states would be of infinitely more importance than they are today. Except in the Senate, Rhode Island would cease to be of any real importance . . . Rhode Island is overrepresented in the electoral college today, based on its population.

PASTORE: I am not going into that question at all. I want to do away with the electoral college. I want to elect my President on election day. I say that when the people go to the polls the man who receives the greatest number of votes should be elected President of the people. He is the President of the people of the United States, and not the President of the states. It makes no difference to me how many electoral votes the people of Rhode Island have. What difference does it make? Why do we talk so much about the power of a state? . . .

KENNEDY: I must say that I disagree with the proposal of the Senator. In fact, it would not have a chance to get by. It would require a two-thirds vote, and the smaller states would not accept it.

PASTORE: I have never worried about what gets by and what does not get by. I am concerned with the principle involved. . . . Most of the people in my state, when they go to the polls on election day, think they are voting for President and Vice President. They do not vote for President if they must elect electors or delegates who meet later in the Governor's office and have a luncheon at 12 o'clock noon and then cast their ballot for President. . . .

KENNEDY: Would the Senator do away with the two electors which his state has by virtue of the fact that it has two Senators of the United States?

PASTORE: I would do away with the whole electoral college. I would do away with it completely. I would have the people elect the President of the United States on election day. I would not care where the candidates came from, whether they came from the North, the South, the West, or the East. They are all Americans. We are all one country. I say let us vote for the best man. Let the man who gets the most votes be President. It is as simple as that. That is my idea of representative government. Everything else beyond that is a gimmick. . . .

The 1960 Presidential election spurred renewed interest in the direct vote alternative. Where only two direct vote amendments had been sponsored in the preceding two sessions of Congress, a total of 12 were proposed in the 87th Congress, which convened in January 1961. The chief sponsors included Senate Majority Leader Mike Mansfield of Montana, Senator Margaret Chase Smith of Maine and Senator Kenneth B. Keating of New York. Their resolutions were debated extensively during the 1961 Senate Judiciary hearings chaired by Kefauver.

"We must see to it," Keating said during the hearings, that "a majority of the American people can and do determine who is to be our nation's Chief Executive. . . . I do not believe that any candidate would want to be elected to the highest office of our land over an opponent who received a larger number of votes." A large portion of the American electorate, the Kefauver subcommittee was told, does not know of the existence of the electoral college, believing that it actually votes directly for President. Professor Paul J. Piccard suggested that the next time the popular vote winner loses in the electoral college, "even the winning party is going to be sufficiently embarrassed to accept direct popular election of the President. I think they will turn to that."[95]

Several witnesses expressed concern that direct national voting would prompt the states to lower their voting qualifications, especially those of age, to swell their vote total and their influence in the Presi-

dential balloting. Congress would have to be given power to fix uniform voting qualifications, Professor Robert G. Dixon argued, "in order
to prevent one state or section of the country from magnifying its voting age to ridiculous levels, or enfranchising its cats and dogs." But
other political scientists differed. Professor Kenneth Kofmehl of Purdue
University suggested that if the voting age, for example, were reduced
to 12, "these 12-year-olds will be picking their mayors, their Governors
and their state legislatures also, and I don't think that the states are
going to commit political hara-kiri for some advantage in the Presidential election."[96] Most direct vote amendments have stipulated that
the voting qualifications for President would be the same as for the
state legislature or Congress, so that a state could not establish a
special broadened voting base for President alone. Even if permitted
to do so, the states would probably not because of the obvious administrative difficulties in a dual-registration system.

The familiar states'-rights arguments were also raised again. "I think
we are a republic," said Senator Thruston B. Morton of Kentucky,
"and as a republic, I think the states, by virtue of being states, should
have some additional weight in the electoral college."[97] But Senator
Mansfield argued that direct vote would complement and strengthen
the federal system, rather than weakening it. "The federal system," he
said, "is not strengthened through an antiquated device which has not
worked as it was intended to work when it was included in the
Constitution and which, if anything, has become a divisive force in the
federal system by pitting groups of states against groups of states. As I
see the federal system in contemporary practice, the House of Representatives is the key to the protection of district interests *as* district
interests, just as the Senate is the key to the protection of state
interests *as* state interests. Those instrumentalities, and particularly the
Senate, are the principal constitutional safeguards of the federal
system, but the Presidency has evolved, out of necessity, into the
principal political office . . . for safeguarding the interests of all the
people in all the states."[98]

Even when they favored direct vote, many witnesses dismissed it as
impossible of adoption because of small-state and particularly South-
ern-state opposition. But a new counterargument was raised: that the
power exercised by large states under the existing system had surely
canceled out any advantage that the small states enjoy through their
two extra electoral votes. "I do not think people in the small states are
terribly anxious to preserve this alleged advantage if they could have a

direct vote for President as the alternative," Professor Paul T. David of the University of Virginia said. Both he and Senator Mansfield suggested that a constitutional amendment instituting the direct vote could be put to special amending conventions chosen by the people of the states, rather than going through the usual state legislature role for ratification. The Constitution gives Congress an option in the matter, and Congress had actually provided for special state conventions to secure repeal of the 18th Amendment to the Constitution in 1933, repealing prohibition. The experience of that year, David said, showed that delegates to the ratifying conventions were usually elected on a statewide basis permitting a clear yes-no vote on the proposed amendment.[99]

No significant move for the direct vote was made in or out of Congress in the wake of the 1961 hearings; indeed, actual sponsorships fell off to only four resolutions in 1963–64, and the reform looked quiescent if not dead. But in other fields, there were major new developments that would have a profound bearing on the political complexion of the country. The Supreme Court reapportionment decisions of 1962 and 1964 pointed to a revolutionary new standard of political equality in state legislature and Congressional districts. The 1964 Presidential election broke down some of the last remnants of old one-party systems, in both the Democratic South and Republican states of the North. The Voting Rights Act of 1965 represented a national assurance that Southern Negroes, within but a few years, would enjoy the full suffrage. Then, in 1966, came four highly significant developments for the direct vote cause.

The Chamber of Commerce of the United States announced on January 31, following a referendum of its member organizations, that it favored abolishing the existing system and shifting to either a nationwide popular vote or a district system. The final vote of the Chamber members for approving the new policy position was 3,877 in favor (91.5 percent) and 362 (8.5 percent) opposed.

A Gallup Poll, released on May 18, showed that 63 percent of the people in a nationwide sampling favored amending the Constitution "to do away with the electoral college and base the election of a President on the total popular vote throughout the nation." The sampling showed 20 percent against the shift, and 17 percent with no opinion. It was the first national poll on direct vote ever published.[100] The electoral college seems to be an institution in which familiarity breeds contempt. Breakdowns of Gallup surveys on the electoral college system show that the more educated a person is—and thus more likely to be familiar with what the electoral college really is—the more likely he is to favor its abolition (see Appendix N).

Senator Birch Bayh of Indiana, who had taken over in 1963 as chairman of the Senate Judiciary Constitutional Amendments Subcommittee after Kefauver's death, announced on May 18 that he was abandoning his support of the automatic system amendment backed by the Johnson Administration and would henceforth work for the adoption of a direct popular vote.[101] This, too, was a "first": the first time that the chairman of a major Congressional committee or subcommittee charged with considering constitutional amendments had allied himself with the popular vote cause. Bayh had already won national prestige as chief Congressional sponsor of the Presidential inability amendment, approved by Congress in 1965. With the ratification of three-fourths of the states, it became the 25th Amendment to the Constitution in 1967.

Senator Bayh's conversion to the direct vote cause was a major surprise, not only because he himself had been the chief sponsor of the Administration's automatic system amendment, but because of his close association with Senators Edward M. and Robert F. Kennedy, both of whom still indicated reservations about a direct vote. Bayh acknowledged he had changed his position only "after a great deal of soul-searching," and that "the Justice Department is not at all happy with us." He had been asked by officials at Justice, Bayh said, why he was shifting to direct vote when it had been defeated so soundly in Senate votes during the 1950s. Bayh said his reply was that "a lot of history has been made since 1956, and a lot of freedoms given to our people since 1956." Specifically, he noted the 24th Amendment abolishing the poll tax in federal elections, the Civil Rights Acts of 1957, 1960 and 1964 and the Voting Rights Act of 1965. "Today, for the first time in our history, we have achieved the goal of universal suffrage regardless of race, religion or station in life," Bayh said.

In July, Delaware, subsequently joined by 12 other states, asked the U.S. Supreme Court to hear a suit challenging the constitutionality under the 14th Amendment of the unit vote or "winner-take-all" method of casting state electoral votes. Delaware asked the Court to "open the door" to reform by granting interim relief that would require the states to divide their electoral votes in a way that would more accurately reflect popular sentiment. The suit acknowledged that a direct vote would be the only permanent remedy to the inequalities built into the electoral college system. On October 17 the Court refused to hear the case, giving no reasons for its action. Delaware's brief, however, served to compare the electoral college system with the "one man, one vote" standard being required by the courts in state legislatures and Congressional districts.[102]

The American Bar Association in February 1966 established a blue-ribbon commission to study the problem of the electoral college and possible reform. Among the panel's members were several former ABA presidents; Paul Freund, constitutional law professor at Harvard Law School; C. Herman Pritchett, professor of political science at the University of Chicago and former president of the American Political Science Association; United Automobile Workers president Walter Reuther; Governors Otto Kerner, Democrat of Illinois, and Henry Bellmon, Republican of Oklahoma; and William T. Gossett, former general counsel to the Ford Motor Company. After a series of meetings the commission decided in the autumn that it would endorse the popular vote alternative. The commission's report, released officially on January 7, 1967, said that "the electoral college method of electing a President of the United States is archaic, undemocratic, complex, ambiguous, indirect and dangerous. . . . While there may be no perfect method of electing a President, we believe that direct, nation-wide popular vote is the best of all possible methods."

The ABA recommendations, ratified by the association's House of Delegates in February 1967, were expected to carry special weight as ABA officials throughout the country brought pressure on members of Congress to consider the direct vote. It was a similar ABA commission, dealing with Presidential inability problems, that had recommended the basic policies spelled out in the 25th Amendment.

Both for Senator Bayh and several members of the ABA commission, the fear of splinter parties appears to have been the major obstacle they had to overcome before accepting direct vote. Early in 1966, Bayh had actually announced his opposition to popular vote because "it would inevitably take this nation down the path of splinter parties that have plagued so many European nations for so many years." In May, Bayh said, "I hate to admit we were wrong, but I think we were." He said that under the constitutional amendment he was proposing, 40 percent of the popular vote, rather than a majority, would be sufficient for election. With that provision, he said, splinter parties would have little incentive to seek votes in the national election—perhaps less than under the existing system, since they would no longer have the hope of depriving both of the major parties of an electoral vote majority and thus putting themselves in a bargaining position. When the ABA commission announced its endorsement of the direct vote, Professor Freund said the fear of a proliferation of parties had been "the great stumbling block," but that "we were persuaded in the end that these fears were exaggerated." The ABA also recommended that 40 percent of the popular vote be required for election, and went a step beyond Bayh's original direct vote proposal, which had provided for a contingent election in a joint session of Congress. The ABA recommended instead that a national popular vote runoff be held if no candidate won 40 percent in the first election. This provision, Freund said, would largely deter the splinter parties, because even if they prevented a decision in the first election, they would have no opportunity to throw an election into Congress with the deals and intrigues that might result. In January 1967, Bayh modified his direct vote amendment to provide for the national direct vote runoff recommended by the ABA.[103]

Professor Freund said the second difficulty the ABA commission had seen in direct vote was its possible impact on the federal system. But in voting for President and Vice President, Freund noted, Americans vote as United States citizens, not as citizens of individual states. If one would preserve the federal system, he added, the Presidential election was not the place to make one's stand. Direct vote, he added, might really strengthen the federal system, by making all votes equal and reducing the conflicts between large and small states.

Stressing the positive aspects of direct vote, the ABA commission said such a system "would do away with the ever-present possibility of a person being elected President with fewer popular votes than his major opponent. . . . It would abolish the office of Presidential elector, which is an anachronism and a threat to the smooth functioning of the elective process. It would minimize the effect of accident and fraud in controlling the outcome of an entire election. It would put a premium on voter turnout and encourage increased political activity throughout the country."

Finally, a poll of the members of the nation's 50 state legislatures, conducted by Senator Quentin N. Burdick of North Dakota, showed a strong majority for direct vote. During the summer of 1966, Burdick wrote to each of the state legislators asking if he or she thought the electoral college should be modified or abolished and, if so, what reform each legislator would favor. The results, based on replies from approximately 2,500 of the nation's 8,000 state legislators, showed a surprising 58.8 percent in favor of complete abolition of the electoral college and substitution of the direct vote. The proportional system was favored by 21.2 percent, the district system by 10.2 percent, and the existing system by only 9.7 percent. In all, 50 percent or more of the legislators replying from 44 of the 50 states supported direct election. And contrary to the judgment of political observers since the early 19th century, the results showed the popular vote just as heavily favored in small states as in large states. Of the seven most heavily populated states, California legislators voted 73.5 percent for direct election, New York legislators 70.0 percent, Pennsylvania 55.8 percent, Michigan 52.4 percent, Ohio 57.1 percent and Texas 52.3 percent. Illinois legislators registered only 37.0 percent for direct election, the lowest percentage among the "big seven." Among the smallest states—those with only three electoral votes—Alaska voted 50.0 percent for direct election, Delaware 53.8 percent, Nevada 62.5 percent, Vermont 68.9 percent and Wyoming 55.5 percent.[104]

The momentum for the direct vote alternative carried into 1967, as the Bayh subcommittee in the Senate launched into a new set of hearings with testimony from ABA officials in favor of their commission's report. Senate Majority Leader Mike Mansfield reiterated his support for direct vote, and the cause won a major convert in the prestigious Senate Minority Leader, Everett Dirksen of Illinois. (For text of Dirksen amendment, drawn up by some of the ABA commission leaders, see Appendix L).

Two political scientists who had previously backed other systems now announced they supported the direct vote—Lucius Wilmerding, Jr., hitherto a major spokesman for the district system, and Professor Joseph E. Kallenbach of the University of Michigan, a backer of the proportional plan in earlier years. On the House side, Judiciary Committee Chairman Emanuel Celler of New York indicated his openness to the direct vote idea by introducing the same amendment drawn up for Dirksen by the ABA. Celler continued to introduce the Administration's automatic system bill as well, however.

The opposition in the Senate hearings tended to come from groups on the right, ranging from the American Good Government Society to the Liberty Lobby. The right-wing multimillionaire, Texas oilman H. L. Hunt, was one of the witnesses opposing a direct vote—because, as Hunt put it, "Dictators extend to their populace the privilege of going to the polls and casting a vote for their dictator and his stooges.

They could laugh up their sleeves if they found the claimants of champions of freedom offering their populace a chance to cast a direct vote." Opposition was also heard from some more moderate conservatives, including Nebraska's Republican Senator Roman L. Hruska and Florida's Democratic Senator Spessard L. Holland. Both professed to fear that a direct vote for President would somehow lead to demands that the states relinquish their equal voting rights in the U.S. Senate.*

Hybrids and Miscellaneous Plans

In addition to the major electoral college reforms proposed over the years, a number of alternative plans have been brought forward, some of them serious attempts to effect a compromise based on the political conditions of the times, others so strange that they can only be described as grotesque imitations of real reform.

The first was suggested in 1808 by Senator James Hillhouse, a Connecticut Federalist who said his intent was to save the country from the evils of parties and party spirit. All United States Senators would hold office for a three-year term, with a third retiring annually. Each year the retiring Senators would assemble and draw balls from a box. One of the balls would be colored, and the man who drew it would be President for a year. Old John Adams commented that the Hillhouse plan "reduces the President's office to that of a mere Doge of Venice, a mere head of wood, a mere tool of the aristocracy of the country."[105] His son, John Quincy Adams, probably reflected prevailing opinion when he wrote in his diary that "a serious discussion of [Hillhouse's] amendments would be ridiculous."[106]

During the 19th century, a few proposals were made to elect the President by geographical sections. Representative Thomas Montgomery of Kentucky introduced the first such resolution in 1822, providing that the country would be divided into four geographical sections, each of which would elect a President in rotation. Montgomery felt impelled to tell his colleagues of his plan: "However laughable it might appear to some gentlemen, [he] considered it a very serious matter." The cause of the amendment was doubtless the

* The idea that the Senate could be "reapportioned" to conform to "one man, one vote" standards in other areas of government is obviously a red herring. Article V of the Constitution, which provides for amendments, stipulates specifically that "no state, without its consent, shall be deprived of its equal suffrage in the Senate." (For further details of 1967 testimony, as it related to big- versus small-state interests, runoff elections and the interests of Negro voters, see Chapter 8.)

jealousy felt in the Middle Atlantic States and New England, and still more in the West, over the fact that all the Presidents up to that time, except for John Adams, had been from Virginia.[107]

Another sectional amendment, introduced by Representative Clement L. Vallandigham of Ohio in 1861 on the eve of the Civil War, was apparently an attempt to change the Constitution in a way that would persuade the South to remain in the Union. Four geographical sections of the country would be established, and to be elected President, a candidate would have to achieve a majority of the votes of the electors in *each* of the regions. A similar amendment, proposed by Andrew Johnson in 1860, would have had the President elected alternately from the North and the South.[108]

One of the most byzantine plans of history was proposed by Senator Lazarus W. Powell of Kentucky in 1864. The electors—from one to seven per state, chosen by district—would all meet in Washington every fourth February and form an electoral college with the Chief Justice presiding. By alphabetical order of their names, the electors would be distributed into six groups, numbered from one to six. Each group would select one man from the next numbered group, and from the six persons so designated two would be selected by lot. The electoral college would then name one of these men as President, the other as Vice President. If no one was elected in 24 hours, then the electoral college would be dissolved and a whole new election ordered. If no President were selected by June 1, then the Senate would choose a President—using the identical system. One of the provisions of Powell's amendment was that electors would declare that they had made no pledges to support any particular candidate or to aid any political party.[109]

In 1862 and on three subsequent occasions, Senator Jarrett Davis of Kentucky suggested that the states should nominate candidates for President in any way they desired and that Congress should then meet as a convention and choose one of the nominees as President. A unanimous vote for election was required. This was to be achieved by dropping candidates from the bottom of the list after a stated time had been reached in the balloting. If no choice were made, then the Supreme Court would pick the President.[110]

Trying to avoid all the problems of getting a specific new plan written into a constitutional amendment, Representative Charles R. Buckalew of Pennsylvania suggested in 1869 an amendment providing simply that "Congress shall have the power to prescribe the manner in which electors shall be chosen by the people." The intent was to assure a popular vote for Presidential electors in each state and to permit Congress to adopt a district system or any other, depending on the times. During Senate discussion the same year on the 15th Amendment (Negro suffrage), Senator Morton of Indiana brought up Buckalew's proposal as an amendment, and the Senate accepted the addition on a 37 to 19 vote. A two-thirds Senate vote (40 to 16) was then obtained for the combined Negro suffrage–Presidential election amendments. The House, however, took strong exception to the Buckalew amendment and refused on a 37 to 133 vote to accept the combined proposals. The 15th Amendment was subsequently submitted to the states without any provision regarding Presidential elections. Similar proposals to let Congress determine the system by which electoral votes are cast were proposed again in 1872 and 1888, but neither made any headway.[111]

An interesting hybrid proposal was brought forward by Senator Hubert H. Humphrey of Minnesota during the electoral reform debate in Congress in 1956. The Humphrey plan, based on a recommendation made to him by Professor Ralph M. Goldman of Michigan State University, retained the total electoral strength based on the number of Senators and Representatives combined, though there would no longer be actual electors. Each state would continue to cast two electoral votes (corresponding to its number of Senators) for the plurality winner in the state. But the remaining electoral votes, corresponding to the number of Representatives in Congress, would be divided on a national proportional basis reflecting the national popular vote for President. Thus the plan would have given predominate weight to the national popular vote but would have allowed some modification based on the traditional federal principle of guaranteeing a minimum of electoral votes to each state. The plan was rejected by voice vote of the Senate during the 1956 debate.[112] Had the Humphrey plan been applied to the 1960 election returns, Nixon would have been elected President, primarily because he carried 26 states to the 22 that went for Kennedy. The vote would have been Nixon, 268.562 electoral votes; Kennedy, 260.159; unpledged, 6.936; and minor parties, 1.377.[113]

Contingent Election

The Constitutional provision for a contingent election in the House of Representatives, which goes into effect if no candidate receives a majority of the electoral vote, has been almost universally condemned (see pages 132–33, above). The various reform proposals over the years have contained a myriad of alternatives. The simplest, of course, is not to require an electoral majority at all, so that the possibility of a contingent election never arises. This was the course advocated by Senator Oliver Morton and a number of reform advocates of the 19th and 20th centuries. Other plans have reduced the electoral vote requirement to one third, or 40 or 45 percent, in the hope of avoiding a contingent election, and some have provided for a repeat election from among the two or three top vote recipients.

The majority of reform proposals in recent years have retained the contingent election in Congress but provided that it will take place in a joint session of Congress with each Senator and Representative having a single vote. This procedure would at least eliminate the undemocratic procedure of each state in the House casting a single vote, as the Constitution currently requires. But it is still open to the objection that any President chosen in Congress could be required to make advance agreements that would limit his independence and power as the Chief Executive.

The other contingent elections proposed over the course of our history have included these alternatives as well: election by the House with each member casting a single vote; a runoff by popular vote but each state to have but one vote in the national tally; the state legislatures to choose; successive national elections until some candidate receives a majority; letting the House choose by any rules it may adopt; or, to prevent deadlock in the House, authorizing the House Speaker to choose a President by lot from the two top-runners after the second ballot.[114]

Conclusion

Constitutional Convention delegate James Wilson told the Pennsylvania ratifying convention late in 1787 that "the Convention [was] perplexed with no part of this plan as much as with the mode of choosing the President of the United States."[115] The founding fathers were well aware that they had failed to create a perfect vehicle for the choice of the Chief Executive, and through the entire course of American history, few men have been willing to defend it. Yet despite lifetimes of exertion by the great reformers, no substantive changes have been made. Why?

First and foremost, the answer lies in the politics of each era. Amending the Constitution of the United States is an arduous process; to succeed, one must form and maintain a broad national consensus. Indeed, no constitutional amendment has much chance of ratification without the support or at least the acquiescence of all the major political forces in the country—the controlling groups in each major political party, spokesmen of each section, state and national party leaders. The stakes in any Presidential election are so high that no political group will consent to a change in the electoral system if it seriously fears that its power and influence will be undercut.

The first great proposed reform, the district system, appears to have lost out in the 19th century because it diluted the power of political leaders who thought they could "deliver" states for one Presidential candidate or the other. And by the time the district plan was revived in the 20th century, it bore so many of the marks of a conservative-rural device to seize the Presidency that it never had a serious chance of adoption. Nor are its chances likely to increase in future years, as the urbanization of America continues. By its very nature, the district system magnifies the power of small states and predominantly one-party areas. Large states and politically marginal areas of the country will never risk it, and they can easily block any proposed constitutional amendment.

For many of the same reasons, the proportional plan clearly seems to have run its course and has little chance of adoption in future years. While fairer in conception and operation than the district system, it still magnifies the power of small states and one-party states against the large competitive ones.* And like the district system, it can quite plausibly elect a minority President.

The automatic system is likewise destined for failure, because it enthrones the most repugnant feature of the electoral college as it operates today, the "winner-take-all" system of casting state electoral votes. As advocated by Presidents Kennedy and Johnson, the automatic system has simply been an effort to prevent the Southern states from casting unpledged electoral votes that could block the election of a national Democratic nominee. Advocates of other systems rightfully detect in the automatic system a substitute for true reform.

---

* Recent computer studies show that citizens of small states would gain a grossly disproportionate power, in terms of actually affecting the outcome of a Presidential election, under either the proportional or district system. (See Appendix O.)

What then of the direct popular vote? Is it also destined to failure because it would "gore the ox" of some major political group in America—the small states, or perhaps just the Southern states, or the minorities in the big pivotal states? A few years ago, the answer would doubtless have been "yes." But the past two decades have witnessed a revolution in the political life of this country—a revolution in party alignment, a revolution in voting rights, a revolution in communications. It is this fundamental alteration in the political landscape of our country that makes the direct popular vote for President a viable alternative today.

N O T E S

1. *N.Y. Times,* March 12, 1950.
2. Computed from Herman V. Ames, "Proposed Amendments to the Constitution of the United States During the First Century of Its History," *Annual Report of the American Historical Association for 1896* (Washington, 1897).
3. Count since 1889 based on various compilations by the Legislative Reference Service of the Library of Congress and Congressional Quarterly Service. Between 1889 and 1946, 109 amendments on Presidential election were offered; between 1947 and 1963, 151 amendments; between 1964 and 1966, 29 amendments.
4. *Annals of Congress,* XLI, p. 170.
5. *Congressional Record,* 1950, p. 883.
6. Max Farrand, ed., *The Records of the Federal Constitutional Convention of 1787,* 4 vols. (New Haven, 1911, 1937), III, p. 459. One hesitates to contradict the "father of the Constitution," but the debates of the Constitutional Convention contain only one fleeting reference to a district system (see p. 43, above), and the question was not raised in the subsequent ratifying conventions.
7. Ames, *op. cit.,* p. 81.
8. Cited by Ames, *op. cit.,* pp. 81–82.
9. *Ibid.,* pp. 83–84.
10. Cited by J. Hampden Dougherty, *The Electoral System of the United States* (New York, 1906), pp. 327, 333. On other occasions, however, Van Buren supported the district plan.
11. Senate Report No. 22, 19th Congress, 1st Session, Jan. 19, 1826, pp. 3, 7–8. Benton reportedly inserted the national runoff in place of a contingent election in Congress on the urging of Andrew Jackson.
12. Giles & Seaton's *Debates,* p. 693, cited by Ames, *op. cit.,* p. 91.
13. House *Journal,* 22nd Congress, 1st Session, Dec. 8, 1829, p. 15.
14. Ames, *op. cit.,* p. 91.

15. Cited by Dougherty, *op. cit.*, pp. 345–46, and Ames, *op. cit.*, p. 93.

16. Cited by Dougherty, *op. cit.*, p. 348.

17. In 1956, Coudert introduced a separate amendment to abolish the office of elector while retaining other provisions of the district plan. But he made no special effort on its behalf.

18. Among those supporting the Mundt-Coudert bill in 1955 Senate hearings was Leander H. Perez, district attorney of Plaquemines–St. Bernard District, La., one of the nation's foremost white supremacy advocates. U.S. Senate, Committee on the Judiciary, *Hearings, Nomination and Election of President and Vice President*, 84th Congress, 1st Session, 1955, p. 122. But from time to time, the district system was advocated by men of more moderate political philosophy, including Senators Thruston B. Morton of Kentucky and Hugh Scott of Pennsylvania.

19. *Congressional Record*, 1956, pp. 5352–53.

20. *Ibid.*, pp. 5150, 5253, 5539–40, 5548.

21. *Ibid.*, p. 5555.

22. U.S. Senate, Committee on the Judiciary, Subcommittee on Constitutional Amendments, *Hearings, Nomination and Election of President and Vice President and Qualifications for Voting*, 87th Congress, 1st Session, 1961, pp. 52, 172, 332–33. Cited hereafter as 1961 Senate *Hearings*.

23. *Ibid.*, pp. 519, 676.

24. *The Electoral College*, a memorandum (Washington, 1961).

25. Letter to James Monroe, Jan. 12, 1800, cited by Lucius Wilmerding, *The Electoral College* (New Brunswick, N.J., 1958), p. 145. Wilmerding disagrees with Jefferson's contention, however, claiming that the disfranchised votes for both candidates would more likely balance out on a multidistrict system than when the states are the smallest unit.

26. District system vote calculations by Congressional Quarterly Service. For comparison with the disparity between the popular and electoral vote under the existing unit vote system, see Appendix D. For actual district system results, see Appendix M.

27. Testimony of Feb. 28, 1966.

28. Ames, *op. cit.*, pp. 95–96.

29. Cited by Ames, *op. cit.*, p. 97.

30. The proportional vote for each state is determined by multiplying the number of popular votes a candidate has received by the state's electoral vote allotment and then dividing the sum derived by the total popular vote of the state. Fractional votes of less than one-thousandth are disregarded. An example, showing the proportional division of Alaska's three electoral votes in the election of 1960:

> For Nixon: 30,953 votes; for Kennedy: 29,809 votes; total: 60,762.
> Nixon proportion: 30,953 × 3 electoral votes = 92,859; 92,859 divided by total popular vote of 60,762 = 1.5282.
> Kennedy proportion: 29,809 × 3 electoral votes = 89,427; 89,427 divided by total popular vote of 60,762 = 1.4717.
> With fractions of less than one-thousandth disregarded, the electoral vote of the state is thus Nixon 1.528; Kennedy 1.471.

31. Cited by Dougherty, *op. cit.*, pp. 352–53.

32. *Ibid.*, pp. 357–58.

33. The proposal was defeated. See p. 178.

34. *Congressional Record*, 1950, p. 884. To allay fears that splinter parties might be encouraged, the Senate accepted an amendment by Scott Lucas of Illinois to require that a candidate receive at least 40 percent of the proportionalized electoral vote to be elected, with the choice of a President going to a joint session of Congress, in which each Senator and Representative would have a single vote, when 40 percent was not achieved.

35. *Congressional Record*, 1950, pp. 1064–65.

36. *Ibid.*, p. 1269.

37. *Ibid.*, p. 886.

38. *Ibid.*, p. 1066.

39. Wright Patman, "Should the United States Abolish the Electoral College? No!," *Rotarian*, July 1949.

40. *Congressional Record*, 1950, p. 886.

41. *Ibid.*, p. 880. Lodge personally favored the direct vote but felt it could not pass because of small-state opposition. See pp. 184–85.

42. *Congressional Record*, 1950, p. 1278; individual votes also recorded in *Congress and the Nation* (Congressional Quarterly Service, Washington, 1965), p. 51a.

43. *Congressional Record*, 1950, p. 10416.

44. *Ibid.*, p. 10417.

45. *Ibid.*, p. 10425.

46. *Ibid.*, p. 10427; *Congress and the Nation*, p. 54a.

47. U.S. House, Committee on the Judiciary, *Hearings, Amending the Constitution With Respect to Election of President and Vice President*, 82nd Congress, 1st Session, 1951, pp. 305–8. Cited hereafter as 1951 House *Hearings*.

48. 1951 House *Hearings*, pp. 308–10.

49. For debate relevant to the district system portion of the Daniel substitute, see pp. 132–34.

50. Figures based on a study by Dr. Ruth Silva of Pennsylvania State University. The Republican electoral vote percentage would have lagged behind the Republican popular vote percentage by percentage point gaps ranging from −.004 in 1904 to −5.316 in 1924. *Congressional Record*, 1956, p. 5564.

51. *Congressional Record*, 1956, p. 5564. Douglas produced figures to show that in the 1952 Presidential election the voting turnout—measured in the percentage of voting-age citizens actually casting ballots for President—was 39.1 percent in the 11 states of the Deep South, 66.4 percent in five border states, and 70.2 percent in the remaining 32 Northern states. *Congressional Record*, 1956, p. 5550.

52. The amendment provided for election of the President in a joint session of Congress, with each member casting a single vote, in cases where the requisite percentage was not achieved. For amendment text, see *Congressional Record*, 1956, pp. 5644–45.

53. *Ibid.*, 1956, pp. 5249–50, 5555, 5558.

54. *Ibid.*, p. 5159.

55. *Ibid.*, p. 5156.

56. *Ibid.*, pp. 5673–74; *Congressional Quarterly Almanac,* 1956, p. 161.

57. 1961 Senate *Hearings,* pp. 169, 466.

58. *Ibid.*, pp. 253–54, 365.

59. Kefauver, "The Electoral College: Old Reforms Take on a New Look," *Law and Contemporary Problems,* Spring 1962, p. 203.

60. A significant distinction between the two kinds of minor or splinter parties was made by Prof. Allan P. Sindler of Duke University in a 1962 essay, "Presidential Election Methods and Urban-Ethnic Interests," *Law and Contemporary Problems,* Spring 1962, pp. 221–24. The "guarantee" of electoral votes under a proportional system would offer no new inducement, he said, to "ideologically-oriented third parties outside the mainstream of national power politics, such as Vegetarians, Socialist Workers, Single Taxers, etc." The real problem, he suggested, was in "blackmail" factional defection such as the 1948 Progressive and Dixiecrat movements, which constituted "a punitive flank attack, from opposite ideological directions, on the Democratic party." Sindler suggested that the existing unit vote system "can be exploited, and in that sense, invites exploitation, by *ad hoc,* transitory third-party activity" of the latter type.

61. 1961 Senate *Hearings,* pp. 509–10.

62. The 1960 figures are based on the arbitrary division of the Democratic electoral vote in Alabama, which was split between pledged and unpledged electors.

63. Testimony of Feb. 28, 1966.

64. Testimony of March 8, 1966.

65. Letter from Jefferson to Gallatin, Sept. 18, 1801, in Jefferson, *Works,* IX, p. 305, cited by Wilmerding, *op. cit.*, p. 170.

66. Ames, *op. cit.*, pp. 94–95.

67. *Ibid.*, pp. 94, 99.

68. House *Journal,* 42nd Congress, 1st Session, pp. 14–15.

69. Norris frequently spoke of the need to abolish the electoral college, but by that he meant simply instituting the automatic system. His words, however, could be used in the direct popular vote cause today. In 1923, he said, "No reason can be given why an independent people, capable of self-government, should not have the right to vote directly for the chief magistrate, who has more power than any other official in our government." Norris said the electoral college was "unnecessary, cumbersome and confusing" and could take from the voter "the right to effectively express his will." *Congressional Record,* 1923, p. 3506.

70. *Ibid.*, 1934, pp. 8944–45, 9127. On reconsideration the day after its initial defeat, the Norris amendment was again defeated, this time 52–29.

71. *Ibid.*, 1950, pp. 1277–78.

72. *Ibid.*, 1956, p. 5574.

73. The Kennedy amendment provided for contingent election by joint session of Congress, with each member having a single vote and a plurality sufficient

to elect, if no candidate won an electoral college majority. Congress would have to elect one of the top three electoral vote winners. For text, see 1961 Senate *Hearings,* pp. 371–72.

74. 1961 Senate *Hearings,* pp. 258–59, 337, 363.
75. *C.Q. Weekly Report,* Feb. 5, 1965, pp. 171, 211.
76. *Ibid.,* Jan. 28, 1966, p. 307; March 11, 1966, pp. 557–58; March 18, 1966, p. 603.
77. Testimony of Donald H. Scott, chairman of the Chamber Study Group on Electoral College Reform, March 9, 1966.
78. *Congressional Record,* 1966, p. 3764 (daily ed.).
79. Technically, Lacock's motion was to recommit the district amendment with instructions to the Senate committee to report an amendment providing for direct election of the President and Vice President by the eligible voters of each state. Before the vote, Lacock modified his motion to require only a committee investigation of the direct vote. *Annals of Congress,* XXIX, p. 220.
80. *Ibid.,* pp. 223–26.
81. House *Journal,* Jan. 3, 1826, p. 115.
82. Ames, *op. cit.,* p. 88.
83. House *Journal,* Dec. 8, 1829, p. 15.
84. In 1838 and 1842, however, Representative Joseph R. Underwood of Kentucky suggested that the state legislatures nominate Presidential candidates, with the final choice in a direct national election. Ames, *op. cit.,* p. 99.
85. Ames, *op. cit.,* pp. 88–89; Dougherty, *op. cit.,* pp. 342–44.
86. *Congressional Record,* 1956, pp. 5137–38.
87. *Ibid.,* 1950, p. 1273.
88. *Ibid.,* pp. 1269–70. Taft had reservations about giving up the state unit vote system, however, and said he would not favor direct vote "unless such a course seemed to be the only solution."
89. *Congressional Record,* 1953, p. 1726.
90. *Ibid.,* 1950, p. 5138.
91. *Ibid.,* 1947, p. 1962.
92. *Ibid.,* 1950, pp. 1276–77.
93. *Ibid.,* 1956, pp. 5159, 5245, 5637, 5657; *Congressional Quarterly Almanac,* 1956, p. 161.
94. *Congressional Record,* 1956, p. 5162.
95. 1961 Senate *Hearings,* pp. 31, 501.
96. *Ibid.,* p. 140, 326, 330.
97. *Ibid.,* p. 114.
98. *Congressional Record,* 1961, p. 350.
99. 1961 Senate *Hearings,* p. 425. A similar provision was included in a direct vote amendment introduced by Senator Everett McKinley Dirksen in 1967, with the assistance of the American Bar Association. See text, Appendix L. For fuller discussion of procedures in calling state ratifying conventions, see 1961 Senate *Hearings,* p. 939.
100. *C.Q. Weekly Report,* May 20, 1966, p. 1042.
101. *Ibid.*
102. *Ibid.,* Aug. 19, 1966, pp. 1811–15.

103. *Ibid.*, Jan. 6, 1967, p. 28.

104. For complete state-by-state table, see *ibid.*, Dec. 16, 1966, p. 3030.

105. Ames, *op. cit.*, pp. 100–101; cited by Charles A. O'Neil, *The American Electoral System* (New York, 1887), pp. 257–58.

106. Ames, *op. cit.*, p. 101.

107. *Ibid.*, p. 103.

108. *Ibid.*, p. 104.

109. *Ibid.*, p. 102.

110. *Ibid.*, p. 100.

111. *Ibid.*, pp. 105, 234–35.

112. *Congressional Record*, 1956, p. 5365. For full discussion, see Ralph M. Goldman, "Hubert Humphrey's S.J. 152: A New Proposal for Electoral College Reform," *Midwest Journal of Political Science*, Feb. 1958, p. 89.

113. *C.Q. Weekly Report*, Feb. 17, 1961, p. 288.

114. Ames, *op. cit.*, pp. 105–11.

115. Farrand, *op. cit.*, III, pp. 166–67.

7 The Right to Vote in America

"THAT THE QUALIFIED VOTERS OF THE STATES OUGHT TO POSSESS THE REAL, as well as the nominal right, to elect the President and Vice President of the United States," Thomas Hart Benton's Select Committee reported to the Senate in 1826, "is a proposition deductible from the rights of man, the nature of the Federal Government, and the proper distribution of its powers. The nature of this government is *free* and *representative*. This is a government of the *people*."[1] But while this ideal appears early in our history—indeed, it derives from the Declaration of Independence, with its clear statement that government must rest on the consent of the governed—the whole course of American history has been occupied with the long and often arduous task of assuring the right to vote to every American. Today the United States *is* approaching universal suffrage, so that every adult American, regardless of wealth, race or residence, will be able to vote, and to have his vote counted equally and fairly. Suddenly, with the civil rights acts of the last decade, the death of the poll tax and the voting decisions of the courts, it is upon us. It is the basic political fact of our times. And it is reflected in every American political institution—except the way we elect our President.

The historical development of the right to vote deserves our attention, for it illustrates how far we have come from the day when an electoral college was reasonable, if not fully justified, as a mechanism to let the privileged few who were allowed to vote in various states make the decision on the President for all the rest of us.

The Expanding Suffrage

The number of Americans who enjoy the privilege to vote and the percentage of voting-age Americans who actually cast their ballots have increased dramatically over the course of American history. National figures showing the number of actual registrants are almost impossible to obtain, since many states have failed to keep records (especially in the early years), and even today many fail to make statewide counts, or have no registration system at all. The best guide is the total vote cast for President over the years. Scattered returns available from the first few Presidential elections show that a minuscule percentage of the adult population actually cast ballots for Presidential electors. In 1804, for instance, a total of 54,393 Presidential elector ballots were cast in Massachusetts out of a total state population (as of 1800) of 422,845. The total Pennsylvania vote in the same year was 23,320 from a population of 602,365, New Jersey's vote was 13,139 from a population of 211,149, and Ohio's 2,453 from a population of 45,365.

The chart below shows the growth of the actual national vote for President from 1824—the year for which the first comprehensive national totals are available—up to the present day. In each instance the vote is shown as a percentage of the total adult population in that year:

Year	Total Adult Population	Total Presidential Vote	Percent Voting
1824	3,964,000*	363,017	9
1840	7,381,000*	2,412,698	33
1860	14,676,000*	4,692,710	32
1880	25,012,000*	9,219,467	37
1900	40,753,000*	13,974,188	35
1920	60,581,000	26,768,613	44
1940	83,512,000	49,900,418	60
1960	107,949,000	69,156,522	64

* Population figures for 1824 through 1900 are based on general estimates from early Census figures, most of which gave no hard count of the population 21 or over. Population shown for 1824 actually based on 1820 Census.

The major advances in the size of the national suffrage can be related to the steady easing of restrictive requirements for voting over American history—from the abolition of early property and tax-paying qualifications to the reforms effected by civil rights legislation in our own day.

PROPERTY RESTRICTIONS IN EARLY AMERICA. Only a small percentage of the people voted in America before the adoption of the Constitution —a narrow voting base attributable both to restrictive suffrage laws and an underdeveloped sense of public participation. Indeed, the suffrage laws of the time appear incredibly narrow on first inspection. The most widely employed qualification for voting was the ownership of a freehold estate in land. This meant that a person had to have absolute ownership of a specified amount of land, often with stipulations of its size or income yield. The leasing of land did not qualify a person to vote, though leasing was common at the time.[2] Connecticut provided that a freehold in land must produce an annual income of at least 40 shillings; in Massachusetts it was 60 shillings. In Maryland the freehold had to be 50 acres regardless of income yield. In Delaware it had to be "well settled"—that is to say, with an occupied house and at least 12 acres cleared and improved.[3] The philosophy behind these restrictions was reflected by this statement of a Pennsylvanian in 1775: "A civil society or state is a number of proprietors of land within certain limits, united by compact of mutual agreement, for making laws and appointing persons to execute these laws for their common benefit."[4]

In some states, however, persons could hold other types of property to qualify to vote. In Connecticut personal property assessed for tax purposes at 40 pounds was sufficient, in Maryland property valued at 30 pounds, in Massachusetts "any estate of the value of 60 pounds." In four states there was no freehold requirement but a voter had to have a certain net worth. In New Jersey a man simply had to be "worth 50 pounds . . . clear estate"; in Pennsylvania and New Hampshire he had to pay poll taxes or other public taxes; in Georgia he had to own ten pounds of value in any taxable property or simply be "of any mechanic trade." The latter provision, more liberal than any other of the time, was dropped in 1789. The only state that adopted a universal manhood suffrage standard before the adoption of the Constitution was Vermont, when it declared its independence of New York in 1777. During the Colonial period, many areas had also imposed religious qualifications on voting, but most of these had been dropped by the time of the Revolution. New York was one of the last, dropping in 1777 the bar on voting imposed on Jews and Catholics. Rhode Island, however, did not permit Jews to vote until 1842.[5]

Despite the seeming stringency of the suffrage laws, however, it appears that in the year leading up to ratification of the Constitution, more than half the free adult males could find a way to vote if they had the interest in doing so. One factor was the easy availability of land in the frontier-like conditions of the Eastern seaboard. Another was the looseness with which the laws were actually applied. Many unqualified persons could vote if they would cast their ballots as election officials or other partisans told them to. In many colonies the prevailing custom was to allow all adult males, if they were known to the community and in any degree respected or liked, to vote. The secret ballot, as we know it today, was virtually unknown, and ruling groups apparently maintained enough control of the whole voting process to make sure no untoward results stemmed from voting. One historian observes that "officials everywhere were variously accused of admitting illegal voters to the polls, denying qualified persons the right to vote, suppressing legal votes in the count, stuffing ballot boxes (as in Pennsylvania), winking at intimidations of electors, opening and closing the polls capriciously, and dropping legal votes to the floor which were later burned with the general debris of electoral activities."[6]

Beyond legal restrictions and polling place irregularities, the size of the vote was limited by sheer voter indifference. The "multitude," stated Ezra Stiles, the Connecticut minister, "will not leave the plow to have a Governor to their taste."[7] Citizens were often discouraged from participating in elections by the many miles that lay between them and the polling place. In New Jersey a voter could conceivably live 25 miles from the polls; the extreme was in South Carolina, where the failure of the Assembly to subdivide large parishes forced some voters to travel 150 miles or more.

The multiplicity of state laws and actual practices makes it difficult to estimate how many Americans really could exercise the franchise before the Constitution was adopted. We do know that women were generally excluded from voting, and that the Negro slaves (well over 600,000) and indentured servants (some 300,000 at the end of the Revolutionary War) were barred from the ballot box. One authority suggests that of the 2,000,000-odd free Americans of all ages immediately after the Revolution, perhaps no more than 120,000 could meet the voting qualifications of their states.[8] Even if loose application of the laws made the real figure substantially larger, the base of popular suffrage was minuscule by modern-day standards.

The Revolutionary period brought the first great wave of interest in suffrage reform in U.S. history. Seeking to justify their break with Great Britain, the colonists turned to the philosophies of natural rights expounded by John Locke and other European writers. The expansive assertion of the Declaration of Independence that "all men are created equal" and "endowed by their Creator with certain unalienable rights" did not trigger an immediate rush to sweep away all suffrage restrictions; indeed, suffrage reform was advanced in a clear-cut fashion by only six states in the Revolutionary period, and in Massachusetts the requirements were actually stiffened. But the seeds of a revolutionary idea had been sown: that voting is not a privilege granted by society to those with the greatest stake, measured by their property holdings, but rather that it is a basic right of a free people.[9]

The Constitutional Convention of 1787 considered but drew back from imposing any national voting qualifications, both because the delegates differed sharply among themselves and because the states would have been loath to ratify a Constitution altering their own suffrage statutes (for an account of debates on suffrage, see pages 37–39, above). The only standard seriously advanced at the Convention was to limit the franchise to freeholders—a necessary defense, as one delegate said, "against those multitudes without property and without principle, with which our country like all others, will in time abound."[10] The nation for which the Constitution was written contained two classes that "counted politically"—those described by James Madison as the "rich and well-born" and the "body of sober and steady people."[11] Perhaps 20 percent of the American people in 1787, it has been estimated, "were mired in a swamp of much poverty and little hope, and thus were victims of a depressing political apathy."

The only voting right granted the people in the Constitution was in its provision that members of the U.S. House would be chosen by the same voters as those who selected the most numerous branch of each state legislature. There was no requirement for popular voting for U.S. Senators, who were to be chosen by the legislatures, or for Presidential electors. To the states was left the decision of who could vote and who could not.

THE STRUGGLE FOR BROADENED SUFFRAGE UP TO THE CIVIL WAR. The early years of the Republic witnessed a gradual erosion of property

qualifications for voting, succeeded either by milder taxpaying requirements or state constitutional provisions that amounted to universal
manhood suffrage. By 1812 both property and taxpaying qualifications
had been erased in Vermont, Maryland, South Carolina, Georgia and
New Hampshire. Kentucky joined the Union in 1792 with a constitution giving the suffrage to all males who had lived in the state for two
years and in a county for one year. Tennessee was the last state to enter
the Union with a real-property requirement, in 1796. Along the Eastern
seaboard, a freehold qualification survived only in Rhode Island and
Virginia for all state elections, and in New York and North Carolina
for some but not all elections. New York continued up to 1821 under
her "balanced" constitution of 1777, allowing men to vote for the
Assembly if they were 20-pound freeholders or 40-shilling renters, but
restricting the vote for the state Senate and Governor to men possess-
ing freeholds worth 100 pounds or more. In 1821 a constitutional
convention in New York extended the franchise to all adult males who
were taxpayers or militiamen, and universal adult suffrage was granted
in an amendment to the state constitution approved in 1826. Massachusetts' freehold requirement survived to 1821, when it was replaced
by a taxpaying qualification. Virginia remained adamant up to 1850 in
requiring that voters possess a stipulated amount of real estate.[12]
Commenting on the situation in Virginia, the *National Advocate* of
New York editorialized in 1825: "That nursery of everything that is
great, the cradle of WASHINGTON himself, has not even a child to offer
to the republic on the side of free suffrage."[13]

Many factors worked toward the broadening of the franchise in the
early 19th century. The emerging political parties were hungry for
votes and sought to broaden the voting base to expand their own
power. More citizens pressed for the vote as interest mounted in
political battles, such as those between seaboard businessmen and
inland farmers. Indignant that many of their number were refused the
ballot, veterans of the War of 1812 joined the battle for manhood
suffrage in their state legislatures and conventions. The Western states,
seeking labor, could use the offer of widened suffrage as inducement.
The Panic of 1819 is said to have accentuated class antagonisms and
increased the pressure for widened voting privileges. Many farmers
had mortgages on their land and found themselves disfranchised in
states with a property test. And in the industrial states of the East, a
growing class of propertyless workers began to press for the franchise.
Of the nine states that entered the Union in the first quarter of the

century, none set up a property qualification and only three—Ohio, Louisiana and Mississippi—chose to establish taxpaying qualifications. After 1817 no new state admitted to the Union required any form of "material interest" in its voters.[14]

With the rise of Jacksonian Democracy in the 1820s, increased pressure was exerted by the landless and debtors to win the right to vote in the states where it was still denied them. According to one writer, the working definition dividing liberals from conservatives in the early 19th century was their "belief or disbelief in universal suffrage, population election of government officials and popular nomination of candidates 'fresh from the people.' "[15] These basic issues were spelled out nowhere so clearly as in the conventions called during the decade to revise the constitutions of Virginia, Massachusetts and New York. The Virginia convention was confronted with petitions of non-freeholders asking to be admitted to the suffrage, while Massachusetts and New York considered changes in the provisions of their original constitutions, which had made the state senates "the guardian of property" or, as one Bay State citizen put it, "the rich man's citadel."[16]

Arguing against an extension of the suffrage to the propertyless in Virginia, Judge Abel P. Upshur said that society consists of persons and property, both of which must be defended, but that the men of property have twice as great a stake in the society—not only their persons but their property as well—and therefore deserve a greater voice in determining its course. Property should be "a leading principle in our Constitution," he said; if a wider franchise is admitted, then the untrustworthy majority will trample the rights of the propertied minority. John Randolph of Roanoke announced incredulously that it was "the first time in my life, that I ever heard of a government which was to divorce property from power." If "King Numbers" should be enthroned, then there would be dire danger "to the great tobacco-growing and slave-holding interest, and to every other interest on this side of the Ridge." It would be foolhardy, he said, to tamper with a constitution "which has shielded us for more than half a century."[17]

Chief Justice John Marshall took it upon himself to argue the case of the non-freeholders seeking the vote in Virginia. "Comprising a very large part, probably a majority of male citizens of mature age," said Marshall, the non-freeholders "have been passed by, like aliens or slaves, as if destitute of interest, or unworthy of a voice, in measures involving their future political destiny." As a result, he said, the freeholders, as "a favored class," had "seized the sovereign authority." Mere land-holding, said Marshall, does not produce virtue and intelligence: "Attachment to property, often a sordid sentiment, is not to be confounded with the sacred flame of patriotism." If the non-freeholders be "so ignorant, so depraved," then why are they called to arms in time of danger? "The muster rolls have undergone no scrutiny, no comparison with the land books, with a view to expunge those who have been struck from the ranks of freemen. If the landless citizens have been ignominiously driven from the polls, in time of peace, they have at least been generously summoned, in war, to the battlefield," Marshall declared. Another Virginia delegate, John R. Cooke, argued that the opponents of widened suffrage were working on "the assumption that men are, by nature, robbers." For himself, Cooke found that man "is an *affectionate,* a *social,* a *patriotic,* a *conscientious* and a *religious* creature," and that little danger existed in giving him the right to control the destiny of his state.[18]

In New York the issue was whether the high land-owning requirements, especially for the gubernatorial and state Senate elections, should be expunged. Chancellor James Kent argued that the Senate "should continue, as heretofore, the representative of the landed interest, and exempted from the control of universal suffrage." The agricultural interests, he said, were "the foundation of national wealth and power" and needed special recognition. "The tendency to universal suffrage," Kent warned, "is to jeopardize the rights of property, and the principles of liberty. . . . Universal suffrage once granted, is granted forever, and never can be recalled. There is no retrograde step in the rear of democracy."[19]

The most powerful rebuttal to Kent came from delegate David Buel, Jr., who discerned a basic difference between Europe and America. In Europe, he said, "it is the policy of the aristocracy to keep the land in few hands," so that the great bulk of the population remains impoverished. The inevitable result is that "the poor envy and hate the rich, and mobs and insurrections sometimes render property insecure." But in America, Buel argued, the laws of descent were causing the steady division of the great landed estates, so that property was inevitably moving into "the hands of the many." Not only would the common ownership of property maintain a stable society in America, but the establishment of common schools and the diffusion of education will be "sure means of establishing these pillars of freedom." He could not imagine the day in America when the poor would be so numerous that they would rise up like the Jacobins of France. "Our community," said Buel, "is an association of persons—of human beings —not a partnership founded on property. . . . Property is only one of the incidental rights of a person who possesses it; and, as such, it must be made secure; but it does not follow, that it must therefore be represented specifically in any branch of the government."[20]

The forces of widened suffrage won only partial victories in the immediate context of the state conventions where they spoke. But their arguments won over the nation, as Andrew Jackson's overwhelming Presidential victories of 1828 and 1832 would amply demonstrate. By the 1840s Rhode Island and Virginia were the only states where the franchise, for all intents and purposes, was not granted to all the adult white males. In Rhode Island the tensions between the dominant landowning groups and the growing numbers of disfranchised factory workers exploded in an actual armed rebellion in 1842. It was led by Thomas W. Dorr, the son of a wealthy China trader who championed the cause of the urban poor. Dorr's rebellion was easily quashed, but a somewhat milder combined freehold-taxpayer requirement was subsequently instituted. Until 1887 Rhode Island maintained a freehold test for the foreign-born, and other restrictions on the franchise existed into the 20th century. Virginia finally achieved universal manhood suffrage except for Negroes in 1851. By the 1850s there was almost complete suffrage for adult white males in America. Indeed, it became a vote-getting tactic for politicians to attack their opponents for having opposed manhood suffrage at any time in their careers.[21]

There were, of course, still some restrictions on voting by adult males. By one device or another, most states managed to exclude paupers, transients and the mentally ill. As immigration rose, Connecticut in 1855 added a provision to its constitution requiring prospective voters to be able to read the constitution or statutes. In 1857 Massachusetts amended its constitution by requiring that all voters be able to read the constitution in the English language and write their names. Massachusetts raised the bars against voting by Irish Catholic immigrants even higher in 1859, requiring that former aliens remain in the state for two years after naturalization before they could vote.[22]

THE VOTE FOR NEGROES. Negro slaves were never allowed to vote, and the few free Negroes found it difficult to exercise the franchise. Between 1792 and 1838, the constitutions of Delaware, Kentucky, Maryland, Connecticut, New Jersey, Virginia, Tennessee, North Carolina and Pennsylvania were altered to exclude Negroes from voting. The Revolutionary-era constitutions of Georgia and South Carolina had already contained explicit provisions limiting suffrage to "white males." All of the states entering the Union between 1800 and the eve of the Civil War, with the sole exception of Maine, denied the ballot to Negroes. New York and the New England states had no specific prohibition on Negro voting, but New York imposed special property-owning and taxpaying qualifications on would-be Negro voters.[23]

By his issuance of the Emancipation Proclamation in 1863, President Abraham Lincoln raised the Civil War to the level of a moral crusade to end Negro slavery. But even with the Northern victory and peace, the American Negro was not assured the right to vote. Indeed, under President Andrew Johnson's conciliatory first plan for the Confederate states, there were no guarantees for basic liberties of Negroes, let alone the right to vote. During 1865 and 1866 conventions or legislative sessions were held in Alabama, Arkansas, Georgia, Florida, Louisiana, North Carolina, South Carolina, Tennessee, Texas and Virginia. Not one of these ten states extended to Negroes the right to vote. Instead, the infamous "Black Codes," severely restricting the Negro's rights to employment and movement, were enacted. The reaction of the radical Republicans in Congress, who were committed to Negro enfranchisement, was almost immediate. The first Civil Rights Act, declaring all persons born in the United States to be citizens, was passed in 1866.[24]

President Johnson issued a proclamation on April 2, 1866, declaring the rebellion at an end, but Congress refused to recognize the credentials of the Southern representatives and said that it would determine when a state should be admitted. The 14th Amendment, a great landmark in assuring basic rights to all Americans, was proposed by Congress on June 13, 1866. It declared in its first section that "all persons born or naturalized in the United States and subject to the jurisdiction thereof, are citizens of the United States and of the state wherein they reside. No state shall make or enforce any law which shall abridge the privileges or immunities of citizens of the United States; nor shall any state deprive any person of life, liberty, or property, without due process of law; nor deny to any person within its jurisdiction the equal protection of the laws." Tennessee ratified the proposed amendment and was readmitted on July 24, 1866, but the other ten former Confederate states rejected the offer to be readmitted upon ratification of the amendment. The basic Reconstruction statute, enacted early in 1867, declared that no governments were in existence in these states, divided the South into five military districts and required of each state, before it could send Senators and Representatives to Congress, that it meet three conditions: first, that Negroes be admitted to suffrage at elections for delegates to constitutional conventions; second, that the new constitutions provide for permanent Negro suffrage; and third, that each of the states ratify the 14th Amendment. Negroes and radical Republicans soon controlled Southern elections, aided by radical Governors in command of Negro militia and carpetbaggers in control of state treasuries.[25]

By July 1868, the required three-quarters of the states had ratified the 14th Amendment and it became part of the Constitution—the first of a great chain of amendments widening the right to vote that would continue to our own day. It was supplemented by the 15th Amendment, ratified in 1870, which provided in its key clause that "the right of citizens of the United States to vote shall not be denied or abridged by the United States or by any state on account of race, color or previous condition of servitude." The Southern states agreed to this amendment as well, in large part because of the presence of Northern troops and large numbers of Negroes in the new Southern legislatures. All the Southern states were readmitted to the Union by 1870. The Reconstruction era stretched on to 1877, when the last federal troops were withdrawn—in part, through the agreements made to secure Southern acquiescence on the accession of Rutherford B. Hayes to the Presidency after the disputed electoral vote count of that year.

The excesses of Reconstruction government in the South had undercut much of the earlier Northern sympathy for the plight of the Southern Negro, however, and there was little public opposition when the U.S. Supreme Court handed down a series of decisions that effectively emasculated the 14th and 15th Amendments and the statutes passed to put them into effect. The Court found, for instance, that the 15th Amendment applied only to the states and their agents and not to private individuals who might seek to prevent equal voting by all races. All the Southern states then had to do to exclude Negroes was to enact statutes that were not discriminatory in their actual wording, regardless of their likely effect.[26]

The moderately conservative Southern leadership that emerged in 1877 was replaced before long by a faction willing to use ingenious and sometimes violent methods to prevent Negroes from voting. As one historian has summarized the practices of the era: "The activities

of the Ku-Klux [Klan] have been immortalized in book and play. Less
dramatic were the practices of brute violence and intimidation, clever
manipulation of ballots and ballot boxes, the deliberate theft of ballot
boxes, false counting of votes, repeating, the use of 'tissue' ballots,
illegal arrests the day before election, and the sudden removing of the
polls."[27]

But Negroes still had the legal right to vote, and controlled Negro
votes played a key role in the struggles during the 1870s and 1880s
between the Southern Democratic party and its opposition, centered in
the Southern Farmers Alliance and the Populist party. Eventually, the
white factions, although they were bitterly at odds with each other,
determined to exclude the Negro from voting altogether. The Jim
Crow statutes, beginning with Florida's in 1889, employed a number
of discriminatory devices: the poll tax, increased residence requirements, literacy tests and the famed "grandfather clauses," which
qualified as voters those who could vote in 1867 or their descendants.
All the 11 states of the old Confederacy adopted variations of these
statutes between 1889 and 1902.[28]

The intent of these statutes was made abundantly clear on many
occasions. At the close of the 1898 Louisiana constitutional convention,
which provided for poll taxes, a property test as an alternative, plus
the infamous "grandfather clause," the convention president stated:
"We have not drafted the exact constitution that we should like to
have drafted; otherwise we should have inscribed in it, if I know the
popular sentiment of this state, universal white manhood suffrage, and
the exclusion from the suffrage of every man with a trace of African
blood in his veins. . . . What care I whether the test we have put be a
new one or an old one? . . . Doesn't it meet the case? Doesn't it let
the white man vote, and doesn't it stop the Negro from voting, and
isn't that what we came here for? (Applause.)"[29] The Louisiana
registration figures show just how successful the constitution writers
were. In 1896, the election immediately preceding the Louisiana
convention, there were 164,088 white and 130,344 Negro registrants.
For the next Presidential election, when the new restrictive amendments went into effect, there were 40,000 fewer whites registered while
Negro registration fell by 125,000, to a total of 5,320 Negroes registered. Between then and the 1930s, the number of Negroes registered
in any election in Louisiana rarely exceeded 2,000.

From the last decades of the 19th century down to the 1940s, the
Democratic party remained absolutely dominant in the states of the

Confederacy. The Republicans had been associated with Reconstruction and the bid to achieve Negro suffrage, and their party declined to insignificant numbers or actually disappeared in many Southern localities. With rare exceptions, victory in the Democratic primary in the South was tantamount to election. This, in turn, opened an additional way to prevent Negroes from voting. Most states delegated the running of primaries entirely to the individual party, giving it also the power to determine who would be eligible to vote. Democratic party leaders predictably decided that Negroes could not be Democrats and excluded them from participation in the primary. Even if Negroes could still vote in the general election, the ballot meant little, since the decision had already been made in the primary. In reality, most Southern Negroes, if they voted at all, voted Republican until the New Deal in the 1930s.

The white primary was challenged on constitutional grounds, and the Supreme Court in 1927 ruled unconstitutional a state law which specifically excluded Negroes from the Democratic party primary.[30] The decision was based not on the 15th Amendment but on the provisions of the 14th Amendment requiring states to give all their citizens equal protection of the laws. The next Southern stratagem was to remove all mention of racial qualifications from the actual state law but still leave the parties free to determine who could participate in their primaries. In 1935 the Supreme Court held that a white primary that resulted from the action of a political party, rather than the state government, was legal.[31] Just nine years later, however, the Court reversed itself and finally outlawed the white primary altogether. In this 1944 decision the Justices held that no matter what part the political party played, by holding a primary it was acting in conformance with state laws and under the state's protection, so that ultimately the white primary rested upon state action.[32] For a while, some of the Southern Democratic parties sought to evade the reasoning of the 1944 decision but gradually gave way and allowed registered Negroes to participate in their primaries. In the meantime, the "grandfather clause," intended to disfranchise Negroes while sparing illiterate whites, was struck down by the Supreme Court in 1915.[33]

The poll tax came under increasingly heavy criticism as a device to restrict voting in general and Negro voting in particular. Almost invariably, the states with poll taxes were those with the lowest voting participation. North Carolina dropped its poll tax in 1920, followed by Louisiana in 1934, Florida in 1937, South Carolina in 1951, Tennessee in 1953 and Arkansas in 1964. Congressional statutes to outlaw poll taxes were passed five times by the U.S. House between 1942 and 1949 but died each time in the Senate as a result of actual or threatened filibusters. Finally, a constitutional amendment barring the poll tax in all federal elections was submitted to the states by Congress in 1962 and ratified in 1964.[34] A Mississippi Negro, testifying before the House Judiciary Committee in 1962, said that in his state the poll tax was used to intimidate Negroes, who had to pay it at the sheriff's office, where they were sometimes warned not to pay. Along with Mississippi, the other states who still had a general poll tax when the poll tax prohibition became the 24th Amendment to the Constitution in 1964 were Alabama, Arkansas, Texas and Virginia. The constitutional amendment, however, still left the states free to impose the poll tax in elections for state and local officials. Moving to plug the loophole, Congress included in the 1965 Voting Rights Act a declaration that poll taxes denied or abridged the right to vote and instructed the Attorney General to start legal proceedings to bar such taxes under the authority of the 14th and 15th Amendments. In the decisive case, *Harper v. Virginia State Board of Elections,* the Supreme Court ruled in March 1966 that the poll tax violated the equal protection clause of the 14th Amendment and was therefore illegal.[35] It seemed unlikely that the states would ever again be able to impose any kind of economic condition for exercise of the franchise.

The abolition of the poll tax in fact constituted only one aspect of a massive federal effort to assure the right to vote to Negroes and other minority groups throughout the United States. The effort had begun in 1939 with the establishment by Attorney General Frank Murphy of a Civil Rights Section in the Justice Department. President Truman in 1948 became the first President to seek the full entry of the federal government in the civil rights field with a comprehensive program of legislation based on the recommendations of his advisory Committee on Civil Rights. The most significant recommendation in the voting-rights field was poll-tax abolition. No action was taken on the Truman proposals, however, and it was not until 1957 that the first Civil Rights Act of the century was passed. This measure, recommended by President Eisenhower, sought to guarantee all citizens their right to vote by giving the Attorney General the power to seek court injunctions against obstruction or deprivation of voting rights. The legislation spoke specifically of "the right to vote . . . for any candidate for the office of President." It also created an executive Commission on

Civil Rights. Acting partially on the comprehensive recommendations of this new commission, Congress in 1960 enacted another Civil Rights Act, setting up procedures by which federal voting referees could be appointed to register Negroes in areas where a pattern or practice of voting discrimination had been established. In 1963, massive Negro demonstrations for widened rights prompted the Administration of President Kennedy to submit comprehensive civil rights legislation to Congress. A number of refinements of the previous voting-rights statutes were included in the resulting legislation, the Civil Rights Act of 1964.[36]

Even with the new legislation, however, state and local officials could still find ways to prevent Negroes from voting. Stiff literacy tests, hostile registrars, prolonged court litigation on challenges, sometimes stretching beyond election day—all continued to restrict Negro suffrage in the South. Hoping to rouse the nation's conscience on the issue, the Reverend Martin Luther King organized massive public voting rights demonstrations in the city of Selma, Alabama, early in 1965. The city was an appropriate one for a number of reasons. By law, registration took place only two days a month. An applicant for registration had to fill in more than 50 blanks, write from dictation a part of the Constitution, answer four questions on the governmental process, read four passages from the Constitution and answer four questions on the passages, and sign an oath of loyalty to the United States and to Alabama. Not surprisingly, the 1960 registration figures showed that while the county was 57.6 percent Negro in population, the 9,877 persons registered to vote there were composed of 9,542 whites and only 335 Negroes. The insensitivity of the Selma and Alabama officials to the challenge at hand led to tragic occurrences during the demonstrations. A young Selma Negro died after an incident in which he said he was shot in the stomach and clubbed by Alabama state troopers. A white Unitarian minister from Boston was clubbed over the head by white men in Selma and died. And Alabama state troopers, acting on orders from Governor George C. Wallace, used tear gas, night sticks and whips to halt a voting-rights march from Selma to Montgomery, severely injuring about 40 marchers.[37]

Newsreel clips of these brutal incidents were flashed on television sets across an aroused nation. Responding to calls for remedial action from both Republican and Northern Democratic Congressional leaders, President Johnson appeared before a nationally televised joint session of Congress on March 15 to ask for rapid enactment of strong voting-rights legislation to "strike down restrictions to voting in all elections—federal, state and local—which have been used to deny Negroes the right to vote." The President declared that "the time for waiting is gone . . . outside this chamber is the outraged conscience of a nation."[38] The resulting legislation, hammered out in conferences between the Justice Department and Republican and Democratic legislative leaders on Capitol Hill, departed significantly from the more modest courtroom remedies of previous voting-rights bills. In all states and counties of the country where less than 50 percent of the voting-age population had registered for the 1964 elections, the new bill authorized the federal government to suspend the use of literacy tests and appoint federal voting examiners to order the registration of Negroes. Another provision established criminal penalties for inter-ference with voting rights. In its scope, the new bill appeared to go as far as the federal government possibly could without taking over all the voter registration functions of the states. In the succeeding two-year period, Negro leaders complained that the Justice Department was not prosecuting the law energetically enough. But in the long run, the Voting Rights Act of 1965 seemed destined to end racial dis-crimination in voting in the United States—probably within a single decade.

The statistics on Negro voter registration in the 11 states of the Confederacy over the 20 years from 1947 to 1967 tell an exciting story. In 1947 about 595,000 Negroes were registered in the area. By 1952 that figure had risen to just over 1.0 million, by 1956 to 1.2 million. Six years later, the figure stood at 1.4 million—little major improvement. But then a concentrated drive was initiated by the leading civil rights groups to register Southern Negro voters. Utilizing the new tools afforded by the 1964 Civil Rights Act, they were able to add 750,000 new Southern Negro registrants by the time of the 1964 Presidential election, making a new total of 2.2 million. In the wake of the Voting Rights Act of 1965, another 500,000 Negroes were registered in the South. By the 1966 Congressional elections, the regional total stood at 2.7 million Negro registrants.

Negro registration in terms of its percentage of the adult Negro population in the South is an equally dramatic story—rising from 12 percent in 1947, 25 percent in 1950 and 43 percent in 1964 to substan-tially more than 50 percent in 1966. Just between 1964 and 1966, the percentage of voting-age Negroes registered to vote rose in Mississippi from 6.7 to 32.9 percent, in Alabama from 23.0 to 51.2 percent and in

South Carolina from 38.8 to 51.4 percent. And not only were Negroes more numerous at the polls, but the growth of real two-party competition in the South put them in a powerful bargaining position.[39]

SUFFRAGE FOR WOMEN. Americans brought no tradition of female suffrage with them from Europe, and the primitive conditions of early Colonial times, when the great mass of American women lived in isolated rural homes and lacked any substantial education, were not conducive to any break in the traditional policy of exclusively male suffrage. Most early laws did not permit women to hold property, so that they were automatically excluded from voting under any circumstances. The only exceptions to the all-male voting rules were in Massachusetts, where women could vote from 1691 to 1780, and in New Jersey, which granted "all inhabitants worth $250"—men and women alike—the right to vote from 1776 to 1807.[40]

As property and taxpaying qualifications for voting were stricken from state constitutions in the first half of the 19th century, the discrimination against women became increasingly apparent. The women's suffrage movement was officially launched with the first Women's Rights Convention at Seneca Falls, New York, in 1848. After ratification of the 14th Amendment, the leaders of the movement felt they could properly demand the ballot under the new law, since to deny it to them would constitute an abridgement by the states of the privileges and immunities guaranteed all United States citizens in the Amendment. In 1871–72, a number of women tried to vote in various states, the great suffragist leader Susan B. Anthony among them. She was arrested, tried and fined. Refused registration in Missouri, Mrs. Virginia L. Minor of St. Louis carried her case to the U.S. Supreme Court. But the plea was rejected in 1875,[41] making it clear that women would have to press for the ballot through state voting-law changes and/or constitutional amendments.

The woman suffrage movements worked with sustained intensity to win the ballot throughout the next decades, trying alternatively to win the ballot through federal constitutional amendment and through changes in state laws. The territories of Wyoming and Utah granted women the right to vote in 1869 and 1870, and carried the same provisions into their permanent constitutions when they entered the Union in the 1890s. Colorado adopted woman suffrage in 1893, Idaho in 1896. But these victories aroused the opposition of party machines, corporations and liquor interests (who were fearful of women's support for temperance), barring any further advances on the state level until 1910. Then the suffragists' efforts of the years began to bear fruit as Washington, Kansas, Oregon, Arizona, Nevada and Montana granted female suffrage in a four-year period. Illinois followed suit, but only in voting for Presidential electors. Woodrow Wilson's antiwar platform in 1916 had a special appeal for women, and the Western states that had extended the vote to women appeared to have turned the balance in his favor in that year's close Presidential election. The next year, a crucial battle for female suffrage ensued in New York state, where more than a million women signed petitions asking for the ballot. In a statewide referendum in November 1917, New York joined the ranks of woman suffrage states by a vote of 703,129 to 600,776.

In a new tactic adopted following the 1916 election, the women sought to persuade the state legislatures to let them have at least the right to vote for Presidential electors—a right the legislatures could grant on their own discretion, without reference to changes in state constitutions. By April 1917, the legislatures of North Dakota, Nebraska, Indiana, Ohio, Michigan and Rhode Island had all complied with this request. More states soon followed suit, and by January 1, 1919, the women of 30 states, controlling 330 of the 531 Presidential electoral votes, had been given the right to vote for President. The implications were not lost on the national politicians.

Since 1869, Congress had conducted periodic hearings on a woman suffrage amendment to the Constitution. First introduced by Senator Aaron A. Sargent of California in 1878, and then by others in every succeeding Congress, the amendment read simply: "The right of citizens of the United States to vote shall not be denied or abridged by the United States or by any state on account of sex." The Senate had twice rejected the amendment—by a 16 to 34 vote in 1887 and by a 35 to 34 vote in 1914, the latter vote 11 short of the required two-thirds. The amendment first reached the House floor in 1915 and was rejected, 174 to 204. But the pressures for passage were becoming irresistible. After a personal appeal from President Wilson to his fellow Democrats for support, it passed the House on January 10, 1918, by a 274 to 136 vote—one more than two-thirds. But the Senate vote, the following October, was two votes short of the necessary two-thirds. Again in February 1919, the Senate fell one short of the required vote. Finally, in a special session of Congress in May 1919, the Senate gave its approval by a 66 to 30 vote and the amendment went to the states for ratification. A rush was made to complete ratification in time for the 1920 elections, and the approval of 29 states came in special sessions called by the state Governors for the purpose of ratifying the amendment. On August 26, 1920, 15 months after its submission, women's suffrage became part of the Constitution as the 19th Amendment.[42]

The nation's women rushed to take advantage of their new right, and the total vote in the 1920 Presidential election was 26,768,613, compared to only 18,536,232 in 1916.

POPULAR ELECTION OF SENATORS. At the Constitutional Convention, James Wilson had made a strong plea for the popular election of Senators, arguing that "if we are to establish a national government, that government ought to flow from the people at large," and that dissensions could arise between the Senate and House if they were to "rest on different foundations." But the overwhelming opinion of the Convention was for appointment by the state legislatures, as the best way to recognize the sovereignty of the states in the national government. John Dickinson of Delaware said a Senate so chosen would better reflect "the sense of the states" than election by the people at large, and expressed the hope that the Senate would "consist of the most distinguished characters, distinguished for their rank in life and their weight in property, and bearing as strong a likeness to the British House of Lords as possible."[43]

From the start, however, state legislature designation of U.S. Senators caused problems. New York had no Senators at all for half of the opening session of the First Congress because of partisan disputes that resulted in a deadlock in the state legislature. Tennessee had only one Senator throughout the 27th Congress (1841–1843) for the same reason. Moreover, it became increasingly clear that the indirect influence of the people over the choice of Senators, exercised through their state legislatures, was often clouded since they generally chose state legislators with an eye to their stands on local and state issues, not national ones. Powerful economic "interests," furthermore, such as railroading, oil, textiles, iron and steel, mining and sugar refining, found it much cheaper to "buy" a United States Senator through use of their influence in the state legislatures than if they had to cultivate the entire electorate of a state.[44]

The direct popular election of Senators fitted in naturally with the reform movements associated with Populism and the Progressive movement around the turn of the century. Starting in the 1890s the platforms of both major parties also urged direct election of Senators. Fearing that the Senate itself would never submit such a constitutional amendment, the legislatures of 31 of the 46 states adopted resolutions between 1893 and 1911 requesting that Congress call a constitutional convention for the purpose of writing an amendment for direct Senatorial election.[45] Presidents Roosevelt, Taft and Wilson all supported the direct vote movement, and by 1912 more than half the states had provided for the expression of the popular will in the election of Senators. This practice was elevated to the status of a Constitutional right in the 17th Amendment, submitted by Congress to the states in 1912 and ratified a year later. The amendment placed the election of Senators on the same basis as that of Representatives in the original Constitution by stipulating that the electors for Senator "shall have the qualifications requisite for electors of the most numerous branch of the state legislatures."

SUFFRAGE FOR THE DISTRICT OF COLUMBIA. The constitutional amendment route was employed again in 1961 to correct one of the glaring deprivations of the right to vote in America: the failure to provide for a vote for President by the people of Washington, D.C., the national capital. The franchise in voting for federal officers had been withdrawn from the federal district in 1802, when it was created out of land ceded by Maryland and Virginia. Under the terms of the 23rd Amendment to the Constitution, submitted to the states by Congress in 1960 and ratified 13 months later, the District was permitted to appoint a number of Presidential electors equal to the number of Senators and Representatives it would have if it were a state, but no more than the least populous state. As long as some states had but one Representative on the national population apportionment, this meant that the District would be limited to three Presidential electors.[46]

The 23rd Amendment failed, however, to assure other fundamental voting rights to the people of the District. No provision was made for them to elect Senators or Representatives, or to elect their own municipal officers, a right denied them by Congress since 1874. Nor was there any apparent justice in the amendment's provision limiting the District to the electoral college representation of the least populous state. In the 1960 Census, for instance, the District had 763,956 inhabitants—a figure that would have entitled it to two Representatives and thus four electoral votes if it had been a state. Hawaii, Idaho, Montana, New Hampshire, North Dakota and South Dakota all had less population but received two Representatives in the apportionment and thus four electoral votes for the decade of the 1960s. But the District was limited by the amendment to the same electoral college apportionment as states like Delaware and Alaska—three votes.

LITERACY TESTS. The requirement that a voter be able to read and understand the prevalent language in his state or the nation would seem to be a reasonable one. A voter unable to understand the presentation of the issues in a campaign can scarcely be expected to cast an intelligent vote and can easily be manipulated by various self-serving political groups. Many of the literacy tests imposed over the course of U.S. history have had political motivation, however, either to exclude foreign immigrant groups from the polls or to prevent Negroes, from voting. The first motive was apparent when Connecticut and Massachusetts, concerned about the vote impact of Irish immigrants, imposed the first education tests in the 1850s. Eleven other Northern states have since imposed literacy tests, the motivations varying substantially from case to case.[47] The most widely respected test was New York's, which included a reasonable reading requirement and uniform state application designed to prevent arbitrary discrimination.

The desire to prevent Negroes or some poor whites from participating in elections was apparently the chief motivation for adoption of literacy tests in eight Southern states between 1890 and 1910.[48] The 1965 Voting Rights Act suspended any literacy tests in areas where less than 50 percent of the voting-age citizens had registered for the 1964 election. The provision automatically suspended the literacy tests in the six Southern states still employing them—Alabama, Georgia, Louisiana, Mississippi, South Carolina and Virginia. The tests can be reinstated in those states only if the states prove in federal court that they have not used literacy tests for five years with the purpose or effect of discrimination.[49]

A controversial provision of the 1965 act also provided that no person who had completed sixth grade in a school under American jurisdiction in which the language of instruction was other than English could be denied the right to vote because of inability to read or write English. This was intended primarily to enfranchise the large Puerto Rican population of New York state, educated in territorial schools where the instruction was in Spanish. The provision was upheld by the U.S. Supreme Court in two decisions handed down in 1966.[50]

The suspension of Southern literacy tests under the Voting Rights Act has contributed significantly to the sharp increase of Negro registration in that area, and with the 1965 act on the books it is unlikely that any state—North or South—will again be able to use literacy tests to restrict the suffrage in any significant way. In a nation with universal compulsory education, the device should not be necessary anyway.

Remaining Restrictions on the Suffrage

Several features of state law still operate to restrict the franchise in the United States, some of them universally recognized as necessary prohibitions—like those against voting by mentally incompetent persons or children—and others of a more disputable nature, such as the variety of residence requirements that exist in the various states.

RESIDENCY REQUIREMENTS. A few of the colonies imposed residency requirements in the pre-Revolutionary period, generally ranging from six months to two years, and three were in existence at the time of the Revolution—in Connecticut, Virginia and South Carolina.[51] During the early years of the Republic, the general assumption in most states was that when a person had resided in a community long enough to meet the property and taxpaying qualifications for voting, he would be sufficiently familiar with local issues to cast an intelligent vote. As the property and taxpaying qualifications were lifted, however, residency requirements were imposed in most of the states. Of the 34 states in the Union in 1860, only two—Indiana and New Hampshire—had no residency requirements. Most states required one year, a few six months and others two years. The Midwestern and Western states, anxious to attract migration, generally set lower requirements, while the Eastern states imposed higher ones. The Southern states that enacted new constitutions in the period from 1890 to 1910 generally imposed heavy residence requirements that were expected to cut down on Negro registration.

Today, all states have residence requirements of some nature. Mississippi's is the most stringent—two years. The most common requirement is one year, imposed by 33 states. Two of these—Alabama and South Carolina—shifted from two years to one in the early 1960s. A residency of six months is required in 12 states, while two others—

New York and New Jersey—shifted to the exceptionally short period of three months, effective in 1967. Pennsylvania voted in 1967 to reduce the state's residence requirement to 90 days. The mildest requirement is West Virginia's, only 60 days. (For state-by-state chart, see Appendix J.) Most states also require a specified term of residency in the county, precinct or ward, in every case less than the requirement for residency in the state itself.

Exact figures are not available on the number of Americans actually barred from voting by residency requirements. Population mobility has always been a prominent feature of American life, and each year about one out of every five Americans moves. But a large proportion of these moves are only on a local basis, so that many citizens can maintain their vote if they will go to the trouble of registering again at their new addresses. Some localities encourage registration by setting up evening registration in local schoolhouses, fire stations and the like. But many require the voter to appear at an inconvenient city hall or courthouse registration office during regular business hours, when he would normally be at his job. Such practices are not an absolute deterrent to registration, but they tend to discourage citizens who lack a keen interest in their government.

Citizens are more likely to be legally barred from voting if they have moved into a new county or precinct close to election time or are one of the three percent of the population that moves across state lines each year. Generally, two types of Americans are most likely to lose their right to vote through the registration laws: corporate employees shifted from one part of the country to another and migrant workers who never stay in one locality long enough to establish residence.

A citizen is not deprived of his residence rights when he is temporarily absent. All of the states' election codes preserve the resident status of members of the Armed Forces, and most states allow federal government employees and students away from home to maintain their residence status.

Estimates of the number of Americans legally barred from voting by the residence laws in any single election have varied from 3 percent, based on a 1924 study in Chicago, to the finding of the American Heritage Foundation that 8 million Americans, or 7.5 percent of those otherwise eligible, were so affected in 1960.[52] A more careful estimate, based on 1960 Census figures on population mobility, indicates that 5.4 million, or 5 percent, of adult Americans were unable to vote in 1960 because of residence requirements.[53]

The justifications for residency requirements range from the suggestion that the voter should have time to familiarize himself with local issues to the desirability of preventing fraud in the balloting. It would seem, however, that the problem of fraud can be solved at least in part by an efficient registration system. The United States is one of the few nations in the world where the voter must qualify himself rather than being included automatically in some type of government enumeration. Given modern-day standards of literacy and communications, a voter should be able to prepare himself to vote on local candidates and issues within a few weeks or, at the most, a few months.

In recent years, increasing opposition has arisen to the disfranchisement of voters in Presidential elections because of changes in residence. Even if a residency requirement can be justified for local elections, the argument goes, can it legitimately be used to prevent citizens from participating in Presidential elections? The mere fact of change of residence does not make a person any less a citizen of the United States, with any less stake in the Presidential election. Connecticut was the first state to enact special legislation to cover this problem, stipulating in a 1953 statute that a citizen who had moved from his prior residence in Connecticut could continue to vote for President from that address until he was eligible at his new address. Four other states subsequently passed statutes of a similar nature—Arizona, Vermont, Wisconsin and Wyoming. Even more popular have been laws permitting new residents of a state to vote for President only, even if their period of residence is far below the normal state requirement. Wisconsin adopted the first statute of this type in 1954, and 24 states have since followed suit. Areas including a substantial majority of the population of the country are now covered by these liberalized new laws (see Appendix J). The popularity of the idea of letting new residents vote for President was demonstrated by the affirmative action of no less than ten states in approving enabling legislation in 1965–1966. A major question remains of the degree with which these special new Presidential voting laws will be utilized, however, since they often involve cumbersome registration procedures designed to prevent fraud. As an example, of the 7,050,985 major party votes cast for President in California in 1964, only 12,284—or one in 500—were in the "new resident" category. In 1967, the Johnson Administration recommended federal legislation that would forbid any state to deny a citizen the right to vote for President if he had been resident in the state since September 1 of the election year. The

Administration bill sought to facilitate absentee registration as well.[54]

State legislatures, by virtue of the discretionary power to regulate the method of choosing Presidential electors granted them in the Constitution, can establish special residence requirements for Presidential voting by simple statute. More cumbersome state constitutional changes are often required to change the registration requirements for voting for local offices, state legislatures and Congress. But given an opportunity, the voters in most states have supported proposals for less stringent registration requirements for voting in virtually all types of elections. The long-term trend seems to be in this direction.

ABSENTEE BALLOTING. In every election millions of Americans are unable to vote in person because of military duty, business trips, sickness, study and vacations. In 1960 about 9.9 million persons were estimated to be in this category.[55] About 3.8 million were institutionalized or so ill that they could not be expected to vote. But 7 million could probably have cast absentee ballots if they had chosen to do so. The nationally recorded absentee ballot total was 3.4 million.

All but three of the states—Mississippi, New Mexico and South Carolina—provide for absentee balloting. Sometimes absentee ballots are not available, however, unless a person is going to be physically absent from the area in which he lives or will be out of the area for one of the specific reasons enumerated in the state's statutes. The American Heritage Foundation proposed that absentee voting by mail be permitted in both primary and general elections for *all* citizens away from their city or state on election day. Safeguards against fraud, the foundation suggested, should include ballots of different colors for military and civilian voters, numbered ballots and the careful checking of signatures. The group also proposed that absentee voting privileges be extended to all the hospitalized and sick persons along the lines of model laws in Colorado and Nebraska.[56]

OVERSEAS BALLOTING. Approximately 500,000 of the estimated 1,500,000 Americans living abroad (exclusive of members of the Armed Forces) were estimated to have lost their right to vote in 1960 through inadequate absentee voting laws or because they no longer had any type of official residence in the United States. The American Heritage Foundation recommended that they be allowed to register and vote by mail, as members of the military are permitted to do.

Thirty-one of the 50 states had enacted laws permitting absentee registration by 1967, with several more considering such a move.[57]

ALIENS. A frequent practice in early America was to extend voting privileges to aliens who declared their intention to become citizens. Twenty-two states and territories followed this policy for all or at least part of the 19th century, and alien voting was not discontinued in Arkansas until 1926. Currently, every state bars aliens from voting, and the propriety of the arrangement is generally acknowledged. One estimate indicates that 2.8 million persons were barred by their alien status from voting in 1960.[58]

MENTAL ILLNESS AND CRIME. Most states bar inmates of mental institutions or persons otherwise deemed unsound of mind from voting, a little-disputed practice. In a majority of the states, a person also loses the right to vote upon conviction of a crime the penalty for which is imprisonment. Some state laws define the point of losing the franchise at "felony," others at "infamous crime" or a similar definition. In most states, a person does not recover the right to vote on release from prison, though some states restore the right to vote after a set number of years, or on release. Executive or legislative clemency, when granted, also restores the right to vote. But it is questionable whether the permanent withdrawal of the right to vote is in accord with modern ideas of criminology and the rehabilitation of former criminals.[59]

VOTING AGE. The Constitution left the question of the minimum voting age, along with all other questions regarding voter qualifications, to the states. The traditional "majority"—21 years—was in effect in all the states in 1787 and was maintained without exception until 1943. In that year Georgia, heeding a war-inspired slogan, "Old enough to fight, old enough to vote," approved a constitutional amendment permitting 18-year-olds to vote in all elections. Kentucky lowered the minimum voting age to 18 in 1955, and Alaska stipulated a minimum age of 19 when she entered the Union in 1958. Admitted to statehood a year later, Hawaii set the figure at 20 years.[60]

Despite continuing pressures, Congress has never responded to pleas that the Constitution be amended to effect an 18-year minimum. A resolution to this effect was reported by the Senate Judiciary Committee in 1952, but it never came to a vote on the floor.

The lack of a uniform minimum voting age has been raised as one of the objections to direct vote for President, although variations in the actual percentage of the voter turnout among various age groups probably play a larger role (see pages 233–34, below).

PRESIDENT'S COMMISSION REPORT. The most comprehensive study of registration and voting during the postwar years was that conducted in 1963 by the President's Commission on Registration and Voting Participation. The ten-man commission was established March 20, 1963, by executive order of President Kennedy, who named as chairman Census Director Richard M. Scammon, an authority on voting and elections. The group was directed to study the causes for the failure of many qualified Americans to exercise their right to vote and to pay particular attention to laws that restricted registration and voting on the basis of residence and absentee voting provisions.

In its report, made public December 20, 1963, the commission placed the blame for low voter turnout in the United States on a number of legal and administrative causes, including inconvenient and burdensome registration and voting procedures; restrictive residence requirements that deprived otherwise eligible voters of their franchise; unreasonable absentee voting provisions; and election day problems, such as crowded or inaccessible polling places, early closing hours and lengthy ballots that discouraged many citizens from voting. In addition, the poll tax and literacy and other voter qualification tests were mentioned as obstacles to registration and voting by some persons, particularly Negroes in the South.

To overcome these obstacles to higher voter turnout in Presidential and Congressional elections, the commission recommended 21 steps:

■ Each state should create a commission on registration and voting participation, or utilize some other existing state machinery to survey in detail its election laws practices.

■ Voter registration should be easily accessible to all citizens.

■ Residence requirements for voting for state officials should not exceed six months.

■ Residence requirements for voting in county and city elections should not exceed 30 days.

■ New state residents should be allowed to vote for President, regardless of their length of residence in the new state, if qualified to vote in the state from which they moved.

■ Voter registration should extend as close to election day as possible, and should not end more than three or four weeks before election day.

- Voter lists should be kept current.
- No citizen's registration should be canceled for failure to vote in any period less than four years.
- Voter registration lists should be used only for electoral purposes.
- States should provide absentee registration for voters who cannot register in person.
- Literacy tests should not be a requisite for voting.
- Election day should be proclaimed a national day of dedication to American democracy. The commission suggested that "the states should consider declaring the day a half-day legal holiday."
- Polling places should be so equipped as to eliminate long waiting periods.
- Polling places should be open throughout the day and remain open until at least 9 P.M.
- The states should provide every possible protection against election fraud.
- Voting by persons when they reach the age of 18 should be considered by the states.
- Candidacy should be open to all.
- The right to vote should be extended to those living on federal reservations.
- Absentee voting by mail should be allowed for all who are absent from home on primary or general election day.
- The poll tax as a qualification for voting should be eliminated.
- Each state should keep informed of other states' practices and innovations in election administration.

With the rapid expansion of their election coverage activities in recent years, the national television networks have taken an active interest in the type of reforms advanced by the President's Commission. Frank Stanton, president of CBS, has proposed that election day be made a national holiday with polls opening simultaneously across the country and remaining open for 24 hours. Stiff residence and registration requirements are relics of an era of poor communications and primitive identification systems, Stanton says, pointing out that the U.S. already has a system of numerical identification of virtually every adult for income and social security tax purposes. Residence requirements for Presidential voting could be eliminated altogether, he proposes, "once a system is devised for automatic, fraud-proof, permanent, nationally-valid registration of voters, making full use of automatic equipment." (South Carolina took a pioneer step in this direction in 1967 through installation of a semi-permanent, centralized state voter registration system with all the data fed into computers.) Stanton claims that the chances for fraud and error in election counts could be materially reduced through installation of electronic voting systems in place of the outmoded paper ballot, still in use in a majority of the nation's 170,375 voting precincts.[61]

Who Actually Votes?

Even with the legal right to vote, a significant percentage of Americans fail to exercise their franchise. The most frequently cited figures show the percentage of the total voting-age population which has participated in a Presidential election. The figure was 63.8 percent in 1960 and 62.1 percent in 1964. These percentages would naturally be greater if there were an accurate method to determine how many voting-age Americans were actually excluded from voting through residency requirements, illiteracy, alien status, systematic discrimination in the Southern states and confinement to institutions. Based on the 1960 election, when there were 107 million Americans of voting age, some studies have suggested that as many as 22 to 23 million Americans may have been barred by such factors.[62] If that many really were excluded, then over 80 percent of the actually eligible voters participated in the 1960 Presidential election.

A more conservative estimate, which seems more in line with the major differences regularly reported between the voter turnout by sex, socioeconomic group and race, would be in the neighborhood of 75 percent. Of the remaining quarter of the American people who fail to vote, indifference and alienation are probably the major factors. But for some, unexpected occurrences—a quickly planned business trip, bad weather or a sudden illness—may account for their failure to vote for President. The percentage participation figures are probably reduced further by the relatively small number of Americans who vote in primary elections but not in the general election, or fail to have their votes for President recorded, either because they deliberately blank that spot on their ballot or spoil their ballots.[63]

VOTING BY AGE GROUPS. Voter turnout tends to be the lowest among young voters and the highest among persons of middle age. This pattern, reported in many earlier surveys, was confirmed by a Census Bureau national sampling of 65,000 persons in all states taken shortly after the 1964 Presidential election. As in virtually all postelection polling results, the Census Bureau found that a greater percentage of the people—69.6 percent—said they voted than the official vote count indicated—62.1 percent.[64] But the population curve was a familiar one to election analysts. Of the 21 to 24 age group, 51.3 percent said they had voted. The figure then rose to 69.0 percent in the 24 to 44 age group and 75.9 percent in the 45 to 64 age group. It then dropped to 66.3 percent for all persons 65 years of age or older. Richard Scammon has commented that "this curving pattern is not difficult to understand, for it measures the integration of young people into our society. Younger people are more mobile and have developed less of a stake in any community than have middle-aged electors."[65]

MEN VERSUS WOMEN. Women consistently register less frequently and vote less frequently than men, a conclusion borne out by virtually every study in the field. The Census figures based on the 1964 election showed that 67.5 percent of all females reported voting, more than 5 percent less than the participation rate of 72.7 percent reported among men. But since there are more women than men in the population, they accounted for 1.7 million more ballots cast than by men in the 1964 election.

INCOME AND EDUCATION. The socioeconomic status of various groups also plays a major role in voter turnout. Better-educated, higher-income persons almost invariably vote in higher percentages than those with less schooling and less income. The Census figures for 1964 showed that only 51.6 percent of the adults with seven or fewer years of school exercised their franchise. The turnout figure rose to 76.5 percent for high school graduates and an astounding 88.2 percent for persons who had completed college. An analagous situation was reported on a division of the population by family income:

Family Income Group	1964 Turnout for President
Under $2,000	50.0%
$2,000 to $2,999	58.2
$3,000 to $4,999	63.1
$5,000 to $7,499	72.8
$7,500 to $9,999	78.7
$10,000 and above	85.2

A typical example of the patterns behind these figures emerges from analysis of the voting for President in 1960 in Hennepin County, Minnesota. On the near north side of Minneapolis, in a 3 to 1 Democratic, predominantly working-class, ethnically mixed neighborhood of about 35,000 persons, 63 percent of the adult population voted. But in the same election, in the suburb of Edina, southwest of Minneapolis, with a wealthy, white and essentially "native" population of 30,000, 92 percent of the adults voted. The Edina vote was about 4 to 1 Republican.[66]

RACE. The common pattern of modern U.S. elections has been for whites to vote in greater percentage than Negroes or other nonwhites, both in the South and in other regions of the country as well. But with the acceleration of the national civil rights movement, combined with Negroes' increased awareness of their political power, the gap has narrowed over the years.

A major reason for Negro nonvoting in past years has been Southern discrimination against Negroes. But Negro voting participation in the North has also lagged behind that of whites, perhaps because of the income and education factors mentioned earlier. The 1964 Census report showed the following regional breakdown on voting by all voters as compared to voting by nonwhites:

Region	Total Adult Population Voting for President	Nonwhite Adult Population Voting for President*
United States	69.9%	58.2%
Northeast	75.1	71.0
South	57.2	44.5
North Central	76.9	80.5
West	72.6	65.1

* The over-all category of "non-white" includes Indians, Japanese, Chinese and other races in addition to Negroes.

The future outlook is for greater and greater Negro voting participation as discriminatory voting devices are removed and Negroes' political awareness increases.

TURNOUT BY STATES. The Southern states, with their more restrictive suffrage laws, have traditionally had a lower voter turnout than the rest of the nation. Northern states have tended to vary in voter turnout according to the stringency of local registration laws, the number of aliens in the population and over-all educational and income levels. Some studies have shown a rather direct relationship between the educational levels of a state's citizens and the over-all voter turnout. High rates of illiteracy, for instance, are frequently associated with low participation levels.[67] Appendix F shows the percentage of the adult population voting by states in several Presidential elections between 1920 and 1964. A general national increase in voter turnout has occurred over these years, but the major rise, as the chart indicates, has been in the Southern states. With implementation of the Voting Rights Act and the death of the poll tax, Southern states are likely to come closer and closer to the national levels in the coming years, creating a relatively uniform national voting base.

The Sanctity of the Ballot

Just as important to the citizen as the basic right to vote is his right to cast his vote freely, without coercion, and to see it counted effectively. Most Americans today take for granted the system of secret voting and assume, except in rare instances, that their votes are counted honestly. But that right has been secured only by a long series of reforms, effected both by state and federal statutes.

In Colonial times, and indeed in many Southern states during a major part of the 19th century, the voter announced his choices orally to the election officials. The historian J. B. McMaster reports that in early elections in Virginia, the electors of an entire county were gathered at one courthouse and polled in the presence of the sheriff. In one Congressional election of the 1790s, conducted at Montgomery Court House, Virginia, one of the contestants was fortunate enough to have a brother in charge of 60 or 70 federal troops camped nearby. On the morning of the election they were paraded, marched to town, led thrice around the courthouse, drawn up before the door and declared themselves for the brother of their chief. They then threatened to beat anyone who wished to vote against their man, knocked down a drunken magistrate and halted the voting until the countrymen stoned them back to camp. A House committee recommended that the Representative so elected be denied his seat, but Southern Congressmen supported him. One Maryland Representative said that comparatively little mischief had taken place in the election under dispute; at his own election, 500 of his constituents had clubs under their coats. If such tactics were enough to unseat a member, he said, the House could begin by unseating him. It was common custom, the Marylander argued, for a man of influence to come to the polls with 200 or 300 of his friends and stop any opponents from voting if he could help it. A Representative from South Carolina expressed surprise, but he was promptly reminded that at his own election a riot had occurred, beginning when a magistrate knocked down a voter and dragged him into the road.[68]

The Revolutionary era witnessed the beginning of an effort to substitute voting by paper ballot, a practice made obligatory by several of the state constitutions adopted in 1776. New York was slower, stipulating paper ballots only for Governor and Lieutenant Governor in 1778 and not extending the system to Legislature elections until 1787. The last state to abandon voice voting was Kentucky in 1891, although it had already been compelled by federal statute to use paper ballots for Congressional elections.[69]

Voting by paper ballot did not necessarily assure a secret ballot, however. During most of the 19th century, politicians managed to ascertain how citizens were voting by requiring voters to sign their ballots, making them show their filled-in ballots to poll officials before placing them in the boxes, or allowing the parties to print ballots on differing colored papers, which citizens actually used instead of a government-printed form. By the 1850s most states required that ballots be cast in sealed envelopes or by some other method that ostensibly made the vote a secret one. But the so-called Australian ballot, issued by the government with the names of all parties' candidates for the various offices printed thereon and providing for absolute secrecy, was not introduced in the United States until the 1880s. The first state to require the Australian ballot for all state elections was Massachusetts, in 1889. Since that time it has been adopted by every state of the Union.[70]

The Constitution gives the state legislatures the power to prescribe "the times, places and manner of holding elections for Senators and Representatives" but provides that "Congress may at any time by law make or alter such regulations" (Article I, Section 4). Congress did little to implement its reserve powers until the decades following the Civil War, when the 14th Amendment gave it clear standards to apply to the honesty of the ballot count. In 1870, as part of the Reconstruction period civil rights acts, legislation was passed by Congress to assure citizens the right to vote without special regard to race questions. The Supreme Court sustained most legislation of this type, in contrast to its reluctance in the late 19th century to implement laws that attempted to protect Negroes' right to vote in the South. In a test case of 1880 the Court upheld the conviction under the 1870 act of state election supervisors in Baltimore who had stuffed ballot boxes in a Congressional election contest.[71] In 1915, in a case involving the false counting of ballots in a Congressional election, the Court reasoned that once the right to vote has been granted, there is a constitutional right to have the vote counted honestly. Justice Oliver Wendell Holmes wrote in this case: "We regard it as . . . unquestionable that the right to have one's vote counted is as open to protection by Congress as the right to put a ballot in the box." The case involved charges that election officers had completely omitted the count of eleven precincts in an Oklahoma Congressional election.[72] The Supreme Court extended the same principle to primary elections for federal office in a 1941 decision, upholding the convictions of New Orleans politicians who had altered and falsely counted ballots in a U.S. House primary.[73] The decision was a major victory for the newly formed Civil Rights Division of the Justice Department.

Little federal effort was made to assure the honesty of the vote count in Presidential elections until recent decades, largely because of the Constitution's apparently exclusive grant to the state legislatures of authority over the method of choosing electors. But even in its 1892 decision declaring the plenary power of state legislatures over the appointment of Presidential electors, the Court made it clear that if the legislature chose the popular election route, then the 14th Amendment guarantees would apply.[74] In 1934 the Supreme Court sustained the right of Congress to pass corrupt practices laws regarding Presidential elections. Justice George Sutherland, speaking for the Court, recognized the premise of earlier decisions that Presidential electors were not federal officers but said that "they exercise federal functions under, and discharge duties in virtue of, authority conferred by the federal Constitution. . . . The power of Congress to protect the election of the President and Vice President from corruption being clear, the choice of means is primarily for the judgment of Congress."[75] Sutherland quoted approvingly from Justice Samuel F. Million in an 1884 decision that spoke in sweeping terms of the right of the federal government to assure the sanctity of the ballot box: "That a government whose essential character is republican, whose executive head and legislative are both elective, has no power by appropriate laws to secure this election from the influence of violence, corruption and fraud, is a proposition so startling as to arrest attention."[76]

Together with subsequent civil rights acts, these court decisions have established a clear federal right to intervene in the conduct of federal elections by the states to assure an honest count—a power the Justice Department has not hesitated to use on occasion.

Compared with that of the 19th century, the incident of vote fraud is remarkably low in modern-day America. Both the secret ballot and voting machines have worked in this direction. Nevertheless, abuses are sometimes claimed. In the wake of the 1960 Presidential election, in which Republicans had charged fraud in a number of states, including Illinois and Texas, the Republican National Committee produced a booklet listing major methods of fraud and the steps to be taken against them. Among the prominent vote-fraud methods enumerated were "tombstone voting," padding voter lists, vote-buying, disqualifying wholesale one party's ballots, deliberate spoiling of ballots (by such devices as a piece of graphite concealed under a counter's fingernail), rigging voting machines, intimidating or bribing election officials, wrongly advising or marking ballots for blind or non-English-speaking voters, removing regularly registered names from registration lists, voting in several locations by the same persons and jamming voting machines.

The booklet recommended numerous preventive steps, including a complete and accurate canvass of the precinct several months prior to election, placing poll watchers armed with cameras to photograph possible "bought" voters or persons voting more than once, moves to tighten up state laws on ballot disqualification, careful surveillance of ballot counting, inspection of voting machines before they are unlocked on election day, quick action to prevent any chicanery at the polls, thorough briefing of poll workers on election laws, recruitment of poll workers able to withstand intimidation or threats of violence in areas where such practices are likely, and recruitment of extra poll-watching staffs in areas with a history of vote frauds.[77] Significantly, most of the Republicans' complaints after the 1960 election had come in areas where they had few poll watchers or where their precinct workers were really controlled by the opposition party. Perhaps the best assurance of an honest vote count throughout the country lies in the expansion of a viable two-party system to every state and subdivision.

The Reapportionment Revolution of the 1960s

One final aspect of the great historical movement toward equal voting rights in America deserves examination: the decisions of the U.S. Supreme Court, starting in 1962, which have assured legislative districts of substantially equal population in the state legislatures and Congressional districts of the country.[78]

Inequality in the population of legislative districts had existed since Colonial times. One of the extreme instances of the early 19th century was in Virginia, where one county with 951 inhabitants had the same representation in the Legislature as another with 22,105—a situation leading Thomas Jefferson to criticize the state's constitution because "among those who share the representation, the shares are unequal." A large proportion of the original state constitutions provided at least in part for population-based apportionment, however, so that malapportionment was not considered a major problem of American government during the first 100 years of the nation's existence.[79]

Massive waves of immigration and the growth of industry, centered in the metropolitan areas, resulted in greater disparities between urban and rural legislative districts around the start of the 20th century and up to the 1960s. The resulting malapportionment of legislatures was magnified even more by the relative decrease of the farm population. The year 1920 was a turning point, when the Census showed more Americans living in urban than in rural areas. Between 1900 and 1950 rural America grew by 16 million in population while urban America expanded by 50 million. But the rural state legislators, reluctant to sacrifice their power, refused in state after state to enact the reapportionment measures necessary to maintain equally populated districts. The immensity of the problem was demonstrated by the 1960 Census figures. In California the smallest Senate district, encompassing three rural mountain counties along the spine of the Sierras, had a population of 14,294. The largest district, encompassing all of Los Angeles County, had 6,038,771 inhabitants—422 times as many. Yet each was represented by one state Senator. Variations of 2 to 1, 5 to 1, 10 to 1 or 100 to 1 were common in many other states. The periodic reapportionment of Congressional seats between the states prevented disparities from mounting to astronomical heights, but they were serious nevertheless. In 1962, two years after the 1960 Census and after all the state legislatures had had the chance to redistrict their Congressional seats, disparities of these magnitudes still existed between the largest and smallest U.S. House districts in various states: 301,872 to 588,933 in California, 278,703 to 552,582 in Illinois, 237,235 to 660,345 in Florida, 216,371 to 951,527 in Texas. [80]

In the 1956 debate on electoral college reform, it had been such inequalities that gave Senators Douglas and Kennedy the basis for arguing that the state legislatures and Congress were malapportioned to benefit rural interests and that the urban voters therefore deserved the extra power of their swing vote in the large pivotal states in the electoral college.

For years the courts were reluctant to interfere in the apportionment area. Up to the 1960s the leading case was the 1946 Supreme Court decision in *Colegrove v. Green,* regarding Congressional redistricting in Illinois.[81] In dismissing the districting challenge, the Supreme Court held that reapportionment matters were not "justiciable"—not appropriate for resolution by a court. "The courts," said Justice Felix Frankfurter in presenting the opinion of a split Court, "ought not to enter this political thicket." There the matter rested for almost 15 years.

THE STATE LEGISLATIVE CASES. In 1959 a group of Tennessee city residents, including the mayor of Nashville and a county judge named Charles W. Baker, filed a suit against Joe C. Carr, Tennessee's secretary of state, challenging Tennessee's apportionment statutes. Under the Tennessee constitution, decennial reapportionment of both houses of the Legislature was required on a strict population base. Yet no apportionment changes had been made since 1901, and tremendous population growth had occurred in the state's urban areas, rendering the constitution's population provision meaningless. By 1960 Tennessee House districts ranged from 3,454 to 79,301 in population—a disparity of 23 to 1. Senate districts varied from 39,727 to 237,905—a sixfold disparity. Rebuffed in the state courts, the plaintiffs took their case into federal court, arguing that the Tennessee Legislature was so unrepresentative that a minority ruled in both houses, contrary "to the philosophy of government of the United States and all Anglo-Saxon jurisprudence in which the legislature has the power to make law only because it has the power and duty to represent people." They charged that there was "a debasement of their votes by virtue of the incorrect, obsolete and unconstitutional apportionment" to such an extent that they were being deprived of their right to "equal protection of the laws" under the 14th Amendment.[82]

A local federal court rejected the Tennessee case, and it was appealed to the U.S. Supreme Court. In March 1961, the U.S. Department of Justice intervened on the side of the urban interests as *amicus curiae*, "a friend of the court." The government's brief said that "numerous states have done nothing with regard to apportionment of their legislature for 25 or 50 years. The only realistic remedy is federal judicial action." In an analysis that ranged beyond the essential points of law, the brief said the state legislatures "have, in very large part, failed to adapt themselves to modern problems and majority needs, and this failure has resulted in public cynicism, disillusionment and loss of confidence." Recommending that the Supreme Court exercise jurisdiction and apply 14th Amendment guarantees, the Justice Department said: "This Court has recognized that a voter has a constitutional right to have his vote counted without its being diluted by fraud. . . . The dilution of one's vote by gross malapportionment is just as unconstitutional."

The decision of the Supreme Court was handed down March 26, 1962, ruling in favor of the Tennessee plaintiffs by a 6 to 2 margin.[83] For the first time in U.S. history, the Court found that the question of apportionment of state legislatures may be reviewed by the federal courts. The decision also made it clear that legislature apportionment might actually violate the equal protection clause of the 14th Amendment and thus be illegal. In a strong dissenting opinion, Justice Frankfurter called the *Baker v. Carr* decision "a massive repudiation of our whole past" and an assertion of "destructively novel judicial power."

The *Baker* decision had left many questions unresolved—whether both or just one house of a legislature must be based on population, how much variation in populations might be permissible, and whether a state could adopt a "little federal system" with one house based on population and the other on geography. In a group of decisions handed down June 15, 1964, the Court resolved all these questions on a strict "one man, one vote" basis. These decisions, known collectively by the name of the first case, *Reynolds v. Sims*,[84] established four major points: First, it was found that the equal protection clause "requires that the seats in both houses of a bicameral state legislature must be apportioned on a population basis." Second, the Court said that "mathematical exactness of precision" in carving out legislative districts might be impossible but that apportionments must be "based substantially on population." Third, the Court refused to recognize the federal analogy as justifying one house based on a principle other than population. And fourth, the Court said that an apportionment failing to provide substantial population equality in both houses, even if such an arrangement is approved by the voters through referendum or initiative measures, is unconstitutional because "a citizen's constitutional rights can hardly be infringed upon because a majority of the people choose to do so." Writing for the majority, Chief Justice Earl Warren said that "legislators represent people, not trees or acres. Legislators are elected by voters, not farms or cities or economic interests."

Rural and conservative forces reacted violently to the 1964 decisions, arguing that the intent of the Constitution had been to provide the states with a much wider degree of discretion in their internal governmental structure than the Supreme Court was permitting. In 1965 and 1966, under the leadership of Senate Minority Leader Everett McKinley Dirksen of Illinois, major efforts were made to win approval of a proposed constitutional amendment granting the states the power, on the approval of a majority of citizens in referendums, to apportion one house of their legislatures on some principle other than population. But the proposed amendment failed to win the required two-thirds affirmative vote by margins of seven votes in the Senate in both 1965 and 1966 and never came to a vote in the House of Representatives.[85]

Rarely in U.S. history has a series of Supreme Court decisions had such a sweeping effect on the nation as the reapportionment orders of the 1960s. Between the 1962 *Baker* decision and mid-1966, some form of reapportionment had taken place in 49 states. (The 50th state, Oregon, had reapportioned on a population base in 1961.) Virtually all 50 states entered the 1966 legislative elections at least roughly on the population standard. In a series of orders early in 1967, the Supreme Court made it plain that population variations from the state average that approached 10 percent would be considered unconstitutional, indicating that many of the states that had already corrected the worst conditions of malapportionment in their legislatures would be obliged to go even further in meeting the "one man, one vote" standard in future years.[86]

CONGRESSIONAL DISTRICT STANDARDS. In a landmark 1964 decision the Supreme Court extended the equal population principle to Congressional districts as well. In this case, *Wesberry v. Sanders*,[87] the Court upheld the claim that Georgia's U.S. House districts—varying from 272,154 population in the rural Ninth District (Northeast Georgia) to 823,680 in the Fifth District (Atlanta and Suburbs)—were unconstitutional. In this case, the Supreme Court decided not to use the 14th Amendment but rested its decision instead on Article I, Section 2 of the Constitution, which provides that "Representatives shall be apportioned among the states according to their respective numbers" and be "chosen by the people of the several states." This language, the Court stated, means that "as nearly as is practicable, one man's vote in a Congressional election is to be worth as much as another's."

Within two years of the *Wesberry* decision, 27 states with a total of 258 Congressional districts had been redistricted to meet the "one man, one vote" rule. As with state legislative districts, the Court indicated early in 1967 that U.S. House districts would not be allowed to vary more than 10 percent, if that much, from the average population figure.[88] Indeed, the bulk of Supreme Court reapportionment decisions were characterized by a "slide rule" approach. By 1967 the Court had yet to come to grips with the problems of gerrymandering and other political manipulation of legislative districts, practices that could in effect deprive a citizen of equal protection of the laws as easily as mere mathematical malapportionment.[89]

One major surprise of the reapportionment revolution of the 1960s was that it did not, in fact, magnify the power of the great cities in the state legislatures and Congress in the way that had been anticipated in earlier years. To read the arguments of Kennedy and Douglas in the 1956 Senate debates, one would have the impression that the basic political division of the country lay between "rural" interests on the one hand and "urban" interests—defined as those of the great cities— on the other. The analysis, in fact, had failed to take into account the growing role of suburban areas in midcentury population patterns. In the decade between 1950 and 1960, for instance, the population of New York City proper went down by 1.4 percent while its suburban areas were increasing 75 percent in population. The trend was essentially the same in major Northern metropolitan areas like Detroit, Baltimore, Chicago and Philadelphia. The only major exceptions were certain Southern and Western cities where original city boundaries contained much unoccupied land and where annexation of new fringe communities was easy. In all, 14 of the 21 largest metropolitan areas of the U.S. witnessed a net decline in center city population between 1950 and 1960, while the suburban population grew in all 21.[90]

Thus the implementation of "one man, one vote" standards in the state legislatures brought the largest gains for the suburbs, not the cities. "The suburbs and, in the long run, only the suburbs will gain in the upheaval resulting from reapportionment of state legislatures on the basis of population," William J. D. Boyd of the National Municipal League reported in June 1965. By 1970, Boyd reported, the overwhelming majority of suburbs would have more population than the center cities that they surround. "No center city contains the necessary 50 percent of the people to dominate the state," Boyd wrote. "It now appears that no city will ever attain that dominance. The United States is an urban nation, but it is not a big-city nation. The suburbs own the future."[91]

The suburbs also turned out to be the big winners in equal population redistricting of Congressional seats. All the major Northern metropolitan center-city areas lost seats in the reshuffle, though gains were made by cities in the South and Far West. A 1964 study by *Congressional Quarterly* indicated that by the time all the states had established districts based on population, there would probably be a *net* shift of only 16 out of the nation's 435 Congressional seats. Suburban areas would gain a net of ten seats, center cities six, all at the expense of rural areas and others with a predominantly mixed population.[92]

"ONE MAN, ONE VOTE" IN A GIVEN CONSTITUENCY. The Supreme Court decision of the 1960s with the greatest direct relevance to the electoral college did not relate directly to state legislature or Congressional districts but rather to Georgia's county-unit, or "little electoral college," system of voting in statewide and Congressional primary elections. The unit vote system gave each county a certain number of votes, usually the number of its seats in the state legislature. The candidate who carried a county won its unit votes. A candidate could easily win the popular vote but lose the nomination by running poorly in the rural areas, which had many more unit votes than the populous cities and suburbs. The system had permitted rural areas to dominate the Georgia state governments and its Congressional delegation for more than half a century.

A challenge to the Georgia system was brought by James O'Hear Sanders, an Atlanta businessman, who was first victorious in a federal court in Atlanta. The state then appealed to the Supreme Court, which decided the case, *Gray v. Sanders,* on March 18, 1963.[93] The Court held that the unit vote system deprived city residents of equal protection of the laws by giving them less than their fair share of the statewide vote. Declaring the system unconstitutional, the Court established the rule that, "Within a given constituency, there can be room for but a single constitutional rule—one voter, one vote."

Rejecting a defense of Georgia's system, based on its similarity to the electoral college, the Supreme Court said it found that such analogies were not pertinent. The electoral college, the Court said, had been included in the Constitution "as the result of specific historical concerns," chiefly the desire to have politically knowledgeable men elect the President, rather than the people directly. An "inherent numerical inequality," the Court said, had been the price of the solution at the Constitutional Convention. "Passage of the 15th, 17th and 19th Amendments shows that this conception of political equality belongs to a bygone day, and should not be considered in determining what the equal protection clause of the 14th Amendment requires in statewide elections," the Court concluded.

In the majority opinion of the *Gray* case, Justice William O. Douglas set down both the rule in the case at hand and a line of argument totally relevant to the electoral college itself. "Once the geographical unit for which a representative is to be chosen is designated," Douglas said, "all who participate in the election are to have an equal vote— whatever their race, whatever their sex, whatever their occupation, whatever their income, and wherever their home may be in that geographical unit. . . . The concept of 'we the people' under the Constitution visualizes no preferred class of voters but equality among those who meet the basic qualifications. . . . The concept of political equality from the Declaration of Independence, to Lincoln's Gettysburg Address, to the 15th, 17th and 19th Amendments can mean only one thing—one person, one vote."

Two actions of the Supreme Court in late 1966 suggested an undercutting of *Gray v. Sanders,* or at least a refusal to follow the decision to its logical conclusions. The first was the Court's refusal in October 1966 to hear arguments in *Delaware v. New York,* a case challenging the constitutionality of the state unit vote method of awarding electoral votes (see pages 190–91, above). Delaware argued that the equal-voter-status principles recognized by the Court in *Gray* and other cases "should nullify all inequitable and unnecessary state policies concerning the casting and counting of the popular vote. This should reach all state laws which have the effect of distorting the popular will, introducing uncertainty into Presidential elections, and differentiating between classes of voters on chance and arbitrary chance factors." Delaware maintained that "it requires little argument to establish that the current general ticket, or state unit vote, system violates contemporary standards of political equality. It is a counterpart to Georgia's county unit system which was invalidated on equal protection grounds in *Gray v. Sanders*." The refusal of the Court even to hold hearings on the Delaware case, however, made it unclear why it would not consider *Gray* in the wider context of the national electoral college.

The second Court action relevant to *Gray* came in *Fortson v. Morris*, the case arising from the disputed Georgia gubernatorial election of 1966. In the November popular election, Republican Howard H. Callaway had received 453,665 votes to 450,626 for Democrat Lester G. Maddox. But Callaway failed to achieve an absolute majority because of the write-in vote for former Governor Ellis G. Arnall, a liberal Democrat, which was reported at 45,603 votes. Both Callaway and Maddox were strong conservatives, though Maddox was known as a violent racist also.

The Georgia constitution provided that when no candidate for Governor receives a majority, the decision shall be made by the Georgia General Assembly. In the wake of the election, Georgia's constitutional provision was challenged in the federal district court on the ground that an election by the legislature would in fact constitute a unit-vote election of the type found unconstitutional in *Gray v. Sanders*. The plaintiffs in the case (including the supporters of Callaway and the American Civil Liberties Union) argued that a state-legislature member voting for Governor would automatically disfranchise disagreeing constituents in his district, and that the principle of "one man, one vote" enunciated in *Gray* was even more vital in the general election, the most important step in the electoral process, than to the nominating procedures to which the original *Gray* decision was addressed. The state of Georgia replied that nothing in the Constitution forbids a state from providing an alternative method of election to popular voting, and that *Gray* had applied to how votes must be counted in a popular election but not to the method of election in the first place or to alternative methods of determining an election when the normal election process fails to produce a winner.

The federal court in Atlanta upheld the contention that throwing the election into the General Assembly would violate the *Gray* decision, but this decision was reversed by the U.S. Supreme Court on a 5 to 4 division. Speaking for the majority, Justice Hugo L. Black said that "there is no provision of the United States Constitution or any of its amendments which either expressly or impliedly dictates the method a state must use to select its Governor." He noted that two other states, Mississippi and Vermont, also provide for state legislature election of a Governor when there is no popular majority. As for *Gray v. Sanders,* Black said, it "did no more than to require the state to eliminate the county-unit machinery from its election system."

In a dissenting opinion, joined in by three other Justices, Douglas said that the central question was not whether Georgia could choose a Governor by legislative election but whether the legislature could make the final choice once the election had been "entrusted to the people" and no majority candidate emerged. All the "vices" outlawed by *Gray* would reappear in an election by the legislature, he said, including the negating of minority sentiment within each legislator's district and the possibility that the candidate who won the most votes in the general election might be defeated.[94]

When the General Assembly met in January 1967 and did elect a Governor, the popular will was in fact frustrated. Heavily Democratic in complexion, the Assembly chose Maddox as Governor, even though Callaway had received more votes in the election.

In the long run, however, the Georgia case may have functioned to strengthen rather than dilute the clear principle of voter equality spelled out in the *Gray* decision. Reflecting the ideology of the reapportionment cases and *Gray v. Sanders* in particular, most U.S. newspapers concluded that a basic injustice had been done. Not a few noted that under the country's archaic electoral college system, exactly the same type of injustice could be perpetrated through a contingent election in Congress if a similar three-way split of votes prevented the candidate who won the most popular votes from winning a majority of the electoral votes.

America had come far since the days of property qualifications for voting, coercion of minorities at the polls, the nonsecret ballot and flagrant vote stealing in disputed elections. Through a climactic series of events in the single decade of the 1960s, gross malapportionment of legislative districts had been ended and the right to vote assured to virtually every adult American. But the sanctity of the ballot and assurance of its equal and full count could not be assured fully until there was a basic reform in the machinery for electing the most important official of all—the President of the United States.

NOTES

1. 1826 Senate Report, p. 6.
2. New York and Virginia, however, had widened the definition of freeholder to include those with estate leases for life. See Chilton Williamson, *American Suffrage from Property to Democracy* (Princeton, N.J., 1960), p. 12.
3. Dudley O. McGovney, *The American Suffrage Medley* (Chicago, 1949), pp. 12–13.
4. Peter Force, *American Archives* (Washington, D.C., 1837–53), II, p. 962, cited by Williamson, *op. cit.*, p. 6.
5. McGovney, *op. cit.*, pp. 13–16.
6. Williamson, *op. cit.*, pp. 49, 57.
7. F. B. Dexter (ed.), *Extracts from the Itineraries of . . . Ezra Stiles . . . 1755–1795* (1916), p. 462, cited by Williamson, *op. cit.*, p. 44.
8. William Miller, *A New History of the United States* (1958), pp. 109–12.
9. In some respects, suffrage was "automatic" in these years as state money depreciated through the economic dislocations of the Revolution and its aftermath. As currency declined in value, the property or tax tests became almost meaningless in a number of states. See Williamson, *op. cit.*, p. 121.
10. John Dickinson of Delaware, cited by Max Farrand (ed.), *The Records of the Federal Constitutional Convention of 1787*, 4 vols. (New Haven, 1911, 1937), II, p. 202.
11. Clinton Rossiter, *1787—The Grand Convention* (New York, 1966), p. 31, quoting a letter from Madison to Jefferson, Dec. 9, 1787, in *Writings of James Madison*, Gaillard Hunt, ed. (New York, 1910), 9 vols., V, p. 66.
12. Williamson, *op. cit.*, pp. 149–50, 156, 202, 204–5, 208–9; also U.S. Commission on Civil Rights, *Report* (Washington, 1959), pp. 23–24. Cited hereafter as Civil Rights Commission *Report*.
13. Cited by Williamson, *op. cit.*, p. 223.
14. Civil Rights Commission *Report*, p. 23.
15. Lee Benson, *The Concept of Jacksonian Democracy* (New York, 1964), p. 7.
16. Alpheus Thomas Mason, *Free Government in the Making* (New York, 1949), p. 383.
17. Cited by Mason, *op. cit.*, pp. 417–22, 423–26.
18. *Ibid.*, pp. 407–17.
19. *Ibid.*, pp. 398–401.
20. *Ibid.*, pp. 406–7.
21. Williamson, *op. cit.*, pp. 242–60, 268.
22. Civil Rights Commission *Report*, p. 25.
23. *Ibid.*, pp. 25–26.
24. *Ibid.*, p. 27.
25. *Ibid.*, p. 28.

26. *United States v. Cruickshank*, 92 U.S. 542 (1876); *United States v. Reese*, 92 U.S. 214 (1876). For full background on Supreme Court cases relating to the right to vote in the era following the Civil War, see Richard Claude, "Constitutional Voting Rights and Early U.S. Supreme Court Doctrine," *The Journal of Negro History*, April 1966, pp. 114–24.

27. K. H. Porter, *A History of Suffrage in the United States* (1918), pp. 196–97.

28. Civil Rights Commission *Report*, pp. 31–32.

29. Cited in Civil Rights Commission *Report*, p. 33.

30. *Nixon v. Herndon*, 272 U.S. 536 (1927).

31. *Grovey v. Townsend*, 295 U.S. 45 (1935).

32. *Smith v. Allwright*, 321 U.S. 649 (1944).

33. *Guinn v. United States*, 238 U.S. 347 (1915).

34. *C.Q. Almanac*, 1962, pp. 404–6; *Congress and the Nation* (Congressional Quarterly Service, Washington, 1965), p. 1641.

35. 383 U.S. 663 (1966). See *C.Q. Weekly Report*, April 1, 1966, p. 715.

36. *Congress and the Nation*, pp. 1596–1642.

37. *C.Q. Almanac*, 1965, p. 538.

38. *Ibid.*, p. 540.

39. Figures from reports of the Commission on Civil Rights and the Southern Regional Council. White registration in the South stood at 14.4 million in 1966, just over 70 percent of the eligible white population.

40. Civil Rights Commission *Report*, p. 20; "Woman Suffrage," *The Encyclopedia Americana* (1953 ed.), XXIX, p. 450.

41. *Minor v. Happersett*, 88 U.S. 162 (1875).

42. "Woman Suffrage," as cited, pp. 452–54.

43. Farrand, *op. cit.*, I, pp. 150–51.

44. Samuel Eliot Morison, *The Oxford History of the American People* (New York, 1966), p. 731.

45. See U.S. House, Committee on the Judiciary, *State Applications Asking Congress to Call a Federal Constitutional Convention*, Committee Print (Washington, 1961), p. 17.

46. *Congress and the Nation*, p. 1516.

47. The years in which Northern states enacted literacy or educational tests: Connecticut 1855, Massachusetts 1857, Wyoming 1889, Maine 1892, California 1896, Delaware 1897, New Hampshire 1902, Arizona 1912, New York 1921, Oregon 1924, Alaska 1958, Hawaii 1959. See McGovney, *op. cit.*, pp. 59–60; also *C.Q. Almanac*, 1965, p. 539.

48. Years of Southern literacy tests: Mississippi 1890, South Carolina 1895, Louisiana 1898, North Carolina 1900, Alabama 1901, Virginia 1902, Georgia 1908, Oklahoma 1910. See McGovney, *op. cit.*, pp. 59–60.

49. *C.Q. Almanac*, 1965, p. 535.

50. *Katzenbach v. Morgan* and *New York City Board of Elections v. Morgan*, 383 U.S. 641 (1966), and *Cardona v. Power*, 384 U.S. 672 (1966). See *C.Q. Weekly Report*, June 17, 1966, p. 1314.

51. For full background on residence laws in U.S. history, see Walter Kravitz, *Residence Requirements on Voting*, report of the Legislative Reference Service, Library of Congress (Washington, 1960), reprinted in 1961 Senate *Hearings*, pp. 844–57.

52. Kravitz, *op. cit.*, pp. 848–49.
53. William G. Andrews, "American Voting Participation," *Western Political Quarterly*, Dec. 1966, pp. 639–52.
54. For background on Administration bill and state laws on absentee voting and registration, see *C.Q. Weekly Report*, July 28, 1967, pp. 1320–23.
55. Andrews, *loc. cit.*, p. 647.
56. 1961 Senate *Hearings*, p. 474.
57. See also remarks of Rep. John Brademas of Indiana, *Congressional Record*, 1967, pp. H 3674–75 (daily ed.).
58. Williamson, *op. cit.*, p. 277; Andrews, *loc. cit.*, p. 642.
59. See McGovney, *op. cit.*, pp. 54–55.
60. For background on shifts in minimum voting age, 1943–60, see 1961 Senate *Hearings*, pp. 859–66.
61. Address to National Association of Secretaries of State, Las Vegas, Nevada, Oct. 5, 1967.
62. 1961 Senate *Hearings*, p. 472; Andrews, *loc. cit.*, p. 651.
63. Andrews, *loc. cit.*, p. 651. Andrews estimates that in 1960 there were 1 million who voted only in primary elections and another 1 million who went to the polls in November but failed to have a Presidential vote recorded.
64. U.S. Census Bureau, *Current Population Reports*, "Voter Participation in the National Election, Nov. 1964," Series P–20, No. 143, Oct. 25, 1965.
65. Richard M. Scammon, "The Electoral Process," *Law and Contemporary Problems*, Spring 1962, p. 301.
66. *Ibid.*, p. 302.
67. See McGovney, *op. cit.*, pp. 89–91.
68. John Bach McMaster, *A History of the People of the United States from the Revolution to the Civil War*, 8 vols. (New York, 1893–1924), I, pp. 14–15; see also *Annals of Congress*, April 29, 1794.
69. See "Ballot," *Encyclopedia Americana* (1953 ed.), III, p. 107.
70. *Ibid.*, p. 108; Williamson, *op. cit.*, pp. 274–75.
71. *Ex parte Siebold*, 100 U.S. 371 (1880).
72. *United States v. Moseley*, 283 U.S. 383 (1915).
73. *United States v. Classic*, 313 U.S. 299 (1941).
74. *McPherson v. Blacker*, 146 U.S. 1 (1892).
75. *Burroughs and Cannon v. United States*, 290 U.S. 534 (1934).
76. *Ex parte Yarbrough*, 110 U.S. 651 (1884).
77. *C.Q. Weekly Report*, June 7, 1963, p. 917.
78. For a full review of the legal development and political effects of the reapportionment cases and related developments, see *Representation and Apportionment* (Congressional Quarterly Service, Washington, 1966).
79. *Ibid.*, p. 87.
80. *Ibid.*, pp. 10–11, 52.
81. 382 U.S. 549 (1946).
82. *Representation and Apportionment*, p. 14.
83. *Baker v. Carr*, 369 U.S. 186 (1962).
84. 377 U.S. 533 (1964).
85. *C.Q. Almanac*, 1965, p. 520; *C.Q. Almanac*, 1966, p. 505. As an alternative to Congressional submission of a constitutional amendment, a number of state

legislatures, following the recommendation of the General Assembly of the States (part of the Council of State Governments), petitioned Congress to call a constitutional convention which would write an amendment similar to Dirksen's for subsequent submission to the states for ratification. By August 1967, 32 of the required 34 states (two thirds of the total) had submitted such resolutions, but serious question remained as to whether they could muster the necessary two additional states, or whether Congress would actually implement the convention call. See *C.Q. Weekly Report*, March 24, 1967, p. 439.

86. *C.Q. Weekly Report*, Jan. 13, 1967, p. 75; Jan. 20, 1967, p. 101. For review of apportionment activity up to mid-1966, see *Representation and Apportionment*, pp. 65–85, or *C.Q. Weekly Report*, June 17, 1966, pp. 1285–1306.

87. 376 U.S. 1 (1964).

88. *C.Q. Weekly Report*, Jan. 20, 1967, p. 101.

89. *Representation and Apportionment*, p. 25.

90. *Ibid.*, p. 39.

91. William J. D. Boyd, "Suburbia Takes Over," *National Civic Review*, June 1965, pp. 294–98. For discussion of city-suburban differences and political impact of the reapportionment decisions, see *Representation and Apportionment*, pp. 38–44.

92. *C.Q. Weekly Report*, Aug. 21, 1964, p. 1784. Many of the center cities had already lost Congressional seats, in redistricting that followed the 1960 Census apportionment, at the time of the study. The C.Q. analysis was based on a standard defining center cities as those with 50,000 population or more, in contrast to the Census Bureau's standard definition of "urban," in effect since 1790, which includes any town of more than 2,500 population.

93. 372 U.S. 368 (1963).

94. *C.Q. Weekly Report*, Dec. 9, 1966, p. 2997; Dec. 16, 1966, p. 3028.

8

Today's Alternative: Direct Vote or the Status Quo

THE EXAMINATION OF ELECTORAL REFORM EFFORTS OVER THE YEARS HAS shown how each halfway measure, from the district system of the 19th century to the proportional system advanced most prominently after World War II, has had its day and been found wanting. The alternatives have failed either because of inherent defects or because they would have wrought fundamental changes in the political power alignments of the nation. Our review of the modern-day trend toward universal adult suffrage has demonstrated that for the first time in U.S. history, a logical electoral base exists for instituting a direct vote of the people for their President. Thus the real choice today is between two alternatives. Either the country will continue with the existing electoral college system, or it will shift to a direct popular vote.

The advantages of a direct vote are immediately apparent. There would no longer be the chance that the man who won the most popular votes could be deprived of the Presidency through the mathematical vagaries of the electoral college. The massive disfranchisement of the minority voters in each state would be ended once and for all, with each person's vote registered directly and equally in the decisive national count. No one's vote would be totally eclipsed or magnified to many times its rightful weight because of the chance factor of state residence. Localized corruption in a single large state would be far less likely to determine the outcome of the national election. The office of elector would disappear, so that no "electoral Benedict Arnold" could take it in his own hands to sway the outcome of an election. Splinter parties would no longer have the ability to shift the outcome in pivotal states or to capitalize on their strength in a handful of states to throw an election into the House of Representatives for decision. If the direct vote system were properly devised, there would no longer be the possibility of a contingent election in Congress where a prospective Chief Executive could be subjected to unconscionable pressures to "sell out" on major issues as the price of his election.

Basic Issues

Even if these apparent advantages are conceded, however, the opponents of direct vote can and do raise serious questions about its implementation: Are our politics advanced to a point where we are ready for a single national vote for President? Would it undermine American federalism and our two-party system? Would it have a disturbing impact on the political balance of the country, on our entire political stability? The historian Clinton Rossiter, a man dubious about the advisability of change, warns that "we should hesitate a long time before replacing a humpty-dumpty system that works with a neat one that will blow up in our faces." Would-be reformers, he cautions, "are digging into the foundations of the state—always a dangerous thing to do."[1]

THE "CONCURRENT MAJORITY" ARGUMENTS. Behind the arguments of Rossiter and other thoughtful opponents of the direct vote is a concern that we would be substituting a kind of naked, unrestrained majoritarianism for a system that obliges the national parties and Presidential candidates to offer moderate programs acceptable to a wide range of economic, geographic and political interests. The electoral college, Carl Becker argued, is a major factor in forcing both political parties to hew close to the middle of the road, in deterring them from the adoption of "pure" ideologies and taking an uncompromising stand in favor of any single economic or class group. "This system," he wrote, "makes it impossible for any political party to win a national election, even though it has a majority of the popular votes cast, unless the votes it polls are properly distributed throughout the country; and no party has much chance of getting such a distribution if it represents exclusively the interests of any section or class. It can get the necessary strategic distribution of the popular vote only if it is willing to appeal to the interests of many sections and to the interests of all classes—agriculture and industry, capital and labor, rich and poor, progressives and conservatives—in a sufficient number of states to win a majority of the electoral votes."[2]

The roots of Becker's argument may be found in John C. Calhoun's theory of the concurrent majority. "There are," Calhoun wrote, "two different modes in which the sense of the community may be taken; one, simply, by the right of suffrage, unaided; the other, by the right through a proper organism. Each collects the sense of the majority. But one regards numbers only and considers the whole community as a unit, having but one common interest throughout, and collects the sense of the greater number of the whole as that of the community. The other, on the contrary, regards interest as well as number—considering the community as made up of different and conflicting interests, as far as the action of the government is concerned—and takes the sense of each, through its majority or appropriate organ, and the united sense of all as the sense of the entire community. The former of these I shall call the numerical, or absolute majority; and the latter, the concurrent or constitutional majority."[3]

Calhoun, of course, developed his theory of the concurrent majority to justify the actions of states in nullifying the acts of the federal government. But the theory is still attractive and valid in many ways. Certainly the entire system of checks and balances, with its distribution of varying powers among federal, state and local governments, is designed to prevent any temporary majority from assuming absolute power and negating the rights of minorities.

But is the theory applicable to the election of a single individual—the President of the United States? Would the direct vote for President in any way negate or restrict the protections built into our constitutional system? The answer is clearly no. A President elected by direct vote would still have to win the approval of Congress for his major programs. Special district and state interests would still have a powerful voice through their regular representation in the U.S. Senate and House. The long chain of constitutional amendments designed to protect the rights of the people, starting with the Bill of Rights and extending into our own century, would remain in full force. The Judiciary would still function as an essential check on unbridled Presidential power. The state and local governments would retain their special preserves of power and authority. One can recognize "concurrent majority" as a touchstone of the American system but still deny that it does or should have anything to do with the process by which the American people elect their Chief Executive.

What then of Carl Becker's argument? Would direct election of the President undermine the forces working for appeasement, for conciliation and for compromise in the American political system? Would rigid ideologies and inflammatory class appeals become more dominant? Again, there is no palpable evidence to support the allegation. In fact, it must be acknowledged that the existing system does not invariably create perfect moderation and balance in our Presidential campaigns. One may admire Harry Truman's political courage in 1948, but by any dispassionate analysis it must be conceded that his campaign was based on blatant class and ethnic appeals. For uncompromising ideology, no Presidential candidate of modern times has outdone Barry Goldwater in the 1964 campaign. These campaigns may be more the exception than the rule, but they have happened—the electoral college notwithstanding.

Secondly, it may be asked if the actual operation of the electoral college has anything to do with the moderation of political life in the United States. If most Americans think they are voting for President directly anyway, it is hard to see how a constitutional legitimization of their direct participation would change their attitude or that of the political leaders. It is suggested that the electoral college makes Presidential candidates and parties appeal to all sections and all classes. Senator Hugh Scott of Pennsylvania, chairman of the Republican National Committee in the 1948 campaign and a strategist in the Eisenhower and Nixon races, suggested in an interview with the author that the necessity of seeking state-by-state victories obliges a Presidential candidate to recognize particular state and regional problems—irrigation and grazing problems in the West, the outmigration of industry in the East, TVA policies in the Tennessee Valley, or East-West trade in the Dakotas. Scott's point is a valid one, but the question arises how this would change under a direct vote system. A candidate would still have to fashion a national majority out of votes from hundreds of geographic areas, class and economic groups and ideological camps. No single group could give him the election. In fact, the candidate might be more willing than now to consider special local problems, since every vote in every state would count—even if the opposing party was all but sure to carry that state.

In the final analysis, it must be recognized that the electoral college today—barring the catastrophe of rebel electors or an election thrown into the House—is nothing more than a counting device. Consciously or not, every candidate for President aims first at winning the support of a majority of the whole American people, because winning an electoral college majority without a popular vote majority is a risky undertaking. Before the 1964 election Barry Goldwater's strategists thought they might achieve an electoral college victory by combining the electoral votes of the South with those of the conservative Western Mountain states and the farm-oriented Midwest. They consciously "wrote off" the popular vote-heavy states like California, New York, Pennsylvania and New Jersey, admitting—at least implicitly—a national popular vote defeat.[4] But the strategy was a bankrupt one from the start and predictably ended in overwhelming defeat. No Presidential candidate is likely to try it again. And if no serious Presidential candidate will consciously design a strategy that admits popular vote defeat in the hope of electoral college victory, would it not be better to have a popular vote alone? Even if there were predictable regional patterns that permitted a candidate to "localize" his campaign to win in the electoral college while losing the popular vote, would we want to accept such a system? Should Westerners or Southerners or people from any region, by the way the electoral votes are distributed, be accorded some special privilege in electing the President that the rest of us are denied? Indeed, if the system *did* operate this way, there would be all the more reason to abolish it posthaste.

If a direct vote really did lead to increased class antagonisms, ideologically oriented campaigns and a lack of political moderation, we should have seen these factors at work already in the states, where every Governor is chosen today by direct vote of the people. The major states especially could be said to be microcosms of the entire nation. The 1960 Census showed that New York and California both had four times as many inhabitants as the entire United States in the first Census, that of 1790. Yet direct vote has not led to extremism in the states; indeed, the overwhelming majority of U.S. Governors have tended to be practical problem-solvers rather than ideological zealots. Nor has the U.S. Senate become a stamping ground for extremists in the wake of the 17th Amendment, which shifted the selection of Senators from the state legislatures to direct vote of the people.

In fact, direct vote of the people is hardly a risky, untried governmental principle that could "blow up in our faces." It is the tried and true way of electing every nonappointive governmental official in the United States today, and for the most part it has been the common rule and practice since the birth of our nation. Norman Thomas stated the case with accuracy a few years ago when he commented that "no one in his right mind would suggest any way of electing the President of the United States, if you were starting *de nova,* other than by straight popular vote."[5]

THE TWO-PARTY SYSTEM. One of the most frequent criticisms of the proposal for direct election of the President is that it would lead to a plethora of ideologically oriented splinter parties and thus undermine the prevailing two-party system and moderate political tone of the United States. Critics of direct vote have argued that splinter parties would be encouraged because they would see their votes, however small, reflected in the decisive national count, or because it might be easier for them to qualify for places on the ballot. The implication of the argument is that splinter parties are now discouraged because they rarely if ever can win a plurality of the popular votes in any state and thus capture electoral votes.

Presumably, if a direct vote plan were written with a requirement that the winner receive an absolute majority of the vote, a significant number of splinter party votes in a close election could deprive both major parties of a majority and throw the election into Congress for decision. Whether the splinter parties would gain anything from such an exercise is dubious, since minor-party Representatives rarely if ever win election to Congress where the choice would be made. The major parties control Congress and would invariably pick a major-party candidate. But to dispel any chance of splinter party exploitation of a direct election system, the American Bar Association recommended that 40 percent, rather than an actual majority of popular votes, be required under a direct election plan and that any runoff be by popular vote rather than by Congress.

Upon serious analysis it appears that any danger to the two-party system through a direct vote for President is chimerical. An extensive body of political research has identified many reasons for Americans' adherence to the two-party system: the electoral college is not among them. The two-party system, one political scientist notes, is "the Rock of Gibraltar of American politics."[6] The reasons for continuation of the system, Rossiter suggests, go far beyond the mere forms of government: "The bounty of the American economy, the fluidity of American society, the remarkable unity of the American people, and, most important, the success of the American experiment have all mitigated against the emergence of large dissenting groups that would seek satisfaction of their special needs through the formation of political parties." Third-party politics is generally radical politics, Rossiter notes, and radical politics has not made much headway in the United States. "Socialism in particular (and in all its varieties) has sailed through rough seas in this country. It foundered long ago, as Werner Sombart remarked despairingly, 'on the shoals of roast beef and apple pie.' "[7]

Many institutional factors also discourage third parties, including the basic American system of elections—electoral laws, campaign practices, social patterns, which make it extremely difficult for minor parties to attain even secondary nationwide influence. Contributing factors are the high cost of political campaigning, the statutory obstacles to getting on the ballot in many states, and the legal status of the major parties as supervisors of elections in many areas.[8] V. O. Key, the noted political scientist, saw the very institution of the Presidency as a major reason for the two-party system: "The Presidency, unlike a multiparty cabinet, cannot be parceled out among minuscule parties. The circumstances stimulate coalition within the electorate before the election rather than in parliament after the popular vote. Since no more than two parties can for long compete effectively for the Presidency, two contending groups tend to develop, each built on its constituent units in each of the 50 states."[9]

Many political scientists define the U.S. system of electing representatives in single-member districts, with the plurality deciding, as the basic support for the two-party system. The Frenchman Maurice Duverger and the American E. E. Schattschneider have been the most prominent advocates of this theory. As Schattschneider develops the case, the higher the percentage of the total vote that a party can win, "the more cheaply"—in terms of votes—can it win seats in Congress. Conversely, the smaller the party's percentage, the more "expensive" will be the seats it wins in terms of votes.[10] As an example, in the 1964 Congressional elections the Democratic party won 57.5 percent of the national vote for the U.S. House, but 67.8 percent of the seats. The Republicans won 42.5 percent of the national House vote, but only 32.2 percent of the seats. When the Republicans have controlled Congress, they have enjoyed the same inflation of their relative power. But while the system discriminates moderately against the runner-up party, the third, fourth and fifth parties see their chances of winning actual seats reduced to the vanishing point. Though several hundred thousand votes are cast for minor parties in most Congressional elections, minor parties have not held more than two of the 435 U.S. House seats at any time since 1944, and the last time that a Representative was elected without regular Democratic or Republican affiliation was 1952.

But why doesn't the single-member district system inflate the leading party's percentage so much that it crushes the second major party as well? The major reason, according to Schattschneider, is that the defeated party is likely to have sufficient sectional strength to protect itself against annihilation even in a crushing defeat. In modern U.S. politics, it may hold certain center-city or rural districts, for instance, that are so impervious to national trends that they will indefinitely continue a party in power. A second reason is that the defeated party is able to retain a "monopoly of opposition" because it is the natural gathering point for critics of the party in power, and because it can claim that any votes cast for minor party candidates are "wasted" votes. In U.S. Presidential politics, sectional third parties, even when they become strong, are probably unable to survive because they cannot make a serious bid for the great prize, the Presidency.[11]

Another political scientist, Allan P. Sindler, says there is merit in the single-member district argument, but that the system alone cannot guarantee the survival of major parties in all circumstances—witness the disintegration of the Federalists and Whigs in earlier years. Nor does the single-member district system, Sindler points out, prevent a one-party regional system such as the U.S. South has had until recently.[12] The broader reason for two-partyism, he suggests, is "the character of social conflict and consensus in the nation." There must be an acceptance of political disagreement to support a two-party system. Where conflicts are bitter and unreconcilable, Sindler says, "the raw materials for unstable multi-partyism are present," and under some circumstances—as in the U.S. in the 1860s—civil war may ensue. On the other end of the spectrum, there may be election areas so united in their political interests that they cannot generate enough conflict to support two parties. The South's involvement with the race problem is given as an example. "The continuance of stable and moderate two-party systems," Sindler concludes, depends "upon a happy balance struck between consensus and conflict." The United States has generally been able to keep the balance, helped in no small part by the federal structure that offers various levels for the release of political pressures that build up in the system.[13]

In short, the suggestion that the two-party system is primarily or even significantly sustained by the electoral college seems to be a classic case of putting the cart before the horse. And it totally ignores the obvious invitation to minor party manipulation that the electoral college, through its requirement of an absolute majority with contingent election in the House, has always afforded.

THE FEDERAL SYSTEM. The direct election of the President, John F. Kennedy warned in 1956, "would break down the federal system under which most states entered the Union, which provides a system of checks and balances to insure that no area or group shall obtain too much power."[14] Kennedy was echoing the warning of critics, repeated thousands of times since the early 19th century, that a direct-vote amendment would be a betrayal of the Great Compromise between the large and small states that was reached at the Constitutional Convention. When the American Bar Association announced early in 1967 that it supported direct popular voting for the Presidency, Senator Karl Mundt rose on the Senate floor to voice the argument once again, warning that the ABA's recommendations "would cut the heart out of our federal union of states" and substitute a "mathematical constituency" for the existing combination of geography and population in the electoral base of the Presidency.[15]

The base of the federal system argument is that the allotment of two extra electoral votes given each state, to correspond with its number of Senators, constitutes a central guarantee of the American system, stemming from the Constitutional Convention itself. Historically, however, the argument stands on shaky ground (see page 36, above). The Great Compromise was devised to settle the dispute over representation in Congress, *not* the electoral college. It was presented to the Convention on July 5, 1787, and constituted the agreement that made the federal Union possible. Today it represents a central pillar of the American federal system which few men have seriously suggested disturbing. On the other hand, the terms of the Great Compromise, applied almost as an afterthought to electoral college apportionment, were not presented to the Constitutional Convention until September 4—a full two months after they had been considered in their essential form, relating to representation in Congress. At no point in the minutes of the Convention can one find any reference to the application of the

Great Compromise to the electoral college's apportionment as important to the federal system or to the over-all structure of the Constitution which was adopted. Indeed, it was never mentioned directly at all. Only in *The Federalist Papers,* where James Madison argued at one point that the electoral base for the Presidency would be a "compound" of national and state factors because of the mixed apportionment base, does the argument appear.[16] But no more than indirect reference was made to the apportionment of the electoral college in the state ratifying conventions, or in fact by any of the nation's leaders until some years after ratification of the Constitution. The argument that the founding fathers viewed the special federal nature of electoral college apportionment as central to the institution of the Presidency, or to the entire Constitution, is simply false. The small states thought they would gain special advantage, but by another provision—their equal votes in the House in contingent elections.

In fact, the fear of small states that they might be "swallowed up" in a titanic struggle with the large ones has never come true in U.S. history. Experience has shown no clear set of interests held by small states as opposed to large ones. None of the great battles of American political history—in Congress or in Presidential elections—has been fought on a basis of small versus large states. The arguments have been ideological, economic and regional but never of the kind that neatly line up the small states on one side and the large ones on the other. The arguments over the years, starting at the Constitutional Convention itself, on the subject of big- versus small-state interests and advantages might well be termed the Great Irrelevancy.

Sometimes it is assumed that the Senate, because of the extra weight it gives to small states, should be a conservative body hostile to the needs of the large states with their large urban population centers. But in our political history—especially in recent decades—this simply has not been the case. In fact, the Senate has generally been more liberal in its composition than the House of Representatives. The chief reason is probably that almost every Senator, except a tiny handful from the most rurally populated states, has one metropolitan center or more within his state and must therefore be responsive to urban needs. On the other hand, there are many Representatives from districts that have no metropolitan centers. These men have the freedom to be more conservative in their voting habits, and many of them are.

On paper, it may be shown that the people of 35 smaller states and the District of Columbia are "overrepresented" in the electoral college

today, because under the existing apportionment fewer of their population correspond to a single electoral vote than the national average of
333,314 persons per electoral vote (see chart, page 139). In Alaska, for
instance, the ratio is one electoral vote for every 75,389 persons; in
South Dakota, one electoral vote for every 170,129 persons. The 39
smallest states (plus the District of Columbia), with only 43.2 percent
of the national population, could theoretically control an electoral
college majority. The special small-state advantages have led observers
to suggest that any direct vote amendment would be "butchered in the
states." The "underrepresented" people are theoretically those in the 15
larger states where the ratio shows more persons per electoral vote
than the national average—from 337,573 per electoral vote in Kentucky to 392,930 per electoral vote in California.

Any advantage this disparity might be said to give to the people of
the smaller states is largely illusory, however. The first reason is that
the people of the 15 states with the least favorable population-to-
electoral-vote ratio still inhabit states with 312 electoral votes, easily a
majority of the national total of 538. In any election the people of the
larger states—if they chose to vote *en bloc*, which they rarely do—
could outvote the people of the 35 smaller states and the District. In
fact, the 12 largest states could elect a President with the 281 electoral
votes they control.* Politicians from the smaller states often complain
that the electoral college, in actual practice, works against them,
because by the very nature of the general ticket "winner-take-all"
system, national candidates concentrate their efforts in the few biggest
states where the shift of just a few hundred or thousand votes may
change large blocs of electoral votes and determine the national
outcome. (Computer studies have actually shown that the citizens of
larger states have a greater chance to cast the decisive votes under the
electoral college system than do citizens of smaller states. See Appendix O.)

A second reason that "overrepresentation" of a state is an illusory
advantage is that the people of a state do not vote unanimously for one
Presidential candidate or another—although the unit vote system of
casting electoral votes may make it look as if they had. But it is *people*
who have preferences, not states. The right to cast one's vote for the
Presidential candidate one prefers—and to see that vote added mean-

* New York, California, Pennsylvania, Illinois, Ohio, Texas, Michigan, New
Jersey, Florida, Massachusetts, Indiana and North Carolina.

ingfully to the votes of like-minded citizens throughout the United States and included in the national count—is the citizen's important right. If a voter finds he is in the minority in his state under the prevailing general ticket system, then he knows his vote will be completely negated in the national electoral vote count. His state may have enjoyed some theoretical right—and in fact cast an electoral vote several times over its actual right by population—but for the individual on the losing side, the alleged "right" is an empty one indeed.

To argue that these supposed mathematical "advantages" of small-state citizens under the federal system are important ones is to make a travesty of the entire federal system itself. For in truth, there are rich benefits for the citizens of all the states stemming from federalism in America. But they stem from entirely different grounds: from the representation each district and state enjoys in Congress, from the right of each state to fashion governmental policies particularly suited to its own citizens, from the protections from overbearing federal power which stem from the special rights of the states under the Constitution. If one wants to preserve "states' rights" and the American federal system, there are many better ways to do so than by preserving the fictional advantages of the electoral college. Improving municipal government, strengthening state legislatures, getting the states to shoulder an increasing share of the complex problems of our modern-day industrialized society—these are the ways to make federalism a viable institution for the benefit of all.

Indeed, if the electoral college has had any real impact on American federalism, it may have been in a way that weakened the role of the small states rather than enlarging or guaranteeing it. For experience has shown that the natural emphasis on the electoral vote blocs of the biggest states under the existing system has eclipsed the Presidential chances of many outstanding public servants who had the misfortune of coming from the smaller states. In its 1966 Supreme Court brief, Delaware pointed out that four states—New York, Ohio, Massachusetts and Virginia—had seen 21 of their citizens elected President for terms with a total of 111 years service. But Delaware pointed out that it was one of 36 states that had never witnessed the election of one of its citizens as President. Confining its analysis to the last century alone, Delaware pointed out that of the 100 major-party nominations for President and Vice President from 1868 through 1964, citizens of New York were nominated in 24 instances and that citizens of five other large states—California, Illinois, Indiana, Massachusetts and Ohio—

had accounted for another 44 of the nominations. But 26 states, itself included, Delaware said, had been totally excluded from nominations. Of the 13 original states, the Delaware brief said, eight had never elected a President in the 45 elections since the founding of the country—Connecticut, Delaware, Georgia, Maryland, North Carolina, Rhode Island, South Carolina and Vermont. In the 1960 Census, these states had a combined population of 18,213,449—substantially more than the 16,782,304 population of New York, the modern-day "mother of Presidents."

The natural rejoinder to Delaware's argument, of course, is that service in the state government of New York or another large state is more likely to train a man for the rigors of the Presidency and give him the national exposure he needs than is service in a small state. But even conceding that such factors may give large-state citizens a better break in many elections, the total exclusion of small-state citizens from the Presidency suggests real inequalities arising from the premium placed on big-state electoral vote blocs.*

Since the earliest days of the Republic, some American statesmen have recognized the dangers of placing states ahead of people in the election of the common national officer, the President. "The question of who shall be elected President is not a state, but a national question," Representative Jabez D. Hammond of New York declared on the House floor in 1816: "The President is an officer who exists for the benefit of the people of the United States, and not for any one state or any part of the states. He ought not, therefore, to be created by the states but by the people."[17] In 1848, President Polk declared: "If both houses represent the states and the people, so does the President. The President represents in the executive department the whole people of the United States, as each member of the legislative department represents portions of them."[18]

In 1956, Senator John Pastore of Rhode Island said that he had never heard—as a member of the Rhode Island Legislature, as Governor or as Senator from that small state—anyone in Rhode Island talk of the state's special power in Presidential elections through its two

---

* Major exceptions to party nominations of large-state candidates in recent times were the 1936 Republican selection of Alfred M. Landon of Kansas and the same party's 1964 nomination of Barry Goldwater of Arizona—ironically, the two biggest "losers" of the last half century. But the emphasis on candidates just because of their big-state ties, which Delaware complained of, may be dissipating in any event (see page 279, below).

extra electoral votes or "the power which would be abandoned if we went to popular elections." But Pastore said he had heard people say what "a shame" it was that the man who gets the most votes might lose the election.[19] At another point in the same year's debate, Pastore denied that his state of Rhode Island would be "making any sacrifice" if the electoral college were discarded for direct vote. "I believe that the power of a Rhode Islander lies in the fact that he has the right of franchise to vote for the President of the United States," Pastore said. "If more Rhode Islanders want a Republican to be President than a Democrat, and more people in the country agree with them than agree with other people who favor a different candidate, the more popular candidate should be elected President. . . . The man who has received the most votes is the man who ought to be President, whether he is from the South or the North or the East or the West. We are all Americans. We are all one nation. . . . The President is the President of all the people, not the President of the states."[20]

The case for disentangling Presidential elections from special state voting power was put another way by Norman Thomas. "Most of us people, when we are stirring up for political purposes, are not such terrific state patriots," Thomas said in 1949. "It seems to me, at least in the climate where I have spent most of my life, that the average American's great ambition is to get to Southern California or Florida or parts of Texas before he dies, perhaps to condition him for the hereafter in one way or another. Now, under those circumstances, I think it is rather ridiculous for us to claim such passion and fervor for 'Delaware über alles,' or something like that."[21]

Indeed, those who would preserve the existing electoral college because of its ties to the federal system ought to consider the effect on American federalism if the electoral college were again to elect a candidate who lost in the popular vote. How could this be explained to the people? That the voters of certain states—any way the mathematical vagaries of the electoral college might misfire—should have more weight in the election of the President than the voters of other states, which make up a majority of the country? That for some mysterious reason connected with the federal system, the votes of men from Wyoming and New Hampshire were to be given more weight than the votes of men from New York and California—or possibly the reverse? How would these inequalities be explained in the day of "one man, one vote"? Past experience suggests there would be no rational explanation for the distribution of electoral votes that caused the system to blow up in our faces again. To preserve such a system seems to be a poor service to federalism.*

Nor would the preservation of the electoral college seem to be an essential element in maintaining the "dual citizenship" of Americans—both as citizens of the United States and as citizens of their particular states. Americans would still be citizens of their own states as they participated in state elections and took part in all the life of their states of residence. Abolishing the electoral college would simply create a direct relationship between the people and their President—who, after all, is a national, not a state, official. In the widest sense, direct voting would not be a contradiction of federalism but its natural culmination in a system of "one man, one vote" for every office, from city councilman to President of the United States, each in its proper sphere.

THE NOMINATING CONVENTIONS. From time to time, the suggestion is made that the Presidential nominating conventions ought to be abolished and replaced with direct national nominating primaries. Some advocates of the direct vote for President, including the late Senator William Langer of North Dakota and Senator Margaret Chase Smith of Maine, have suggested that the direct national primary would be the natural companion of the popular vote for President. One of the earliest supporters of the direct primary was President Woodrow Wilson, who advanced the idea in his first annual message to Congress in 1913.[22]

On first blush, the national primary idea seems to offer many advantages. It would permit the people in each party to play a direct role in the nomination of their candidate, rather than filtering their choice through the circus-like atmosphere of the national convention with all its invitations to horse-trading and corruption. "Is it not a far better thing," Senator William Proxmire of Wisconsin has argued, "to choose our Presidential nominees in a national primary, where the candidates and their ideas are on display and are contending openly,

---

* Defenders of the existing electoral vote system are rarely candid about the inequalities they want to preserve. As an exception, Senator Holland of Florida in 1967 Senate hearings said he opposed direct election because one of its results would be to give citizens of the District of Columbia more voting power than the citizens of 11 states with less population—Alaska, Delaware, Hawaii, Idaho, Montana, Nevada, New Hampshire, North Dakota, South Dakota, Vermont and Wyoming. Holland's reason for wanting to dilute the voting power of District residents: the fact that the District "does not have any of the duties or responsibilities of sovereign statehood." Holland apparently believed District citizens should have less of a right to choose their President because of their residence.

than it is to choose them in the narrow, emotional, cynical, rumor-filled, bandwagon-rolling, shouting, no-one listening climate of a party convention?" The rank and file of the parties' membership, Proxmire said, "do not have a meaningful voice in the selection of the Presidential candidate." A handful of political leaders usually dominate the state conventions and party committee meetings called to select delegates, and even in the primary states those contests "are not responsive instruments for carrying out the wishes of the mass of the party membership." Proxmire suggested a common national primary date, with each candidate given the number of electoral votes his state is entitled to, and a runoff if no candidate won the nomination in the first primary.[23]

A closer examination, however, reveals many deleterious effects that could stem from an abandonment of the convention system in favor of national primaries. The national convention, for all its faults, does provide the forum in which the disparate elements of a national party must reach the necessary compromises to hammer out a party platform. This process, Malcolm Moos has commented, "compels both parties to try to bring together all the discordant elements all over the country. And, in the long process, it seems to me that that's one of the best ways of cementing our political life."[24] Since the candidates for President and Vice President are chosen at the same convention, there is a natural pressure to select men who can run on the platform as written and a subsequent pressure on the candidates to live up to the broad principles and policies spelled out in the platform.

The convention has other distinct advantages. While it is composed of party professionals, it does have to bear in mind the importance of selecting a candidate who will appeal not just to convinced party members but to a broad base of independent voters as well. The independent voters would presumably be excluded from the party nominating primaries. Also, there are years when none of the candidates who have advanced themselves and run in the various state primaries have been able to build a really broad base of national support. Under such circumstances, the convention can "draft" a candidate like Charles Evans Hughes in 1916 (while he was sitting on the Supreme Court) or Governor Adlai E. Stevenson of Illinois in 1952.

National primaries would also raise a new set of thorny problems. There would often be multiple entries, making it impossible for any man to win a clear majority. Even if a runoff were held between the top two contenders, there is no assurance that they might not represent

the extreme positions in the party, while a more moderate contender—
representing everyone's second choice but no one's first choice—would
be eliminated in the first round. There would be no opportunity, as
there is in the national nominating convention, for the competing
forces to reshuffle themselves again and again until they were able
to reach a consensus in favor of a single candidate. Thus a proposal
"designed to locate and amplify the voice of the real majority might
instead gag it," Sidney Hyman comments.[25]

Moreover, the men chosen to run together for President and Vice
President in a national primary might represent sharply contrasting
points of view or even be antagonistic toward each other. The result
would be continuing embarrassments in the general election campaign,
and even if the team was elected, highly undesirable discord in the
new administration. Under the convention system as it operates today,
the Presidential candidate is almost invariably accorded the privilege
of selecting his own Vice Presidential nominee—a sound principle
recognized in the 25th Amendment, which gives a President the right
to nominate a new Vice President when the latter office becomes
vacant.

Thus the national party conventions, which the late V. O. Key saw
as "part and parcel of the magic by which men rule," play a vital role
in the American system of bringing together, tempering and compro-
mising the factions of continental political parties. Rather than the
electoral college, the conventions should be recognized as an institution that produces a "concurrent majority" in American Presidential
politics. There may be a time in the future when devices can be found
to overcome the apparent drawbacks of the national primary—perhaps
by requiring candidates to subscribe to a platform already written by a
convention or even permitting the Presidential candidate chosen in a
national primary to nominate his own Vice Presidential running mate,
subject to certain limitations. But as Senator Thruston Morton of
Kentucky suggests, the nation may need a half-generation or more of
experience with the direct popular election before it seriously considers
discarding the proven convention system in favor of direct nominating
primaries.[26]

The Nationalization of U.S. Politics

The electoral college system of choosing the President is predicated
on the treatment of states as separate voting blocs. The system could
be said to make some sense in a country where various regions and

states are essentially one party in nature. If the people of Vermont vote in election after election for the Republican candidate and Alabamians are unswervingly Democratic in their loyalties, then there may be little reason for not alloting the electoral votes of those states to the national candidates of the dominant party in each case, no matter how small the voter turnout in these "safe" states may be.

Until recent years a substantial number of the states were essentially "one party" in nature. The entire Southland voted Democratic without exception. As recently as 1949, then-Representative Brooks Hays of Arkansas could complain: "I was over 21 years of age before I ever saw a candidate for the Presidency. My people never really shared in the selection of the President. They do not yet share in it."[27] Senator Kefauver pointed out that until 1928, when Herbert Hoover made a journey to Elizabethton, Tennessee, no major candidate for President had ventured below the Mason-Dixon line for many, many years.[28] From the end of Reconstruction until 1928, eight Southern states never once cast their electoral votes for a Republican candidate. It was not until 1964 that Alabama, Georgia, Mississippi and South Carolina finally went Republican in a Presidential race. On the other side, six states voted Republican in every Presidential election from the Civil War to New Deal days, with the exception of 1912, when the Bull Moose movement split the GOP vote. These states were Iowa, Maine, Michigan, Minnesota, Pennsylvania and Vermont. Vermont actually remained true to the Grand Old Party in every election until 1964. Another six states—Illinois, Massachusetts, New Hampshire, Ohio, Oregon and Rhode Island—strayed from the Republican fold only twice in the 16 elections between the end of the Civil War and the advent of the New Deal in 1932.

This one-party complexion of major regions and states has evaporated in the past decades. Since 1932, only two states—Arkansas and North Carolina—have voted unfailingly for the Presidential candidates of one party (the Democratic), and the recent increase of Republican strength in the North Carolina House delegation and the election of a Republican Governor in Arkansas promise that these states too will soon join the others as real battlegrounds in any close election. Looking to the future, it is hard to detect any "safe" states or regions anywhere in the United States. In Presidential politics, and increasingly in local and state politics as well, each state is a two-party battleground. Compartmentalizing voters into state voting blocs is no longer desirable or necessary. Combined with the trend toward universal adult suffrage, the nationalization of U.S. politics means that the national electoral base for a direct vote of all the people for their President already exists.

These fundamental changes in the political landscape have not, of course, taken place in a vacuum. They are closely related to the revolution in educational standards, the American standard of living, population mobility and communications that the United States has experienced in the past decades and that forms the basis for a continuing widening of the suffrage and development of viable national two-party politics in the years to come.

EDUCATION. The principle of universal compulsory education, born in Massachusetts in the early 19th century, has spread to every state and community in the United States. Not only is every child in the United States now entitled to free education through the 12th grade, but many states provide for free junior colleges or all-the-way-through state-supported colleges. As a result of this movement, illiteracy has been virtually eliminated in the United States. The years since World War II have seen a vast expansion in public education and in the broadening of the numbers of Americans continuing to higher education. The figures below, based on Census data, show the sharp rise in recent decades of the number of median school years completed by all Americans over 25, with a projection to the future:

Census Year	Median School Years Completed
1940	8.6
1960	10.5
1970 (projection)	12.0
1980 (projection)	12.3

One authority estimates that by the year 2000 the median number of school years attained by Americans may well have reached 14.0 years—the equivalent average education through the sophomore year in college.[29]

The inevitable result of this steady upward climb in education is an increasingly sophisticated electorate, able to make its own decisions about national issues and the candidates for public office and inevitably more willing—despite the many ties of family and economic group political loyalty—to split tickets on election day and to pick the man rather than the party when it comes to voting for President.

STANDARD OF LIVING. The fears of some of the founding fathers that a majority of the American people would one day be without property or any other stake in their community, and thus hostile to the established order, have not been borne out by the course of U.S. history, especially in recent decades. Instead, there has been a dramatic rise in the standard of living of the people, combined with phenomenal growth in home ownership and the possession of wealth of every kind. In a single 16-year period, from 1947 to 1963, there was a rise of about 50 percent in the dollar income of the average American family, from $4,165 to $6,249 a year—measured in "constant" 1963 dollars. In 1947 a typical family earned $80 a week; in 1963 its counterpart was earning $120 a week in constant dollars. Ben J. Wattenberg, in his analysis of Census data, estimated that by the year 2000 the median family income in the United States will certainly have exceeded $10,000 a year, again in constant dollars. "Even $15,000 is not too wild a guess," he adds, "for after all, real family income climbed by 37 percent in one decade from 1950 to 1960."[30]

These rosy economic projections are not intended to deny the presence of hardcore, brutal poverty in the United States today. About a quarter of the families of the nation subsist on less than $4,000 a year, considered by some authorities to be the threshold of real poverty. But after allowance is made for students, farm families without rent to pay and retirees among the 25 percent of U.S. families earning the least money, Wattenberg estimates that no more than one in ten families is afflicted by "true poverty." "We are not a nation with huge numbers of seething, shuffling poor people who invisibly tramp through our streets with neither hope nor health," he comments. The problem of hunger, present in many parts of America as recently as the 1930s, has been largely conquered. Social Security gives virtually all Americans an assurance of support in their old age. The median wages of service workers and laborers rose by four times between 1939 and 1960, those of semiskilled factory workers by the same factor. In recent years the relative income increases for the professional and manager class have exceeded that of blue-collar workers, but in an era when the income of every group is rising at a rapid pace, the poorest segment of the population may be gaining the most in human terms. For the wealthy, more income may mean a larger house, more vacations or more securities owned. But for the poor family it may mean moving from a slum to an unpretentious suburb, a better diet, pension rights, better medical care or an automobile—the kinds of things that make life livable and pleasant.[31] Moreover, income figures do not reflect the major redistribution of wealth effected by federal mortgage insurance, unemployment compensation benefits, scholarship funds and the wide variety of other federal and state grant-in-aid programs. The days when citizens' votes were exchangeable for minor jobs, Christmas baskets or other petty favors are long since past.

The most serious economic problems for the country to solve in the coming decades clearly stem from the dilemma of the American Negro, especially in the crowded ghetto areas of the great cities. Many Negroes in America have achieved wages and status equal to or greater than those of the average white man. But there are still millions more to whom these advantages are denied, who suffer through substandard housing, poor education, discrimination in job placement and income below their real worth in our society.

In the long run, however, the problems of the American Negro must and will be solved—as equally formidable problems have been solved before in U.S. history. Indeed, Wattenberg points to the Census figures, which now show the Negro at the bottom of virtually every index, as evidence of the country's proven ability to solve its major social problems. A comparison of where the country stood half a century ago and where it stands today suggests the fantastic rate of progress that has been achieved. Today, Wattenberg points out, "there is a great 'absence of misery' in that number of children who don't die and in all those missing unskilled laborers; in the millions of marriages that aren't barren, millions of women who aren't spinsters, millions of families now undoubled, millions of children not at work, tens of millions of once-certain illiterates who instead can read and write, millions of Negroes now in the middle class, millions of children who'll go to kindergarten, millions of men who will retire healthy and compensated at 65 or 62, hundreds of thousands of women who will never be sleep-in domestics, and hundreds of farmers who own their farms and do not have to share-crop." The Census figures of the past show, he says, that these problems are not insurmountable. "Here is a nation," Wattenberg concludes, "dedicated to individualism, to economic mobility and egalitarianism and to the nobility of men—a nation that delivers many of those promises—and a nation that when it falls short of its world-shattering ideals subjects itself to tough and stinging self-scrutiny."[32] The plight of the ghetto Negro might seem to belie such optimism today. But given a choice between increasingly bitter racial tensions on the one hand and the massive and perhaps agonizing efforts necessary to achieve equity for the Negro on the other, the whole American experience suggests the nation in the long run will opt for the latter course.

If this analysis is correct, then the United States in the coming decades may look forward to increasing wealth, an end to poverty and, if its racial crises can be weathered, a high degree of political stability. And as Americans gain in wealth and leisure time, they will have more and more time to take part in politics.

POPULATION MOBILITY. One of the most important factors contributing to the nationalization of U.S. politics has been the mobility of the country's population. This is not merely the result of permanent moves of individuals and families across state lines, though as many as 10 percent of the population may change its state of residence in a single five-year period. The more important factor is the familiarity the vast majority of Americans have with people and places far from their own homes, a reflection of the increased travel made possible by greater wealth and modern means of transportation. As unpleasant as the wars of our century may have been, they have given millions of Americans a view of other portions of their own country and places abroad they would never have had in more placid times. The highly interdependent nature of the modern American economy promises to keep us a nation "on the move" into the foreseeable future. In the process, New Englanders are no longer strangers to the West, most Californians have met and know Easterners, and even Southerners have broken out of their ancient insularity. All of this has served to heighten all Americans' understanding of the Presidency as a national office responsible to all the people as Americans first, an office they view from their special vantage as citizens of one state or another in a very minor way.

MASS MEDIA. Probably no factor has contributed so much to the nationalization of American politics as the mass media: newspapers, national magazines, radio, and first and foremost in our own times, the phenomenon of television. Today the President of the United States can project himself into the vast majority of American homes any day he chooses to make a major pronouncement through television. His activities and his policies are reported and interpreted by *national* news organizations, so that the individual voter no longer has a view filtered through the biases of his Congressman or Senator reporting back from Washington, or the particular slant of his local newspaper alone. He can watch and judge the President on his own. And the President, in turn, knows that when he speaks out in public, he is speaking out to a national audience. He cannot tailor his remarks to please farmers one day, industrialists the next or unionists on another occasion. In the interests of his own political survival, he must remain the President of all the people—for they are watching him all the time.

Television has also raised the level of argument in Presidential primary and general election campaigns through the question-and-answer format of press conferences, interviews and panel shows. Candidates are obliged to take responsibility for the arguments they have advanced and to discuss them in some substance. The ultimate example was the series of "Great Debates" in the Kennedy-Nixon race of 1960, each of which was viewed by between 61 million and 75 million Americans. The debates forced the two candidates to clarify the many areas in which they agreed with each other, and sharpened the issue in areas where they really disagreed. Even more importantly, it gave the people of the country a chance to view the two men under the strain and pressure of the event. Nixon entered the debates with the reputation of being a skilled debater and a man with superior knowledge and depth through his eight years as Vice President. But his performance, especially in the first debate, disappointed even his warmest supporters. Kennedy, on the other hand, showed coolness under fire and an ability to deal with complex issues and make his points rapidly and clearly. In view of the close outcome of the 1960 election, it is generally believed that the debates were crucial in the election of Kennedy.

The future of the "Great Debates" is in doubt because any incumbent President—as Lyndon Johnson demonstrated in 1964—will be highly reluctant to expose himself to the political dangers, and the possibility of a "slip" on a point of national security, inherent in a live nationally televised confrontation with his opponent. But the whole array of other possibilities for television appearances—ranging from aired press conferences to paid political time—is likely to fill most of the real needs of Americans to watch and judge the candidates for the Presidency.

In every sense of the word, the Presidency has become a national office. The only aspect of it which is not national is the electoral college, a system devised for a poorer, less educated, less informed, less sophisticated nation and devised in an era when it was thought we would view the Chief Executive in our capacity as state patriots rather than the way we view him today—as the man of all the people.

The Direct Vote and National Politics

Precisely because the popular vote corresponds so closely to the way the American people already think about their President and appears to coincide so well with the existing political institutions of the United States, its institution would not likely cause any major change in the political alignments of the country or in the way that Presidential campaigns are conducted. In this respect the direct vote parts company with the district and proportional systems proposed in earlier years, which opponents could claim—with substantial evidence— would do much to alter the political balance of the nation.

In a series of interviews with national party professionals, men who had managed or advised in Presidential campaigns of the last decades, the author asked for their analysis of the impact that a direct vote might have. Almost without exception, they replied that they saw few if any substantive changes that might result in Presidential campaigns, and none felt that a direct vote would pose any special threat—or give any special advantage—to his party.

On the Democratic side, Postmaster General Lawrence O'Brien, a key strategist of two Democratic campaigns—the 1960 Kennedy effort and President Johnson's reelection campaign in 1964—said the direct vote "would not alter the basics of organizing a national political campaign." The candidate and his managers, O'Brien said, "would still concentrate their efforts where the votes are." While the major emphasis on New York City and other great metropolitan centers of the nation would continue, O'Brien indicated, visits would still be made to the smaller states—because there are votes there, too, even if not so many. O'Brien did recall that in the final week of the 1960 campaign, Kennedy and his managers decided to cancel a planned overnight tour of Indiana because they had decided that Nixon would carry the state and its electoral votes anyway. "With a popular vote, we might have gone through" with the Indiana tour, O'Brien said. But he thought such adjustments would be relatively minor. "Basically," he said, the direct vote system would have "no significant effect on the process of getting a majority."

Kentucky's Senator Thruston B. Morton, who was chairman of the Republican National Committee and a member of Nixon's strategy board in the 1960 campaign, took essentially the same view. In recent campaigns, he said, the candidates had gone frequently into California and New York because of their huge blocs of electoral votes. Under direct election, he thought, the candidates would continue to concentrate on the big states where the greatest masses of voters are located. But he felt that the smaller states would continue to receive some measure of attention.

On balance, Morton thought the direct vote might aid the Republicans because in the suburbs—where Republican strength tends to concentrate—it is easier to get the voters registered and to the polls than in center-city or rural areas. "We would have reason to redouble our vote effort in the suburbs," Morton said.

But Morton and the other political managers interviewed agreed that a direct vote would also increase the pressure to register the greatest pool of voters who do not yet participate fully in U.S. Presidential elections—the Negroes of the South. They also anticipated an effort to reach the "missing million" of Negro males (mostly in Northern cities) who have never been registered and to register the migrating citizen and get him to the polls.

Theodore C. Sorensen, who had been a close adviser to Kennedy and White House general counsel during the Kennedy Administration, said he was "inclined to believe there would be comparatively little difference in the campaigns, except that even less attention would be given to sparsely settled areas of the rural West and possibly more attention would be given to clusters of population (such as Omaha or Brattleboro) in states which presently have a small number of electoral votes."

A dissenting view was entered by Senator Hugh Scott of Pennsylvania, chairman of the Republican National Committee in 1948 and a strategist in subsequent Republican campaigns (with the notable exception of Barry Goldwater's effort in 1964). Scott said a direct vote system might favor the incumbent, lead to more emotional campaign appeals and increase the influence of immediate events on the course of a campaign. The candidates, Scott said, would concentrate, centralize and computerize their campaigns. More television and radio would be used, and candidates might do less national traveling—certainly nothing on the scale of Nixon's visits to all 50 states in 1960. The candidates would still feel obliged to make key speeches to veterans, labor and business conventions, Scott said, but the minor "prop stops" would be cut from schedules.

Scott's suggestion that television would increase in importance was supported by Richard M. Scammon, director of the Elections Research Center of the Governmental Affairs Institute, who saw an increasing reliance on that media as candidates sought "to project the issues to a universal constituency."[33] But O'Brien said that as a political organizer he would see little reason to increase television usage over its present levels.

Scott was concerned that the direct vote system might lead candidates to emphasize "glamor" issues instead of serious fiscal or other substantive problems, and that emotional class or racial appeals could increase. But he acknowledged that the dangers of such a downgrading in the quality of Presidential campaign discussion would be less likely than in earlier years because of the increasing educational levels and political sophistication of the country. Despite the possible disadvantages that he discerned in direct Presidential voting, Scott said he might well support the proposal—especially in view of the ABA recommendation—to rid the country of the evils of the existing electoral college setup. Scott has sponsored a district system amendment in Congress.

One of the most delicate balances in U.S. politics is that between the national party structures and the state political organizations beneath them. Most of the men interviewed envisioned little change in the existing balance—presuming that the national convention method of nominating Presidential candidates, with the special power and influence it gives to state party organizations, was retained.[34] Some of the political managers interviewed believed the Presidential candidate might be more distant from state leaders, since he would be a "national" candidate instead of a contender for any state's specific electoral votes. But the preponderant opinion was that the role of the state organizations might become even more important because of the vital function they would play in maximizing voter registration and election day turnout under a direct vote system. Substantial additional funds might flow from national headquarters in Washington to the state organizations to help them in this function. Increased emphasis on voter registration and turnout efforts emerged as the most important effect the party professionals expected to see stem from institution of a direct vote.

Both political managers and political scientists analyzing the potential impact of a direct vote agree that it would serve to foster two-party competition in all the states of the Union. The basic goal of any Presidential campaign in future years would be to get every possible vote in every state, since each vote would count. Simply "carrying" a state would no longer be of such paramount importance. Instead, the basic question would be a candidate's margin of victory—the net "plus" any state's votes would give him in the national tally. And even if a candidate had little hope of winning a plurality in a given state, he would be vitally concerned with the size of the vote cast for him in the state, bending every effort to minimize any margin against him.

The growing nationalization of U.S. politics in recent decades has already served to minimize the traditional emphasis on a potential candidate's home state and the bloc of electoral votes it can swing in the fall election. The Presidential election of 1948 may well have been the last one in which the home state of one of the Presidential candidates—in that case, Thomas E. Dewey of New York—played an appreciable role in winning a major party Presidential nomination. Dwight D. Eisenhower, Adlai E. Stevenson, John F. Kennedy, Richard M. Nixon, Lyndon B. Johnson, Barry Goldwater—all were chosen because of their national stature or regional strength, not because they represented a certain state with a mighty bloc of electoral votes. This trend could be expected to continue under a direct vote system. The talents and leadership qualities of candidates would count much more than their state of origin. It would still be easier, of course, for a Governor of New York or California to win a Presidential nomination than for the chief executive of Vermont or Wyoming. But citizens of the latter states—especially if they distinguish themselves in Congress or in other national service—would no longer be almost automatically excluded as was once the case in U.S. politics.

A final concern with the institution of direct voting for President is whether it would work substantially to the detriment of one political party or one political bloc—conservatives or liberals, civil rights advocates or white supremacists. Ideally, this should not be a paramount concern, for the important question in establishing a Presidential election system is more properly which system corresponds best to the standards of political democracy held by most Americans, and which system best guarantees that the popular will is reflected in the final outcome. But if it *could* be shown that one political group would lose out seriously through institution of the direct vote, then the proposal might be doomed from the start.

In the American Bar Association's panel on electoral reform, a strong consensus for direct vote was obtained from representatives of every political hue—Republicans and Democrats, "big state" and "little state" men, Northerners and Southerners, management representatives and labor union men (see page 191, above). The Congressional support for direct vote, ranging from conservatives like Illinois' Everett Dirksen to liberals like Indiana's Birch Bayh, suggests that in Congress, as in the ABA commission, the direct vote has not emerged as a partisan political issue. Among informed political leaders, there seems to be a growing consensus that there is no longer a "solar system" of balanced injustices in U.S. politics, requiring preservation of the electoral college for the kind of reasons John Kennedy advanced in the 1950s (see page 159, above). "One man, one vote" decrees have destroyed any special conservative advantages in legislatures and Congressional districts, and the broadening of national suffrage has created a base for national Presidential voting in which all groups, liberal and conservative alike, can have a fair voice.

When the ABA House of Delegates debated the direct vote proposal in February 1967, however, opposition did emerge—from the far right. Former ABA president Loyd Wright of Los Angeles said the proposal was but "another step down the road to socialism" and an attempt "to force down the throats of the American people a democracy." Supporters of former Alabama Governor George C. Wallace's planned 1968 Presidential bid were reported among the chief opponents at the ABA meeting. The opposition failed, as the House of Delegates voted to endorse its commission recommendation for the popular vote by a vote of 171 to 57. But the debate had made it clear that opposition could be expected from the right-wing fringes of American politics, and that conservative Southerners of the Wallace variety had identified the direct vote—probably correctly—as a clear threat to the Southern independent-elector strategy. Such manipulative tactics would simply not be open to splinter parties and groups under a direct vote system. On the other hand, a third-party movement could conceivably influence the outcome of the national election under a direct vote system by siphoning off a few million votes from one of the leading candidates and thus helping his opponent to win. The maneuver would be successful, however, only if the third party drew most of its votes from one of the major parties. If it drew equally from both, it would be of little importance.

As our earlier analysis suggested, the direct vote system—rationally analyzed—should do little to harm the political interests of small states and rural areas, since they already see their supposed special influence in the electoral college eclipsed by the pivotal power of the big states. But fears still exist in this camp. Several came to light at a May 1967 meeting of the Chamber of Commerce of the U.S. in Washington, when a proposal was brought forward to drop the Chamber's standing policy in favor of either direct vote *or* the district system in favor of support for the direct vote alone. But the fears of a number of conservative small-state delegates about the direct vote were not even allayed by the news that one of their favorites, Senator Dirksen, had introduced the ABA direct vote amendment in Congress. One delegate warned of the "despotism of the majority" under direct vote. A South Dakotan, Burt Tolefson of the American Corn Millers' Federation, told his fellow Chamber delegates that they should not desert the district system alternative because "99 percent of the people in this room would do better under a district system," which he said would elect "a moderate conservative" to the Presidency. By a vote of 195 to 192, the Chamber delegates voted to stick with their old policy favoring either the popular vote or the district system.

Thus the cause of electoral reform seems to be endangered by two age-old threats—the unwillingness of reformers to agree on a single system and the insistence of some that they could reform the system for their own partisan advantage. But most opinion samplings, even in small states, have suggested that a wide range of the people would not oppose the direct election on narrow grounds of self-interest. A nationwide poll of members of the national Federation of Independent Business, conducted in the spring of 1967, showed 75 percent in favor of the direct vote alternative, with only 18 percent opposed and 7 percent undecided. About 85 percent of the group's membership was reported to live outside the large metropolitan centers of the nation, and there was not a single state in which less than two-thirds of the businessmen polled did not favor the direct vote proposal.

But looking at the other side of the coin, should the big states fear a diminution of their power under direct voting? In their capacity as states, they would lose the special pivotal power assigned to them today. The election of the President would no longer swing on the turn of a few thousand votes in California, Illinois or New York. But this is not to say that *the people* of the big states would have anything to lose. Indeed, individual citizens of the large states would know that their votes would be counted meaningfully, even if they found themselves in a minority in their own state.

Moreover, it seems certain that no Presidential candidate—almost regardless of the election system in effect—will ever risk ignoring the vital interests of citizens in the large metropolitan areas of the country, which form the bulk of the big-state populations. An exclusive appeal to rural or small-town voters would have little viability in a country where the vast (and increasing) preponderance of the population lives in the cities and their immediate suburbs.

But what then of the "minority" groups—Catholics, unionists, Negroes, Jews, assorted ethnic blocs—who are said to have a special "swing" power in modern Presidential elections because of their alleged ability to shift a few thousand votes one way or the other and thus determine the outcome in pivotal states? Would these groups lose a special privilege they enjoy today? The answer is clearly "no"—for three specific reasons.

First, while it is true that a handful of votes can swing pivotal states in some (but certainly not all) elections, there are clearly limits to the ability of leaders of special ethnic, religious or economic groups, in the heat of an election campaign, to persuade their followers to break radically from their traditional political loyalties and vote in any other way than they were planning to in the first place. Actually, studies on the voting behavior of such groups over several elections indicate a remarkable stability in their political preferences—in recent years, overwhelmingly Democratic. Over decades, these groups may make basic shifts in political allegiance, and their support for any party will naturally fluctuate slightly from election to election. But to suggest that they can shift more rapidly than other groups in the population for immediate political bargaining purposes in the midst of a campaign is to disregard the conclusions of most responsible political science analysis of recent years.[35] One could argue just as logically that suburbanites or American Legionnaires or Rotarians or Episcopalians—or any group imaginable—constitute the "swing" vote in the great "pivotal" states and thus control the Presidential elections.

Second, even if one were to concede that certain groups in big states could mobilize to shift their votes back and forth for purposes of controlling large blocs of electoral votes, it is not clear that it would always be "liberals" who enjoy that special advantage. In fact, the "white backlash" vote among foreign ethnic groups in the big cities could presumably be mobilized to defeat a Presidential candidate who took a strong civil rights stand. Or some militant right-wing group like the John Birch Society might suddenly seize the "swing" position in the pivotal states that Negroes, Jews and a whole multitude of hyphenated Americans have been said to occupy in the past. A look at the political complexion of modern-day California suggests that this possibility may not be so remote.

A third reason that the nation's minority groups would not be losing any special advantage in direct voting is that they would be able to transfer their voting strength to the national stage instead—and be just as effective there. Scattered labor union members in the South would suddenly find themselves able to unite their votes with those of unionists from the great industrialized states of the North. The newly enfranchised Negroes from Southern states like Georgia and Alabama would be able to combine their Presidential votes with Negroes from New York, Illinois and Michigan and thus constitute a formidable national voting bloc that the parties would ignore at their peril. Of course, men owning $50,000 homes would also be able to unite their voting strength across state lines if they wanted to, and so would migrant workers (if they could ever manage to establish residence long enough to vote) or schoolteachers or retirees or segregationists. But there is nothing inherently evil about this process, for politics in the long run must be, and is, the process by which the competing demands and needs of a pluralistic society are met. The direct vote for President simply means that everyone would approach the game on equal terms.[36]

The voice in Presidential elections of America's most deprived minority group, its Negro citizens, was discussed in the 1967 Senate hearings by Clarence Mitchell, director of the Washington bureau of the National Association for the Advancement of Colored People. Mitchell said his organization would be prepared to support the direct vote proposal of the American Bar Association, but with one important proviso—that there be "absolute and foolproof safeguards against discrimination in registering and voting." Mitchell suggested that Congress be given not only a reserve power, but the duty and obligation to act to regulate elections to prevent discriminatory practices where they still restrict Negro voting in the South. Under the existing electoral college system, Mitchell said, the voting power of Negroes in the pivotal states of the North tended to balance out "the segregation bloc" of Southern states. He said the NAACP would be willing to see Northern Negroes lose their special swing power only if Southern Negroes were given full access to the ballot box so that Negroes could participate in the election on an equal footing with other citizens.

Implementing the Direct Vote

Because of its very simplicity, the direct vote for President would pose few difficulties in administration. But there are three problem areas that must be dealt with, both by Congress as it seeks to frame a direct vote amendment to the Constitution and later in terms of actual operation. They relate to the actual counting of popular votes, the qualifications of voters, and the percentage of the national vote to be required for election and methods of contingent election.

OBTAINING AN ACCURATE NATIONAL VOTE COUNT. Each state today has a well-established, reliable method of counting the votes for local and state officials and certifying the winners. The popular vote for President would simply constitute the addition of the popular votes cast in each state and the District of Columbia to obtain a national total.

The only problem that could arise under this system would relate to certifying the winner in an exceptionally close election. "The possibility of close elections," Senator Kefauver commented a few years ago, "will always be with us, and in a federation of 185 million people from Maine to Hawaii, uncertainty and suspense will attend the final determination under any system."[37] Some observers have suggested that the problem of local fraud would be magnified under the direct vote system, since any irregularity in the voting in any state could influence—and if great enough, actually determine—the outcome of the national election. Some have contended that actual federal administration of elections would be necessary.

On balance, such fears are probably exaggerated. The argument could as easily be made that federal administration of election laws is already necessary, since fraud in a closely contested state with a large bloc of electoral votes may already be enough to swing the entire national election. Some Republicans, indeed, suggested that an honest count in Illinois, Texas and other states would have shifted the outcome of the 1960 contest. Regardless of the system of election employed, there has always been and will always be a possibility that irregularities could influence the outcome. Mathematically, there is probably no greater—and possibly, much less—chance that there can be enough irregularities to cloud the outcome under the direct vote system than there is today, when the shift of a few hundred or thousand votes in crucial states can determine who will be the next President.

A legitimate question may be raised, however, about determining the winner in an exceedingly close election. Recalling the suspense of election night 1960 and the hair-breadth popular vote margin that separated Nixon and Kennedy, some have suggested that the process of recounting, challenging and litigation might have gone on well beyond inauguration day in January.

As an objection to popular voting, the problem of determining the winner falls on two points. First (as previously noted), the uncertainty of the outcome in one or just a handful of pivotal electoral vote states could easily create the same conditions of uncertainty about the winner under the electoral college system. Indeed, it was many weeks after the 1960 election before it was known who had carried Hawaii, and several days after the election before the California outcome was clear. Secondly, the chances that the two major candidates would come within a few hundred or thousand votes of each other are minuscule when 70 million or more persons are participating in the election. Tom Wicker of *The New York Times* points out that there was only one other U.S. Presidential election—the Garfield-Hancock contest of 1880—when the popular vote was "so close that counting a winning total would have been difficult, or that any but the most massive and wholesale fraud could have changed the outcome."[38] Garfield's actual plurality was 9,457 out of 9.2 million votes cast. Proportionately, that would have been a 69,036-vote plurality out of the total of 70.6 million votes cast in the most recent national election (1964). Admittedly, this is a narrow margin on a national basis. But it would still be a clear and unambiguous national plurality, barring allegations of voting irregularity on a scale that the country has in fact not experienced in modern times. More than 1,000 votes would have to be stolen or lost in every state to change the outcome. Long-term projections of the growth of the total U.S. population, and the size of the electorate, suggest increasingly less likelihood that only a few thousand votes might separate candidates in a Presidential election:[39]

Year	National Population	Voting-Age Population†	Presidential Vote*
	Actual Census and Vote Cast		
1960	180,676,000	108,830,000	68,838,000
	Projected Figures		
1970	206,110,000	123,260,000	80,119,000
1980	236,474,000	144,597,000	93,998,000
1990	271,426,000	169,259,000	110,018,000
2000	308,517,000	194,999,000	126,749,000
2010	352,189,000	224,739,000	146,080,000

* Figures for 1970 through 2010 are based on the assumption that 65 percent of the adult population will vote. In 1960, 63.8 percent participated. Actually, the percentage turnout is likely to go far beyond the 65 percent in the coming decades.

† Based on all residents 21 years or older through 1980, and all 20 years or older thereafter.

By 1980, a difference between candidates of a narrow half of one percent would be a substantial 468,890 votes, and by 2010, 730,400 votes. A difference of a tiny one-tenth of a percentage point would be 93,998 in 1980 and 146,080 in 2010.

Statistically, it is doubtful whether there would be more than one election in a century—and probably not more than one every three or four centuries—in which the popular vote would be so close that there could be real dispute about the outcome. And the fact of the matter is that the American people are accustomed to witnessing razor-thin vote margins in individual state races: witness the 91-vote margin by which Karl Rolvaag won the Minnesota Governorship in 1962 and the 84-vote margin by which Senator Howard W. Cannon won reelection to the Senate from Nevada in 1964. Recounts are invariably ordered in all such close races, but it is rare indeed that the results of the first canvass—no matter how narrow—are upset. An exception was the 1960 Presidential race in Hawaii, where the Republican electors led by 141 votes on the first official count but trailed by 115 after a recount.*

* One of the more unusual arguments advanced against a direct vote has been that the system could result in a shifting of the "center of political gravity" of the country if accidental factors such as a great storm in the Northwestern states materially reduced the vote from one region.[40] Presumably, storms could influence the outcome only if the national vote balance was exceedingly close. Under the existing system, bad weather was reported to have reduced the upstate Republican vote in New York in 1884, helping the Democrats carry the state and, be-

If Americans are able to accept the results of official canvasses and recounts in close state races, there is no reason they should not accept the same process, if it ever became necessary, in Presidential balloting.* Indeed, the temptations to fraud in ballot-counting are probably stronger in state and local elections, where the jobs of election officials may ride on the outcome, than they are in Presidential elections. The chief difficulties in establishing a definitive national popular vote count under the existing system have stemmed from phenomena like the divided Alabama elector slate in 1960. Such difficulties would be avoided by obliging each voter to cast a single, unambiguous vote for one national candidate. And the exceedingly remote possibility that local frauds could affect the national outcome under a direct vote system pales rapidly when one recalls that under the existing electoral college system, the greatest fraud of all can be perpetrated, legally— the elevation of a man to the Presidency who was specifically rejected by the people, even by a margin that could go as high as *several million* votes. A proportionate extension of the 1876 and 1888 vote counts to 1964 turnout levels indicates that Tilden would have won in 1876 by 2.1 million votes and Cleveland by 590,000 votes in 1888, despite the fact that the electoral college elected their opponents.

Short shrift may also be given to the argument that the existing electoral college should be retained because in a close and bitterly contested election its normally inflated majorities give the impression that the country stands overwhelmingly behind the winner, thus promoting national unity. Senator Margaret Chase Smith of Maine suggests that of all the arguments for the existing system, this is "the most fatuous and guilty of sheer sophistry."[41] The argument takes no account of the possibility that the man whose electoral victory looks so substantial may actually have lost in the popular vote, or of the possibility that the electoral vote (as in 1876) may also be sufficiently close to throw the country into turmoil. Nor can it be seriously suggested that very many of the people are fooled by an inflated electoral college majority when they know the popular vote margin

---

cause of it, the entire nation. In the days of the automobile and perfected mass transit, Americans are less likely to be deterred from voting by bad weather. But if weather really were the stumbling block in the way of adopting a national direct vote, alternative solutions like an extended 24-hour voting period in a storm-hit area could be instituted.

* Although the chances of an absolute tie in the popular vote are only one in many million, a constitutional amendment or enabling legislation should make provision for it—presumably through the device of a second election.

was narrow. Former President Truman, himself a defender of the electoral college, suggests that "there is something to be said for the narrow margin of victory in a Presidential election. It makes the new President realize in a very dramatic and material way that there is more than one side to a question. And where there are two strong major parties, there are bound to be reasonable differences of opinion on many issues and conflicts of interest." In the eyes of the President-elect, Truman said, the "voices and ideas" of the millions who voted for the losing candidate should be "just as important as those of the victorious millions."[42]

While close elections are always possible, the chances of uncertain outcomes in elections are being reduced by the trend toward better regulated, more scientific ballot counting in the United States. The possibilities of irregularities in the count have been reduced materially as communities have shifted from paper ballots to mechanical voting machines—a change that more than half the country has made already. As electronic voting machines are perfected, they are likely to reduce even further the possibilities of fraud and error in vote counting. Viewed in terms of the technological advances made in other areas of American life, the country's voting procedures and laws are terribly antiquated. Elmer W. Lower, president of ABC News, notes that paper ballots are "a relic of the 19th century, inefficient and inaccurate." He recommends using the latest electronic voting devices and suggests that within a few years such methods as push-button telephone balloting, with the results recorded on a master computer, may be possible. But even if one dismisses voting by telephone as somewhat visionary, it does seem entirely feasible to establish a national electronic voting system that would completely eliminate errors in counting paper ballots or reading the returns on individual voting machines. Then the only possibilities for fraud will exist before the ballot is cast—in tombstone balloting, double voting or other abuses that can creep in where both parties fail to maintain vigorous local precinct organizations to check abuses by the opposition as the vote is actually cast. The direct vote for President, by encouraging healthy two-party competition in every state, should also encourage the parties to man each precinct with vigilant poll watchers. Modernized and simplified registration laws should further guarantee to each American one vote—no more, no less.

Modern voting equipment should also help to solve another problem in American elections—the slowness of the count, recount and challenge procedure, which can sometimes delay certification of the winner in an election for weeks or, in the most extreme cases, months after an election. In contrast to Great Britain, where a change of government takes place within hours of the popular mandate, the pace of the official ballot count in the United States (as opposed to the unofficial counts reported by networks and news services) is torturously slow. Many states are unable to report an official vote count until several weeks after election day, as local boards of elections languidly carry out their duties. If recounts are necessary or challenges reach the courts, the process of establishing an official final count can drag on well into the term of the official who has been elected. It is in this area of the speed in the count and challenge procedure, rather than in obtaining, finally, a conclusive national count, that the direct vote for President raises the most serious problems. The Presidential election takes place early in November, but the welfare of the country cannot permit slow vote count and challenge procedures that would prevent official certification of the new President until the eve of inauguration day, the next January 20, or beyond. A new President needs to know if he is elected almost immediately after election day, so that he can begin the delicate and difficult business of choosing a Cabinet and other top aides, formulating a program for Congress, and letting foreign powers know what they may expect in the future international policy of the United States. No competent observer would doubt that prolonged uncertainty about the outcome of a Presidential election could be injurious to the welfare of the entire nation.

Most recommendations for a direct vote, including that of the American Bar Association, contemplate leaving the operation and regulation of Presidential voting in the hands of the states but with a reserve Congressional power to legislate in the field. Presumably Congress, itself consisting of representatives from the individual states, would be loath to exercise its reserve power and interfere with the states' discretion in election regulation in the absence of gross misuse by the states of their power. But this should not deter Congress from passing legislation to expedite rapid and fair resolution of disputed Presidential votes in a close election.

An interesting proposal in this regard was advanced by L. Kinvin Wroth in the *Dickinson Law Review*.[43] Wroth's proposal was advanced for use under the existing electoral college system to determine disputes in the popular vote that might affect the casting of state electoral votes. But it would be equally applicable to a direct vote system. He suggested that while the states continue to conduct elections, the federal courts be given exclusive jurisdiction in the event of contested Presidential vote returns. The federal courts would be more appropriate than state courts in this regard, Wroth said, because they enjoy immunity from political pressures, stemming from the life tenure of federal judges, which state courts—where the judges are often subject to periodic reelection—do not enjoy. Congress, he said, could provide a schedule for the filing, hearing and decision of all contests, including the selection of federal judges on an impartial basis determined in advance, perhaps by requiring each circuit to establish an election contest calendar prior to the election. The importance of the matter, Wroth said, might well justify special three-judge federal courts. They would have "jurisdiction of all questions arising out of the popular election which affect the validity of votes and the accuracy and fairness of the count and canvass." But the federal courts, he suggested, would be instructed to apply *state* election law in these matters. They would have express power to order the preservation of the ballots for a recount under the direction of a court-appointed master, Wroth proposed. Provision could be made for direct appeal to the Supreme Court—but all within a specified time limit that would result in a final determination of all contests before an appointed date.

"The President of the United States will increasingly require strength based on national and international respect if he is to guide the nation through times of mounting crisis," Wroth said. "This respect will not come to one who is elected under the slightest suspicion of error or fraud. To insure that no electoral contest will mar or disrupt the orderly succession of the Presidency in the difficult future, Congress must give to the federal courts the power to reach a timely, final and binding decision of all controversies."[44]

Unless the outcome in a national Presidential election were exceedingly close, there would be little incentive for the parties or individual citizens to bring suits in the federal courts under the special procedures suggested by Kinvin Wroth. But the presence of such legislation on the books would act as a powerful deterrent to irregularities at the polls and do much to assure the sanctity of the votes Americans cast for their President.

QUALIFICATIONS FOR VOTERS. A major danger to any direct vote amendment, as it is considered by Congress and later by the states, would be to infringe too far on the states' traditional right to set voting qualifications, especially by becoming immersed in the debate over whether young Americans should be permitted to vote at 18 or not until the traditional age of 21. The ABA and other chief Congressional backers of the direct vote thus recommend a relatively simple formula: To vote for President, a person must have met his state's requirements to vote for Members of Congress. Thus the voter for President would be subjected to the traditional state residence and age limitations, which, as noted earlier, are approaching universal adult suffrage today (see Chapter 7). Any state could specifically provide less stringent residence requirements for Presidential elections alone, however. This would preserve the 24 state laws already passed that set much shorter residence requirements for Presidential balloting. Congress would be given a reserve power to set uniform residence and age requirements. "It is probable that, as with other reserve powers, Congress might not have to exercise this power particularly in view of the increasing tendency on the part of the states to make uniform their qualifications for voting in elections," the ABA Report noted. Senator Bayh states the case in less formal language: "If we see some mad scramble by the states to lower voter qualifications willy-nilly, then Congress can step in and establish uniform standards."

A familiar argument of opponents of the direct vote is that the states would embark on a race to debase their voting qualifications. But since the qualifications for voting for Congress in the U.S. are almost invariably the same as those for state legislators, it is doubtful that this would really happen. Local politicians who lowered the voting age just to increase a state's influence in Presidential voting "would be cutting off their noses to spite their faces," Senator Pastore remarked a few years ago. "Does any Senator mean to tell me that he is going to say, 'Let us do this, because we in Rhode Island will control the election of the President of the United States'? The minute he gets himself into setting up such reckless and callous qualifications, he destroys the efficacy and the effectiveness and the dignity of his own local government," Pastore said.[45]

Most likely, adoption of the direct vote amendment would act as a spur to states considering reducing their minimum voting age to 18, or reducing their residence qualifications—especially for Presidential elections. But it is highly doubtful that 12- and 15-year-olds would be allowed to vote or that voting qualifications would be lowered to a point where fraud would be invited. The fact that 18-year-olds could vote in some states but not in others would of course create some minor inequalities in the Presidential voting base from state to state. But at least theoretically the reduced voting age in four states today (Georgia, Kentucky, Alaska and Hawaii) could shift the political balance in those states and in a close national electoral vote count determine the outcome. Compared to the inequalities of the electoral college system, with its disfranchisement of all minority voters in the states, the minor differences in voting age and residence requirements from state to state dwindle in significance—though there is sure to be a lot of debate about them when Congress finally gets to serious discussion on a direct-vote amendment.

Opponents of the direct vote may well argue that even if Congress fails to exercise its reserve power, there will be subtle influences on the states to conform to uniform age and residence requirements—thus reducing, to some extent, the states' traditional discretion in this field and the full extent of state sovereignty. The argument may be a fair one; indeed, Professor Paul Freund of the ABA commission acknowledged in 1967 Senate hearings that the logic of direct popular vote would draw in its train the concept of uniform voting qualifications prescribed by Congress, although he thought that step would be unnecessary if the states maintained relatively uniform requirements. Another direct-vote proponent, Professor Robert G. Dixon, Jr., said a direct-vote amendment ought to include "standards and national police power regarding uniform voting qualifications and open, honest, unintimidated balloting," or that Congress should at least be required to prescribe such standards by law. There seemed to be little immediate likelihood of Congress's taking the steps Dixon recommended, especially in view of the high standards of fair count and universal suffrage being attained by the states. But even if some regulatory action by Congress were necessary, one might ask whether a minor diminution of state sovereignty—in a field where, at least in earlier years, the states were guilty of gross abuses—would be too high a price to pay for achieving an equal and fair system by which all Americans will choose their Chief Executive.

QUALIFYING FOR THE BALLOT. The people of all the states should certainly have the right to vote for any major-party candidate, and the ABA suggested that Congress be given the power to deal with cases where a state seeks to exclude the Presidential candidate of one of the major parties from the ballot, as Alabama did in 1948 and 1964. With Congress given this reserve right, it is likely that the states themselves would see to it that major-party candidates were given places on their general election ballots—if for no other reason, to avoid Congressional intervention. There might, of course, be considerable debate in Congress about which parties are "major" enough to be entitled to inclusion on all states' ballots. Should modern replicas of the 1948 Dixiecrat and Progressive parties, for instance, be guaranteed ballot positions by Congress? In all likelihood, Congress—itself dominated by the two major parties—would leave this problem where it is now, in the hands of the states, where election laws generally make it fairly difficult for new parties to qualify.

PLURALITIES, MAJORITIES AND RUNOFFS. The system of plurality election, in which the man with the most votes is declared elected—regardless of his percentage—now applies almost uniformly in the U.S., with rare exceptions such as Georgia, which requires a majority vote for all state and federal offices, and Mississippi and Vermont, which require a majority vote for Governor. In practice, the plurality system has worked well in the United States. In the vast majority of elections, the winner receives a clear majority anyway. In a very close election one or more minor-party candidates on the ballot may pull him below 50 percent, but real three- or four-way splits are rare, and the plurality system has not encouraged minor parties in U.S. politics.

Nevertheless, there has been a feeling in the country that the President should be chosen by majority vote. Thus the Constitution requires a majority of the electoral college ballots to elect a man President. In actual popular voting, there have been 14 Presidents who failed to achieve an absolute majority—including Lincoln, Wilson and Kennedy (see chart, Appendix A). But only in one election—1860— has one of the candidates failed to win at least 40 percent. Lincoln is credited with 39.8 percent but would certainly have received more than 40 percent if his name had not been kept off the ballot in ten states.

In company with many other constitutional amendments to reform the electoral college, direct vote proposals over the years have often maintained the majority requirement with a provision that Congress choose the President if no candidate were to achieve a majority, with each member accorded a single vote. In 1966, Senator Bayh recommended that the requirement be reduced to 40 percent with the contingent election in Congress. In 1967 the ABA suggested that the 40 percent figure be used but that the contingent election consist of a national runoff instead of submitting the issue to Congress. Senator Bayh shifted to the national runoff in the direct vote amendment he offered in January 1967, cosponsored by 19 other Senators.

The reasons for turning to a national runoff instead of having a contingent election in Congress are obvious. As Wicker of *The New York Times* summed up the case, "Congress would not necessarily be controlled by the party of the leading Presidential vote-getter; its members might choose the second man, just as Georgia's Legislature did [January 10, 1967] in choosing Lester G. Maddox for Governor. In a closely divided Congress there might be excessive log-rolling, arm-twisting, promise-making, wheeling and dealing and even fraud to win the necessary votes. And particularly after such an episode, Congress might then be able to exert an undue influence over a President it had directly and specifically chosen, thus breaching the doctrine of separation of powers."[46]

The ABA suggested that the 40 percent figure, combined with a national runoff, would assure a reasonable mandate to any man elected President and function to discourage splinter parties from trying to influence the outcome of the election. The 40 percent figure, the ABA said, "would render extremely remote the possibility of having to resort to the contingent election procedure." Based on the experience of the American past, there would probably be no more than one election in a century when a runoff was actually required under the ABA system.

Nevertheless, the runoff does pose some problems. At the end of an already lengthy campaign, it would place added burdens on the Presidential candidates and especially their already depleted campaign treasuries. This disadvantage could, of course, be alleviated in part by a generous allowance of free national television time before the runoff. There would be no "equal time" requirements after all the minor-party candidates had been eliminated in the first election.

Second, a runoff would require an even more rapid count and certification of ballots, including the resolution of all disputes, than would otherwise be necessary. This would probably not be an insurmountable obstacle, however. The 11 states that now provide for runoff elections in their primaries currently allow between two and five weeks after the first primary.[47]

The states might also be reluctant to undergo the major expense involved in a special runoff. This objection, though, could be met by a special Congressional appropriation to cover costs at a reasonable figure per vote cast.

There is also the problem of whether the leading candidates might be tempted to make unconscionable concessions to the runners-up in a runoff. Experience shows this often occurs in Southern primary run-offs, but it may be argued that if a candidate cannot garner 40 percent of the vote in the first Presidential election, his appeal is too narrow and he should be obliged to accommodate the minority candidates and the feelings of their followers before submitting himself to the people again in the runoff.

Runoff elections often tend to be a contest in which the voters whose candidates were eliminated on the first round simply vote against the man they like the least. But if there is to be a contingent election at all, it is unquestionably preferable to let the people make that judgment rather than Congress.

Finally, there is the problem of whether there would be a significant vote drop-off in the runoff. On the average, the vote is somewhat lighter in runoffs. In the most recent gubernatorial runoffs in ten Southern states, the total vote was less than that of the first primary in five instances and greater in five instances. Over-all, however, the runoff vote was off only 2.38 percent from the first primary in these states. In a Presidential election, with all the interest it arouses, the problem might not be too great. In October 1962, France adopted direct election of its President with the requirement of an "absolute majority" for election. In the December 1965 Presidential election, Charles de Gaulle received only 43.96 percent of the vote to 32.04 percent for his closest competitor, François Mitterrand, candidate of the left wing. In the subsequent runoff, De Gaulle polled 55.2 percent. The total vote in the first election was 23,891,391; in the runoff, only 0.77 percent less—23,708,654.[48]

On balance, a runoff election provision is probably not necessary. An analysis of 170 gubernatorial elections, occurring in the 30 most competitive states between 1952 and 1964, showed that the winning candidate polled less than 45 percent of the total vote in only two cases and less than 40 percent in no case at all.[49]

Doing away with the contingent election requirement altogether would be in the tradition of the great 19th-century electoral college reform effort in the United States. "Dispense with the requirement of a majority and adopt the plurality system, and avoid an election by the House altogether," Senator Oliver P. Morton of Indiana proposed in 1875. "The plurality rule is adopted by all the states except three in the election of state officers," Morton noted, "and by all in regard to election of Members of Congress. . . . It has worked well in the states and no state now proposes to go back from the plurality to the majority system."[50]

Even if the runoff provision is not particularly necessary, however, the ABA and other modern reformers may have been wise to adopt it as a counterploy to anticipated charges that they are undermining the two-party system. Minor parties would have to obtain at least 20 percent of the vote, and probably more in most years, to prevent one of the major candidates from winning election. Their incentives for making an effort at the Presidential level would be reduced drastically from what they are today. The very fact that the Constitution provided for a runoff might mean that the country would never have to go through one.*

RUNNING AS A TEAM. Most modern direct vote amendments require that the candidates for President and Vice President run as a team. The advantages of this are obvious. It would prevent the distractions of separate appeals by Presidential and Vice Presidential candidates in the general election, would prevent any chance that these two officials might be from opposing parties, and would assure reasonable harmony between the President and his Vice President in the new administration.

"A More Perfect Union"

In one respect, the proposal for abolishing the rickety old electoral college and substituting a direct vote of the people seems to be little more than a housekeeping item on the agenda of pressing national and international problems that face the American people as they enter the closing decades of the 20th century. Yet the importance of the Presidency in American life can scarcely be underestimated, and thus the

---

* In a 1967 statement endorsing the ABA direct vote recommendations, the New York City Bar Association commented that a runoff system could conceivably encourage third parties to enter candidates in the hopes of forcing a runoff and then wringing concessions from front-runners in return for their support. "On balance, however, we believe that the 40-percent runoff provision is necessary to avoid the possibility of a relatively small minority electing a President," the Bar group said. Not only would runoffs be extremely unlikely, but "so uncertain a prospect of 'leverage in the sky' would be unlikely to induce a proliferation of political parties, particularly in view of the manifold difficulties, monetary and otherwise, in the way of mounting a serious Presidential campaign."

way that office is filled must be a matter of major national concern. As Estes Kefauver commented in 1961, "Every four years the electoral college is a loaded pistol aimed at our system of government. Its continued existence is a game of Russian roulette. Once its antiquated procedures trigger a loaded cylinder, it may be too late for the needed corrections."[51]

Of course, it is possible that even if the electoral college sent the popular-vote loser to the White House, the people would find a way to live with the situation—even though the authority of the Presidency and the quality of American democracy would certainly be undermined. But even if one assumes that the country *could* somehow exist with a President the people had rejected, the question still remains: What good reason is there to continue such an irrational voting system in an advanced democratic nation, where the ideal of popular choice is the most deeply ingrained of governmental principles?

Democratic elections do not always guarantee that the best man will win. Even when we have shed the barnacles of the electoral college from the ship of state, there is no guarantee that we or our descendants may not one day elect a charlatan or an ideologue to the Presidency. For all our talk of great American Presidents, we have elected some pretty grim mediocrities to that office, and we could again—although the modern levels of education and political sophistication in the United States today make it far less likely. But even when one admits that the *vox populi* may err, the fact remains that through our entire national experience we have learned that there is no safer, no better way to elect our public officials than by the choice of the people, with the man who wins the most votes being awarded the office. This is the essence of "the consent of the governed." And no matter how wisely or foolishly the American people choose their President, he *is* their President. No one has been able to show how the preservation of a quaint 18th-century voting device, the electoral college, with all its anomalies and potential "wild cards," can serve to protect the Republic. The choice of the Chief Executive must be the people's, and it should rest with none other than them.

The framers of the Constitution sought to embody the essence of American nationality in the opening words of the Preamble: "We the People of the United States, in order to form a more perfect Union . . ." Yet the perfection of the Union has more than once been marred by the workings of the electoral college, and every four years the nation runs the risk that a malfunction of the Presidential voting system could disrupt "the domestic tranquillity" and threaten "the general welfare" of which the Preamble also spoke. By amending the Constitution to provide a direct vote of all the people for their President, the nation would strike a serious defect from its charter of government. And it would lay a sound foundation for a fuller realization of that "more perfect Union" in the times to come.

N O T E S

1. Clinton Rossiter, *The American Presidency* (New York, 1956), pp. 144–45.
2. Carl Becker, "The Will of the People," *Yale Review,* March 1945, pp. 393–94.
3. Cited by Sidney Hyman, *The American President* (New York, 1954), pp. 155–56; see also Margaret L. Coit, *John C. Calhoun* (Boston, 1950), pp. 235–36.
4. *C.Q. Weekly Report,* April 12, 1963, p. 575.
5. U.S. House, Committee on the Judiciary, Subcommittee No. 1, *Hearings, Amending the Constitution with Respect to Election of President and Vice President,* 81st Congress, 1st Session, 1949, p. 163. Cited hereafter as 1949 House *Hearings.*
6. E. E. Schattschneider, *Party Government* (New York, 1960; orig. ed., 1941), p. 69.
7. Rossiter, *Parties and Politics in America* (Ithaca, N.Y., 1962), p. 8.
8. *Ibid.,* p. 10.
9. V. O. Key, *Parties and Pressure Groups* (New York, 5th ed., 1964), p. 209.
10. Schattschneider, *op. cit.,* p. 75.
11. *Ibid.,* pp. 81–83.
12. Allan P. Sindler, *Political Parties in the United States* (New York, 1966), pp. 53–54.
13. *Ibid.,* pp. 57–59.
14. *Congressional Record,* 1956, p. 5159.
15. *Ibid.,* 1967, p. S 1587 (daily ed.).
16. *Federalist* No. 39: "The executive power will be derived from a very compound source. The immediate election (by electors) is to be made in the states in their political characters. The votes allotted to them are in a compound ratio, which considers them partly as distinct coequal societies, partly as unequal members of the same society." *The Federalist,* Jacob E. Cooke, ed., (Middletown, Conn., 1961), p. 255.
17. *Annals of Congress,* XXX, p. 309.
18. Polk's Fourth Annual Message to Congress, Dec. 5, 1848.
19. *Congressional Record,* 1956, p. 5642.
20. *Ibid.,* pp. 5163, 5648.
21. 1949 House *Hearings,* p. 163.

22. *President Wilson's State Papers and Addresses* (New York, 1916), p. 43.

23. U.S. Senate, Committee on the Judiciary, Subcommittee on Constitutional Amendments, *Hearings, Nomination and Election of President and Vice President and Qualifications for Voting*, 87th Congress, 1st Session, 1961, pp. 279–85. Cited hereafter as 1961 Senate *Hearings*. For review of other proposals for a direct national nominating primary, see James W. Davis, *Presidential Primaries: Road to the White House* (New York, 1967), pp. 261–65.

24. *U.S. News & World Report*, Sept. 14, 1964, p. 70.

25. Hyman, *op. cit.*, p. 161.

26. Interview with author, Jan. 20, 1967.

27. 1949 House *Hearings*, p. 155.

28. 1961 Senate *Hearings*, p. 379.

29. Ben J. Wattenberg, in collaboration with Richard M. Scammon, *This U.S.A.— An Unexpected Family Portrait of 194,067,296 Americans Drawn from the Census* (New York, 1965), pp. 231, 301.

30. *Ibid.*, p. 302.

31. *Ibid.*, pp. 141–42.

32. *Ibid.*, pp. 307–8.

33. See David S. Broder, "Direct Vote: Who Would Be Losers?," *Washington Post*, Jan. 8, 1967.

34. Some observers believe there might be pressure to do away with the equal state voting power now enjoyed by the states and territories in the Democratic and Republican National Committees. See Lyle Denniston, "A Suggestion That Could Strengthen National Parties," Washington *Sunday Star*, Jan. 15, 1967. The party managers interviewed did not believe this would necessarily ensue, however.

35. This conclusion is based on a survey of prominent studies in the field of voter behavior by Angus Campbell, Warren E. Miller, V. O. Key and others, reported by Ralph M. Goldman in "Hubert Humphrey's S.J. 152: A New Proposal for Electoral College Reform," *Midwest Journal of Political Science*, Feb. 1958, p. 95. Exceptions to the rule might be the unusually strong movement of Catholics to the Democratic column when John F. Kennedy ran for President, or of Negroes to the Democrats when the Republicans nominated Barry Goldwater, an open opponent of civil rights legislation. These strong voter shifts, however, took place spontaneously under the special conditions of those campaigns and were probably due only secondarily to open urgings of Catholic and Negro leaders.

36. See Alexander Bickel, "The Case for the Electoral College," *New Republic*, Jan. 28, 1967, pp. 15–16, and Neal R. Peirce, "The Case Against the Electoral College," *New Republic*, Feb. 11, 1967, pp. 12–13.

37. Estes Kefauver, "The Electoral College: Old Reforms Take on a New Look," *Law and Contemporary Problems*, Spring 1962, pp. 188–89.

38. Tom Wicker, "In the Nation: Graduating from the Electoral College," *N. Y. Times*, Jan. 10, 1967.

39. Figures based on U.S. Census Bureau, *Current Population Reports*, "Projections of the Population of the United States by Age and Sex, 1964 to 1985, with Extensions to 2010," Series P-25, No. 286, July 1964. The Census reports include four alternative series of projections, ranging from the most

conservative estimate (321,916,000 by 2010) to the most liberal (437,578,-000 by 2010). Projections in this chart are based on Census Series C, the next to the most conservative.

40. Statement of the American Good Government Society, *Congressional Record,* 1967, p. S 1588 (daily ed.), in remarks of Sen. Mundt. Sen. Holland of Florida advanced the same argument in July 12, 1967, testimony before the Senate Judiciary Constitutional Amendments Subcommittee. According to Weather Bureau data on storms and unusual weather phenomena during the first week of November in recent years, Holland reported, voters might have been hindered from going to the polls in certain areas of three states in 1960, in nine states in 1961, in all of one state and parts of five others in 1962, in all of two states and parts of eight others in 1963, in certain areas of four states in 1964, in all of four states and parts of three others in 1965, and in all of two states and parts of ten others in 1966.

41. 1961 Senate *Hearings,* p. 61.

42. Washington *Post,* Nov. 14, 1960.

43. L. Kinvin Wroth, "Election Contests and the Electoral Vote," *Dickinson Law Review,* June 1961, p. 321.

44. *Ibid.,* p. 353.

45. *Congressional Record,* 1956, p. 5648. For fuller discussion on this point, see pp. 187–88, above.

46. *N.Y. Times,* Jan. 12, 1967.

47. The primary runoff states are Alabama, Arkansas, Georgia, Florida, Louisiana, Mississippi, Oklahoma, South Carolina and Texas. North Carolina and Virginia also provide for runoffs, but only if they are requested by the second-running candidate.

48. The other nations with runoff provisions for their chief executives, according to study papers prepared for the ABA Commission on Electoral College Reform, include Costa Rica, Gabon, the Ivory Coast and Malagasy. The only one of these that requires 40 percent rather than a majority in the first election is Costa Rica. An interesting provision of the Costa Rican Constitution provides that if there is a tie, the older candidate is considered elected President.

49. Testimony of Donald E. Stokes, Department of Political Science, University of Michigan, before the U.S. Senate Judiciary Subcommittee on Constitutional Amendments, July 18, 1967. Even in Southern primaries, which tend to be free-for-alls with none of the restraining influences exercised by prior official nominating conventions, a study showed that 84.2 percent of 3,105 contests resulted in a candidate's receiving a majority, and thus the nomination, in the first primary. The percentage of first primary winners would doubtless have been much higher if the requirement had been 40 percent rather than an absolute majority. See Cortez A. M. Ewing, *Primary Elections in the South* (Norman, Okla., 1953), p. 96.

50. Cited by J. Hampden Dougherty, *The Electoral System of the United States* (New York, 1906), pp. 346–47.

51. 1961 Senate *Hearings,* pp. 1–2.

Appendices

APPENDIX A

The National Vote for President, 1789–1964

The United States has entrusted no single national agency with the official tabulation of the popular votes cast for Presidential electors, although the electoral vote itself is certified every four years before a joint session of Congress. The chart below records the official electoral vote and indicates the best available tallies of the national popular vote, based on the method of translating votes for electors into a popular count which is described in Chapter 5 (pages 136–37). Sources[*] for the popular vote: for the elections of 1824 (the year for which the first national count could be compiled) through 1916, Svend Petersen, *A Statistical History of the American Presidential Elections* (Frederick Ungar Publishing Co., New York, 1963); for the elections of 1920 through 1964, Richard M. Scammon, *America at the Polls* (University of Pittsburgh Press, Pittsburgh, 1965); for the refinements of the 1960 vote, where a split Democratic elector slate in Alabama raised difficult problems in evaluation, Congressional Quarterly Service.

In the elections of 1789 through 1800, each Presidential elector cast two equal votes, without distinguishing the person he favored for President from his choice for Vice President. The candidate with the most electoral votes was elected President if his total constituted a majority of the number of electors. The runner-up, without a majority requirement, was elected Vice President. The 12th Amendment to the Constitution, adopted in 1804 and applicable to the election of that year and all subsequent elections, required the electors to cast separate votes for President and Vice President.

[*] Material reprinted with permission of the indicated authors or publishers.

The elections of 1800 and 1824 were decided by the House of Representatives because no candidate for President received a majority of electoral votes.

The name of the winning candidate is given first for each election year.

Key to party designations:

F Federalist	CU Constitutional Union
D Democratic	G Greenback
NR National Republican	P Prohibition
AM Anti-Masonic	PO Populist
W Whig	S Socialist
L Liberty	PR Progressive
FS Free Soil	U Union
R Republican	SR States' Rights
LR Land Reform	

Party designations pose special problems in the early years, when national political parties in the sense understood in modern times were still emerging. The designation (D) for Democrat is used in this chart for the factions called Anti-Federalist, later Republican and eventually known as Democratic by the 1820s.

Year	Candidates	Popular Vote Total Percentage	Electoral Votes Received
*1789	George Washington (F)	Not Available	69
	John Adams (F)	" "	34
	John Jay (F)	" "	9
	Others	" "	26
*1792	George Washington (F)	" "	132
	John Adams (F)	" "	77
	George Clinton (D)	" "	50
	Others	" "	5
*1796	John Adams (F)	" "	71
	Thomas Jefferson (D)	" "	68
	Thomas Pinckney (F)	" "	59
	Aaron Burr (D)	" "	30
	Samuel Adams (F)	" "	15
	Oliver Ellsworth (F)	" "	11
	Others	" "	22
*1800	Thomas Jefferson (D)	" "	73
	Aaron Burr (D)	" "	73

(See p. 308 for explanation of symbols * and †.)

Year	Candidates	Popular Vote Total Percentage		Electoral Votes Received
	John Adams (F)	"	"	65
	Charles C. Pinckney (F)	"	"	64
	John Jay	"	"	1
1804	Thomas Jefferson (D)	"	"	162
	Charles C. Pinckney (F)	"	"	14
1808	James Madison (D)	"	"	122
	Charles C. Pinckney (F)	"	"	47
	George Clinton (F)	"	"	6
1812	James Madison (D)	"	"	128
	DeWitt Clinton (F)	"	"	89
1816	James Monroe (D)	"	"	183
	Rufus King (F)	"	"	34
1820	James Monroe (D)	"	"	231
	John Quincy Adams (D)	"	"	1
*1824	John Quincy Adams (D)	115,696	31.9	84
	Andrew Jackson (D)	152,933	42.2	99
	William H. Crawford (D)	46,979	13.0	41
	Henry Clay (D)	47,136	13.0	37
1828	Andrew Jackson (D)	647,292	56.0	178
	John Quincy Adams (NR)	507,730	44.0	83
1832	Andrew Jackson (D)	688,242	54.5	219
	Henry Clay (NR)	473,462	37.5	49
	William Wirt (AM)	101,051	8.0	7
	John Floyd (D)	———	———	11
1836	Martin Van Buren (D)	764,198	50.9	170
	William H. Harrison (W)	549,508	36.6	73
	Hugh L. White (W)	145,352	9.7	26
	Daniel Webster (W)	41,287	2.8	14
	Willie P. Mangum (D)	———	———	11
1840	†William H. Harrison (W)	1,275,612	52.9	234
	Martin Van Buren (D)	1,130,033	46.8	60
	James G. Birney (L)	7,053	0.3	———
1844	James K. Polk (D)	1,339,368	49.6	170
	Henry Clay (W)	1,300,687	48.1	105
	James G. Birney (L)	62,197	2.3	———
1848	†Zachary Taylor (W)	1,362,101	47.3	163
	Lewis Cass (D)	1,222,674	42.5	127
	Martin Van Buren (FS)	291,616	10.1	———
	Gerrit Smith (L)	2,733	0.1	———

Year	Candidates	Popular Vote Total	Percentage	Electoral Votes Received
1852	Franklin Pierce (D)	1,609,038	50.9	254
	Winfield Scott (W)	1,386,629	43.8	42
	John P. Hale (FS)	156,297	4.9	———
	Others	12,445	0.4	———
1856	James Buchanan (D)	1,839,237	45.6	174
	John C. Frémont (R)	1,341,028	33.3	114
	Millard Fillmore (W)	849,872	21.1	8
	Gerrit Smith (LR)	484		
1860	Abraham Lincoln (R)	1,867,198	39.8	180
	Stephen A. Douglas (D)	1,379,434	29.4	12
	John C. Breckinridge (D)	854,248	18.2	72
	John Bell (CU)	591,658	12.6	39
	Gerrit Smith	172		
1864	†Abraham Lincoln (R)	2,219,362	55.2	212
	George B. McClellan (D)	1,805,063	44.9	21
1868	Ulysses S. Grant (R)	3,013,313	52.7	214
	Horatio Seymour (D)	2,703,933	47.3	80
1872	Ulysses S. Grant (R)	3,597,375	55.6	286
	†Horace Greeley (D)	2,833,711	43.8	———
	Others	35,052	0.6	63
*1876	Rutherford B. Hayes (R)	4,035,924	47.9	185
	Samuel J. Tilden (D)	4,287,670	50.9	184
	Others	94,935	1.1	———
1880	†James A. Garfield (R)	4,454,433	48.3	214
	Winfield S. Hancock (D)	4,444,976	48.2	155
	James B. Weaver (G)	308,649	3.4	———
	Others	11,409	0.1	———
1884	Grover Cleveland (D)	4,875,971	48.5	219
	James G. Blaine (R)	4,852,234	48.3	182
	Benjamin F. Butler (G)	175,066	1.7	———
	John P. St. John (P)	150,957	1.5	———
*1888	Benjamin Harrison (R)	5,445,269	47.8	233
	Grover Cleveland (D)	5,540,365	48.6	168
	Clinton B. Fisk (P)	250,122	2.2	———
	Others	154,083	1.4	———
1892	Grover Cleveland (D)	5,556,982	46.0	277
	Benjamin Harrison (R)	5,191,466	43.0	145
	James B. Weaver (PO)	1,029,960	8.5	22
	Others	292,672	2.4	———

Year	Candidates	Popular Vote Total	Percentage	Electoral Votes Received
1896	William McKinley (R)	7,113,734	51.0	271
	William J. Bryan (D)	6,516,722	46.7	176
	Others	317,219	2.3	——
1900	†William McKinley (R)	7,219,828	51.7	292
	William J. Bryan (D)	6,358,160	45.5	155
	Others	396,200	2.8	——
1904	Theodore Roosevelt (R)	7,628,831	56.4	336
	Alton B. Parker (D)	5,084,533	37.6	140
	Eugene V. Debs (S)	402,714	3.0	——
	Silas C. Swallow (P)	259,163	1.9	——
	Others	149,357	1.1	——
1908	William H. Taft (R)	7,679,114	51.6	321
	William J. Bryan (D)	6,410,665	43.1	162
	Eugene V. Debs (S)	420,858	2.8	——
	Eugene W. Chafin (P)	252,704	1.7	——
	Others	127,379	0.9	——
1912	Woodrow Wilson (D)	6,301,254	41.9	435
	Theodore Roosevelt (PR)	4,127,788	27.4	88
	William H. Taft (R)	3,485,831	23.2	8
	Eugene V. Debs (S)	901,255	6.0	——
	Others	238,934	1.6	——
*1916	Woodrow Wilson (D)	9,131,511	49.3	277
	Charles E. Hughes (R)	8,548,935	46.1	254
	Allan L. Benson (S)	585,974	3.2	——
	Others	269,812	1.5	——
1920	†Warren G. Harding (R)	16,153,115	60.3	404
	James M. Cox (D)	9,133,092	34.1	127
	Eugene V. Debs (S)	915,490	3.4	——
	Others	566,916	2.1	——
1924	Calvin Coolidge (R)	15,719,921	54.0	382
	John W. Davis (D)	8,386,704	28.8	136
	Robert M. LaFollette (PR)	4,832,532	16.6	13
	Others	155,866	0.5	——
1928	Herbert C. Hoover (R)	21,437,277	58.2	444
	Alfred E. Smith (D)	15,007,698	40.8	87
	Others	360,976	1.0	——
1932	Franklin D. Roosevelt (D)	22,829,501	57.4	472
	Herbert C. Hoover (R)	15,760,684	39.6	59
	Norman M. Thomas (S)	884,649	2.2	——
	Others	283,925	0.8	——

Year	Candidates	Popular Vote Total	Percentage	Electoral Votes Received
1936	Franklin D. Roosevelt (D)	27,757,333	60.8	523
	Alfred M. Landon (R)	16,684,231	36.5	8
	William Lemke (U)	892,267	2.0	———
	Others	320,932	0.7	———
1940	Franklin D. Roosevelt (D)	27,313,041	54.7	449
	Wendell Willkie (R)	22,348,480	44.8	82
	Others	238,897	0.5	———
1944	†Franklin D. Roosevelt (D)	25,612,610	53.4	432
	Thomas E. Dewey (R)	22,017,617	45.9	99
	Others	346,443	0.7	———
*1948	Harry S Truman (D)	24,179,345	49.6	303
	Thomas E. Dewey (R)	21,991,291	45.1	189
	J. Strom Thurmond (SR)	1,176,125	2.4	39
	Henry A. Wallace (PR)	1,157,326	2.4	———
	Others	289,739	0.6	———
1952	Dwight D. Eisenhower (R)	33,936,234	55.1	442
	Adlai E. Stevenson (D)	27,314,992	44.4	89
	Others	299,692	0.5	———
1956	Dwight D. Eisenhower (R)	35,590,472	57.4	457
	Adlai E. Stevenson (D)	26,022,752	42.0	73
	Unpledged Elector Slates	196,318	0.3	———
	Others	217,366	0.3	1
*1960	†John F. Kennedy (D)	34,220,984	49.5	303
	Richard M. Nixon (R)	34,108,157	49.3	219
	Unpledged Elector Slates	638,822	0.9	15
	Others	188,559	0.3	———

ALTERNATE COMPUTATION: This method avoids a major defect of the method used above, which counted Alabama Democratic votes twice, once for Kennedy and once for unpledged slates. The alternate computation credits 5/11ths of Alabama's Democratic votes to Kennedy and 6/11ths to the unpledged electoral slate totals. (See pages 100–109).

	John F. Kennedy (D)	34,049,976	49.2	303
	Richard M. Nixon (R)	34,108,157	49.3	219
	Unpledged Elector Slates	491,527	0.7	15
	Others	188,559	0.3	———
1964	Lyndon B. Johnson (D)	43,129,484	61.1	486
	Barry M. Goldwater (R)	27,178,188	38.5	52
	Others	336,838	0.4	———

* ELECTION YEAR NOTES:

1789—for further background, see pp. 58–61. 1876—see pp. 86–92.
1792—see pp. 61–62. 1888—see pp. 92–93.
1796—see pp. 62–65. 1916—see pp. 93–95.
1800—see pp. 65–71. 1948—see pp. 95–100.
1824—see pp. 82–86. 1960—see pp. 100–109.

† NOTES ON CANDIDATES:

William Henry Harrison died in office April 4, 1841, and was succeeded by Vice President John Tyler.

Zachary Taylor died in office July 9, 1850, and was succeeded by Vice President Millard Fillmore.

Abraham Lincoln was shot April 14, 1865, and died the following day. He was succeeded by Vice President Andrew Johnson.

Horace Greeley died Nov. 29, 1872, before the counting of the electoral votes, which the Democratic electors divided among a scattering of candidates.

James A. Garfield was shot July 2, 1881, and died Sept. 19, 1881. He was succeeded by Vice President Chester A. Arthur.

William McKinley was shot Sept. 6, 1901, and died Sept. 14, 1901. He was succeeded by Vice President Theodore Roosevelt.

Warren G. Harding died in office Aug. 2, 1923, and was succeeded by Vice President Calvin Coolidge.

Franklin D. Roosevelt died in office April 12, 1945, and was succeeded by Vice President Harry S Truman.

John F. Kennedy was assassinated Nov. 22, 1963, and was succeeded by Vice President Lyndon B. Johnson.

APPENDIX B

The Choice of Presidential Electors, 1788–1836

THE NUMBER OF STATES USING EACH METHOD OF ELECTOR SELECTION

| Election Year | Legislature Selected | Popular Election | | | Mixed Systems |
		By General Ticket	By Districts	Total	
1788–89	4	2	2	4	2
1792	9	3	2	5	1
1796	7	2	4	6	3
1800	10	2	3	5	1
1804	6	6	5	11	——
1808	7	6	4	10	——
1812	9	5	4	9	——
1816	9	7	3	10	——
1820	9	9	6	15	——
1824	6	12	5	17	1
1828	2	18	3	21	1
1832	1	22	1	23	——
1836	1	25	——	25	——

STATE-BY-STATE BREAKDOWN ON METHODS OF CHOOSING ELECTORS,
1789–1836

KEY: L   chosen by legislature   G   general ticket (at-large)
      P   chosen by popular vote   D   district system
      C   combination of methods

Election Year

State	1789	1792	1796	1800	1804	1808	1812
Connecticut	L	L	L	L	L	L	L
Delaware	P/D	L	L	L	L	L	L
Georgia	L	L	P/G	L	L	L	L
Maryland	P/G	P/G	P/D	P/D	P/D	P/D	P/D
Massachusetts	C	C	C	L	P/D & G	L	P/D
New Hampshire	C	P/G	C	L	P/G	P/G	P/G
New Jersey	L	L	L	L	P/G	P/G	L
Pennsylvania	P/G	P/G	P/G	L	P/G	P/G	P/G
South Carolina	L	L	L	L	L	L	L
Virginia	P/D	P/D	P/D	P/G	P/G	P/G	P/G
Kentucky		P/D	P/D	P/D	P/D	P/D	P/D
New York		L	L	L	L	L	L
North Carolina			P/D	P/D	P/D	P/D	P/D
Rhode Island			L	P/G	P/G	P/G	P/G
Vermont		L	L	L	L	L	L
Tennessee			C	C	P/D	P/D	P/D
Ohio					P/G	P/G	P/G
Louisiana							L

State						
Connecticut	—	L	P/G	P/G	P/G	P/G
Delaware	L	L	L	L	P/G	P/G
Georgia	L	L	P/G	P/G	P/G	P/G
Maryland	P/D	P/D	P/D	P/D	P/D	P/D
Massachusetts	L	L & G	P/G	P/G	P/G	P/G
New Hampshire	P/G	P/G	P/G	P/G	P/G	P/G
New Jersey	P/G	P/G	P/G	P/G	P/G	P/G
Pennsylvania	P/G	P/G	P/G	P/G	P/G	P/G
South Carolina	L	L	L	L	L	L*
Virginia	P/G	P/G	P/G	P/G	P/G	P/G
Kentucky	P/D	P/D	P/D	P/G	P/G	P/G
New York	L	L	L	C	P/G	P/G
North Carolina	P/G	P/G	P/G	P/G	P/G	P/G
Rhode Island	P/G	P/G	P/G	P/G	P/G	P/G
Vermont	L	L	L	L	P/G	P/G
Tennessee	P/D	P/D	P/D	P/D	P/G	P/G
Ohio	P/G	P/G	P/G	P/G	P/G	P/G
Louisiana	L	L	L	L	P/G	P/G
Indiana	L	L	P/G	P/G	P/G	P/G
Alabama	—	L	P/G	P/G	P/G	P/G
Illinois	—	P/D	P/D	P/G	P/G	P/G
Maine	—	P/D & G	P/D & G	P/D	P/G	P/G
Missouri	—	L	C	P/G	P/G	P/G
Mississippi	—	P/G	P/G	P/G	P/G	P/G
Arkansas	—	—	—	—	—	P/G
Michigan	—	—	—	—	—	P/G

* South Carolina chose electors by the legislature until 1860.

SOURCE: Adapted from data in Charles A. Paullin, "Political Parties and Opinions, 1788–1930," *Atlas of the Historical Geography of the United States* (Washington, 1932).

APPENDIX C

Electoral College Membership

TOTAL MEMBERSHIP OF THE ELECTORAL COLLEGE SINCE 1789

(together with totals for selected states)

Election Years*	Number of States†	Total Electoral Vote†	Calif.	Ill.	N.Y.	Va.
1789	13	91	—	—	8	12
1792–1800	16	138	—	—	12	21
1804–1808	17	176	—	—	19	24
1812–1820	23	232	—	3	29	25
1824–1828	24	261	—	3	36	24
1832–1840	26	294	—	5	42	23
1844–1848	31	294	—	9	36	17
1852–1860	33	303	4	11	35	15
1864–1868	36	315	5	16	33	13
1872–1880	38	369	6	21	35	11
1884–1888	44	420	8	22	36	12
1892–1900	45	447	9	24	36	12
1904–1908	46	483	10	27	39	12
1912–1928†	48	531	13	29	45	12
1932–1940	48	531	22	29	47	11
1944–1948	48	531	25	28	47	11
1952–1960	50	537§	32	27	45	12
1964–1968	50	538‖	40	26	43	12
1972–1980 (estimate)	50	538‖	46	25	42	12

(*See p. 314 for explanation of symbols.*)

SOURCES: *Biographical Directory of the American Congress* (Washington, 1961), p. 45; *Representation and Apportionment* (Congressional Quarterly Service, 1966), pp. 53, 61.

ELECTORAL COLLEGE MEMBERSHIP, STATE BY STATE, 1904–1980*

State	1904–1908	1912–1928‡	1932–1940	1944–1948	1952–1960	1964–1968	(estimate) 1972–1980
Alabama	11	12	11	11	11	10	10
Alaska					3	3	3
Arizona		3	3	4	4	5	6
Arkansas	9	9	9	9	8	6	6
California	10	13	22	25	32	40	46
Colorado	5	6	6	6	6	6	6
Connecticut	7	7	8	8	8	8	8
Delaware	3	3	3	3	3	3	3
District of Columbia	—	—	—	—	—	3	3
Florida	5	6	7	8	10	14	16
Georgia	13	14	12	12	12	12	12
Hawaii					3	4	4
Idaho	3	4	4	4	4	4	4
Illinois	27	29	29	28	27	26	25
Indiana	15	15	14	13	13	13	13
Iowa	13	13	11	10	10	9	8
Kansas	10	10	9	8	8	7	7
Kentucky	13	13	11	11	10	9	9
Louisiana	9	10	10	10	10	10	10
Maine	6	6	5	5	5	4	4
Maryland	8	8	8	8	9	10	10
Massachusetts	16	18	17	16	16	14	14
Michigan	14	15	19	19	20	21	20
Minnesota	11	12	11	11	11	10	10
Mississippi	10	10	9	9	8	7	7
Missouri	18	18	15	15	13	12	12
Montana	3	4	4	4	4	4	4
Nebraska	8	8	7	6	6	5	5
Nevada	3	3	3	3	3	3	3
New Hampshire	4	4	4	4	4	4	4
New Jersey	12	14	16	16	16	17	18
New Mexico		3	3	4	4	4	4
New York	39	45	47	47	45	43	42
North Carolina	12	12	13	14	14	13	13
North Dakota	4	5	4	4	4	4	3
Ohio	23	24	26	25	25	26	25
Oklahoma	7	10	11	10	8	8	7
Oregon	4	5	5	6	6	6	6
Pennsylvania	34	38	36	35	32	29	27

State	1904–1908	1912–1928‡	1932–1940	1944–1948	1952–1960	1964–1968	(estimate) 1972–1980
Rhode Island	4	5	4	4	4	4	4
South Carolina	9	9	8	8	8	8	8
South Dakota	4	5	4	4	4	4	4
Tennessee	12	12	11	12	11	11	11
Texas	18	20	23	23	24	25	26
Utah	3	4	4	4	4	4	4
Vermont	4	4	3	3	3	3	3
Virginia	12	12	11	11	12	12	12
Washington	5	7	8	8	9	9	9
West Virginia	7	8	8	8	8	7	6
Wisconsin	13	13	12	12	12	12	11
Wyoming	3	3	3	3	3	3	3
Total†	483	531	531	531	537§	538‖	538‖

* Apportionments are based on the last decennial Census preceding the actual year of the election. Thus the electoral college membership for the Presidential elections of 1792 through 1800 was based on the 1790 Census, that of 1804 and 1808 on the 1800 Census, etc. The electoral college membership for the first Presidential election, in 1789, was based on the temporary apportionment specified in the Constitution.

† Figures given are those at the end of the decade, including temporary apportionment for states that may have joined the Union since the preceding Census.

‡ Congress made no reapportionment following the 1920 Census.

§ Total rose temporarily to 537 for 1960 election to allow newly admitted states of Alaska and Hawaii to cast electoral votes.

‖ Increase to 538 from 535, which would be the normal 50-state base, accounted for by the 23rd Amendment, giving the District of Columbia a minimum of 3 electoral votes.

APPENDIX D

Comparison of Popular and Electoral Vote Percentages, 1824–1964

Year	Winning Candidate	Percent of Popular Vote	Percent of Electoral Vote	Disparity (In Percentage Points)
1824	John Quincy Adams (D)	32	32	0
1828	Andrew Jackson (D)	56	68	12
1832	Andrew Jackson (D)	55	77	22
1836	Martin Van Buren (D)	51	58	7
1840	William H. Harrison (W)	53	80	27
1844	James K. Polk (D)	50	62	12
1848	Zachary Taylor (W)	47	56	9
1852	Franklin Pierce (D)	51	86	35
1856	James Buchanan (D)	46	59	13
1860	Abraham Lincoln (R)	40	59	19
1864	Abraham Lincoln (R)	55	91	36
1868	Ulysses S. Grant (R)	53	73	20
1872	Ulysses S. Grant (R)	56	82	26
1876	Rutherford B. Hayes (R)	48	50	2
1880	James A. Garfield (R)	48	58	10
1884	Grover Cleveland (D)	49	55	6
1888	Benjamin Harrison (R)	48	58	10
1892	Grover Cleveland (D)	46	62	16
1896	William McKinley (R)	51	61	10
1900	William McKinley (R)	52	65	13
1904	Theodore Roosevelt (R)	56	71	15

Year	Winning Candidate	Percent of Popular Vote	Percent of Electoral Vote	Disparity (In Percentage Points)
1908	William H. Taft (R)	52	66	14
1912	Woodrow Wilson (D)	42	82	40
1916	Woodrow Wilson (D)	49	52	3
1920	Warren G. Harding (R)	60	76	16
1924	Calvin Coolidge (R)	54	71	17
1928	Herbert C. Hoover (R)	58	84	26
1932	Franklin D. Roosevelt (D)	57	89	32
1936	Franklin D. Roosevelt (D)	61	98	37
1940	Franklin D. Roosevelt (D)	55	85	30
1944	Franklin D. Roosevelt (D)	53	81	28
1948	Harry S Truman (D)	50	57	7
1952	Dwight D. Eisenhower (R)	55	83	28
1956	Dwight D. Eisenhower (R)	57	86	29
1960	John F. Kennedy (D)	50	62	12
1964	Lyndon B. Johnson (D)	61	90	29

APPENDIX E

Elections in Which Minor Vote Shifts Could Have Changed the Outcome

Listed below are a number of elections in U.S. history in which a strategically placed shift in the popular vote, amounting to less than one percent of the national vote cast, could have changed the outcome of the contest for the Presidency.

In each case, however, a vote shift larger over-all than the mathematical minimum first indicated would undoubtedly have been necessary, since any significant change in voting patterns would have been general, not selective in a few crucial states. To give some idea of the magnitude of the national vote shifts that would have changed election results, an additional percentage is noted: the percentage of switched votes required in the key states. In most elections a similar shift of the over-all natural popular vote would have been required actually to change the outcome of the election. In 1892, for instance, a shift of 37,364 votes in five states would have elected Harrison instead of Cleveland. Those 37,364 votes constituted 0.317 percent of the national popular vote. But the shift in the five key states alone would have been 1.349 percent. Thus it is likely that a general national shift of between 1.0 and 1.5 percent of the popular vote would actually have had to take place for the five closest states to change, giving Harrison the election.

Pioneer research in the field of "hairbreadth" elections appears in Svend Petersen, *A Statistical History of American Presidential Elections* (New York, 1963). The listing below, however, also contains a number of computations not made by Petersen, and rests on data other than his for Presidential elections since 1920.

1828.   Andrew Jackson received 647,292 popular and 178 electoral votes, while John Quincy Adams received 507,730 popular and 83 electoral votes. A shift from Jackson to Adams of 11,517 votes in five states (Ohio, Kentucky, New York, Louisiana and Indiana) would have elected Adams. The required shift was 0.997 percent of the national vote cast. But a shift of 2.189 percent in the five crucial states would have been needed to change the indicated number of electoral votes.

1836.   Martin Van Buren received 764,198 popular and 170 electoral votes, while William Henry Harrison received 549,508 popular and 73 electoral votes. A shift from Van Buren to Harrison of 14,061 votes in one state—New York—would have deprived Van Buren of an electoral college majority and probably would have encouraged the Whigs to unify their electoral votes behind Harrison and thus make him President. As it was, two other Whig candidates received a total of 40 electoral votes. The required shift was 0.937 percent of the national vote cast. But a shift of 4.600 percent in New York would have been needed to change the indicated number of electoral votes.

1840.   Harrison received 1,275,612 popular and 234 electoral votes and Van Buren 1,130,033 popular and 60 electoral votes. A shift from Harrison to Van Buren of 8,386 votes in four states (New York, Pennsylvania, Maine and New Jersey) would have elected Van Buren. The required shift was 0.349 percent of the national vote cast; a shift of 0.949 percent in the four crucial states would have been needed to change the indicated number of electoral votes.

1844.   James K. Polk received 1,339,368 popular and 170 electoral votes, while Henry Clay received 1,300,687 popular and 105 electoral votes. A shift of 2,555 votes from Polk to Clay in one state—New York— would have made Clay President. The required shift was 0.097 percent of the national vote cast; a shift of 0.544 percent in New York would have been needed to change the indicated number of electoral votes.

1848.   Zachary Taylor received 1,362,101 popular and 163 electoral votes, while Lewis Cass received 1,222,674 popular and 127 electoral votes. A shift from Taylor to Cass of 3,227 votes in three states (Georgia, Maryland and Delaware) would have given Cass the Presidency. The required shift was 0.125 percent of the national vote cast; a shift of 1.824 percent in the three crucial states would have been needed to change the indicated number of electoral votes.

1856.   James Buchanan received 1,839,237 popular and 174 electoral votes, while John C. Frémont received 1,341,028 popular and 114 electoral votes; Millard Fillmore received 849,872 popular and 8 electoral votes. A shift of 17,427 votes from Buchanan to Frémont in two states (Indiana and Illinois) and from Fillmore to Frémont in one state (Delaware) would have deprived Buchanan of an electoral majority and thrown the election into the House of Representatives for decision. The required shift was 0.432 percent of the national vote cast; a shift of 3.554 percent in the three crucial states alone would have been needed to change the indicated number of electoral votes.

1860.   Abraham Lincoln received 1,867,198 popular and 180 electoral votes, while Stephen A. Douglas received 1,379,434 popular and 12 electoral votes; John C. Breckinridge received 854,248 popular and 72 electoral votes, and John Bell received 591,658 popular and 39 electoral votes. A shift of 18,050 votes from Lincoln to Douglas in four states (California, Oregon, Illinois and Indiana), or of 25,069 votes from Lincoln to Douglas in New York, would have deprived Lincoln of an electoral college majority and thrown the election into the House, where Lincoln's Republicans controlled only 15 of the 34 state delegations. The required shift of 18,050 votes was 0.772 percent of the national vote cast; a shift of 2.677 percent in the four crucial states alone—or a shift of 3.713 percent in New York— would have been needed to change the indicated number of electoral votes.

1864.   Lincoln received 2,219,362 popular and 212 electoral votes, while George B. McClellan received 1,805,063 popular and 21 electoral votes. A shift of 38,111 votes in seven states (New York, Pennsylvania, Indiana, Wisconsin, Maryland, Connecticut and Oregon) would have elected McClellan. The required shift was 0.947 percent of the national vote cast; a shift of 1.994 percent in the seven crucial states would have been needed to change the indicated number of electoral votes.

1868.   Ulysses S. Grant received 3,013,313 popular and 214 electoral votes, while Horatio Seymour received 2,703,933 popular and 80 electoral votes. A shift of 29,862 votes in seven states (Pennsylvania, Indiana, North Carolina, Alabama, Connecticut, California and Nevada) would have elected Seymour. The required shift was 0.522 percent of the national vote cast; a shift of 1.923 percent in the seven crucial states would have been needed to change the indicated number of electoral votes.

1876.   After the disputed ballot count in several states was settled, Rutherford B. Hayes received 4,035,924 popular and 185 electoral votes, while Samuel J. Tilden received 4,287,670 popular and 184 electoral votes. A shift of 116 votes in South Carolina would have transferred one electoral vote from Hayes to Tilden and made Tilden President. The required shift was 0.0056 percent of the national vote cast; a shift of 0.0635 percent in the South Carolina balloting would have been needed to change the electoral vote.

1880.   James A. Garfield received 4,454,433 popular and 214 electoral votes, while Winfield S. Hancock received 4,444,976 popular and 155 electoral votes. A shift of 10,517 votes in New York would have elected Hancock. The required shift was 0.118 percent of the national total; a shift of 0.965 percent in New York would have been needed to change the indicated number of electoral votes.

1884.   Grover Cleveland received 4,875,971 popular and 219 electoral votes, while James G. Blaine received 4,852,234 popular and 182 electoral votes. A shift of 575 votes in one state—again New York—would have made Blaine President. The required shift was 0.006 percent of the national vote; a shift of 0.051 percent in New York would have been needed to change the indicated number of electoral votes.

1888.   Benjamin Harrison received 5,445,269 popular and 233 electoral votes, while Grover Cleveland received 5,540,365 popular and 168 electoral votes. A switch of New York's electoral votes, in this instance through a shift of 7,189 votes from Harrison to Cleveland, would have elected Cleveland. The required shift was 0.065 percent of the national vote; a shift of 0.589 percent in New York would have been needed to change the indicated number of electoral votes.

1892.   Cleveland received 5,556,982 popular and 277 electoral votes, while Harrison received 5,191,466 popular and 145 electoral votes. A shift of 37,364 votes from Cleveland to Harrison in five states (New York, Indiana, Wisconsin, New Jersey and California) would have reelected Harrison. The required shift was 0.317 percent of the national vote; a shift of 1.349 percent in the five states would have been needed to change the indicated number of electoral votes.

1896.   William McKinley received 7,113,734 popular and 271 electoral votes, while William Jennings Bryan received 6,516,722 popular and 176 electoral votes. A shift of 20,296 votes in six states (Indiana, Kentucky, California, West Virginia, Oregon and Delaware) would have given the election to Bryan. The required shift was 0.150 percent of the national vote; a shift of 1.207 percent in the six states would have been needed to change the indicated number of electoral votes.

1900.   McKinley received 7,219,828 popular and 292 electoral votes, while Bryan received 6,358,160 popular and 155 electoral votes. A shift of 74,755 votes in seven states (Ohio, Indiana, Kansas, Nebraska, Maryland, Utah and Wyoming) would have elected Bryan. The required shift was 0.551 percent of the national vote cast; a shift of 2.848 percent in the seven crucial states would have been needed to change the indicated number of electoral votes.

1908.   William Howard Taft received 7,679,114 popular and 321 electoral votes, while Bryan received 6,410,665 popular and 162 electoral votes. A shift of 75,041 votes in eight states (Ohio, Missouri, Indiana, Kansas, West Virginia, Delaware, Montana and Maryland) would have given Bryan a majority in the electoral college. The required shift was 0.533 percent of the national vote; a shift of 2.204 percent in the eight states would have been needed to change the indicated number of electoral votes.

1916.   Woodrow Wilson received 9,131,511 popular and 277 electoral votes, while Charles Evans Hughes received 8,548,935 popular and 254 electoral votes. A shift of 1,983 votes from Wilson to Hughes in California would have cost Wilson the election. The required shift was 0.0112 percent of the national vote cast; a shift of 0.0214 percent in California would have been needed to change the indicated number of electoral votes.

1948.   Harry S Truman received 24,179,345 popular and 303 electoral votes, while Thomas E. Dewey received 21,991,291 popular and 189 electoral votes. A shift of 29,294 votes in three states (Illinois, California and Ohio) would have made Dewey President. A switch of 12,487 votes in California and Ohio would have denied both candidates an electoral college majority and would have thrown the election into the House, where neither candidate was favored by a clear majority of states. The shift required to elect Dewey was 0.063 percent of the national vote cast; a shift of 0.275 percent in the three states would have elected Dewey, and an 0.186 percent shift in the two states would have sent the election to the House for decision.

1960.   John F. Kennedy received 34,220,984 popular and 303 electoral votes, while Richard M. Nixon received 34,108,157 popular and 219 electoral votes. A shift of 11,424 votes in five states (Illinois, Missouri, New Mexico, Hawaii and Nevada) would have elected Nixon. A shift of only 8,971 popular votes from Kennedy to Nixon in Illinois and Missouri would have prevented either man from receiving an electoral college majority and given the balance of power to the unpledged electors who eventually voted for Harry F. Byrd of Virginia. If the election had gone to the House for decision, neither Kennedy nor Nixon would have been assured of a clear majority of the states. The shift required to elect Nixon was 0.0167 percent of the national vote cast; a shift of 0.157 percent in the five crucial states would have been needed to change the indicated number of votes, and a shift of 0.134 percent in the two states would have been enough to prevent either candidate from gaining an electoral college majority.

APPENDIX F

The Voter Turnout by State for Presidential Elections, 1920–1964

Figures show the percentage of the civilian population of voting age in each state that cast votes for Presidential electors. The states and the District of Columbia are ranked in the order of their turnout in 1964.

State	*Percentage Turnout*					
	1964	*1960*	*1948*	*1940*	*1932*	*1920*
Utah	78.6	80.0	74.7	80.3	75.1	63.8
Minnesota	76.9	77.0	65.5	69.6	62.7	53.3
Idaho	76.5	80.8	65.3	75.1	73.4	57.9
Iowa	74.8	76.6	62.8	74.1	67.8	62.7
South Dakota	74.4	78.2	66.7	79.5	73.4	52.8
West Virginia	74.4	77.4	67.5	81.4	78.5	67.8
Wyoming	74.4	73.6	62.2	72.2	71.3	45.4
Indiana	73.9	76.9	65.3	79.8	76.4	71.0
Illinois	73.7	75.7	68.1	78.4	68.6	53.1
New Hampshire	71.9	79.3	67.3	72.4	68.5	56.6
Massachusetts	71.8	76.1	65.9	69.5	58.0	41.2
Washington	71.8	72.3	61.4	66.5	59.9	46.5
North Dakota	71.7	78.4	64.0	75.2	71.4	63.7
Connecticut	71.4	76.8	63.7	67.4	58.3	43.6
Rhode Island	71.3	75.0	62.3	67.4	62.9	47.3
Wisconsin	70.8	73.5	59.2	69.6	60.7	45.9
Montana	70.4	71.4	65.4	69.6	67.4	55.8
Vermont	70.3	72.4	54.1	62.7	62.0	41.4
Delaware	70.2	73.4	66.9	76.8	72.8	69.5
Oregon	69.4	72.3	55.9	64.3	57.5	48.2
Colorado	69.3	71.4	64.4	76.9	71.5	51.7

Percentage Turnout

State	1964	1960	1948	1940	1932	1920
New Jersey	68.9	71.8	59.2	69.6	62.3	48.0
Michigan	68.6	72.4	52.4	61.8	56.6	47.3
Pennsylvania	68.1	70.5	54.6	64.2	48.8	36.7
Nebraska	67.2	71.5	59.6	73.6	69.1	51.8
Missouri	66.6	71.8	61.2	73.3	68.7	65.4
Ohio	66.4	71.3	55.8	72.4	61.3	56.8
Maine	65.7	72.6	47.6	60.2	60.2	41.6
Kansas	64.8	70.3	64.1	74.0	68.9	55.7
California	64.7	67.4	58.9	66.9	55.9	40.7
New York	63.5	67.0	60.8	67.4	56.0	44.5
New Mexico	63.4	62.0	57.1	64.4	66.2	56.9
Oklahoma	62.7	63.8	56.2	60.3	53.7	47.6
Arizona	55.8	54.4	44.0	52.0	46.6	35.4
Maryland	55.7	57.2	40.7	55.7	49.1	49.7
Nevada	54.3	61.3	59.2	70.6	63.7	52.1
Florida	53.3	50.0	34.5	39.8	30.2	36.0
Kentucky	52.9	59.2	49.8	59.3	67.4	71.2
North Carolina	51.8	53.5	36.7	42.6	43.7	44.5
Hawaii	51.5	51.3	—	—	—	—
Tennessee	51.2	50.3	28.5	30.6	26.1	35.3
Arkansas	49.9	41.0	22.8	18.2	22.5	21.2
Alaska	48.3	45.3	—	—	—	—
Louisiana	47.2	44.8	27.1	27.1	22.5	13.6
Texas	44.4	41.8	24.7	27.0	25.8	19.8
Georgia	43.2	30.4	20.4	17.6	16.4	10.4
Virginia	41.1	33.4	22.1	22.0	21.7	19.1
District of Columbia	39.4	—	—	—	—	—
South Carolina	38.7	30.5	13.4	10.1	12.1	8.6
Alabama	35.9	31.0	12.7	18.9	17.6	20.8
Mississippi	33.2	25.5	16.7	14.7	13.8	9.4
Average total U.S.	62.1	63.8	56.3	59.7	52.9	44.2

SOURCES: Report of the President's Commission on Registration and Voting Participation (Nov. 1963); Congressional Quarterly Service.

APPENDIX G

Constitutional Provisions
Relating to Presidential Election
and Succession and the
Elective Franchise

ARTICLE II

Section 1. The executive Power shall be vested in a President of the United States of America. He shall hold his Office during the Term of four Years, and, together with the Vice President, chosen for the same Term, be elected, as follows

Each State shall appoint, in such Manner as the Legislature thereof may direct, a Number of Electors, equal to the whole Number of Senators and Representatives to which the State may be entitled in the Congress: but no Senator or Representative, or Person holding an Office of Trust or Profit under the United States, shall be appointed an Elector.

*[The Electors shall meet in their respective States, and vote by Ballot for two Persons, of whom one at least shall not be an Inhabitant of the same State with themselves. And they shall make a List of all the Persons voted for, and of the Number of Votes for each; which List they shall sign and certify, and transmit sealed to the Seat of the Government of the United States, directed to the President of the Senate. The President of the Senate shall, in the Presence of the Senate and House of Representatives, open all the Certificates, and the Votes shall then be counted. The Person having the greatest Number of Votes shall be the President, if such Number be a Majority of the whole Number of Electors appointed; and if there be more than one who have such Majority, and have an equal Number of Votes,

* Paragraph in brackets superseded by the 12th Amendment (see below).

then the House of Representatives shall immediately chuse by Ballot one of them for President; and if no Person have a Majority, then from the five highest on the List the said House shall in like Manner chuse the President. But in chusing the President, the Votes shall be taken by States, the Representation from each State having one Vote; a quorum for this Purpose shall consist of a Member or Members from two thirds of the States, and a Majority of all the States shall be necessary to a Choice. In every Case, after the Choice of the President, the Person having the greatest Number of Votes of the Electors shall be the Vice President. But if there should remain two or more who have equal Votes, the Senate shall chuse from them by Ballot the Vice President.]

The Congress may determine the Time of chusing the Electors, and the Day on which they shall give their Votes; which Day shall be the same throughout the United States.

No Person except a natural born Citizen, or a Citizen of the United States, at the time of the Adoption of this Constitution, shall be eligible to the Office of President; neither shall any person be eligible to that Office who shall not have attained to the Age of thirty five Years, and been fourteen Years a Resident within the United States.

In Case of the Removal of the President from Office, or of his Death, Resignation, or Inability to discharge the Powers and Duties of the said Office, the Same shall devolve on the Vice President, and the Congress may by Law provide for the Case of Removal, Death, Resignation or Inability, both of the President and Vice President, declaring what Officer shall then act as President, and such Officer shall act accordingly, until the Disability be removed, or a President shall be elected.

The President shall, at stated Times, receive for his Services, a Compensation, which shall neither be encreased nor diminished during the Period for which he shall have been elected, and he shall not receive within that Period any other Emolument from the United States, or any of them.

Before he enter on the Execution of his Office, he shall take the following Oath or Affirmation:—"I do solemnly swear (or affirm) that I will faithfully execute the Office of President of the United States, and will to the best of my Ability, preserve, protect and defend the Constitution of the United States."

Section 2. The President shall be Commander in Chief of the Army and Navy of the United States, and of the Militia of the several States, when called into the actual Service of the United States; he may require the Opinion, in writing, of the principal Officer in each of the executive Departments, upon any Subject relating to the Duties of their respective Offices, and he shall have Power to grant Reprieves and Pardons for Offenses against the United States, except in Cases of Impeachment.

He shall have Power, by and with the Advice and Consent of the Senate, to make Treaties, provided two thirds of the Senators present concur; and he shall nominate, and by and with the Advice and Consent of the Senate, shall appoint Ambassadors, other public Ministers and Consuls, Judges of the supreme Court, and all other Officers of the United States, whose Appointments are not herein otherwise provided for, and which shall be established by Law: but the Congress may by Law vest the Appointment of such inferior Officers, as they think proper, in the President alone, in the Courts of Law, or in the Heads of Departments.

The President shall have Power to fill up all Vacancies that may happen during the Recess of the Senate, by granting Commissions which shall expire at the End of their next Session.

Section 3.   He shall from time to time give to the Congress Information of the State of the Union, and recommend to their Consideration such Measures as he shall judge necessary and expedient; he may, on extraordinary Occasions, convene both Houses, or either of them, and in Case of Disagreement between them, with Respect to the Time of Adjournment, he may adjourn them to such Time as he shall think proper; he shall receive Ambassadors and other public Ministers; he shall take Care that the Laws be faithfully executed, and shall Commission all the Officers of the United States.

Section 4.   The President, Vice President and all Civil Officers of the United States, shall be removed from Office on Impeachment for, and Conviction of, Treason, Bribery, or other high Crimes and Misdemeanors.

AMENDMENT XII
(*Declared ratified Sept. 25, 1804*)

The Electors shall meet in their respective states and vote by ballot for President and Vice-President, one of whom, at least, shall not be an inhabitant of the same state with themselves; they shall name in their ballots the person voted for as President, and in distinct ballots the person voted for as Vice-President, and they shall make distinct lists of all persons voted for as President, and of all persons voted for as Vice-President, and of the number of votes for each, which lists they shall sign and certify, and transmit sealed to the seat of the government of the United States, directed to the President of the Senate;—The President of the Senate shall, in the presence of the Senate and House of Representatives, open all the certificates and the votes shall then be counted;—The person having the greatest number of votes for President, shall be the President, if such number be a majority of the whole number of Electors appointed; and if no person have such majority, then from the persons having the highest numbers not exceeding three on the list of those voted for as President, the House of Representatives shall choose immediately, by ballot, the President. But in choosing the President, the votes shall be taken by states, the representation from each state having one vote; a quorum for this purpose shall consist of a member or members from two-thirds of the states, and a majority of all the states shall be necessary to a choice. And if the House of Representatives shall not choose a President whenever the right of choice shall devolve upon them, before the fourth day of March next following, then the Vice-President shall act as

President, as in the case of the death or other constitutional disability of the President—The person having the greatest number of votes as Vice-President, shall be the Vice-President, if such number be a majority of the whole number of Electors appointed, and if no person have a majority, then from the two highest numbers on the list, the Senate shall choose the Vice-President; a quorum for the purpose shall consist of two-thirds of the whole number of Senators, and a majority of the whole number shall be necessary to a choice. But no person constitutionally ineligible to the office of President shall be eligible to that of Vice-President of the United States.

A M E N D M E N T   X I V
(Declared ratified July 28, 1868)

Section 1.   All persons born or naturalized in the United States and subject to the jurisdiction thereof, are citizens of the United States and of the State wherein they reside. No State shall make or enforce any law which shall abridge the privileges or immunities of citizens of the United States; or shall any State deprive any person of life, liberty, or property, without due process of law; nor deny to any person within its jurisdiction the equal protection of the laws.

Section 2.   Representatives shall be apportioned among the several States according to their respective numbers, counting the whole number of persons in each State, excluding Indians not taxed. But when the right to vote at any election for the choice of electors for President and Vice President of the United States, Representatives in Congress, the Executive and Judicial officers of a State, or the members of the Legislature thereof, is denied to any of the male inhabitants of such State, being twenty-one years of age, and citizens of the United States, or in any way abridged, except for participation in rebellion, or other crime, the basis of representation therein shall be reduced in the proportion which the number of such male citizens shall bear to the whole number of male citizens twenty-one years of age in such State.*

Section 3.   No person shall be a Senator or Representative in Congress, or elector of President and Vice President, or hold any office, civil or military, under the United States, or under any State, who, having previously taken an oath, as a member of Congress, or as an officer of the United States, or as a member of any State legislature, or as an executive or judicial officer of any State, to support the Constitution of the United States, shall have engaged in insurrection or rebellion against the same, or given aid or comfort to the enemies thereof. But Congress may by a vote of two-thirds of each House, remove such disability. . . .

Section 5.   The Congress shall have power to enforce, by appropriate legislation, the provisions of this article.

* The sections of this amendment which would reduce a state's Congressional representation (and thus its votes in the electoral college) have never been enforced.

A M E N D M E N T   X V
(*Declared ratified March 30, 1870*)

Section 1. The right of citizens of the United States to vote shall not be denied or abridged by the United States or by any State on account of race, color, or previous condition of servitude.

Section 2. The Congress shall have power to enforce this article by appropriate legislation.

A M E N D M E N T   X V I I
(*Declared ratified May 31, 1913*)

The Senate of the United States shall be composed of two Senators from each State, elected by the people thereof, for six years; and each Senator shall have one vote. The electors in each State shall have the qualifications requisite for electors of the most numerous branch of the State legislatures. . . .

A M E N D M E N T   X I X
(*Declared ratified Aug. 26, 1920*)

The right of citizens of the United States to vote shall not be denied or abridged by the United States or by any State on account of sex.

Congress shall have power to enforce this article by appropriate legislation.

A M E N D M E N T   X X
(*Declared ratified Feb. 6, 1933*)

Section 1. The terms of the President and Vice President shall end at noon on the 20th day of January, and the terms of Senators and Representatives at noon on the 3d day of January, of the years in which such terms would have ended if this article had not been ratified; and the terms of their successors shall then begin.

Section 2. The Congress shall assemble at least once in every year, and such meeting shall begin at noon on the 3d day of January, unless they shall by law appoint a different day.

Section 3. If, at the time fixed for the beginning of the term of the President, the President elect shall have died, the Vice President elect shall become President. If a President shall not have been chosen before the time fixed for the beginning of his term, or if the President elect shall have failed to qualify, then the Vice President elect shall act as President until a President shall have qualified; and the Congress may by law provide for the case wherein neither a President elect nor a Vice President elect shall have qualified, declaring who shall then act as President, or the manner in which one who is to act shall be selected, and such person shall act accordingly until a President or Vice President shall have qualified.

Section 4. The Congress may by law provide for the case of the death of any of the persons from whom the House of Representatives may choose a President whenever the right of choice shall have devolved upon them, and for the case of the death of any of the persons from whom the Senate may choose a Vice President whenever the right of choice shall have devolved upon them. . . .

AMENDMENT XXII
(*Declared ratified Feb. 26, 1951*)

Section 1. No person shall be elected to the office of the President more than twice, and no person who has held the office of President, or acted as President, for more than two years of a term to which some other person was elected President shall be elected to the office of the President more than once. But this Article shall not apply to any person holding the office of President when this Article was proposed by the Congress, and shall not prevent any person who may be holding the office of President, or acting as President, during the term within which this Article becomes operative from holding the office of President or acting as President during the remainder of such term. . . .

AMENDMENT XXIII
(*Declared ratified March 29, 1961*)

Section 1. The District constituting the seat of Government of the United States shall appoint in such manner as the Congress may direct:

A number of electors of President and Vice President equal to the whole number of Senators and Representatives in Congress to which the District would be entitled if it were a State, but in no event more than the least populous State; they shall be in addition to those appointed by the States, but they shall be considered, for the purposes of the election of President and Vice President, to be electors appointed by a State; and they shall meet in the District and perform such duties as provided by the twelfth article of amendment.

Section 2. The Congress shall have power to enforce this article by appropriate legislation.

AMENDMENT XXIV
(*Declared ratified Jan. 23, 1964*)

Section 1. The right of citizens of the United States to vote in any primary or other election for President or Vice President, for electors for President or Vice President, or for Senator or Representative in Congress, shall not be denied or abridged by the United States or any State by reason of failure to pay any poll tax or other tax.

Section 2. The Congress shall have power to enforce this article by appropriate legislation.

AMENDMENT XXV
(Declared ratified Feb. 10, 1967)

Section 1.   In case of the removal of the President from office or of his death or resignation, the Vice President shall become President.

Section 2.   Whenever there is a vacancy in the office of the Vice President, the President shall nominate a Vice President who shall take office upon confirmation by a majority vote of both houses of Congress.

Section 3.   Whenever the President transmits to the President pro tempore of the Senate and the Speaker of the House of Representatives his written declaration that he is unable to discharge the powers and duties of his office, and until he transmits to them a written declaration to the contrary, such powers and duties shall be discharged by the Vice President as Acting President.

Section 4.   Whenever the Vice President and a majority of either the principal officers of the Executive departments or of such other body as Congress may by law provide transmit to the President pro tempore of the Senate and the Speaker of the House of Representatives their written declaration that the President is unable to discharge the powers and duties of his office, the Vice President shall immediately assume the powers and duties of the office as Acting President.

Thereafter, when the President transmits to the President pro tempore of the Senate and the Speaker of the House of Representatives his written declaration that no inability exists, he shall resume the powers and duties of his office unless the Vice President and a majority of either the principal officers of the executive departments or of such other body as Congress may by law provide transmit within four days to the President pro tempore of the Senate and the Speaker of the House of Representatives their written declaration that the President is unable to discharge the powers and duties of his office. Thereupon Congress shall decide the issue, assembling within forty-eight hours for that purpose if not in session. If the Congress, within twenty-one days after receipt of the latter written declaration, or, if Congress is not in session, within twenty-one days after Congress is required to assemble, determines by two-thirds vote of both houses that the President is unable to discharge the powers and duties of his office, the Vice President shall continue to discharge the same as Acting President; otherwise, the President shall resume the powers and duties of his office.

APPENDIX H

Federal Law Relating to Presidential Election Procedures

UNITED STATES CODE, 1964 EDITION

TITLE 3 — THE PRESIDENT
Chapter 1—Presidential Elections and Vacancies (Excerpts)

§ 1. Time of appointing electors.

The electors of President and Vice President shall be appointed, in each State, on the Tuesday next after the first Monday in November, in every fourth year succeeding every election of a President and Vice President.

§ 4. Vacancies in electoral college.

Each State may, by law, provide for the filling of any vacancies which may occur in its college of electors when such college meets to give its electoral vote.

§ 7. Meeting and vote of electors.

The electors of President and Vice President of each State shall meet and give their votes on the first Monday after the second Wednesday in December next following their appointment at such place in each State as the legislature of such State shall direct.

§ 9. Certificates of votes for President and Vice President.

The electors shall make and sign six certificates of all the votes given by them, each of which certificates shall contain two distinct lists, one of the votes for President and the other of the votes for Vice President, and shall annex to each of the certificates one of the lists of the electors which shall have been furnished to them by direction of the executive of the State.

§ 11. Disposition of certificates.

The electors shall dispose of the certificates so made by them and the lists attached thereto in the following manner:

First.   They shall forthwith forward by registered mail one of the same to the President of the Senate at the seat of government.

Second.   Two of the same shall be delivered to the secretary of state of the State, one of which shall be held subject to the order of the President of the Senate, the other to be preserved by him for one year and shall be a part of the public records of his office and shall be open to public inspection.

Third.   On the day thereafter they shall forward by registered mail two of such certificates and lists to the Administrator of General Services at the seat of government, one of which shall be held subject to the order of the President of the Senate. The other shall be preserved by the Administrator of General Services for one year and shall be a part of the public records of his office and shall be open to public inspection.

Fourth.   They shall forthwith cause the other of the certificates and lists to be delivered to the judge of the district in which the electors shall have assembled.

§ 15. Counting electoral votes in Congress.

Congress shall be in session on the sixth day of January succeeding every meeting of the electors. The Senate and House of Representatives shall meet in the Hall of the House of Representatives at the hour of 1 o'clock in the afternoon on that day, and the President of the Senate shall be their presiding officer. Two tellers shall be previously appointed on the part of the Senate and two on the part of the House of Representatives, to whom shall be handed, as they are opened by the President of the Senate, all the certificates and papers purporting to be certificates of the electoral votes, which certificates and papers shall be opened, presented, and acted upon in the alphabetical order of the States, beginning with the letter A; and said tellers, having then read the same in the presence and hearing of the two Houses, shall make a list of the votes as they shall appear from the said certificates; and the votes having been ascertained and counted according to the rules in this subchapter provided, the result of the same shall be delivered to the President of the Senate, who shall thereupon announce the state of the vote, which announcement shall be deemed a sufficient declaration of the persons, if any, elected President and Vice President of the United States, and, together with a list of the votes, be entered on the Journals of the two Houses. Upon such reading of any such certificate or paper, the President of the Senate shall call for objections, if any. Every objection shall be made in writing, and shall state clearly and concisely, and without argument, the ground thereof, and shall be signed by at least one Senator and one Member of the House of Representatives before the same shall be received. When all objections so made to any vote or paper from a State shall have been received and read, the Senate shall thereupon withdraw, and such objections shall be submitted to the Senate for its decision; and the Speaker of the House of Representatives shall, in like manner, submit such objections to the House of Representatives for its decision; and no electoral vote or votes from any State which shall have been regularly given by electors whose appointment has been lawfully certified to according to section 6° of this title from which but one return has been received shall be rejected, but the two Houses concurrently may reject the vote or votes when they agree that such vote or votes have not been so regularly given by electors whose appointment has been so certified. If more than one return or paper purporting to be a return from a State shall have been received by the President of the Senate, those votes, and those only, shall be counted which shall have been regularly given by the electors who are shown by the determination mentioned in section 5† of this title to have been appointed, if the determination in said section provided for shall have been made, or by such successors or substitutes, in case of a vacancy in the board of electors so ascertained, as have been appointed to fill such vacancy in the mode provided by the laws of the State; but in case there shall arise the question which of two or more of such State authorities determining what electors have been appointed, as mentioned in section 5 of this title, is the lawful tribunal of such State, the votes regularly given of those electors, and those only, of such State shall be counted whose title as electors the two Houses, acting separately, shall concurrently decide is supported by the decision of such State so authorized by its law; and in such case of more than one return or paper purporting to be a return from a State, if there shall have been no such determination of the question in the State aforesaid, then those votes, and those only, shall be counted which the two Houses shall concurrently decide were cast by lawful electors appointed in accordance with the laws of the State, unless the two Houses, acting separately, shall concurrently decide such votes not to be the lawful votes of the legally appointed electors of such State. But if the two Houses shall disagree in respect of the counting of such votes, then, and in that case, the votes of the electors whose appointment shall have been certified by the executive of the State, under the seal thereof, shall be counted. When the two Houses have voted, they shall immediately again meet, and the presiding officer shall then announce the decision of the questions submitted. No votes or papers from any other State shall be acted upon until the objections previously made to the votes or papers from any State shall have been finally disposed of.

§ 16. Same; seats for officers and Members of two Houses in joint meeting.

At such joint meeting of the two Houses seats shall be provided as follows: For the President of the Senate, the Speaker's chair; for the Speaker, immediately upon his left; for the Senators, in the body of the Hall upon the right of the presiding officer; for the Representatives, in the body of the Hall not provided for the Senators; for the tellers, Secretary of the Senate,

° Section 6 provides for certification of votes by electors by state Governors.

† Section 5 provides that if state law specifies a method for resolving disputes concerning the vote for Presidential electors, Congress must respect any determination so made by a state.

and Clerk of the House of Representatives, at the Clerk's desk; for the other officers of the two Houses, in front of the Clerk's desk and upon each side of the Speaker's platform. Such joint meeting shall not be dissolved until the count of electoral votes shall be completed and the result declared; and no recess shall be taken unless a question shall have arisen in regard to counting any such votes, or otherwise under this subchapter, in which case it shall be competent for either House, acting separately, in the manner hereinbefore provided, to direct a recess of such House not beyond the next calendar day, Sunday excepted, at the hour of 10 o'clock in the forenoon. But if the counting of the electoral votes and the declaration of the result shall not have been completed before the fifth calendar day next after such first meeting of the two Houses, no further or other recess shall be taken by either House.

§ 17. Same; limit of debate in each House.

When the two Houses separate to decide upon an objection that may have been made to the counting of any electoral vote or votes from any State, or other question arising in the matter, each Senator and Representative may speak to such objection or question five minutes, and not more than once; but after such debate shall have lasted two hours it shall be the duty of the presiding officer of each House to put the main question without further debate.

§ 18. Same; parliamentary procedure at joint meeting.

While the two Houses shall be in meeting as provided in this chapter, the President of the Senate shall have power to preserve order; and no debate shall be allowed and no question shall be put by the presiding officer except to either House on a motion to withdraw.

APPENDIX I

Rules for Election

of a President in the

House of Representatives

The following rules* were adopted by the House of Representatives on February 7, 1825, for the election of a President when the electoral college failed to produce a majority for any candidate following the Presidential election of 1824. No subsequent election has ever gone to the House for decision. These rules would be the governing precedent if the House should again be called upon to elect a President, though the House might alter the rules at any time.

1. In the event of its appearing, on opening all the certificates, and counting the votes given by the electors of the several States for President, that no person has a majority of the votes of the whole number of electors appointed, the same shall be entered on the Journals of this House.

2. The roll of the House shall then be called by States; and, on its appearing that a Member or Members from two-thirds of the States are present, the House shall immediately proceed, by ballot, to choose a President from the persons having the highest numbers, not exceeding three, on the list of those voted for as President; and, in case neither of those persons shall receive the votes of a majority of all the States on the first ballot, the House shall continue to ballot for a President, without interruption by other business, until a President be chosen.

3. The doors of the Hall shall be closed during the balloting, except against the Members of the Senate, stenographers, and the officers of the House.

* Hinds' *Precedents of the House of Representatives,* Vol. III, pp. 292–93 (Washington, 1907).

4. From the commencement of the balloting until an election is made no proposition to adjourn shall be received, unless on the motion of one State, seconded by another State, and the question shall be decided by States. The same rule shall be observed in regard to any motion to change the usual hour for the meeting of the House.

5. In balloting the following mode shall be observed, to wit:

The Representatives of each State shall be arranged and seated together, beginning with the seats at the right hand of the Speaker's chair, with the Members from the State of Maine; thence, proceeding with the Members from the States, in the order the States are usually named for receiving petitions,* around the Hall of the House, until all are seated.

A ballot box shall be provided for each State.

The Representatives of each State shall, in the first instance, ballot among themselves, in order to ascertain the vote of their State; and they may, if necessary, appoint tellers of their ballots.

After the vote of each State is ascertained, duplicates thereof shall be made out; and in case any one of the persons from whom the choice is to be made shall receive a majority of the votes given, on any one balloting by the Representatives of a State, the name of that person shall be written on each of the duplicates; and in case the votes so given shall be divided so that neither of said persons shall have a majority of the whole number of votes given by such State, on any one balloting, then the word "divided" shall be written on each duplicate.

After the delegation from each State shall have ascertained the vote of their State, the Clerk shall name the States in the order they are usually named for receiving petitions; and as the name of each is called the Sergeant-at-Arms shall present to the delegation of each two ballot boxes, in each of which shall be deposited, by some Representative of the State, one of the duplicates made as aforesaid of the vote of said State, in the presence and subject to the examination of all the Members from said State then present; and where there is more than one Representative from a State, the duplicates shall not both be deposited by the same person.

When the votes of the States are thus all taken in, the Sergeant-at-Arms shall carry one of said ballot boxes to one table and the other to a separate and distinct table.

One person from each State represented in the balloting shall be appointed by the Representatives to tell off said ballots; but, in case the Representatives fail to appoint a teller, the Speaker shall appoint.

The said tellers shall divide themselves into two sets, as nearly equal in number as can be, and one of the said sets of tellers shall proceed to count the votes in one of said boxes, and the other set the votes in the other box.

When the votes are counted by the different sets of tellers, the result shall be reported to the House; and if the reports agree, the same shall be ac-

---

* Petitions are no longer introduced in this way. This old order of calling the States began with Maine and proceeded through the original 13 States and then through the remaining States in the order of their admission.

cepted as the true votes of the States; but if the reports disagree, the States shall proceed, in the same manner as before, to a new ballot.

6. All questions arising after the balloting commences, requiring the decision of the House, which shall be decided by the House, voting per capita, to be incidental to the power of choosing a President, shall be decided by States without debate; and in case of an equal division of the votes of States, the question shall be lost.

7. When either of the persons from whom the choice is to be made shall have received a majority of all the States, the Speaker shall declare the same, and that that person is elected President of the United States.

8. The result shall be immediately communicated to the Senate by message, and a committee of three persons shall be appointed to inform the President of the United States and the President-elect of said election.

On February 9, 1825, the election of John Quincy Adams took place in accordance with these rules.

APPENDIX J

State Laws on Ballots, Elector Nominations, Residence Requirements for Voting

Type of General Election Ballot for Choosing Presidential Electors

Short ballot, with names of electors excluded (35 states): Alaska, Arkansas, California, Colorado, Connecticut, Delaware, Florida, Georgia (areas with voting machines), Hawaii, Illinois, Indiana, Iowa, Kentucky, Maine, Maryland, Massachusetts, Michigan, Minnesota, Missouri, Nebraska, Nevada, New Hampshire, New Jersey, New Mexico, New York (where voting machines or short ballots are authorized), North Carolina, Ohio, Oregon, Pennsylvania, Rhode Island (on voting machines), Texas, Utah, Washington, West Virginia, Wisconsin and the District of Columbia. The laws of these states contain a provision to the effect that a vote cast for President and Vice President is deemed to be a vote cast for the electors of the party which the candidates represent.

Long ballot, with both the names of Presidential candidates and the electors (14 states): Arizona, Idaho, Kansas, Louisiana, Mississippi, Montana, North Dakota, Oklahoma, South Carolina (if requested in certification), South Dakota, Tennessee, Vermont, Virginia and Wyoming. In addition, Georgia uses this system in areas without voting machines, and New York uses the system in areas without voting machines or where short ballots are not authorized.

Long ballot, showing the names of Presidential electors and their party designation but no names of Presidential candidates (one state): Alabama.

SOURCE: Robert L. Tienken, *Proposals to Reform Our Electoral System,* report of Legislative Reference Service, Library of Congress (Washington, 1966).

State Law Requirements on the Method of Nominating Candidates for Presidential Elector

By state party conventions (35 states): Arkansas, California, Colorado, Connecticut, Hawaii, Idaho, Illinois, Indiana, Iowa, Kansas, Maine, Maryland, Michigan, Minnesota, Missouri, Nebraska, Nevada, New Hampshire, New Jersey, New Mexico, North Carolina, North Dakota, Ohio, Oklahoma, Oregon, Rhode Island, South Dakota, Texas, Utah, Vermont, Virginia, Washington, West Virginia, Wisconsin, Wyoming.

By state party committees (five states): Georgia, Massachusetts, New York, South Carolina, Tennessee; also the District of Columbia by party executive committee.

By method to be stipulated by state party committees (five states): Delaware, Louisiana, Alaska, Kentucky, Montana.

By Governor on recommendation of state party committee (one state): Florida.

By primary election (two states): Arizona, Alabama.

By mixed convention-primary system (one state): Mississippi. Under that state's law, each party's convention has the option of designating directly the elector nominees for the general election ballot or of requesting a primary between an unpledged elector slate and a slate pledged to the party's national nominee. A request of 10 percent of the convention delegates necessitates a primary.

By the party's Presidential nominee (one state): Pennsylvania.

SOURCE: Tienken, *op. cit.*

RESIDENCE REQUIREMENTS FOR VOTING IN THE STATES, 1967

State	All Offices	Reduced Requirements for President Only		State	All Offices	Reduced Requirements for President Only	
		New Residents*	Old Residents†			New Residents*	Old Residents†
Ala.	1 year			Mont.	1 year		
Alaska	1 year			Neb.	6 months	X	
Ariz.	1 year	X	X	Nev.	6 months		
Ark.	1 year			N.H.	6 months	X	
Calif.	1 year	X		N.J.	3 months	X	
Colo.	1 year	X		N.M.	1 year		
Conn.	1 year	X	X	N.Y.	3 months	X	
Del.	1 year			N.C.	1 year	X	
Fla.	1 year	X		N.D.	1 year	X	
Ga.	1 year			Ohio	1 year	X	
Hawaii	1 year			Okla.	1 year	X	
Idaho	6 months	X		Ore.	6 months	X	
Ill.	1 year	X		Pa.	90 days		
Ind.	6 months			R.I.	1 year		
Iowa	6 months			S.C.	1 year		
Kan.	6 months	X		S.D.	1 year		
Ky.	1 year			Tenn.	1 year		
La.	1 year			Texas	1 year	X	
Maine	6 months	X		Utah	1 year		
Md.	1 year	X		Vt.	1 year		X
Mass.	1 year	X		Va.	1 year		
Mich.	6 months			Wash.	1 year	X	
Minn.	6 months	X		W.Va.	60 days		
Miss.	2 years			Wis.	6 months	X	X
Mo.	1 year	X		Wyo.	1 year		X
				D.C.	1 year		

* States that permit new residents to vote for President only, before the regular residence requirement has been met (see pages 228–29).

† States that permit previous residents to vote for President until they have qualified in their new state of residence.

SOURCE: Elizabeth Yadlosky, *Proposals for Federal Legislation to Enable a Citizen to Vote Who Cannot Meet the Residence Requirements of the State into Which He Has Moved,* report of Legislative Reference Service, Library of Congress (Washington, 1965); Congressional Quarterly Service.

APPENDIX K

Presidential Election Documents

I—Legislative Election Tally Sheet

The official tally sheet showing the votes cast by members of the South Carolina Senate and House when they chose the Presidential electors directly, in 1812.

II—Early Elector Tickets

(a) The ticket for Adams electors in Virginia in 1824. Along with the other anticaucus candidates in that year, Adams had no specific Vice Presidential running mate. Thus voters were told only that the Adams electors would support "some tried and approved Patriot" for Vice President.

(b) The ticket for Breckinridge and Lane in Virginia in 1860. Though the names of the elector candidates are given by districts, they were all elected at-large in the state under the general ticket system.

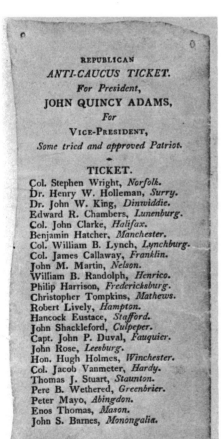

(c) The ticket for Grant and Wilson in Massachusetts, along with other Republican candidates, in 1872. Electors were all elected by general ticket, despite the individual district designations.

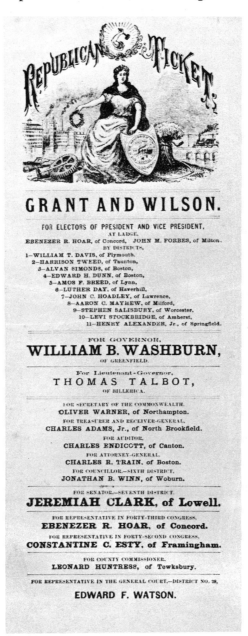

REPUBLICAN TICKET

GRANT AND WILSON.

FOR ELECTORS OF PRESIDENT AND VICE PRESIDENT,
AT LARGE,
EBENEZER R. HOAR, of Concord, JOHN M. FORBES, of Milton.
BY DISTRICTS,
1—WILLIAM T. DAVIS, of Plymouth,
2—HARRISON TWEED, of Taunton,
3—ALVAN SIMONDS, of Boston,
4—EDWARD H. DUNN, of Boston,
5—AMOS F. BREED, of Lynn,
6—LUTHER DAY, of Haverhill,
7—JOHN C. HOADLEY, of Lawrence,
8—AARON C. MAYHEW, of Milford,
9—STEPHEN SALISBURY, of Worcester,
10—LEVI STOCKBRIDGE, of Amherst,
11—HENRY ALEXANDER, Jr., of Springfield.

FOR GOVERNOR,
WILLIAM B. WASHBURN,
OF GREENFIELD.

For Lieutenant-Governor,
THOMAS TALBOT,
OF BILLERICA.

FOR SECRETARY OF THE COMMONWEALTH,
OLIVER WARNER, of Northampton.
FOR TREASURER AND RECEIVER-GENERAL,
CHARLES ADAMS, Jr., of North Brookfield.
FOR AUDITOR,
CHARLES ENDICOTT, of Canton.
FOR ATTORNEY-GENERAL,
CHARLES R. TRAIN, of Boston.
FOR COUNCILLOR.—SIXTH DISTRICT,
JONATHAN B. WINN, of Woburn.

FOR SENATOR.—SEVENTH DISTRICT,
JEREMIAH CLARK, of Lowell.

FOR REPRESENTATIVE IN FORTY-THIRD CONGRESS,
EBENEZER R. HOAR, of Concord.
FOR REPRESENTATIVE IN FORTY-SECOND CONGRESS,
CONSTANTINE C. ESTY, of Framingham.

FOR COUNTY COMMISSIONER,
LEONARD HUNTRESS, of Tewksbury.

FOR REPRESENTATIVE IN THE GENERAL COURT.—DISTRICT NO. 28,

EDWARD F. WATSON.

III—Modern Ballot Arrangements

(a) The New York state voting machine diagram for 1964, typical of the increasingly popular "short ballot," on which no names of electors appear on the ballots at all.

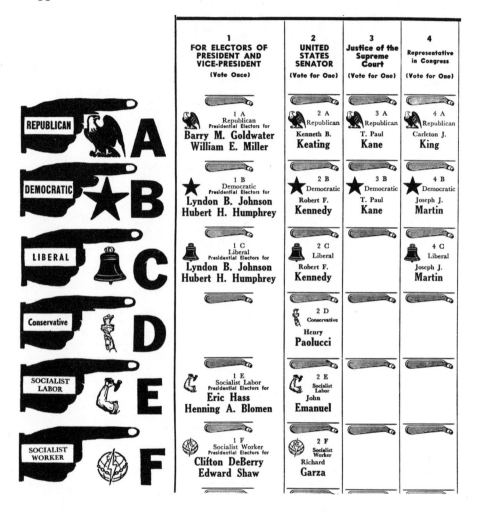

(b) The Hawaiian ballot for 1960, a short ballot type in which the words "Presidential electors for . . ." have even been dropped. Note voter instructions are in both English and Hawaiian.

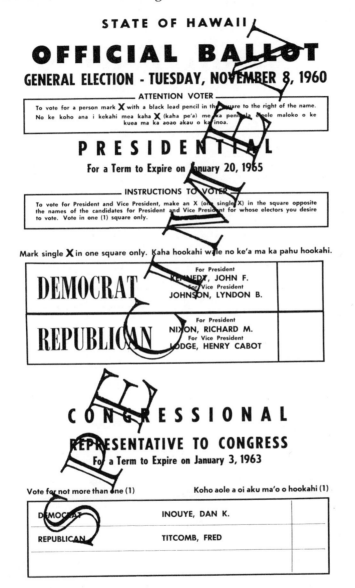

STATE OF HAWAII

OFFICIAL BALLOT

GENERAL ELECTION - TUESDAY, NOVEMBER 8, 1960

ATTENTION VOTER

To vote for a person mark **X** with a black lead pencil in the square to the right of the name. No ke koho ana i kekahi mea kaha **X** (kaha pe'a) me ka penikala keele maloko o ke kuea ma ka aoao akau o ka inoa.

PRESIDENTIAL

For a Term to Expire on January 20, 1965

INSTRUCTIONS TO VOTER

To vote for President and Vice President, make an X (one single X) in the square opposite the names of the candidates for President and Vice President for whose electors you desire to vote. Vote in one (1) square only.

Mark single **X** in one square only. Kaha hookahi wale no ke'a ma ka pahu hookahi.

DEMOCRAT	For President KENNEDY, JOHN F. For Vice President JOHNSON, LYNDON B.	
REPUBLICAN	For President NIXON, RICHARD M. For Vice President LODGE, HENRY CABOT	

CONGRESSIONAL

REPRESENTATIVE TO CONGRESS

For a Term to Expire on January 3, 1963

Vote for not more than one (1)   Koho aole a oi aku ma'o o hookahi (1)

DEMOCRAT	INOUYE, DAN K.	
REPUBLICAN	TITCOMB, FRED	

(c) The Kansas ballot for 1960, showing the form by which elector names are listed on the ballot with an indication of the Presidential candidate to whom they are pledged. The voter, in effect, is obliged to vote for an entire elector slate by the single box arrangement (unless he wants to go to the trouble of writing in another complete elector slate).

State of Kansas

GENERAL BALLOT

FIRST DIVISION

NATIONAL AND STATE TICKET

List of Candidates Nominated to be Voted for in the County of Shawnee

CITY OF TOPEKA

NOVEMBER 8, 1960

NATIONAL TICKET

If you wish to vote for the group of electors nominated by one of the political parties place a cross ✕ in the square opposite the names of the candidates of that party for president and vice-president.

If you do not wish to vote for the group of electors nominated by any of the political parties you may write in the following blank spaces the names of all the electors for whom you wish to vote, placing a cross ✕ in the square at the right of each.

For President and Vice-President

DECKER AND MUNN   Prohibition ☐

Presidential Electors,
RAYMOND BALTY, Burr Oak
MERLE M. FAWLEY, Milford
ADRIAN G. FIELDS, Bucklin
SHELDON G. JACKSON, Haviland
WILBUR ST. JOHN POMEROY, Emporia
STEWART REED, Emporia
ALBERT E. SMITH, McPherson
DALE YOCUM, Overland Park

For President and Vice-President

KENNEDY AND JOHNSON   Democratic ☐

Presidential Electors,
EDITH BECKMAN, Hoxie
J. DONALD COFFIN, Council Grove
REA CRESS, Junction City
MRS. MARIE HARDING, Ottawa
JOHN D. HENDERSON, Topeka
KARL C. PARKHURST, Wichita
JOHN B. SANDERS, Tonganoxie
ROBERT L. SHUMWAY, El Dorado

For President and Vice-President

NIXON AND LODGE   Republican ☐

Presidential Electors,
DONALD O. CONCANNON, Hugoton
HARRY R. HORNER, Wichita
R. E. JACOBS, Lenora
HENRY B. JAMESON, Abilene
SADIE JURNEY, Kingman
HENRY OTTO, Manhattan
WILLIAM H. VERNON, Larned
EMMETT E. WILSON, Independence

For Presidential Electors

☐
☐
☐
☐
☐
☐
☐
☐

To vote for a person, mark a cross ✕ in the square at the right of the party name or political designation.

For Governor	**Vote for One**
J. J. STEELE, Coffeyville	Prohibition ☐
JOHN ANDERSON, JR., Olathe	Republican ☐
GEORGE DOCKING, Lawrence	Democrat ☐
	☐
For Lieutenant Governor	**Vote for One**
SAM WALKER, Junction City	Prohibition ☐
HAROLD H. CHASE, Salina	Republican ☐
JACK GLAVES, Wichita	Democrat ☐
	☐
For Secretary of State	**Vote for One**
K. L. SMITH, Wichita	Democrat ☐
MARIE HADIN, Leonardville	Prohibition ☐
PAUL R. SHANAHAN, Salina	Republican ☐
	☐
For State Auditor	**Vote for One**
CLAY E. HEDRICK, Newton	Republican ☐
WILLIAM A. BELL, Franklin	Democrat ☐
ROLLAND FISHER, Kansas City	Prohibition ☐
	☐
For State Treasurer	**Vote for One**
WALTER H. PEERY, Topeka	Republican ☐
NATHAN De YOUNG, Manhattan	Prohibition ☐
GEORGE HART, Wichita	Democrat ☐
	☐
For Attorney General	**Vote for One**
DALE A. SPIEGEL, Emporia	Democrat ☐
WILLIAM M. FERGUSON, Wellington	Republican ☐
	☐
For State Superintendent of Public Instruction	**Vote for One**
A. F. THROCKMORTON, Wichita	Republican ☐

(d) The Vermont ballot for 1960, an example of the ballot form in which the voter has an option of voting a "straight" ticket for one party's electors or of splitting his votes.

Electors of President and Vice-President of the United States

To vote a straight party ticket, make a cross (X) in the square at the head of the party column of your choice.

If you desire to vote for a person whose name is not on the ballot, fill in the name of the candidate of your choice in the blank space provided therefor.

If you do not wish to vote for every person in a party column, make a cross (X) opposite the name of each candidate of your choice; or you may make a cross (X) in the square at the head of the party column of your choice which shall count as a vote for every name in that column, except for any name through which you may draw a line, and except for any name representing a candidate for an office to fill which you have otherwise voted in the manner heretofore prescribed.

REPUBLICAN PARTY	DEMOCRATIC PARTY
For President	**For President**
RICHARD M. NIXON of California	JOHN F. KENNEDY of Massachusetts
For Vice-President	**For Vice-President**
HENRY CABOT LODGE of Massachusetts	LYNDON B. JOHNSON of Texas
☐	☐

For Electors of President and Vice-President of the United States — Vote for THREE		For Electors of President and Vice-President of the United States — Vote for THREE	
DEANE C. DAVIS, Republican, Montpelier		FREDERICK J. FAYETTE, Democratic, South Burlington	
JOSEPH B. JOHNSON, Republican, Springfield		ROBERT W. LARROW, Democratic, Burlington	
MRS. MORTIMER R. PROCTOR, Republican, Proctor		WILLIAM J. RYAN, Democratic, Montpelier	

(e) The Alabama voting machine and paper ballot diagram for 1960—the only one in the U.S. on which the names of electors are given without the names of the Presidential and Vice Presidential candidates for whom they intend to vote. For review of the difficulties that arose

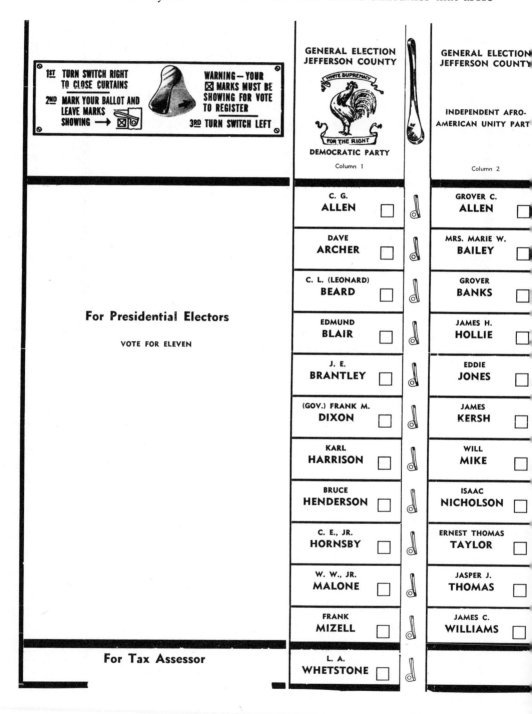

1ST TURN SWITCH RIGHT TO CLOSE CURTAINS
2ND MARK YOUR BALLOT AND LEAVE MARKS SHOWING →
WARNING—YOUR ☒ MARKS MUST BE SHOWING FOR VOTE TO REGISTER
3RD TURN SWITCH LEFT

GENERAL ELECTION JEFFERSON COUNTY

WHITE SUPREMACY
FOR THE RIGHT
DEMOCRATIC PARTY
Column 1

GENERAL ELECTION JEFFERSON COUNTY

INDEPENDENT AFRO-AMERICAN UNITY PART
Column 2

For Presidential Electors

VOTE FOR ELEVEN

Column 1		Column 2	
C. G. ALLEN	☐	GROVER C. ALLEN	☐
DAVE ARCHER	☐	MRS. MARIE W. BAILEY	☐
C. L. (LEONARD) BEARD	☐	GROVER BANKS	☐
EDMUND BLAIR	☐	JAMES H. HOLLIE	☐
J. E. BRANTLEY	☐	EDDIE JONES	☐
(GOV.) FRANK M. DIXON	☐	JAMES KERSH	☐
KARL HARRISON	☐	WILL MIKE	☐
BRUCE HENDERSON	☐	ISAAC NICHOLSON	☐
C. E., JR. HORNSBY	☐	ERNEST THOMAS TAYLOR	☐
W. W., JR. MALONE	☐	JASPER J. THOMAS	☐
FRANK MIZELL	☐	JAMES C. WILLIAMS	☐
L. A. WHETSTONE	☐		

For Tax Assessor

from ascertaining a popular vote total from this state in 1960, see pp. 102–04. In 1966 the Alabama Democratic party discontinued its use of the slogan, "White Supremacy—For The Right."

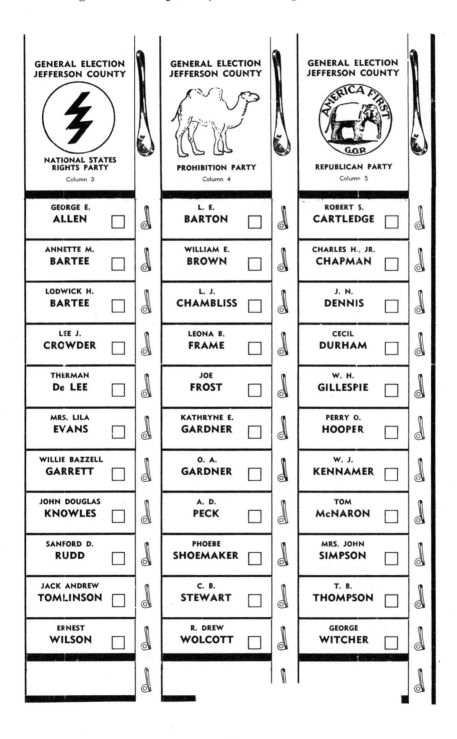

GENERAL ELECTION JEFFERSON COUNTY	GENERAL ELECTION JEFFERSON COUNTY	GENERAL ELECTION JEFFERSON COUNTY
NATIONAL STATES RIGHTS PARTY — Column 3	PROHIBITION PARTY — Column 4	REPUBLICAN PARTY — Column 5
GEORGE E. ALLEN	L. E. BARTON	ROBERT S. CARTLEDGE
ANNETTE M. BARTEE	WILLIAM E. BROWN	CHARLES H., JR. CHAPMAN
LODWICK H. BARTEE	L. J. CHAMBLISS	J. N. DENNIS
LEE J. CROWDER	LEONA B. FRAME	CECIL DURHAM
THERMAN De LEE	JOE FROST	W. H. GILLESPIE
MRS. LILA EVANS	KATHRYNE E. GARDNER	PERRY O. HOOPER
WILLIE BAZZELL GARRETT	O. A. GARDNER	W. J. KENNAMER
JOHN DOUGLAS KNOWLES	A. D. PECK	TOM McNARON
SANFORD D. RUDD	PHOEBE SHOEMAKER	MRS. JOHN SIMPSON
JACK ANDREW TOMLINSON	C. B. STEWART	T. B. THOMPSON
ERNEST WILSON	R. DREW WOLCOTT	GEORGE WITCHER

(a) A Certificate of Ascertainment of the election of Presidential electors, from Ohio in 1964. The electors who received 2,498,331 votes were the Democrats pledged to Johnson and Humphrey; the electors who received 1,470,865 votes were the Republican electors pledged to Goldwater and Miller. Signatures are those of Governor James A. Rhodes and Secretary of State Ted W. Brown.

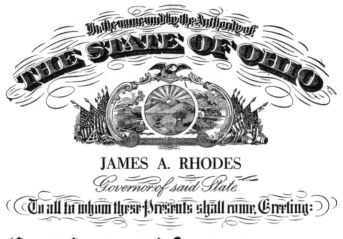

In the name and by the Authority of

THE STATE OF OHIO

JAMES A. RHODES
Governor of said State

To all to whom these Presents shall come, Greeting:

Certificate of Ascertainment

Pursuant to the act of Congress approved June twenty-fifth, 1948, and amended October 31, 1951, entitled "An act to fix the day for the meeting of the Electors of President and Vice-President, and to provide for and regulate the counting of the votes for President and Vice-President and the decision of questions arising thereon," I, JAMES A. RHODES, Governor of the State of Ohio, do hereby certify that at the election held in the several voting precincts of the State of Ohio, on the Third day of November, A. D. 1964, the following named persons were voted for, for the office of Elector of President and Vice-President of the United States and that each received the number of votes set opposite his name:

Vincent H. Beckman ... 2,498,331	Mark McElroy ... 2,498,331	Letha C. Astry ... 1,470,865	Lloyd C. Moreland ... 1,470,865
William M. Cafaro ... 2,498,331	Anthony M. Rogers ... 2,498,331	Loren M. Berry ... 1,470,865	H. Richard P. Niehoff ... 1,470,865
William L. Coleman ... 2,498,331	Herman J. Rosselott ... 2,498,331	Albert S. Close ... 1,470,865	Roy Odenkirk ... 1,470,865
Carlos A. Cordova ... 2,498,331	James W. Shocknessy ... 2,498,331	William H. Deddens ... 1,470,865	Jessie Semple O'Donnell ... 1,470,865
Michael V. DiSalle ... 2,498,331	Raymond R. Spitler ... 2,498,331	John K. Da'farnon ... 1,470,865	Judy Othersen ... 1,470,865
John J. Gilligan ... 2,498,331	William J. Timmins, Jr. ... 2,498,331	Homer M. Edwards ... 1,470,865	Walter R. Oxley ... 1,470,865
George A. Green ... 2,498,331	Joseph A. Ujhelyi ... 2,498,331	Harley Gardell ... 1,470,865	Catharine Pennell ... 1,470,865
Greg Holbrock ... 2,498,331	Frank A. Vannelle ... 2,498,331	Redmond Greer ... 1,470,865	Leonard G. Richter ... 1,470,865
Dorothy E. Holden ... 2,498,331	Robert C. Weaver ... 2,498,331	Philip S. Hamilton ... 1,470,865	Ferald Ritchie ... 1,470,865
Helen B. Karpinski ... 2,498,331	William H. H. Wertz ... 2,498,331	Fred L. Hoffman ... 1,470,865	Windle Roose ... 1,470,865
John P. Kelly ... 2,498,331	Milton J. Weston ... 2,498,331	Albert H. James ... 1,470,865	William Schneider ... 1,470,865
Carl W. Lehman ... 2,498,331	Clyde Wharton ... 2,498,331	Vincent B. Linn ... 1,470,865	John A. Skipton ... 1,470,865
E. E. Leonard ... 2,498,331	Stephen M. Young ... 2,498,331	Joseph E. L. MacAdam ... 1,470,865	Everett E. Taylor ... 1,470,865

I further certify that at a canvass of the official returns of said election, duly made according to law on the 1st day of December, A. D. 1964, at the office of the Secretary of State of Ohio, by said Secretary of State, it was duly ascertained that the following named persons received the highest number of votes cast at said election for said office of Elector of President and Vice-President of the United States, and were duly declared to have been elected to such office, and that they have been duly certified, commissioned and appointed as such, viz:

VINCENT H. BECKMAN	GREG HOLBROCK	MARK McELROY	JOSEPH A. UJHELYI
WILLIAM M. CAFARO	DOROTHY E. HOLDEN	ANTHONY M. ROGERS	FRANK A. VANNELLE
WILLIAM L. COLEMAN	HELEN B. KARPINSKI	HERMAN J. ROSSELOTT	ROBERT C. WEAVER
CARLOS A. CORDOVA	JOHN P. KELLY	JAMES W. SHOCKNESSY	WILLIAM H. H. WERTZ
MICHAEL V. DiSALLE	CARL W. LEHMAN	RAYMOND R. SPITLER	MILTON J. WESTON
JOHN J. GILLIGAN	E. E. LEONARD	WILLIAM J. TIMMINS, JR.	CLYDE WHARTON
GEORGE A. GREEN			STEPHEN M. YOUNG

In Testimony Whereof, I have hereunto subscribed my name, and caused to be affixed the Great Seal of the State of Ohio, at Columbus, the ......day of December in the year of our Lord one thousand nine hundred and sixty-four and in the one hundred and eighty-ninth year of the independence of the United States of America.

_____ Governor.

By the Governor:

_____ Secretary of State.

(b) Official ballots cast by Presidential electors: Ohio in 1936; Ohio,
New York and California in 1948.

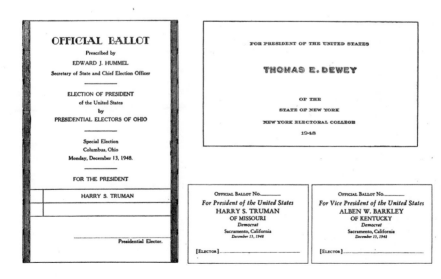

OFFICIAL BALLOT

Prescribed by

George S. Myers,

Secretary of State and Chief Election Officer

ELECTION OF PRESIDENT
of the United States
by
PRESIDENTIAL ELECTORS

Election
Columbus, Ohio
Monday, December 14, 1936
by
Presidential Electors of Ohio

FOR THE PRESIDENT

FRANKLIN D. ROOSEVELT

Presidential Elector.

OFFICIAL BALLOT
Prescribed by
EDWARD J. HUMMEL
Secretary of State and Chief Election Officer

ELECTION OF PRESIDENT
of the United States
by
PRESIDENTIAL ELECTORS OF OHIO

Special Election
Columbus, Ohio
Monday, December 13, 1948.

FOR THE PRESIDENT

HARRY S. TRUMAN

Presidential Elector.

FOR PRESIDENT OF THE UNITED STATES

THOMAS E. DEWEY

OF THE
STATE OF NEW YORK
NEW YORK ELECTORAL COLLEGE
1948

OFFICIAL BALLOT No.	OFFICIAL BALLOT No.
For President of the United States	*For Vice President of the United States*
HARRY S. TRUMAN	ALBEN W. BARKLEY
OF MISSOURI	OF KENTUCKY
Democrat	*Democrat*
Sacramento, California	Sacramento, California
December 13, 1948	December 13, 1948
[ELECTOR]	[ELECTOR]

Electors' Certificate of Their Votes

State of Ohio, ss.

We, the undersigned, Electors of President and Vice-President of the United States of America, for the respective terms of four years, beginning on the Fourth day of March, in the year of our Lord one thousand nine hundred and____Twenty Nine____, being Electors duly and legally appointed and qualified by and for the State of Ohio, as appears by the annexed list of Electors, made, certified, and delivered to us by the Executive of the State, having met and convened at the State House, in the City of Columbus, in the State of Ohio, in pursuance of the direction of the Legislature of said State, on the First Wednesday, being the____2nd____ day of January, in the year of our Lord one thousand nine hundred and____Twenty Nine____;

Do Hereby Certify. That, being so assembled and duly organized, we proceeded to vote by ballot, and balloted first for such President, and then for such Vice-President, by distinct ballots;

And We Further Certify. That the following are two distinct lists; one, of the votes cast for President, and the other, of the votes for Vice-President, so cast as aforesaid.

LIST OF ALL PERSONS VOTED FOR AS PRESIDENT. WITH THE NUMBER OF VOTES FOR EACH

NAMES OF PERSONS VOTED FOR	NUMBER OF VOTES
HERBERT C. HOOVER	24

LIST OF ALL PERSONS VOTED FOR AS VICE-PRESIDENT. WITH THE NUMBER OF VOTES FOR EACH

NAMES OF PERSONS VOTED FOR	NUMBER OF VOTES
CHARLES C. CURTIS	24

In Witness Whereof, We have hereunto set our hands, at the State House, in the City of Columbus, in the State of Ohio, on the First Wednesday, being the____2nd____ day of January, in the year of our Lord, one thousand nine hundred and____Twenty Nine____

APPENDIX L

Proposed
Constitutional Amendments

I—Direct Popular Vote

The text of a proposed amendment for direct popular vote, prepared by three attorneys associated with the American Bar Association's Commission on Electoral College Reform and introduced in 1967 by Senate Republican Leader Everett McKinley Dirksen of Illinois and House Judiciary Committee Chairman Emanuel Celler, Democrat of New York. The ABA attorneys who developed the language in the amendment were Paul Freund, professor of law at the Harvard Law School; James C. Kirby, Jr., professor of law at Northwestern University Law School; and John D. Feerick, a New York attorney who served as advisor to the ABA Commission. The proposed amendment contains the same substance as, but is somewhat more simply worded than, a similar amendment proposed by Senator Birch Bayh, Democrat of Indiana and Chairman of the Senate Judiciary Committee's Subcommittee on Constitutional Amendments. Bayh proposed, however, that the amendment be submitted to the state legislatures for ratification, while Dirksen and Celler favored submitting it to special conventions of the people in the states for ratification. Bayh's proposal had been co-sponsored by 19 other Senators.

ARTICLE —

Section 1. The President and Vice President shall be elected by the people of the several States and the district constituting the seat of government of the United States.

Section 2. The electors in each State shall have the qualifications requisite for electors of Senators and Representatives in Congress from that State, except that the legislature of any State may prescribe lesser qualifications with respect to residence and Congress may establish uniform residence and age qualifications.

353

Section 3.   The persons having the greatest number of votes for President and Vice President shall be elected, if such number be at least 40 per centum of the whole number of votes cast for such offices. If no persons have such number, a runoff election shall be held in which the choice of President and Vice President shall be made from the persons who received the two highest numbers of votes for each office.

Section 4.   The times, places, and manner of holding such election and entitlement to inclusion on the ballot shall be prescribed in each State by the legislature thereof; but the Congress may at any time by law make or alter such regulations. The Congress shall prescribe by law the time, place, and manner in which the results of such elections shall be ascertained and declared.

Section 5.   Each elector shall cast a single vote jointly applicable to President and Vice President. Names of candidates shall not be joined unless they shall have consented thereto and no candidate shall consent to his name being joined with that of more than one other person.

Section 6.   The days for such elections shall be determined by Congress and shall be uniform throughout the United States.

Section 7.   The Congress may by law provide for the case of the death of any candidate for President or Vice President before the day on which a President-elect or a Vice President-elect has been chosen; and for the case of a tie in any election.

Section 8.   This article shall be inoperative unless it shall have been ratified as an amendment to the Constitution by conventions of three-fourths of the States within seven years from the date of its submission to the States by the Congress.

II—The Proportional Plan

Text of the Lodge-Gossett plan for proportional division of each state's electoral votes to reflect the popular vote division, in the form that it passed the Senate (but was rejected by the House) in 1950. The major sponsors were Senator Henry Cabot Lodge, Republican of Massachusetts, and Representative Ed Gossett, Democrat of Texas. As originally proposed, the plan had stipulated no minimum percentage of the electoral vote for winning election. But the plan was amended in the Senate to require that the winner receive at least 40 percent of the electoral vote, with contingent election in Congress if no candidate won 40 percent or more. Proportional plans introduced by other Senators in subsequent years were essentially the same as this plan.

A R T I C L E —

Section 1.   The executive power shall be vested in a President of the United States of America. He shall hold his office during the term of 4 years, and together with the Vice President, chosen for the same term, be elected as provided in this Constitution.

The electoral college system of electing the President and Vice President of the United States is hereby abolished. The President and Vice President shall be elected by the people of the several States. The electors in each State shall have the qualifications requisite for electors of the most numerous branch of the State legislature. Congress shall determine the time of such election, which shall be the same throughout the United States. Until otherwise determined by the Congress, such election shall be held on the Tuesday next after the first Monday in November of the year preceding the year in which the regular term of the President is to begin. Each State shall be entitled to a number of electoral votes equal to the whole number of Senators and Representatives to which such State may be entitled in the Congress.

Within 45 days after such election, or at such time as the Congress shall direct, the official custodian of the election returns of each State shall make distinct lists of all persons for whom votes were cast for President and the number of votes for each, and the total vote of the electors of the State for all persons for President, which lists he shall sign and certify and transmit sealed to the seat of the Government of the United States, directed to the President of the Senate. On the 6th day of January following the election, unless the Congress by law appoints a different day not earlier than the 4th day of January and not later than the 10th day of January, the President of the Senate shall in the presence of the Senate and House of Representatives open all certificates and the votes shall then be counted. Each person for whom votes were cast for President in each State shall be credited with such proportion of the electoral votes thereof as he received of the total vote of the electors therein for President. In making the computations fractional numbers less than one one-thousandth shall be disregarded. The person having the greatest number of electoral votes for President shall be President if such number be at least 40 percent of the whole number of such electoral votes. If no person have at least 40 percent of the whole number of electoral votes, then from the persons having the two highest numbers of electoral votes for President the Senate and the House of Representatives sitting in joint session shall choose immediately by ballot the President. A majority of the votes of the combined authorized membership of the Senate and the House of Representatives shall be necessary for a choice.

The Vice President shall be likewise elected at the same time and in the same manner and subject to the same provisions as the President, but no person constitutionally ineligible for the office of President shall be eligible to that of Vice President of the United States.

The Congress may by law provide for the case of the death of any of the persons from whom the Senate and the House of Representatives may choose a President whenever the right of choice shall have devolved upon them, and for the case of the death of any of the persons from whom the Senate and the House of Representatives may choose a Vice President whenever the right of choice shall have devolved upon them.

Section 2. Paragraphs 1, 2, and 3 of section 1, article II, of the Constitution, the twelfth article of amendment to the Constitution, and section 4 of the twentieth article of amendment to the Constitution, are hereby repealed.

Section 3. This article shall take effect on the 10th day of February following its ratification.

Section 4. This article shall be inoperative unless it shall have been ratified as an amendment to the Constitution by the legislatures of three-fourths of the States within 7 years from the date of its submission to the States by the Congress.

III—The District Plan

Text of the district plan for electing Presidential electors, in the form that it was proposed by its chief Senate sponsor, Karl Mundt, Republican of South Dakota, in 1965 and 1967.

ARTICLE —

Section 1. Each State shall choose a number of electors of President and Vice President equal to the whole number of Senators and Representatives to which the State may be entitled in the Congress; but no Senator or Representative, or person holding an office of trust or profit under the United States, shall be chosen an elector.

The electors to which a State is entitled by virtue of its Senators shall be elected by the people thereof, and the electors to which it is entitled by virtue of its Representatives shall be elected by the people within single-elector districts established by the legislature thereof; such districts to be composed of compact and contiguous territory, containing as nearly as practicable the number of persons which entitled the State to one Representative in the Congress; and such districts when formed shall not be altered until another census has been taken. Before being chosen elector, each candidate for the office shall officially declare the persons for whom he will vote for President and Vice President, which declaration shall be binding on any successor. In choosing electors of President and Vice President the voters in each State shall have the qualifications requisite for electors of the most numerous branch of the State legislature, except that the legislature of any State may prescribe lesser qualifications with respect to residence therein.

The electors shall meet in their respective States, fill any vacancies in their number as directed by the State legislature, and vote by signed ballot for President and Vice President, one of whom, at least, shall not be an inhabitant of the same State with themselves; they shall name in their ballots the person voted for as President, and in distinct ballots the person voted for as Vice President; and they shall make distinct lists of all persons voted for as President, and of all persons voted for as Vice President, and of the number of votes for each, excluding therefrom any votes for persons other than those named by an elector before he was chosen, unless one or both of the persons so named be deceased, which lists they shall sign and certify, and transmit sealed to the seat of government of the United States, directed to the President of the Senate; the President of the Senate shall, in the presence of the Senate and the House of Representatives, open all the certificates and the votes shall then be counted; the person having the greatest number of votes for President shall be the President, if such number be a majority of the whole number of electors chosen; and the person having the greatest number of votes for Vice President shall be the Vice President, if such a number be a majority of the whole number of electors chosen.

If no person voted for as President has a majority of the whole number of electors, then from the persons having the three highest numbers on the lists of persons voted for as President, the Senate and the House of Representatives, assembled and voting as individual Members of one body, shall choose immediately, by ballot, the President; a quorum for such purpose shall be three-fourths of the whole number of the Senators and Representatives, and a majority of the whole number shall be necessary to a choice; if additional ballots be necessary, the choice on the fifth ballot shall be between the two persons having the highest number of votes on the fourth ballot.

If no person voted for as Vice President has a majority of the whole number of electors, then the Vice President shall be chosen from the persons having the three highest numbers on the lists of persons voted for as Vice President in the same manner as herein provided for choosing the President. But no person constitutionally ineligible to the office of President shall be eligible to that of Vice President of the United States.

Section 2. The Congress may by law provide for the case of the death of any of the persons from whom the Senate and the House of Representatives may choose a President or a Vice President whenever the right of choice shall have devolved upon them.

Section 3. This article supersedes the second and fourth paragraphs of section 1, article II, of the Constitution, the twelfth article of amendment to the Constitution and section 4 of the twentieth article of amendment to the Constitution. Except as herein expressly provided, this article does not supersede the twenty-third article of amendment.

Section 4. Electors appointed pursuant to the twenty-third article of amendment to this Constitution shall be elected by the people of such district in such manner as the Congress may direct. Before being chosen as such elector, each candidate shall officially declare the persons for whom he will vote for President and Vice President, which declaration shall be binding on any successor. Such electors shall meet in the district and perform the duties provided in section 1 of this article.

Section 5. This article shall take effect on the 1st day of July following its ratification.

APPENDIX M

Allocation of Electoral Votes

under Alternative Systems

PROPORTIONAL SYSTEM—1864–1964
(Figures in parentheses show vote actually cast under existing
unit vote system.)

Year	Republican	Democratic	Other
1864	129.8 (212)	103.2 (21)	—— ——
1868	156.1 (214)	132.9 (80)	—— ——
1872	205.0 (286)	159.1 (63)	1.9 ——
1876	177.1 (185)	188.1 (184)	3.8 ——
1880	175.1 (214)	181.9 (155)	12.0 ——
1884	189.7 (182)	200.5 (219)	10.8 ——
1888	185.8 (233)	202.9 (168)	12.3 ——
1892	186.2 (145)	202.7 (277)	55.1 (22)
1896	215.3 (271)	221.3 (176)	10.4 ——
1900	217.3 (292)	217.2 (155)	12.5 ——
1904	268.5 (336)	179.0 (140)	28.5 ——
1908	230.8 (321)	226.9 (162)	25.3 ——
1912	113.9 (8)	246.7 (435)	170.4 (88)
1916	222.1 (254)	284.3 (277)	24.6 ——
1920	299.9 (404)	212.6 (127)	18.5 ——
1924	258.8 (382)	191.4 (136)	80.8 (13)
1928	291.9 (444)	231.6 (87)	7.5 ——
1932	189.6 (59)	327.6 (472)	13.8 ——
1936	175.6 (8)	340.3 (523)	15.1 ——
1940	214.6 (82)	310.0 (449)	6.4 ——
1944	223.8 (99)	294.7 (432)	12.5 ——
1948	221.4 (189)	258.0 (303)	51.6 (39)
1952	288.5 (442)	239.8 (89)	2.7 ——
1956	296.7 (457)	227.2 (73)	7.1 (1)
1960	266.1 (219)	265.6 (303)	5.3 (15)
1964	213.6 (52)	320.0 (486)	3.9 ——

SOURCES: 1864–1956: Legislative Reference Service, Library of Congress; 1960–64: Congressional Quarterly Service.

DISTRICT SYSTEM—1952–64

(Figures for previous years unavailable. Figures in parentheses
show vote under existing unit vote system.)

Year	Republican	Democratic	Other
1952	375 (442)	156 (89)	—— ——
1956	411 (457)	120 (73)	—— (1)
1960	278 (219)	245 (303)	14* (15)
1964	72 (52)	466 (486)	—— ——

* 1960 votes won by Unpledged Electoral Slates.

SOURCE: Congressional Quarterly Service.

NOTE: Caution must be exercised in interpreting the possible outcome of alternative electoral count systems in past elections, since the campaigns might well have been conducted in a different manner as the Presidential candidates and their managers sought to exploit the differing types of electoral bases that would have been involved.

APPENDIX N

Gallup Poll on Instituting
Direct National Vote

Results of a national Gallup Poll sampling of February 1967, asking the following question: "Would you approve or disapprove of an amendment to the Constitution which would do away with the electoral college and base the election of a President on the total popular vote cast throughout the nation?"

	Approve	*Disapprove*	*No Opinion*
National	58%*	22%	20%
SEX			
Men	64	23	13
Women	54	20	26
RACE			
White	62	21	17
Non-white	†	†	†
EDUCATION			
College	68	23	9
High School	62	22	16
Grade School	46	20	34
OCCUPATION			
Prof. & Bus.	66	24	10
White Collar	59	24	17
Farmers	64	17	19
Manual	55	22	23
AGE			
21–29 years	50	32	18
30–49 years	62	21	17
50 & over	59	18	23

National	Approve	Disapprove	No Opinion
RELIGION			
Protestant	56	24	20
Catholic	63	19	18
Jewish	†	†	†
POLITICS			
Republican	62	22	16
Democrat	53	23	24
Independent	67	20	13
REGION			
East	58	22	20
Midwest	61	21	18
South	52	23	25
West	66	20	14
INCOME			
$10,000 & over	69	24	7
$7,000 & over	66	24	10
$5,000–$6,999	58	23	19
$3,000–$4,999	51	19	30
Under $3,000	47	19	34
COMMUNITY SIZE			
1,000,000 & over	58	20	22
500,000 & over	57	23	20
50,000–499,999	59	23	18
2,500–49,999	56	23	21
Under 2,500, Rural	61	19	20

* The 58 percent affirmative response reflected in this particular Gallup survey is slightly lower than the 63 percent answering in the affirmative in an identical Gallup Poll question in April–May 1966, and the 65 percent answering in the affirmative in a subsequent Gallup Poll of November 1967. In the November 1967 survey, 22 percent disapproved of the proposal to substitute a direct vote for the electoral college system, while 13 percent had no opinion. The scores for direct vote were up to 70 percent among college graduates, 67 percent among high school graduates and 54 percent among persons with grade school or less education.

The slightly higher scores for abolishing the electoral college in the November 1967 survey may be attributed either to normal sampling tolerances, or possibly to increased public concern over the possibility of a George Wallace-led third party in 1968 which could throw that year's election into the House of Representatives.

† Indicates population group for which sampling was not large enough to provide sufficiently accurate results.

APPENDIX O

Computer Analysis of Large-
versus Small-State Power
in the Electoral College

With the advent of the computer age and the development of the mathematical theory of games, studies have recently been undertaken to determine—through analysis of thousands of vote combinations under the existing electoral college system—whether it is the large or small states that actually have more chance, in relation to their electoral votes, to be decisive in the attainment of an electoral college majority. Studies by Irwin Mann and L. S. Shapley, using RAND Corporation computers, found that the powers of states of various sizes in the electoral college are *not* out of accord, to any significant extent, with the electoral college voting strength actually accorded the states. Based on the 1960 Census apportionment, for instance, it was found that New York state, with 43 electoral votes (8.0 percent of the total electoral vote pool of 538), had a power index of 8.406 (out of 100). On the other end of the scale, the states with three electoral votes—each controlling .538 percent of the electoral vote—were found to have a power index of .5416 each. Medium-sized states were also found to have a power index roughly equivalent to their percentage of total electoral college membership.*

* Irving Mann and L. S. Shapley, *Values of Large Games, VI: Evaluating the Electoral College Exactly* (The RAND Corp., Santa Monica, Calif., Memorandum RM-3158-PR, May 1962). See also Paul T. David, Ralph M. Goldman and Richard C. Bain, *The Politics of National Party Conventions* (Washington, 1960), pp. 174–75.

Significantly different results were produced by John F. Banzhaf III, a New York attorney and expert on weighted voting. Banzhaf extended the concept of state voting power in the electoral college to the level of the individual voter in the state. He concluded through a computer study that the citizens of the larger states have a disproportionately larger power, through their votes, to influence the national election outcome than the citizens of the smaller states. Banzhaf based his conclusion on a finding that the chance of an individual citizen-voter to determine the outcome of the election in his state is not halved if the population is doubled or divided by three if the population is tripled. Rather, he showed mathematically that the chance of a voter to affect his state's electoral vote decreases as the inverse of the square root of the population. An example used the states of New York and Alaska, the former with 74 times the population of the latter. One might suppose that a New Yorker would have 1/74th the chance of affecting New York's 43 electoral votes that an Alaskan would have to affect Alaska's three votes. But since voter effectiveness actually depends on the square root of the population ratio, a New Yorker really has about one-ninth as much chance of affecting his state's electoral votes. Because a New Yorker may potentially affect 43 votes as compared with the Alaskan's potential effect on only three votes, however, the New Yorker actually has almost twice as much chance of affecting the overall election as has the Alaskan. Citizens in 32 states (including all the smallest) were found to have less than average voting power in the electoral college. Shapley and Mann have subsequently agreed to the correctness of extending the power analysis, as Banzhaf did, to the individual voter.

Banzhaf also applied his analysis to the proportional system, finding that it would benefit small-state voters (giving Alaskans four times as much chance to affect the election as New Yorkers). The district system would also give citizens of the smallest states more than two-and-a-half times the voting power of citizens in the larger states. Only the direct election method, he found, would give all U.S. citizens an equalized voting power in the election of the President.*

* Testimony before the U.S. Senate Judiciary Subcommittee on Constitutional Amendments, July 14, 1967. A full statement of Banzhaf's findings, together with tables showing the relative voting power of citizens of each of the states under the various electoral systems, was scheduled for publication in an early 1968 edition of the *Villanova Law Review*.

A Selected Bibliography

CONSTITUTIONAL ORIGINS OF THE ELECTORAL COLLEGE

Max Farrand (ed.), *The Records of the Federal Convention of 1787,* 4 vols. (New Haven: Yale University Press, 1911, 1937). The standard work on the proceedings of the Constitutional Convention, with an excellent index referring to all relevant debate.

The Federalist, Jacob E. Cooke (ed.) (Middletown, Conn.: Wesleyan University Press, 1961).

John P. Roche, "The Founding Fathers: A Reform Caucus in Action," *American Political Science Review,* Dec. 1961, pages 799–816. A perceptive essay showing the pragmatic political considerations—rather than abstract theories—that lay behind decisions of the Constitutional Convention on the electoral college and other issues.

Clinton Rossiter, *1787—The Grand Convention* (New York: The Macmillan Company, 1966). The work of the Constitutional Convention seen in the context of its time.

Charles C. Thach, Jr., *The Creation of the Presidency, 1775–1789* (Baltimore: The Johns Hopkins Press, 1922). A view of the struggle for a strong executive at the Constitutional Convention and in the first years of the Republic.

Charles Warren, *The Making of the Constitution* (Boston: Little, Brown and Company, 1928).

THE ELECTORAL COLLEGE IN GENERAL

Herman V. Ames, "The Proposed Amendments to the Constitution of the United States During the First Century of its History," *Annual Report of the American Historical Association for 1896* (Washington: Government Printing Office, 1897). Valuable for its review and documentation regarding all constitutional amendments proposed up to 1889.

J. Hampden Dougherty, *The Electoral System of the United States* (New York: G. P. Putnam's Sons, 1906). A general discussion of the electoral college, including the most comprehensive review available on the problem of how disputed electoral votes should be handled in Congress, with documentation on the vote disputes of the 19th century.

Charles A. O'Neil, *The American Electoral System* (New York: G. P. Putnam's Sons, 1887). Substantial detail on the problems of the electoral college during its first 100 years.

U.S. Senate, *Report 22*, 19th Congress, 1st Session, Jan. 19, 1826. Report of a select Senate committee on electoral college reform, headed by Thomas Hart Benton of Missouri. A classic evaluation of the electoral college in practice and the case for change by one of the great reform advocates.

Lucius Wilmerding, Jr., *The Electoral College* (New Brunswick, N.J.: Rutgers University Press, 1958). Especially valuable for its comprehensive account of the early history of the electoral college, including the national trend toward use of the general ticket (unit vote) system of choosing electors in the early 19th century.

PRESIDENTIAL ELECTIONS

Congress and the Nation, 1945–1964 (Washington: Congressional Quarterly Service, 1965). Ch. 1, "Politics and National Issues," includes a comprehensive chronology and detail on Presidential elections since World War II.

John Bach McMaster, *A History of the People of the United States from the Revolution to the Civil War,* 8 vols. (New York: D. Appleton and Company, 1893–1924). A general history of the early United States with colorful detail on the first Presidential elections.

Eugene H. Roseboom, *A History of Presidential Elections* (New York: The Macmillan Company, 1959). A general history of Presidential elections, up to 1956.

Edward Stanwood, *A History of the Presidency from 1788 to 1897* (Boston: Houghton Mifflin Company, 1898), and *A History of the Presidency from 1897 to 1916* (Boston: Houghton Mifflin Company, 1916). These two volumes contain a detailed history of Presidential elections through 1912, with valuable charts showing electoral and popular votes, convention balloting, etc.

THE ELECTORAL COLLEGE TODAY AND REFORM PROPOSALS

Congressional Documents:

1949—Senate, Committee on the Judiciary, *Hearings on S.J. Res 2, An Amendment to the Constitution of the United States Providing for the Election of President and Vice President,* 81st Congress, 1st Session (Washington: Government Printing Office, 1949).

1949—House, Committee on the Judiciary, Subcommittee No. 1, *Hearings, Amending the Constitution with Respect to Election of President and Vice President,* 81st Congress, 1st Session (Washington: Government Printing Office, 1949).

1951—House, Committee on the Judiciary, Subcommittee No. 1, *Hearings, Amending the Constitution to Abolish the Electoral College System,* 82nd Congress, 1st Session (Washington: Government Printing Office, 1951).

1955—Senate, Committee on the Judiciary, *Hearings, Nomination and Election of President and Vice President,* 84th Congress, 1st Session (Washington: Government Printing Office, 1955).

1961—Senate, Committee on the Judiciary, Subcommittee on Constitutional Amendments, *Hearings, Nomination and Election of President and Vice President and Qualifications for Voting,* 87th Congress, 1st Session (Washington: Government Printing Office, 1961). The most comprehensive hearings of recent decades, with extensive documentation (reprints of prominent articles, historical material, etc.).

1961—Staff of the Subcommittee on Constitutional Amendments, Senate Committee on the Judiciary, *The Electoral College,* a memorandum (Washington: Government Printing Office, 1961). A thorough review of the likely effects of various electoral college reform proposals, prepared by the Subcommittee's chief counsel, James C. Kirby, Jr.

1963—Senate, Committee on the Judiciary, Subcommittee on Constitutional Amendments, *Hearings, Nomination and Election of President and Vice President,* 88th Congress, 1st Session (Washington: Government Printing Office, 1963).

General Materials:

Congress and the Nation, 1945–1964 (Washington: Congressional Quarterly Service, 1965). Ch. 13, "Election Law," includes arguments for and against each major plan for Presidential election, and a review of the legislative history of electoral college reform efforts since World War II.

Robert G. Dixon, Jr., "Electoral College Procedure," *The Western Political Quarterly,* June 1950, pp. 214–24. The best modern review of the actual procedure of the electoral colleges on the state level.

Joseph E. Kallenbach, "Presidential Election Reform," paper inserted in the *Congressional Record* by Senator Henry Cabot Lodge, April 13, 1949 (pp. 4448–53). A short history of reform efforts and statement of the case for electoral college reform.

———, "Our Electoral College Gerrymander," *Midwest Journal of Political Science,* May 1960, pp. 162–91.

Estes Kefauver, "The Electoral College: Old Reforms Take on a New Look," *Law and Contemporary Problems,* part of a two-part symposium, "The Electoral Process," Spring 1962, pp. 188–212. A perceptive analysis of electoral college reform problems.

James C. Kirby, Jr., "Limitations on the Power of State Legislatures Over Presidential Elections," *Law and Contemporary Problems,* Spring 1962, pp. 495–509. A careful review of state law regarding Presidential electors.

Neal R. Peirce, "The Electoral College Goes to Court," *The Reporter,* Oct. 6, 1966, pp. 34–37. The development of Delaware's court case against the unit vote system of casting state electoral votes.

Allan P. Sindler, "Presidential Election Methods and Urban-Ethnic Interests," *Law and Contemporary Problems,* Spring 1962, pp. 213–33. An excellent analysis of the political consequences of various reform proposals.

Robert L. Tienken, *Proposals to Reform Our Electoral System,* report of Legislative Reference Service, Library of Congress, Jan. and April 1966. Pros and cons of various reform plans; listing of constitutional amendments proposed, with sponsors, in each Congress since World War II; full bibliography.

L. Kinvin Wroth, "Election Contests and the Electoral Vote," *Dickinson Law Review,* June 1961, pp. 321–53. An imaginative proposal for resolution of conflicts in Presidential voting.

THE PRESIDENCY

Edward S. Corwin, *The President—Office and Powers* (New York: New York University Press, 4th rev. ed., 1957). The classic modern volume on the Presidency and its base in the Constitution and statutes.

Clinton Rossiter, *The American Presidency* (New York: Harcourt, Brace and Company, Inc., 1956). A perceptive examination of the Presidency in history and today.

THE NOMINATING PROCESS

Paul T. David, Ralph M. Goldman and Richard C. Bain, *The Politics of National Party Conventions* (Washington: The Brookings Institution, 1960). See especially Ch. 2, "Origins of the National Convention System," and Ch. 19, "The Nominating Process and the Future of the Party System." This is the most comprehensive book available on national party conventions and the nominating process in general.

Paul T. David, "Reforming the Presidential Nominating Process," *Law and Contemporary Problems,* Spring 1962, pp. 159–77.

James W. Davis, *Presidential Primaries: Road to the White House* (New York: Thomas Y. Crowell Co., 1967). An excellent analysis of the Presidential primaries, with charts showing complete Presidential primary returns by state, 1912–64.

THE TWO-PARTY SYSTEM

Several books contain valuable material on the reasons for the two-party system in the United States:

William Goodman, *The Two-Party System in the United States* (Princeton: D. Van Nostrand Co., Inc., 1956).

V. O. Key, *Politics, Parties and Pressure Groups* (New York: Thomas Y. Crowell Company, 5th ed., 1964).

Howard R. Penniman, *Sait's American Parties and Elections* (New York: Appleton-Century-Crofts, Inc., 5th ed., 1952).

Clinton Rossiter, *Parties and Politics in America* (Ithaca, N.Y.: Cornell University Press, 1962).

E. E. Schattschneider, *Party Government* (New York: Farrar & Rinehart, 1960, orig. ed., 1941).

Allan P. Sindler, *Political Parties in the United States* (New York: St. Martin's Press, 1966).

SUFFRAGE AND VOTER PARTICIPATION

Dudley O. McGovney, *The American Suffrage Medley* (Chicago: University of Chicago Press, 1949). General review of suffrage problems in the United States.

Report of the President's Commission on Registration and Voting Participation, Nov. 1963 (Washington: Government Printing Office, 1963). A survey of the reasons for low voter turnout, and recommendations of ways to increase it, prepared by a special Presidential commission headed by Richard M. Scammon.

Representation and Apportionment (Washington: Congressional Quarterly Service, 1966). A full review of the Supreme Court's reapportionment decisions of the 1960s and their impact.

Richard M. Scammon, "The Electoral Process," *Law and Contemporary Problems,* Spring 1962, pp. 299–306. A discussion of voter participation patterns.

U.S. Census Bureau, "Voter Participation in the National Election, November 1964," *Current Population Reports,* Series P-20, No. 143 (Washington: Government Printing Office, 1965). Results of a national survey showing the voter turnout by region, age, sex, economic group, race, etc.

U.S. Commission on Civil Rights, *Report* (Washington: Government Printing Office, 1959). An excellent short history of suffrage requirements in the U.S., especially in regard to the American Negro.

Chilton Williamson, *American Suffrage from Property to Democracy, 1760–1860* (Princeton: Princeton University Press, 1960). This study, based on extensive original research in 18th- and 19th-century government documents, indicates that suffrage may not have been as limited in early years as is often assumed.

PRESIDENTIAL SUCCESSION

John D. Feerick, *From Failing Hands—The Story of Presidential Succession* (New York: Fordham University Press, 1965). The definitive work in its field.

PRESIDENTIAL ELECTION STATISTICS

Richard M. Scammon, *America at the Polls—A Handbook of American Presidential Election Statistics, 1920–1964* (Pittsburgh: University of Pittsburgh Press, 1965). The most authoritative modern reporting of official Presidential election statistics, broken down to the state and county levels.

———, *America Votes, A Handbook of Contemporary American Election Statistics,* 7 vols., official figures for President, Governor, U.S. Senate and U.S. House seats, published every two years. (First ed. 1956; current publisher, Congressional Quarterly Service, Washington.)

Svend Petersen, *A Statistical History of the American Presidential Elections* (New York: Frederick Ungar Publishing Co., 1963). A carefully compiled volume of Presidential election statistics, showing both popular and electoral votes, nationally and by state, for all elections through 1960.

NOTE: The state-by-state and national popular vote returns in each Presidential election, as furnished by official state sources, are published by Congressional Quarterly Service in *C.Q. Weekly Reports* following each election. The official Presidential returns, broken down by state and Congressional district, are published in a *C.Q. Weekly Report* the spring after the election, and subsequently in the *C.Q. Almanac.* The figures are prepared for *Congressional Quarterly* by the Elections Research Center, Governmental Affairs Institute, of which Richard M. Scammon is director.

I N D E X